Family Relationships

Family Relationships

An Evolutionary Perspective

Edited by
Catherine A. Salmon and Todd K. Shackelford

OXFORD
UNIVERSITY PRESS

2008

OXFORD
UNIVERSITY PRESS

Oxford University Press, Inc., publishes works that further
Oxford University's objective of excellence
in research, scholarship, and education.

Oxford   New York
Auckland   Cape Town   Dar es Salaam   Hong Kong   Karachi
Kuala Lumpur   Madrid   Melbourne   Mexico City   Nairobi
New Delhi   Shanghai   Taipei   Toronto

With offices in
Argentina   Austria   Brazil   Chile   Czech Republic   France   Greece
Guatemala   Hungary   Italy   Japan   Poland   Portugal   Singapore
South Korea   Switzerland   Thailand   Turkey   Ukraine   Vietnam

Copyright © 2007 by Oxford University Press

Published by Oxford University Press, Inc.
198 Madison Avenue, New York, New York 10016

www.oup.com

Library of Congress Cataloging-in-Publication Data
Family relationships : an evolutionary perspective / edited by Catherine A. Salmon and
Todd K. Shackelford.
   p. cm.
Includes bibliographical references and index.
ISBN 978-0-19-532051-0
1. Family. 2. Interpersonal relations. I. Salmon, Catherine. II. Shackelford,
Todd K. (Todd Kennedy), 1971–
HQ734.F2417 2008
306.87—dc22   2007000224

9 8 7 6 5 4 3 2 1

Printed in the United States of America
on acid-free paper

ACKNOWLEDGMENTS

Catherine Salmon thanks, for their intellectual support, encouragement, and conversations, Kingsley Browne, Charles Crawford, Martin Daly, A.J. Figuerado, Maryanne Fisher, Maria Janicki, Dennis Krebs, Anna Napoli, Francisco Silva, and Margo Wilson. Special thanks to Todd Shackelford for all his work on this volume and for suggesting the idea in the first place.

Todd K. Shackelford thanks, for their scholarly support and encouragement, John Alcock, Robin Baker, Mark Bellis, Iris Berent, Jesse Bering, Tim Birkhead, Dave Bjorklund, April Bleske-Rechek, Becky Burch, David Buss, Martin Daly, Alastair Davies, Josh Duntley, Judy Easton, Harald Euler, Gordon Gallup, Steve Gangestad, Aaron Goetz, Steve Hecht, Erika Hoff, Craig LaMunyon, Brett Laursen, Bill McKibbin, Rick Michalski, Gary Perry, Steve Platek, Danielle Popp, Nick Pound, Harry Reis, Joe Rodgers, Monica Rosselli, Luke Schipper, Dave Schmitt, Valerie Starratt, Emily Stone, Jaime Thomson, Randy Thornhill, Robin Vallacher, Charles White, Margo Wilson, and Dave Wolgin. Special thanks to Catherine Salmon, for her hard work and persistence in bringing this volume to fruition. Finally, my deepest thanks to Viviana Weekes-Shackelford, for her unwavering support and encouragement, professional and personal.

The editors thank Jennifer Rappaport and Brian Desmond at Oxford University Press for their direction, support, and encouragement.

Contents

CONTRIBUTORS

Jay Belsky
School of Psychology
Birkbeck University of London

David F. Bjorklund
Department of Psychology
Florida Atlantic University

Athanasios Chasiotis
Faculty of Social & Behavioral
  Sciences
Tilburg University

Kevin A. Chavarria
Department of Psychology
California State University,
  Fullerton

Kathryn Coe
Mel and Enid Zuckerman College
  of Public Health
University of Arizona

Harald A. Euler
Department of Psychology
University of Kassell

Helen E. Fisher
Department of Anthropology
Rutgers University

Mark V. Flinn
Department of Anthropology
University of Missouri, Columbia

Amy Gardiner
Department of Psychology
Florida Atlantic University

David C. Geary
Department of Psychology
University of Missouri, Columbia

Aaron T. Goetz
Department of Psychology
Florida Atlantic University

Sarah Blaffer Hrdy
Department of Anthropology
University of California at
  Santa Barbara

Heide D. Island
Department of Psychology
Pacific University

Sarah E. Johns
Department of Anthropology
University of Kent

Heidi Keller
Universitat Osnabruck

Debra Lieberman
Department of Psychology
University of Hawaii

Daniel Marchalik
East Brunswick, NJ

Richard L. Michalski
Department of Psychology
Hollins University

Robert J. Quinlan
Department of Anthropology
Washington State University

Jonathan Rich
Irvine, CA

Catherine A. Salmon
Department of Psychology
University of Redlands

Nancy L. Segal
Department of Psychology
California State University,
 Fullerton

Todd K. Shackelford
Department of Psychology
Florida Atlantic University

Joanne Hoven Stohs
Department of Psychology
California State University,
 Fullerton

Frank J. Sulloway
Institute of Personality and Social
 Research
University of California,
 Berkeley

Ilanit Tal
Department of Psychology
University of New Mexico

Carol V. Ward
School of Medicine
University of Missouri,
 Columbia

PART I

Introduction and Overview

1 Toward an Evolutionary Psychology of the Family

Catherine A. Salmon and Todd K. Shackelford

Relationships with family are at the heart of human lives. As infants, we are dependent on our families for our survival, for helping us learn about the world around us. At some point, most people move out of the circle of their kin to form families of their own, and yet most retain strong ties to their natal kin. Family relationships are important to our emotional health and our social success. They are a source of great joy and sometimes a source of great pain. Family can be our strongest allies and our most persistent opponents. There are hundreds of popular-press books devoted to helping us understand and manage our family relationships: *Why Can't We Get Along? Healing Adult Sibling Relationships, The World's Easiest Guide to Family Relationships, The Baffled Parent's Guide to Sibling Rivalry,* and *Parenting with Love and Logic.* Most of these works consider the hows, the possible ways to deal with family processes. The current volume addresses the whys, the reasons behind people's behavior, and how a greater understanding of "whys" can help us better understand our own behavior and that of our family members.

When we refer to the evolved "reasons" or motivations behind people's behavior, we are not making a judgment about whether the behavior itself is good or bad or right or wrong in any moral sense. Behaviors exist, and evolutionary psychologists are interested in understanding why certain behaviors evolved and why they appear in certain circumstances. Making a claim or giving evidence that a behavior has evolved (infanticide on the part of mothers, for example) says nothing about how such a behavior should be viewed from a moral stance. In fact, using what is to justify what ought to be is referred to as the *naturalistic fallacy*. Empirical data and the moral realm are logically distinct. No matter how desirable some behavior may be, wishing will not make it so; likewise, the existence of a behavior does not necessarily make it desirable. A better understanding of the evolutionary forces that shaped a behavior and the cues to which the underlying mechanisms are sensitive may allow us to better shape behavior in the direction society considers more moral or desirable (for a more complete discussion of the naturalistic fallacy and evolutionary moral psychology, see Holcomb, 2004).

EVOLUTIONARY PSYCHOLOGY

In many areas, early-20th-century forward thinkers interested in human behavior embraced Darwinism. However, the past 75 years have seen the de-biologizing of the study of human behavior. In psychology, neo-behaviorism, social learning theory, cognitive theory, modern psychoanalysis, and a variety of postmodernist explanations have come to dominate many academics' thinking. We suggest that a new approach is needed, a return to a consideration of our ancestral history and the forces that shaped not only our physical forms but also our mental forms. To do this, we first review briefly what natural selection is, what role kinship plays in evolutionary analyses, and how adaptations can function as decision makers, particularly with regard to kinship.

Natural Selection

An adaptation is an anatomical structure, a physiological process, or a behavior pattern that contributed to ancestral individuals' ability to survive and reproduce in competition with other members of their species. Natural selection, the process that shapes adaptations, is the differential production or survival of offspring by genetically different members of the population (Williams, 1966). Darwin's (1859) logic may be explained through the following assumptions and inferences:

> Assumption 1: Species are capable of overproducing offspring.
> Assumption 2: The size of populations of individuals is relatively stable over time.
> Assumption 3: Resources for supporting individuals are limited.
> > Inference 1: A struggle for existence among individuals ensues.
> Assumption 4: Individuals differ on traits (i.e., adaptations) that enable them to survive and reproduce.
> Assumption 5: At least some of the variation in these traits is heritable.

Inference 2: There is differential production or survival of offspring by genetically different members of the population, which is by definition natural selection.

Inference 3: Through many generations, evolution of traits that are more adaptive than others will occur through natural selection. (Crawford & Salmon, 2004)

In other words, some feature of the environment poses a problem for an organism. Genetically based variants contribute to reproduction and survival. Individuals with those variants will be more successful, passing on their "good genes" and, in many cases, the resulting behavioral repertoire to their offspring.

Although Darwin's logic of natural selection provides the basis for all evolutionary explanations, a number of concepts that were not fully developed in his work have been more completely refined in recent years. Particularly relevant for this volume on the family is kinship theory.

Kinship Theory

Kinship (or the family network) has been a central construct in evolutionary biological analyses of social behavior since Hamilton (1964) demonstrated that altruistic behavior (behavior performed at a cost to oneself and a benefit to others) could evolve if the individuals involved were related. Even though the direct reproductive fitness of the donor is reduced, if his actions aid his own genetic kin, then he receives an indirect fitness benefit. Typically, this idea is expressed by the equation:

$$Br_1 > Cr_2$$

Where

B = the benefit to the recipient

r_1 = the genetic correlation between the donor and the recipient's offspring

C = the cost to the donor

r_2 = the genetic correlation between the donor and its own offspring (Crawford & Salmon, 2004)

In the equation, r represents the probability that the two individuals each have an allele that is a copy of one in a common ancestor. Such an allele is called identical by common descent, and the probability of such is called a genetic correlation or a coefficient of relatedness between individuals. Br_1 is the indirect benefit to the donor through the recipient's additional offspring, and Cr_2 is the direct cost to the helper because of decreased offspring. Both sides of the equation refer to changes in the donor's fitness as a result of his or her actions. This was a revolutionary concept. No longer were organisms simply reproductive strategists, they were also nepotistic strategists. If an individual's genes are just as likely to be reproduced in a sister as in a daughter, one would expect the evolution of sororal investment in the same way one expects maternal investment. This concept revolutionized the way biologists understand social interaction and influence.

Consider within-family conflict. Trivers (1974) used Hamilton's argument that the behavior of an individual is shaped by natural selection to maximize the probability that copies of alleles the individual carries are replicated through her behavior, to analyze within-family conflict. Because the probability of a focal individual replicating her allele(s) through her own offspring is 0.5, whereas replicating it through a sibling's offspring (a niece or nephew) is only 0.25, natural selection will favor individuals who seek a greater share of a parent's resources. Because the parent is equally related to all their children and future grandchildren, they will be selected to resist a particular offspring's demands.

When the child is young, the parent can maximize the child's fitness by investing in him at the expense of additional offspring, who would be the child's future siblings. When the child is older, he can maximize his fitness by deferring parental investment in himself in favor of parental investment in additional younger siblings. Conflict is most intense during the period in which the parent's fitness is increased more by investing in additional children, whereas a particular child's fitness is increased more by continued parental investment. Thus, the intensity of within-family conflict varies both as a function of genetic relationship and according to the relative ages of individuals in the family. Weaning conflict is a well-known example of this.

Haig (1993, 2002) applied Trivers's concept to another level of analysis by considering three sets of genes that may have different interests: genes in the mother, maternally derived genes in the child, and paternally derived genes in the child. Because maternal genes have an equal stake in each child, they will be selected to transfer resources to children as a function of the children's likelihood of reproducing. Genes in the current child have a greater interest in the current child than in future children and will be selected to maximize transfer of resources to the current child. Some genes can be imprinted with information about their paternal origin. This fact makes the situation more complicated if the mother has children by different fathers insofar as paternally active genes in the current child have no stake in children fathered by different men. Haig provided arguments and evidence addressing how these conflicts have influenced the evolution of the female reproductive system and how they can lead to serious health problems for mothers, such as gestational diabetes and preeclampsia.

Adaptations as Decision Makers

An adaptation can be an anatomical structure, a physiological process, or a behavior pattern that contributed to ancestral survival and reproduction (Williams, 1966; Wilson, 1975). The beaks of Darwin's finches, which can be used to characterize the different species of finches living on the Galapagos, provide a classic example of an adaptation that is an anatomical structure. But adaptations can also be understood in terms of processes for carrying out the cost–benefit analyses an ancestral organism required to survive its daily encounters with environmental problems. The fever adaptation, for example, can be considered as a set of decision processes for dealing with certain kinds of invading bacteria. For example, if bacteria A is invading, raise body temperature by X degrees. Harmful bacteria may be destroyed if the body temperature is raised X degrees, which is beneficial to the individual (on the other hand, harmful bacteria cannot be destroyed when fever is blocked by drugs, and resistance to infection appears lowered). But the adaptation has costs as well. Energy is required to raise the body temperature. Moreover, the rise in body temperature can damage other systems of the body if it is excessive and prolonged (Williams & Nesse, 1991).

Thus, a good working definition of an adaptation is: a "set of genetically-coded decision processes that enabled ancestral organisms to carry out cost–benefit analyses in response to a specific set of environmental contingencies, and that organized the effector processes for dealing with those contingencies in such a way that gene(s) producing the decision processes would be reproduced better than alternate sets of genes" (Crawford, 1998, p. 279).

When considering the behavioral domain, sets of decision rules can be thought of as mental mechanisms designed by natural selection for producing the different behaviors required for ancestral survival, growth, and reproduction. Buss (1999) offered the term "evolved psychological mechanisms" for mental mechanisms shaped by natural selection. These are specialized learning mechanisms that organize experience into adaptively meaningful schemas. When activated by the appropriate problem content, they focus attention, organize perception and memory, and call up specialized procedural knowledge that leads to domain-appropriate inferences, judgments, and choices.

KINSHIP AND PSYCHOLOGY

Kinship has long played a central role in anthropological analyses of social behavior, and one might have assumed it to play a similarly strong role in psychology. A focus on the family has been important in such areas as developmental psychology, whereas it has largely been deemed unimportant in other areas such as, for the most part, social psychology (see Daly, Salmon, & Wilson, 1997, for a discussion, and see Burnstein, Crandall, & Kitayama, 1994, for an example of evolutionarily informed social–psychological research).

Although some areas of psychology (such as family studies) appreciate the importance of understanding familial relationships, most areas have suffered from a lack of attention to the qualitatively distinct types of close relationships found within the realm of family. Family psychology is relationship-specific. Humans have evolved specialized mechanisms for processing information and motivating behavior that deal with the distinct demands of being a mate, father, mother, sibling, child, grandparent, and so on Such an evolutionary perspective on family dynamics can provide insight into our behavior in a way that no other perspective offers.

RELATIONSHIP-SPECIFIC ADAPTATIONS

Family, or kinship, is not one relationship but many. The challenges that have faced human mothers, for example, are different from those confronting fathers or offspring or siblings.

Motherhood

The most intimate of mammalian relationships is that between mother and child, and it is the one with the greatest number of special-purpose anatomical, physiological, and psychological mechanisms. But the tasks of motherhood are far more complex than the demands of conception, gestation, and nursing imply. Because not all children are equally capable of translating parental nurture into the long-term survival of parental genes, there has been intense selection for subtle discriminations in the allocation of maternal effort. As a result, the evolved motivational mechanisms regulating maternal investment decisions are contingent on variable attributes of the young, of the material and social situation, and of the mother herself (Daly & Wilson, 1995).

Maternal allocation of investment can also be influenced by other interested parties, particularly the children themselves. Parent–child conflict (Trivers, 1974) is endemic to sexually reproducing species because of genetic asymmetries in family relationships. A mother is equally related genetically to any two of her children, but each of those children is more closely related to themselves than to their sibling (unless they are identical twins). Thus, mother and child are selected to see the relative fitness value of children, and hence the allocation of maternal resources, somewhat differently. This conflict over allocation of maternal resources accounts for the otherwise-puzzling existence of various aspects of mother–child interaction, including weaning conflict (Trivers, 1974) and the sometimes dangerously high levels of substances of fetal origin in the blood of pregnant women, such as placental lactogen, which up-regulates the fetus's access to maternal glucose stores, resulting in gestational diabetes (Haig, 1993). Such areas of conflict between parent and child are explored further in a later chapter (Salmon, this volume).

Many researchers interested in family psychology have focused on the maternal relationship and its special nature. But the sources of variation in maternal feeling and behavior have often been ignored, perhaps because of a lack of exposure to an evolutionary framework capable of making sense of such variation (Daly & Wilson, 1988). Attention to these issues has focused largely on the impact of maternal behavior on the developing child (Howes, Matheson, & Hamilton, 1994) and on maternal style as a personality attribute (Belsky, Fish, & Isabella, 1991), rather than on maternal behaviors as adaptively contingent responses (but see Belsky, 2000, and Bjorklund & Pellegrini, 2002, for examples of evolutionary developmental psychology). Heidi Keller and Athanasios Chasiotis focus on maternal investment in chapter 5.

Fatherhood

There are clear parallels between paternal solicitude and maternal solicitude, but there are also crucial differences. In both mothers and fathers, parental solicitude evolved to vary adaptively in relation to cues of the expected impact of any parental investment on the child's future success, so both parents are selected to assess child quality and need. And both father and mother are selected to discriminate with respect to available cues that the child is the parent's own. However, for mammalian mothers, the evidence is clear: if you gave birth to it, it's yours. Because of internal fertilization and, in humans in particular, concealed ovulation, men can never be certain of paternity. Fathers must rely on sources of information about the mother's probable fidelity, or the child's phenotypic resemblance to his relatives or to himself. One prediction from this logic is that paternal affection is influenced by paternal perceptions of resemblance. Consistent with this prediction, people pay more attention to paternal resemblance than to maternal resemblance, and mothers and their relatives actively promote perceptions of paternal resemblance (Daly & Wilson, 1982; Regalski & Gaulin, 1993). The issues fathers face, in terms of investing in their children, are discussed by David Geary in chapter 6.

Sibship

An understanding of sibling relations also can benefit from a selectionist perspective (Mock & Parker, 1996). Sisterhood was at the heart of Hamilton's (1964) analysis of the evolution of sociality and altruism in haplodiploid insects. But if siblings are major social allies by virtue of relatedness, they are also major competitors, especially for limited maternal resources. As a result, sibling relationships are often ambivalent. Richard Michalski and Harald Euler elaborate on the nature of sibling relationships in chapter 9. And in chapter 14, Nancy Segal, Kevin Chavarria, and Joanne Hoven Stohs discuss a special type of sibling relationship, that of twins.

Our sibships are the social environment into which we are born, with associated opportunities, costs, and niches, and it would be extraordinary if we did not have evolved psyches to deal with the peculiarities of sibling relationships. Sulloway (1995) has used an evolutionary framework to explore niche differentiation with regard to how one deals with one's birth order within a sibship. He elaborates on this idea in chapter 8. Evolutionary considerations suggest that parents will favor their eldest child when resources are scare, and there is evidence that they do just that (Daly & Wilson, 1984). So it is not surprising that firstborn children are supporters of the status quo (Sulloway, 1995, 1996, 1999). There is some theoretical and empirical support for the notion of parental indulgence of lastborns as well, which suggests that it may be the middle children who derive the least benefit from parental investment. In support of this, Salmon (1999, 2003) has found firstborn and lastborn Canadians to differ from middleborns on measures of family solidarity and identity, suggesting that sibling behavioral strategies are shaped by the parental-investment environment. Sulloway has suggested that many sibling differences in personality traits are best explained as arising "because birth order is correlated with differences in age, size, power, and status within the family. These physical and social disparities cause siblings to experience family relationships in dissimilar ways and to pursue differing ways of optimizing their parents' investment in their welfare" (Sulloway, 1999, p. 190).

Grandparenthood

Is grandparenthood a relationship for which we have specific adaptations? It is a cross-culturally general fact that postmenopausal women contribute significantly to their grandchildren's welfare (Lancaster & King, 1985; Sears, Mace, & McGregor, 2000), and it is therefore plausible that mental processes specific to the task of adaptive allocation of grandparental investment have been targets of natural selection (Hawkes, O'Connell, Blurton Jones, Alvarez, &

Charnov, 1998; Smith, 1988). Noting that paternity certainty could influence grandparental investment in particular, and paternal investment generally, Euler and Weitzel (1996) asked adults to rate the degree of grandparental solicitude they experienced from each of their four grandparents. The results demonstrated a strong link with relatedness and paternity certainty, with mother's mother showing the highest solicitude, followed by mother's father, father's mother, and father's father. A maternal grandmother has the greatest certainty that her grandchild is indeed related to her. A father's father, in contrast, has two uncertain links: the grandchild might not be his son's child, and his son might not be his own biological child (see also Michalski & Shackelford, 2005). Harald Euler and Richard Michalski address, in chapter 11, the nature of grandparental and extended-kin relationships.

Mateship

Although mates are not usually close genetic relatives (see Ilanit Tal and Debra Lieberman's discussion of incest in chapter 10 for exceptions to this rule), their relationship is usually considered a family one. Both parties typically have a shared genetic interest in their children. The longer-lasting the relationship, the more likely it is that the optimal allocation of resources for one is the optimal allocation for the other. Issues surrounding mating, marriage, divorce, and love are addressed by Helen Fisher and colleagues in chapter 13. The transition to parenthood that often accompanies a committed mateship is discussed by Sarah Johns and Jay Belsky in chapter 4.

But there is an important difference between mateship and genetic kinship in that extrapair relations can shatter the commonality of interests. Daly and Wilson's studies of marital conflict and violence make this point clear. Suspected or actual infidelity is a uniquely potent source of severe conflict and spousal violence (Daly & Wilson, 1988; Wilson & Daly, 1993).

Step-relationships are such that a child raised by a couple is a potential contributor to the fitness of one partner but not the other. This relatedness asymmetry is known to both parties (unlike in instances of female infidelity and subsequent cuckoldry) before or very early in the relationship. Nevertheless, stepchildren are at an elevated risk of neglect, abuse, and homicide (Daly & Wilson, 1988, 1995), reinforcing the point that the motivational mechanisms of parental feeling are designed to channel affection and investment preferentially toward one's own offspring.

According to Daly and Wilson (1984), motivational differences generate differences in the methods by which stepparents and genetic parents kill a child. Using Canadian and British national-level databases, Daly and Wilson found that stepfathers were more likely than genetic fathers to commit filicide by beating and bludgeoning, arguably revealing stepparental feelings of bitterness and resentment not present to the same degree in genetic fathers. Genetic fathers, in contrast, were more likely than stepfathers to commit filicide by shooting or asphyxiation, methods which often produce a relatively quick and painless death. Weekes-Shackelford and Shackelford (2004) sought to replicate and extend these findings using a United States national-level database of more than four hundred thousand homicides. The results replicated those of Daly and Wilson for genetic fathers and stepfathers. In addition, Weekes-Shackelford and Shackelford identified similar differences in the methods by which stepmothers and genetic mothers committed filicide. In chapter 12, Aaron Goetz discusses the nature and incidence of violence and abuse within families, with a special focus on intimate-partner violence.

CONCLUSIONS

This volume is intended to illustrate the many ways in which an evolutionary perspective on the family can contribute to our understanding of behavior, and the many ways in which this kind of understanding may help us handle the unique aspects of these relationships in our everyday lives. Many of the conflicts and disagreements and the more-enjoyable aspects of family life have been with us since the beginning. Our modern behavior is the product of our evolutionary response to those pressures. Further explorations of what evolutionary theory as a perspective brings to the study of the family can be found in chapter 2, in which Mark Flinn, Robert Quinlan, Kathryn Coe, and Carol Ward present evolutionary anthropological perspectives on the family, and in chapter 3, in which Sarah Blaffer Hrdy addresses the evolutionary context of human development. In chapter 15, Amy Gardiner and David Bjorklund address the future of evolutionary applications to family psychology.

REFERENCES

Belsky, J. (2000). Conditional and alternative reproductive strategies: Individual differences in susceptibility to rearing experience. In J. Rodgers and D. Rowe (Eds.), *Genetic influences on fertility and sexuality* (pp. 127–146). Boston: Kluwer Academic.

Belsky, J., Fish, M., & Isabella, R. A. (1991). Continuity and discontinuity in infant negative and positive emotionality: Family antecedents and attachment consequences. *Developmental Psychology, 27*, 421–431.

Bjorklund, D. F., & Pellegrini, A. D. (2002). *The origins of human nature: Evolutionary developmental psychology.* Washington, DC: American Psychological Association.

Burnstein, E., Crandall, C., & Kitayama, S. (1994). Some neo-Darwinian decision rules for altruism: Weighing cues for inclusive fitness as a function of the biological importance of the decision. *Journal of Personality and Social Psychology, 67,* 773–789.

Buss, D. M. (1999). *Evolutionary psychology: The new science of the mind* (1st ed.). New York: Allyn & Bacon.

Crawford, C. B., & Salmon, C. (2004). The essence of evolutionary psychology. In C. Crawford & C. Salmon (Eds.), *Evolutionary psychology, public policy and personal decisions* (pp. 23–49). Mahwah, NJ: Erlbaum.

Crawford, C. B. (1998). Environments and adaptations: Then and now. In C. B. Crawford & D. Krebs (Eds.), *Handbook of evolutionary psychology: Ideas, issues and applications.* Hillsdale, NJ: Erlbaum.

Daly, M., & Wilson, M. (1982). Whom are newborn babies said to resemble? *Ethology and Sociobiology, 3,* 69–78.

Daly, M., & Wilson, M. (1984). A sociobiological analysis of human infanticide. In G. Hausfater & S. B. Hrdy (Eds.), *Infanticide: Comparative and evolutionary perspectives* (pp. 487–502). Hawthorne, NY: Aldine.

Daly, M., & Wilson, M. (1988). The Darwinian psychology of discriminative parental solicitude. *Nebraska Symposium on Motivation, 35,* 91–144.

Daly, M., & Wilson, M. (1995). Discriminative parental solicitude and the relevance of evolutionary models to the analysis of motivational systems. In M. Gazzaniga (Ed.), *The cognitive neurosciences* (pp. 1269–1286). Cambridge, MA: MIT Press.

Daly, M., Salmon, C., & Wilson, M. (1997). Kinship: The conceptual hole in psychological studies of social cognition and close relationships. In J.A. Simpson and D.T. Kenrick (Eds.), *Evolutionary Social Psychology* (pp. 265–296). Mahwah, NJ: Erlbaum.

Darwin, C. (1859). *On the origin of species by means of natural selection or the preservation of favored races in the struggle for life.* London: John Murray.

Euler, H., & Weitzel, B. (1996). Discriminative grandparental solicitude as reproductive strategy. *Human Nature, 7,* 39–59.

Haig, D. (1993). Genetic conflicts in human pregnancy. *Quarterly Review of Biology, 68,* 495–532.

Haig, D. (2002). *Genomic imprinting and kinship.* New Brunswick, NJ: Rutgers University Press.

Hamilton, W. D. (1964). The genetical evolution of social behaviour. I and II. *Journal of Theoretical Biology, 7,* 1–52.

Hawkes, K., O'Connell, J. F., Blurton Jones, N. G., Alvarez, H., & Charnov, E. L. (1998). Grandmothering, menopause, and the evolution of human life histories. *Proceedings of the National Academy of Sciences of the United States, 95,* 1336–1339.

Holcomb, H. (2004). Darwin and evolutionary moral psychology. In C. Craw-ford & C. Salmon (Eds.), *Evolutionary Psychology, Public Policy and Personal Decisions* (pp.73–95). Mahwah, NJ: Erlbaum.

Howes, C., Matheson, C. G., & Hamilton, C. E. (1994). Maternal, teacher, and child care history correlates of children's relationships with peers. *Child Development, 65,* 264–273.

Lancaster, J. B., & King, B. J. (1985). An evolutionary perspective on meno-pause. In J. K. Brown & V. Kern (Eds.), *In her prime: A new view of middle aged women* (pp. 13–20). Boston: Bergin and Garvey.

Michalski, R. L., & Shackelford, T. K. (2005). Grandparental investment as a function of relational uncertainty and emotional closeness with parents. *Human Nature, 16,* 292–304.

Mock, D. W., & Parker, G. A. (1996). *The evolution of sibling rivalry.* New York: Oxford University Press.

Regalski, J. M. & Gaulin, S. J. C. (1993). Whom are Mexican infants said to resemble? Monitoring and fostering paternal confidence in the Yucatan. *Ethology and Sociobiology, 14,* 97–113.

Salmon, C. (1999). On the impact of sex and birth order on contact with kin. *Human Nature, 10,* 183–197.

Salmon, C. (2003). Birth order and relationships: Family, friends, and sexual partners. *Human Nature, 14,* 73–88.

Sears, R., Mace, R., & McGregor, I. A. (2000). Maternal grandmothers improve nutritional status and survival of children in rural Gambia. *Proceedings of the Royal Society of London. Series B. Biological Sciences, 267,* 1641–1647.

Smith, M. S. (1988). Research in developmental sociobiology: Parenting and family behavior. In K. MacDonald (Ed.), *Sociobiological perspectives on human development* (pp. 271–292). New York: Springer.

Sulloway, F. J. (1995). Birth order and evolutionary psychology: A meta-analytic overview. *Psychological Inquiry, 6,* 75–80.

Sulloway, F. J. (1996). *Born to rebel: Birth order, family dynamics, and creative lives.* New York: Pantheon.

Sulloway, F. J. (1999). Birth order. In M.A. Runco & S. Pritzker (Eds.), *Encyclopedia of Creativity* (Vol.1, pp. 189–202). San Diego, CA: Academic Press.

Trivers, R. L. (1974). Parent–offspring conflict. *American Zoologist, 14,* 249–264.

Weekes-Shackelford, V. A., & Shackelford, T. K. (2004). Methods of filicide: Stepparents and genetic parents kill differently. *Violence and Victims, 19,* 75–81.

Williams, G. C. (1966). *Adaptation and natural selection: A critique of some current evolutionary thought.* Princeton, NJ: Princeton University Press.

Williams, G. C., & Nesse, R. (1991). The dawn of Darwinian medicine. *Quarterly Review of Biology, 66,* 1–22.

Wilson, E. O. (1975). *Sociobiology: The new synthesis*. Cambridge, MA: Harvard University Press.

Wilson, M., & Daly, M. (1993). An evolutionary psychological perspective on male sexual proprietariness and violence against wives. *Violence and Victims, 8,* 271–294.

2 Evolution of the Human Family: Cooperative Males, Long Social ·Childhoods, Smart Mothers, and Extended Kin Networks

Mark V. Flinn, Robert J. Quinlan, Kathryn Coe, and Carol V. Ward

THE HUMAN FAMILY: KEY EVOLUTIONARY PUZZLES

Humans are characterized by a distinctive set of traits, including: (1) large brains, (2) long periods of juvenile dependence, (3) extensive bi-parental care including large transfers of information, (4) multigenerational bilateral kin networks, (5) habitual bipedal locomotion, (6) use of the upper limbs for handling tools, including throwing projectile weapons, (7) concealed, or "cryptic," ovulation, (8) menopause, (9) culture including language, and (10) lethal competition among kin-based coalitions. A few other species exhibit several of these traits; only humans, however, are characterized by the entire combination (Alexander, 2005). The evolution and co-evolution of this suite of traits present several evolutionary questions or puzzles that are central to understanding the human family. Here we first briefly describe these puzzles and then suggest a resolution based on the importance of social competition during human evolution. Afterward we turn to the developmental issue of how the family social environment may affect the timing of reproductive maturation and how this timing is essential to an understanding of the family.

Paternal Care in Multi-Male Groups

Mammals that live in groups with multiple males—such as chimpanzees (*Pan troglodytes*)—usually have little or no paternal care, because the non-exclusivity of mating relationships obscures paternity (Clutton-Brock, 1991). In contrast, it is common for human fathers to provide protection, information, food, and social status for their children. Paternal care in humans appears to be facilitated by relatively stable pair bonds, which not only involves co-operation between mates that often endures over the lifespan, but which requires an unusual type of cooperation among co-residing males—respect for each other's mating relationships.

The relatively exclusive mating relationships that are characteristic of humans generate natural factions within the group. Mating relationships also can create alliances in human groups, linking two families or clans together. By way of comparison, in chimpanzee communities it is difficult for even the most dominant male to monopolize an estrous female; most of the males in a community mate with most of the females (Goodall, 1986). Chimpanzee males in effect "share" a common interest in the community's females and their offspring. Human groups, in contrast, are composed of family units, each with distinct reproductive interests. Men do not typically share mating access to all the group's women; consequently, there are usually reliable cues identifying which children are their genetic offspring and which are those of other men (for exceptions, see Beckerman & Valentine, 2002). Because humans live in multi-male groups yet maintain fairly stable mating relationships, the potential for fission along family lines is high. Still, human groups overcome this inherent conflict between family units to form large, stable coalitions.

This unusual tolerance among co-residential men stands in contrast to the norm of polygamous mate competition in non-human primates. Selection pressures favoring such tolerance are uncertain but likely involve the importance of both male parental investment (Geary & Bjorklund, 2000) and male coalitions for intra-specific conflict (Bernhard, Fischbacher, & Fehr, 2006; Geary & Flinn, 2001; Wrangham, 1999). We term this evolutionary puzzle "cooperative males."

An Extended Period of Juvenile Dependence and Child Development

The human baby is unusually altricial (helpless). Infants must be carried, fed, and protected for a long period in comparison with other primates. Human childhood and adolescence are also lengthy (Bogin, 1999; Leigh, 2004; Smith, 1994).

This extension of the juvenile period that delays reproduction for much longer than for other hominoids appears costly in evolutionary terms. Parental and other kin investment continues for an unusually long time, often well into adulthood and sometimes even after parents die (Coe, 2003).

The selective pressures responsible for this unique suite of life-history characteristics appear central to understanding human evolution (Alexander, 1990a, 1990b; Bjorklund & Pellegrini, 2002; Kaplan, Hill, Lancaster, & Hurtado, 2000; Rosenberg, 2004). The delay of reproduction until at least 15 years of age involves prolonged exposure to extrinsic causes of mortality and longer generational intervals. What advantages of an extended childhood could have outweighed the heavy costs of reduced fecundity and late reproduction (Stearns, 1992; Williams, 1966) for our hominin ancestors? We term this evolutionary puzzle "long social childhoods."

Intelligence, Information, and Female Social Power

The human brain is an astonishing organ. Its cortex comprises 30 billion neurons of 200 different types, each of which are interlinked by about 1,000 synapses, resulting in a million billion connections working at rates of up to 10 billion interactions per second (Edelman, 2006). Quantifying the transduction of these biophysical actions into specific cognitive activities—for example, thoughts and emotions—is difficult, but it is likely that humans have more information-processing capacity than does any other species (Roth & Dicke, 2005).

The human brain evolved rapidly: hominin cranial capacity tripled (from an average of about 450cc to 1,350 cc) in less than 2 million years (Lee & Wolpoff, 2003), or roughly 100,000 neurons and supportive cells per generation. Structural changes such as increased convolutions, thickly myelinated cortical neurons, lateral asymmetries, von Economo neurons, expansion of the neo-cortex, and enhanced integration of the cerebellum also appear significant (Allman, 1999; Amodio & Frith, 2006). In comparison with most other parts of the human genome, selection on genes involved with brain development was especially intense (Gilbert, Dobyns, & Lahn, 2005).

The human brain has high metabolic costs: about 50% of an infant's and 20% of an adult's energetic resources are used to support this neurological activity (Aiello & Wheeler, 1995). The obstetric difficulties associated with birthing a large-headed infant generate additional problems (Rosenberg & Trevathan, 2002). The selective advantages of increased intelligence must have been correspondingly high to overcome these costs.

The human brain is, in short, a big evolutionary paradox. It is developmentally and metabolically expensive; evolved rapidly; enables uniquely human cognitive abilities such as language, empathy, foresight, consciousness, and theory of mind; and generates unusual levels of novelty. The advantages of a larger brain may include enhanced information-processing capacities to contend with ecological pressures that involve sexually dimorphic activities such as hunting and complex foraging (Kaplan & Robson, 2002). There is little evidence, however, of sufficient domain-specific enlargement of those parts of the brain associated with selective pressures from the physical environment (Adolphs, 2003; Geary & Huffman, 2002). Indeed, human cognition has little to distinguish itself in the way of specialized ecological talents. A large brain may have been sexually selected because it was an attractive trait for mate choice (Gavrilets & Vose, 2006; Miller, 2000). However, there is little sexual dimorphism in encephalization quotient or intelligence psychometrics (Jensen, 1998).

One area in which humans are truly extraordinary is sociality. Humans are able to mentally represent the feelings and thoughts of others. Humans have unusually well-developed mechanisms for theory of mind (Amodio & Frith, 2006; Leslie, Friedmann, & German, 2004) and associated specific pathologies in this domain (Baron-Cohen, 1995; Gilbert, 2001). We have exceptional linguistic abilities for transferring information from one brain to another (Pinker, 1994), enabling complex social learning. Social and linguistic competencies are roughly equivalent in both men and women, although human mothers appear to have especially important roles in the development of their children's socio-cognitive development (Deater-Deckard, Atzaba-Poria, & Pike, 2004; Simons, Paternite, & Shore, 2001). In apparent contrast with chimpanzees and gorillas, women have substantial social influence or power, based not only on modeling a behavior, but on the use of information transmitted via language (see Hess & Hagen, 2006). We term this evolutionary puzzle of large brains, female social power, and the associated development of social competency "smart mothers."

We use the term "smart" here to describe mental capabilities and the resulting behavioral repertoire required for complex social life. Human interactions, influenced initially largely by male physical strength, were increasingly coming to be based on social information and skill. Intense inter-group competition created pressure for within-group social cohesion (Flinn, Geary, & Ward, 2005), which required not only strength but complex social strategies.

Among contemporary "tribal" populations, increased inter-group aggression is associated with decreased levels of bi-parental care (Ember & Ember, 2002; Whiting & Whiting, 1975). Bi-parental care implies, to some extent, skills for promoting enduring social relationship between a man and a woman. Such relationships, as current divorce records make clear, are not something that comes naturally to humans. Moral systems, across cultures, provided step-by-step procedures for maintaining enduring social relationships (Edel & Edel, 1959). If the ecological dominance–social competition scenario is correct (Flinn, Geary, & Ward, 2005), fathers may often have been absent, with the mother largely responsible for the development of social competence favored by intense pressure for within-group cohesion. If we wish to understand human families, we must understand how mothers prepared their altricial children for a "world that [was becoming] socially complex" (Coe, 2003, p. 110).

Kin Networks and Multiple Caretakers

All human societies recognize kinship (Brown, 1991) as a key organizational principle. All languages have kinship terminologies and concomitant expectations of nepotism (Fortes, 1969; Murdock, 1949). Human kinship systems appear unique in the consistency of both bilateral (maternal and paternal) and multigenerational structure. These aspects of human kinship link families into broader cooperative systems and provide additional opportunities for alloparental care during the long social childhood. Human grandparents stand out as unusually important in this regard (Flinn & Leone, 2006, 2007; Hrdy, 2005).

Grandparents and grand-offspring share 25% of their genes (identical by descent), a significant opportunity for kin selection. Few species, however, live in groups with multiple overlapping generations of kin. Fewer still have significant social relationships among individuals two or more generations apart. Humans appear rather exceptional in this regard. Grandparenting is cross-culturally ubiquitous and pervasive (Murdock, 1967; Sear, Mace, & McGregor, 2000). Our life histories allow for significant generational overlaps, including an apparent, extended post-reproductive stage facilitated by the unique human physiological adaptation of menopause (Alexander, 1987; Hawkes, 2003).

The neuroendocrinological mechanisms guiding attachment processes in grand-relationships are uncertain. The maternal neuropeptide oxytocin and dopamine system is a likely candidate (for review, see Fleming, O'Day, & Kraemer, 1999; Insel, 2000). Regardless, the significance of emotional bonding between grandparents and grandchildren is beyond doubt. The evolved functions are uncertain but likely involve the exceptional importance of long-term extensive and intensive investment for the human child. The emotional and cognitive processes that guide grand-relationships must have evolved because they enhanced the survival and eventual reproductive success of grandchildren. In addition to the physical basics of food, protection, and hygienic care, development of the human child is strongly influenced by the dynamics of the social environment (Dunn, 2004; Hetherington, 2003a,

2003b; Konner, 1991). Grandparents may have knowledge and experience that are important and useful for helping grandchildren and other relatives succeed in social competition (Coe, 2003). Humans are unusual in the role of kin in alloparental care and group coalitions. We term this evolutionary puzzle "extended kin networks."

THE SOCIAL ENVIRONMENT AS A KEY SELECTIVE PRESSURE

Information Processing Is a Core Human Adaptation

Children are especially tuned to their social world and the information it provides. The social world is a rich source of useful information for cognitive development. The human brain appears designed by natural selection to take advantage of this bonanza of data (Belsky, 2005; Bjorklund & Pellegrini, 2002; Tooby & Cosmides, 1992). "Culture" may be viewed as a highly dynamic information pool that co-evolved with the extensive information-processing abilities associated with our flexible communicative and socio-cognitive competencies (Alexander, 1979). With the increasing importance and power of information in hominin social interaction, culture and tradition may have become an arena of social cooperation and competition (Baumeister, 2005; Coe, 2003; Flinn, 2004, 2006a).

The key issue is *novelty*. One of the most difficult challenges to understanding human cognitive evolution and its handmaiden culture is the unique informational arms race that underlies human behavior. The reaction norms posited by evolutionary psychology to guide evoked culture within specific domains may be necessary but insufficient (Chiappe & MacDonald, 2005). The mind does not appear limited to a pre-determined Pleistocene set of options—such as choosing mate A if in environment X, but choose mate B if in environment Y—analogous to examples of simple phenotypic plasticity (MacDonald & Hershberger, 2005).

Keeping up in the hominin social chess game required imitation. Getting ahead favored creativity to produce new solutions to beat the current winning strategies. Random changes, however, are risky and ineffective. Hence the importance of cognitive abilities to hone choices among imagined innovations in ever-more-complex social scenarios. The theater of the mind that allows humans to "understand other persons as intentional agents" (Tomasello, 1999, p. 526) provides the basis for the evaluation and refinement of creative solutions to the never-ending novelty of the social arms race. This process of filtering the riot of novel information generated by the creative mind favored the cognitive mechanisms for recursive pattern recognition in the "open" domains of both language (Nowak, Komarova, & Niyogi, 2001; Pinker, 1994) and social dynamics (Flinn, 2006a; Geary, 2005). Cultural "traditions" passed down through the generations also help constrain the creative mind (Coe, 2003; Flinn & Coe, 2007). The evolutionary basis for these psychological mechanisms underlying the importance of social learning and culture appears rooted in a process of "runaway social selection" (Alexander, 2005; Flinn & Alexander, 2007).

Runaway Social Selection

Darwin (1871) recognized that there could be important differences between (1) selection occurring as a consequence of interaction with ecological factors such as predators, climate, and food, and (2) selection occurring as a consequence of interactions among conspecifics, that is, members of the same species competing with each other over resources such as nest sites, food, and mates. The former is termed "natural selection" and the latter "social selection," of which sexual selection may be considered a special subtype (West-Eberhard, 1983). The pace and directions of evolutionary changes in behavior and morphology produced by these two types of selection—natural and social—can be significantly different (Fisher, 1930; West-Eberhard, 2003).

Selection that occurs as a consequence of interactions between species can be intense and unending—for example with parasite-host red-queen evolution (Hamilton, Axelrod, & Tanese, 1990) and other biotic arms races. Intra-specific social competition may generate selective pressures that cause even more rapid and dramatic evolutionary changes. Relative to natural selection, social selection has the following characteristics (West-Eberhard, 1983): (1) The intensity of social selection (and consequent genetic changes) can be very high because competition among conspecifics can have especially strong effects on differential reproduction. (2) Because the salient selective pressures involve competition among members of the same species, the normal ecological constraints are often relaxed for social selection. Hence, traits can evolve in seemingly extreme and bizarre directions before counterbalancing natural selection slows the process. (3) Because social competition involves *relative* superiority among conspecifics, the bar can be constantly and consistently raised generation after generation in an unending arms race. (4) Because social competition can involve multiple iterations of linked strategy and counterstrategy among interacting individuals, the process of social selection can become autocatalytic, its pace and directions partly determined from within, generating what might be termed "secondary red queens." For example, reoccurrence of social competition over lifetimes and generations can favor flexible phenotypic responses such as social learning that enables constantly changing strategies. Phenotypic flexibility of learned behavior to contend with a dynamic target may benefit from enhanced information-processing capacities, especially in regard to foresight and scenario building.

Human evolution appears characterized by these circumstances generating a process of runaway social selection (Alexander, 2005; Flinn & Alexander, 2007). Humans, more so than any other species, appear to have become their own most potent selective pressure via social competition involving coalitions (Alexander, 1989; Geary & Flinn, 2002), and dominance of their ecologies involving niche construction (Laland, Odling-Smee, & Feldman, 2000). The primary functions of the most extraordinary and distinctive human mental abilities—language, imagination, self-awareness, theory of mind, foresight, and consciousness—involve the negotiation of social relationships (Flinn, Geary, & Ward, 2005; Siegal & Varley, 2002; Tulving, 2002). The multiple-party reciprocity and shifting nested sub-coalitions characteristic of human sociality generate especially difficult information-processing demands for these cognitive facilities that underlie social competency. Hominin social competition involved increasing amounts of novel information and creative strategies. Culture emerged as a new selective pressure on the evolving brain.

Evolution of the Cultural Brain

As noted above, the human brain is a big evolutionary paradox. It has high metabolic costs, takes a long time to develop, evolved rapidly, enables behavior to change quickly, has unique linguistic and social aptitudes, and generates unusual levels of informational novelty. Its primary functions include dealing with other human brains (Adolphs, 2003; Alexander, 2005; Amodio & Frith, 2006). The currency is not foot-speed or antibody production, but the generation and processing of data in the social worlds of the human brains' own collective and historical information pools. Some of the standout features of our brains that distinguish us from our primate relatives are asymmetrically localized in the prefrontal cortex, including especially the dorsolateral prefrontal cortex and frontal pole (Ghazanfar & Santos, 2004; for review, see Geary, 2005). These areas appear to be involved with "social-scenario building" or the ability to "see ourselves as others see us so that we may cause competitive others to see us as we wish them to" (Alexander, 1990b, p. 7) and are linked to specific social abilities such as understanding sarcasm (Shamay-Tsoory, Tomer, & Aharon-Peretz, 2005) and morality (Moll, Zahn, Oliveira-Souza, Krueger, & Grafman, 2005). An extended childhood seems to enable the development of these necessary social skills (Joffe, 1997).

Evolution of the Human Family as a Nest for the Child's Social Mind

To summarize our argument, we view the human family as the nexus for the suite of extraordinary and unique human traits. Humans are the only species to live in large multi-male groups with complex coalitions and extensive paternal and alloparental care, and the altricial infant is indicative of a protective environment with intense parenting and alloparental care in the context of kin groups (Chisholm, 1999). The human baby does not need to be physically precocial, instead, the brain continues rapid growth and the corresponding cognitive competencies largely direct attention toward the social environment. Plastic neural systems adapt to the nuances of the local community, such as its language (Alexander, 1990a; Bjorklund & Pellegrini, 2002; Fisher, 2005; Geary & Bjorklund, 2000). In contrast to the slow development of the ecological skills of movement, fighting, and feeding, the human infant rapidly acquires skill with the complex communication system of human language (Pinker, 1994; Sakai, 2005). The extraordinary information-transfer abilities enabled by linguistic competency provide a conduit to the knowledge available in other human minds. This emergent capability for intensive and extensive communication potentiates the social-dynamics characteristic of human groups (Deacon, 1997; Dunbar, 1998) and provides a new mechanism for social learning and culture.

An extended childhood appears useful for acquiring the knowledge and practice to hone social skills and to build coalitional relationships necessary for successful negotiation of the increasingly intense social competition of adolescence and adulthood. Ecologically related play and activities (e.g., exploration of the physical environment) are also important (see Geary, Byrd-Craven, Hoard, Vigil, & Numtee, 2003) but appear similar to those of other primates. The unusual scheduling of human reproductive maturity, including an "adrenarche" (patterned increases in adrenal activities preceding puberty) and a delay in direct mate competition among men appears to extend the period of practicing social roles and extends social ontogeny.

The advantages of intensive parenting, including paternal protection and other care, require a most unusual pattern of mating relationships: moderately exclusive pair bonding in multiple-male groups. No other primate (or mammal) that lives in large, cooperative multiple-reproductive-male groups has extensive male parental care, although some protection by males is evident in baboons (Buchan, Alberts, Silk, & Altmann, 2003). Competition for females in multiple-male groups usually results in low confidence of paternity (e.g., chimpanzees). Males forming exclusive pair bonds in multiple-male groups would provide cues of non-paternity to other men, and hence place their offspring in great danger of infanticide (Hrdy, 1999).

Paternal care is most likely to be favored by natural selection in conditions where men can identify their offspring with sufficient probability to offset the costs of investment, although reciprocity with mates is also likely to be involved (Geary & Flinn, 2001; Smuts & Smuts, 1993). Humans exhibit a unique "nested family" social structure, involving complex reciprocity among men and women to restrict direct competition for mates among group members.

Foraging men "provide a considerable portion of the energy consumed by juveniles and reproductive-aged women.... It is the partnership between men and women that allows long-term juvenile dependence and learning and high rates of survival" (Kaplan et al., 2000, p. 173). Bi-parental care may be particularly important during the period of lactation that coincides with attachment, a key component in the development of social competence. Among the Hadza foragers of Tanzania, Marlowe (2003) found that husbands appear to compensate for their wives' diminished foraging return when they have young children. Similarly, among the Ache and Hiwi foragers, women's time spent foraging and in childcare were inversely related; nursing women spent less time foraging than did non-nursing women, and women's foraging time was inversely related to their husbands foraging (Hurtado, Hill, Kaplan, & Hurtado, 1992). Based on these findings Marlowe (2003) suggests that pair bonds in human evolution may function to provision a mate and children during a "critical period" coinciding with lactation.

Among foragers "divorce or paternal death leads to high rates of child mortality among the Ache, the Hiwi, and the !Kung, but not the Hadza" (Kaplan et al., [2000], p. 173). Similar to findings for foragers, in the world's large-scale "industrial" populations, public health studies consistently find that single mothers tend to wean their children earlier than do women living with a mate (Bar-Yam & Darby, 1997; Pande, Unwin, & Haheim, 1997). This association is probably related to the tradeoff between breastfeeding and women's work (Arlotti, Cottrell, Lee, & Curtin, 1998) that may be particularly pressing among single mothers. Prolonged nursing may have a positive influence on long-term psychomotor and neural development in well-nourished populations (Clark et al., 2006; Horwood, Darlow, & Mogridge, 2001). Breastfeeding duration has also been associated with long-term reduction in children's stress-hormone levels (Quinlan, Quinlan, & Flinn, 2003), and increased "developmental stability" (Leone, Quinlan, Hayden, Stewart, & Flinn, 2004). Nursing can be important to the mother–child bond, associated with positive emotions and attachment linked to maternal hormones, including prolactin and oxytocin (Ellison, 2001, pp. 83–126). Maternal responsiveness, related to nursing, appears to influence the development of children's attachment styles and later conjugal relations as an adult (Belsky, 1997; Chisholm, 1999). Ecological exigencies for social competence may drive the evolution of human pair bonds and regulate pair-bond stability in contemporary populations.

It is difficult to imagine how this system could be maintained in the absence of another unusual human trait: concealed, or "cryptic," ovulation (Alexander & Noonan, 1979). Human groups tend to be male philopatric (men tend to remain in their natal groups), resulting in extensive male-kin alliances, useful for competing against other groups of male kin (LeBlanc, 2003; Wrangham & Peterson, 1996). Women also have complex alliances but usually are not involved directly in the overt physical aggression characteristic of inter-group relations (Campbell, 2002; Geary & Flinn, 2002). Parents and other kin may be especially important for the child's mental development of social and cultural maps because they can be relied upon as landmarks to provide relatively honest information. From this perspective, the evolutionary significance of the human family in regard to child development is viewed more as a nest from which social skills may be acquired than merely an economic unit centered on the sexual division of labor (Flinn, Ward, & Noone, 2005).

Evolution of the Human Family: The Fossil Evidence

A prolonged childhood in the latter part of human evolution can be seen in delayed dental maturation rates occurring after the early evolution of *Homo*. The teeth of early *Homo erectus* (1.6 million years) developed at similarly relatively rapid rates as those of apes and australopithecines (Dean et al., 2001; Smith, 1993). However, they are modern in pattern by 800,000 years ago (Bermudez de Castro, Rosas, Carbonell, Nicolas, Rodriguez, & Arsuaga, 1999), and certainly in rate by 150,000 years ago (Guatelli-Steinberg, Reid, Bishop, & Larsen, 2005; see also Dean et al., 2001). Thus, by the appearance of *Homo sapiens*, at least, rates of juvenile development appear to have slowed to modern human levels.

During this time period, brain size increased roughly 50%, from 800–900 cc to 1,200–1,600 cc. At this same time, female body size increased markedly from about three to four feet in stature to four to five feet, with a corresponding estimated 50% increase in body mass (McHenry 1992a, 1992b; Ruff, Trinkaus, Walker, & Larsen, 1993). These brain size increases were associated with a change in pelvic structure permitting the birth of larger-brained infants (Ruff, 2002). It may be that this change in body size and pelvic structure permitted the initial brain size increase without altering selection on timing of birth and rate of brain growth. Subsequent brain size increase, then, would have necessitated more altricial infants with a greater percentage of brain growth occurring post-natally (Portman, 1941). This, and the slowing rates of development during this period, may reflect intensified selection for a long period of dependency and learning throughout the evolution of *Homo erectus*, appearing in roughly modern human form by the appearance of *Homo sapiens*.

With the origins of *Homo*, female body size increased dramatically, and although men increased in size, the change was not as pronounced, resulting in a decrease in sexual dimorphism (McHenry 1992a, 1992b; Ruff et al., 1993). Selection for larger women may have been due to increasing fecundity and the ability to produce larger, higher-quality infants, perhaps facilitated by increasing ability to extract higher-quality resources from the environment more consistently (Ungar, Grine, Teaford, & El Zaatari, 2006). A lack of concomitant selection for a similar magnitude of increasing male size is what probably reflects changing male reproductive strategies. Although its magnitude is the subject of current debate, most indications are that *Australopithecus* species were more dimorphic in body mass than later hominins (Cunningham, Cole, Jungers, Ward, & Wescott, 2005; Plavcan, Lockwood, Kimbel, Lague, & Harmon, 2005; but see Reno, Meindl, McCollum, & Lovejoy, 2005). This change in dimorphism likely reflects changing patterns of social behavior (e.g., Plavcan & Van Schaik, 1997a, 1997b). High levels of sexual dimorphism are associated with extensive and intense mate competition in extant primates (Plavcan, 2000). Reduced dimorphism in hominoids is associated with stable male–female mating relationships (hylobatids, humans) (Plavcan, 2000; Plavcan & Van Schaik, 1997a) and also with male–male coalitions (chimpanzees, humans) (Pawlowski, Lowen, & Dunbar, 1998; Plavcan & Van Schaik, 1997a, 1997b). Both of these systems offer less relative advantage for large male size than do other hominoid social systems. It is reasonable to hypothesize that either, and perhaps both, of these social changes were taking place early in the evolution of *Homo*. An increase in infant altriciality necessitates greater social support for women, and almost certainly paternal and alloparental care. Fairly exclusive mating relationships and cooperative kin networks would have permitted both of these changes.

Ecological Variation in Parenting, Pair Bonds, and Life-History Development

Social competence is developmentally expensive in time, instruction, and parental care. Costs are not equally justified for all expected adult environments. The human family may help children adjust development in response to environmental exigencies for appropriate tradeoffs in life-history strategies. Life history reflects two basic "decisions" (see Roff, 2002): whether to reproduce now or later, and how much to invest in each offspring. If all else is equal, then organisms should begin to reproduce as soon as possible to maximize fitness. But when fitness hinges on accumulation of resources and skills (including social skills), delaying reproduction is appropriate (Roff, 2002; Geary & Bjorklund, 2000). Long delays, however, can reduce fitness through a shortened reproductive span, discounted reproduction, and mortality exposure. Parental care in early childhood appears to affect life-history strategies in humans (Chisholm, Quinlivan, Petersen, & Coall, 2005; Draper & Harpending, 1982; Quinlan, 2003), suggesting a "rule of thumb" for development (Belsky, Steinberg, & Draper, 1991). Direct parental care received during childhood may determine whether development continues or not and indicates appropriate adult strategies. If a child perceives that "parental investment" (PI) is consistent and forthcoming, then she should delay reproduction and emphasize high levels of PI herself. High levels of PI indicate an environment in which offspring success is sensitive to parental care, and a long developmental period should improve offspring social competency. Delayed reproduction coupled with high parental investment is called a "parenting-effort strategy." If PI is not forthcoming, then the child should accelerate reproductive development. Low levels of PI may indicate that success is not dependent on parenting, because environmental risks cannot be avoided through additional parental care (Chisholm, 1999; Quinlan, 2003, 2006). If PI is not forthcoming, then delaying reproduction may reduce fitness. Therefore, limited PI should predict accelerated maturation. A strategy characterized by early maturity coupled with low parental investment is called "mating effort."

The nature of risk in an environment should influence strategic choices. "Risk" can be defined as "unpredictable variability in the outcome of an adaptively significant behavior" (Winterhalder & Leslie, 2002, p. 61). If risk is high, then parental effort might be wasted because child outcomes are determined by chance rather than parenting (Quinlan, 2007; see also Scheper-Hughes, 1992). Hence, high fertility and lower levels of parental investment per child are predicted to enhance parents' fitness. But if extrinsic risk is low, then more children survive to reproduce, and responsive parenting can promote children's ultimate success as members of their society. If knowledge, skill, and social competence lead to success (Flinn, 2004; Kaplan et al., 2000), then low fertility and higher levels of parental investment are predicted to enhance parents' long-term fitness (Mace, 2000). The nature of parental care during childhood may indicate appropriate adult strategies and affect developmental pathways tuned to socio-environmental risk.

The quality of pair bonds is a key feature in theories of human life-history development. Pair-bond stability and father involvement may be reliable indicators of local resource stability and the long-term benefits of parental care.

This hypothesis is based in parental investment theory (Clutton-Brock, 1991; Trivers, 1972). Parental investment is defined as expenditures (cash, time, attention, etc.) benefiting one offspring at a cost to parents' ability to invest in other offspring or reproductive opportunities (Clutton-Brock, 1991, p. 9). The theory predicts father abandonment in environments where paternal care does not benefit men's fitness (Trivers, 1985). "Aloofness" between women and their mates may influence socialization practices that shape adult behavior (Draper & Harpending, 1982).

Stress response systems may link parenting to reproductive development (Cameron, Champagne, Parent, Fish, Ozaki-Kuroda, & Meaney, 2005; Chisholm, 1999; Ellis, 2004). Unresponsive parenting is positively associated with children's stress-hormone levels (cortisol) (Ellis, Essex, & Boyce, 2005; Flinn, 2006b) and autonomic reactivity (reviewed in Boyce & Ellis, 2005). Early life stress has been associated with difficulty in bonding and "affiliative" behavior as adults (Henry & Wang, 1998). Although pathologically high stress may significantly delay reproductive development (Henry & Wang, 1998), moderately stressful family environments are associated with accelerated maturation in healthy, well-nourished populations (Ellis & Garber, 2000; Moffitt, Caspi, Belsky, & Silva, 1992). Timing of stressful family events may influence the strength of developmental effects because organizational influences are strongest in early childhood (West-Eberhard, 2003).

Rodent models of adaptive stress-response systems and related behavioral and reproductive strategies have identified maternal behavior as a mechanism that communicates ecological conditions to offspring (e.g., Cameron et al., 2005). Children's experience of maternal behavior throws regulatory switches associated with a developmental cascade, including sympathetic adrenomedullary (autonomic) and adrenocortical (cortisol) reactivity, timing of puberty, defensive responses, and reproductive behavior.

Among humans, warm and supportive family environments have been found to predict heightened autonomic reactivity (Ellis et al., 2005), early puberty (reviewed in Ellis, 2004), and development of high parenting-effort life-history strategies (Quinlan, 2003). Pair bonds apparently support warm, affectionate family environments (Quinlan, 2003). Mothers often face a critical choice between childcare and work. Tradeoffs between parenting and production create pressure for cooperative childrearing among humans. Nursing often taxes mothers' time and energy in ways that other childcare does not; hence, parental cooperation may be particularly important during lactation (Marlowe, 2003). A child's father may be especially well situated to assist the nursing mother because he and the mother share identical genetic interest in their children's success. Other potential helpers may not share such "symmetrical" interests with a child's mother.

SUMMARY AND CONCLUDING REMARKS

Human childhood is a life-history stage that appears necessary and useful for acquiring the information and practice to build and refine the mental algorithms critical for negotiating the social coalitions that are key to success in our species. Mastering the social environment presents special challenges for the human child. Social competence is difficult because the target is constantly changing and similarly equipped with theory of mind and other cognitive abilities. Here we suggest that family environment, including care from fathers, siblings, and grandparents, is a primary source and mediator of the ontogeny of social competencies.

Following the ecological-dominance/social-competition model, human family systems and child-development strategies may have evolved in response to a cycle of inter-group conflict on a multigenerational time scale. Human developmental plasticity appears consistent with cycling on "cultural" time scales—that is, over the course of generations that coincide with violent population expansions followed by periods (generations) of stasis in which competition becomes more subtle and social rather than violent. Bi-parental care enhances children's social competence during non-warfare periods, but mothers may take on increased socialization responsibilities, perhaps with the help of grandmothers, during times of intense inter-group conflict.

An evolutionary developmental perspective of the family can be useful in these efforts to understand this critical aspect of a child's world by integrating knowledge of physiological causes with the logic of adaptive design by natural selection. Human biology has been profoundly affected by our evolutionary history as unusually social creatures, including, perhaps, a special reliance upon smart mothers, cooperative fathers, and helpful grandparents. Indeed, the mind of the human child may have design features that enable its development as a group project, guided by the multitudinous informational contributions of its ancestors and co-descendants (Coe, 2003).

REFERENCES

Adolphs, R. (2003). Cognitive neuroscience of human social behavior. *Nature Reviews, Neuroscience, 4*, 165–178.

Aiello, L. C., & Wheeler, P. (1995). The expensive-tissue hypothesis: The brain and the digestive system in human and primate evolution. *Current Anthropology, 36*, 199–221.

Alexander, R. D. (1979). *Darwinism and human affairs.* Seattle: University of Washington Press.

Alexander, R. D. (1987). *The biology of moral systems.* Hawthorne, NY: Aldine.

Alexander, R. D. (1989). Evolution of the human psyche. In P. Mellars & C. Stringer (Eds.), *The human revolution* (pp. 455–513). Chicago: University of Chicago Press.

Alexander, R. D. (1990a). Epigenetic rules and Darwinian algorithms: The adaptive study of learning and development. *Ethology and Sociobiology, 11*, 1–63.

Alexander, R. D. (1990b). *How humans evolved: Reflections on the uniquely unique species.* Museum of Zoology (Special Publication No. 1). Ann Arbor: The University of Michigan.

Alexander, R. D. (2005). Evolutionary selection and the nature of humanity. In V. Hosle & C. Illies (Eds.), *Darwinism and philosophy* (chap. 15). South Bend, IN: University of Notre Dame Press.

Alexander, R.D., & Noonan, K.M. (1979). Concealment of ovulation, parental care, and human social evolution. In N. Chagnon & W. Irons (Eds.), *Evolutionary Biology and Human Social Behavior.* North Scituate, MA: Duxbury Press.

Allman, J. (1999). *Evolving Brains.* New York: Scientific American Library.

Amodio, D. M., & Frith, C. D. (2006). Meeting of minds: The medial frontal cortex and social cognition. *Nature Reviews Neuroscience, 7*, 268–277.

Arlotti, J. P., Cottrell, B. H., Lee, S. H., & Curtin, J. J. (1998). Breastfeeding among low-income women with and without peer support. *Journal of Community Health Nursing, 15*, 163–78.

Bar-Yam, N. B., & Darby, L. (1997). Fathers and breastfeeding: A review of the literature. *Journal of Human Lactation, 13*, 45–50.

Baron-Cohen, S. (1995). *Mindblindness: An essay on autism and theory of mind.* Boston, MA: MIT/Bradford Books.

Baumeister, R. F. (2005). *The cultural animal: Human nature, meaning, and social life.* New York: Oxford University Press.

Beckerman, S., & Valentine, P. (Eds.) (2002). *Cultures of multiple fathers: The theory and practice of partible paternity in South America.* Gainesville, FL: University of Florida Press.

Belsky, J. (1997). Attachment, mating, and parenting: An evolutionary interpretation. *Human Nature, 8*, 361–381.

Belsky, J. (2005). Differential susceptibility to rearing influence: An evolutionary hypothesis and some evidence. In B. J. Ellis & D. F. Bjorklund (Eds.), *Origins of the social mind: Evolutionary psychology and child development* (pp. 139–163). New York, NY: Guilford Press.

Belsky, J., Steinberg, L., & Draper, P. (1991). Childhood experience, interpersonal development, and reproductive strategy: an evolutionary theory of socialization. *Child Development, 62*, 647–670.

Bermudez de Castro, J. M., Rosas, A., Carbonell, E., Nicolas, M. E., Rodriguez, J., & Arsuaga, J. L. (1999). A modern human pattern of dental development in lower Pleistocene hominids from Atapuerca–TD6 (Spain). *Proceedings of the National Academy of Sciences, 96*(7), 4210–4213.

Bernhard, H., Fischbacher, U., & Fehr, E. (2006). Parochial altruism in humans. *Nature, 442*(7105), 912–915.

Bjorklund, D. F., & Pellegrini, A. D. (2002). *The origins of human nature: Evolutionary developmental psychology.* Washington, DC: APA Press.

Bogin, B. (1999). *Patterns of human growth* (2nd ed.). Cambridge: Cambridge University Press.

Boyce, W. T., & Ellis, B. J. (2005). Biological sensitivity to context: I. An evolutionary-developmental theory of the origins and functions of stress reactivity. *Development & Psychopathology, 17,* 271–301.

Brown, D. E. (1991). *Human universals.* Philadelphia: Temple University Press.

Buchan, J. C., Alberts, S. C., Silk, J. B., & Altmann, J. (2003). True paternal care in a multi-male primate society. *Nature, 425,* 179–181.

Cameron, N. M., Champagne, F. A., Parent, C., Fish, E. W., Ozaki-Kuroda, K., & Meaney, M. J. (2005). The programming of individual differences in defensive responses and reproductive strategies in the rat through variations in maternal care. *Neuroscience and Biobehavioral Reviews, 29,* 843–865.

Campbell, A. (2002). *A mind of her own: The evolutionary psychology of women.* London: Oxford University Press.

Chiappe, D., & MacDonald, K. (2005). The evolution of domain-general mechanisms in intelligence and learning. *Journal of General Psychology, 132,* 5–40.

Chisholm, J. S. (1999). *Death, hope, and sex.* Cambridge: Cambridge University Press.

Chisholm, J. S., Quinlivan, J. A., Petersen, R. W., & Coall, D. A. (2005). Early stress predicts age at menarche and first birth, adult attachment, and expected lifespan. *Human Nature, 16*(3), 233–265.

Clark, K. M., Castillo, M., Calatroni, A., Walter, T., Cayazzo, M., Pino, P., et al. (2006). Breast-feeding and mental and motor development at 5½ years. *Ambulatory Pediatrics, 6,* 65–71.

Clutton-Brock, T. H. (1991). *The evolution of parental care.* Princeton, NJ: Princeton University Press.

Coe, K. (2003). *The ancestress hypothesis: Visual art as adaptation.* New Brunswick: Rutgers University Press.

Cunningham, D. L., Cole, T., III, Jungers, W. L., Ward, C. V., & Wescott, D. (2005). Patterns of postcranial and body mass dimorphism in hominoids. *American Journal of Physical Anthropology Supplement, 40,* 90.

Darwin, C. R. (1871). The descent of man and selection in relation to sex. London: John Murray.

Deacon, T. W. (1997). *The symbolic species: The co-evolution of language and the brain.* New York: Norton.

Dean, C., Leakey, M. G., Reid, D., Schrenk, F., Schwartz, G. T., Stringer, C., et al. (2001). Growth processes in teeth distinguish modern humans from *Homo erectus* and earlier hominins. *Nature, 414,* 628–631.

Deater-Deckard, K., Atzaba-Poria, N., & Pike, A. (2004). Mother– and father–child mutuality in Anglo and Indian British families: A link with lower externalizing behaviors. *Journal of Abnormal Child Psychology, 32,* 609–620.

Draper, P., & Harpending, H. (1982). Father absence and reproductive strategy: An evolutionary perspective. *Journal of Anthropological Research, 38*, 255–279.

Dunbar, R. I. M. (1998). The social brain hypothesis. *Evolutionary Anthropology, 6*, 178–190.

Dunn, J. (2004). Understanding children's family worlds: Family transitions and children's outcome. *Merrill-Palmer Quarterly, 50*, 224–235.

Edel, M., & Edel, A. (1959). *Anthropology and ethics.* Springfield, IL: Charles C. Thomas.

Edelman, G. M. (2006). *Second nature: Brain science and human knowledge.* New Haven: Yale University Press.

Ellis, B. J. (2004). Timing of pubertal maturation in girls: an integrated life history approach. *Psychological Bulletin, 130*, 920–958.

Ellis, B. J., Essex, M. J., & Boyce, W. T. (2005). Biological sensitivity to context: II. Empirical explorations of an evolutionary-developmental theory. *Development & Psychopathology, 17*, 303–328.

Ellis, B. J., & Garber, J. (2000). Psychosocial antecedents of variation in girls' pubertal timing: maternal depression, stepfather presence, and marital and family stress. *Child Development, 71*, 485–501.

Ellison, P. T. (2001). *On fertile ground, A natural history of human reproduction.* Cambridge, MA: Harvard.

Ember, C. R., & Ember, M. (2002). Father absence and male aggression: a re-examination of the comparative evidence. *Ethos, 29*, 296–314.

Fisher, R. A. (1930). *The genetical theory of natural selection.* Oxford: Clarendon Press.

Fisher, S. E. (2005). On genes, speech, and language. *New England Journal of Medicine, 353*, 1655–1657.

Fleming, A. S., O'Day, D. H., & Kraemer, G. W. (1999). Neurobiology of mother–infant interactions: Experience and central nervous system plasticity across development and generations. *Neuroscience and Biobehavioral Reviews, 23*, 673–685.

Flinn, M. V. (2004). Culture and developmental plasticity: Evolution of the social brain. In K. MacDonald & R. L. Burgess (Eds.), *Evolutionary perspectives on child development* (pp. 73–98). Thousand Oaks, CA: Sage.

Flinn, M. V. (2006a). Cross-cultural universals and variations: The evolutionary paradox of informational novelty. *Psychological Inquiry, 17*, 118–123.

Flinn, M. V. (2006b). Evolution and ontogeny of stress response to social challenge in the human child. *Developmental Review, 26*, 138–174.

Flinn, M. V., & Alexander, R. D. (2007). Runaway social selection. In S. W. Gangestad & J. A. Simpson (Eds.), *The evolution of mind* (pp. 249–255). New York: Guilford Press.

Flinn, M. V., & Coe, M. K. (2007). The linked red queens of human cognition, coalitions, and culture. In S. W. Gangestad & J. A. Simpson (Eds.), *The evolution of mind* (pp. 339–347). New York: Guilford Press.

Flinn, M. V., Geary, D. C., & Ward, C. V. (2005). Ecological dominance, social competition, and coalitionary arms races: Why humans evolved extraordinary intelligence. *Evolution and Human Behavior, 26*, 10–46.

Flinn, M. V., & Leone, D. V. (2006). Early trauma and the ontogeny of glucocorticoid stress response: Grandmother as a secure base. *Journal of Developmental Processes, 1*, 31–68.

Flinn, M. V., & Leone, D. V. (2007). Alloparental care and the ontogeny of glucocorticoid stress response among stepchildren. In G. Bentley & R. Mace (Eds.), *Alloparental care in human societies* (Biosocial Society Symposium Series). Oxford: Berghahn Books.

Flinn, M. V., Ward, C. V., & Noone, R. (2005). Hormones and the human family. In D. Buss (Ed.), *Handbook of evolutionary psychology* (chap. 19, pp. 552–580). New York: Wiley.

Fortes, M. (1969). *Kinship and the social order.* Chicago, IL: Aldine.

Gavrilets, S., & Vose, A. (2006). The dynamics of Machiavellian intelligence. *Proceedings of the National Academy of Sciences, 103*, 16823–16828.

Geary, D. C. (2005). *The origin of mind: Evolution of brain, cognition, and general intelligence.* Washington: American Psychological Association.

Geary, D. C., & Bjorklund, D. F. (2000). Evolutionary developmental psychology. *Child Development, 71*, 57–65.

Geary, D. C., Byrd-Craven, J., Hoard, M. K., Vigil, J., & Numtee, C. (2003). Evolution and development of boys' social behavior. *Developmental Review, 23*, 444–470.

Geary, D. C., & Flinn, M. V. (2001). Evolution of human parental behavior and the human family. *Parenting: Science and Practice, 1*, 5–61.

Geary, D. C., & Flinn, M. V. (2002). Sex differences in behavioral and hormonal response to social threat. *Psychological Review, 109*, 745–750.

Geary, D. C., & Huffman, K. J. (2002). Brain and cognitive evolution: Forms of modularity and functions of mind. *Psychological Bulletin, 128*, 667–698.

Ghazanfar, A. A., & Santos, L. R. (2004). Primate brains in the wild: The sensory bases for social interactions. *Nature Reviews Neuroscience, 5*, 603–616.

Gilbert, P. (2001). Evolutionary approaches to psychopathology: The role of natural defences. *Australian & New Zealand Journal of Psychiatry, 35*, 17–27.

Gilbert, S. L., Dobyns, W. B., & Lahn, B. T. (2005). Genetic links between brain development and brain evolution. *Nature Reviews Genetics, 6*, 581–590.

Goodall, J. (1986). *The chimpanzees of Gombe: Patterns of behavior.* Cambridge, MA: Belknap Press of Harvard University Press.

Guatelli-Steinberg, D., Reid, D. J., Bishop, T. A., & Larsen, C. S. (2005). Anterior tooth growth periods in Neandertals were comparable to those of modern humans. *Proceedings of the National Academy of Sciences, 102*(40), 14197–14202.

Hamilton, W. D., Axelrod, R., & Tanese, R. (1990). Sexual reproduction as an adaptation to resist parasites (a review). *Proceedings of the National Academy of Sciences, 87*, 3566–3573.

Hawkes, K. (2003). Grandmothers and the evolution of human longevity. *American Journal of Human Biology, 15*, 380–400.

Henry, J. P., & Wang, S. (1998). Effect of early stress on adult affiliative behavior. *Psychoneuroendocrinology, 23*, 863–875.

Hess, N. H, & Hagen, E. H. (2006). Sex differences in indirect aggression: Psychological evidence from young adults. *Evolution and Human Behavior, 27*, 231–245.

Hetherington, E. M. (2003a). Intimate Pathways: Changing patterns in close personal relationships across time. *Family Relations: Interdisciplinary Journal of Applied Family Studies, 52*, 318–331.

Hetherington, E. M. (2003b). Social support and the adjustment of children in divorced and remarried families. *Childhood: A Global Journal of Child Research, 10*, 217–236.

Horwood, L. J., Darlow, B. A., & Mogridge, N. (2001). Breast milk feeding and cognitive ability at 7–8 years. *Archives of Disease in Childhood: Fetal & Neonatal Edition, 84*, F23-27

Hrdy, S. B. (1999). *Mother Nature: A history of mothers, infants, and natural selection.* New York: Pantheon.

Hrdy, S. B. (2005). Evolutionary context of human development: The cooperative breeding model. In C. S. Carter & L. Ahnert (Eds.), *Attachment and bonding: A new synthesis* (Dahlem Workshop 92). Cambridge, MA: MIT Press.

Hurtado, A. M., Hill, K., Kaplan, H., & Hurtado, I. (1992). Trade-offs between female food acquisition and child care among Hiwi and Ache foragers. *Human Nature, 3*, 185–216.

Insel, T. R. (2000). Toward a neurobiology of attachment. *Review of General Psychology, 4*, 176–185.

Jensen, A. R. (1998). *The g factor: The science of mental ability.* New York: Praeger.

Joffe, T. H. (1997). Social pressures have selected for an extended juvenile period in primates. *Journal of Human Evolution, 32*, 593–605.

Kaplan, H., Hill, K., Lancaster, J., & Hurtado, A. M. (2000). A theory of human life history evolution: Diet, intelligence and longevity. *Evolutionary Anthropology, 9*, 156–183.

Kaplan, H. S., & Robson, A. J. (2002). The emergence of humans: The coevolution of intelligence and longevity with intergenerational transfers. *Proceedings of the National Academy of Sciences, 99*, 10,221–10,226.

Konner, M. (1991). *Childhood.* Boston, MA: Little, Brown.

Laland, K. N., Odling-Smee, J., & Feldman, M. W. (2000). Niche construction, biological evolution, and cultural change. *Behavioral & Brain Sciences, 23*, 131–175.

Leblanc, S. A. (2003). *Constant battles: The myth of the peaceful, noble savage.* New York: St. Martin's Press.

Lee, S. H., & Wolpoff, M. H. (2003). The pattern of evolution in Pleistocene human brain size. *Paleobiology, 29*, 186–196.

Leigh, S. R. (2004). Brain growth, cognition, and life history in primate and human evolution. *American Journal of Primatology, 62*, 139–164.

Leone, D. V., Quinlan, R. J., Hayden, R., Stewart, J., & Flinn, M. V. (2004). Long-term implications for growth of prenatal and early postnatal environment [Abstract]. *American Journal of Human Biology, 16,* 212–213.

Leslie, A. M., Friedmann, O., & German, T. P. (2004). Core mechanisms in 'theory of mind'. *Trends in Cognitive Sciences, 8,* 529–533.

MacDonald, K., & Hershberger, S. L. (2005). Theoretical issues in the study of evolution and development. In R. L. Burgess & K. MacDonald (Eds.), *Evolutionary perspectives on human development* (chap. 2, pp. 21–72). Thousand Oaks, CA: Sage.

Mace, R. (2000). Evolutionary ecology of human life history. *Animal Behaviour, 59,* 1–10.

Marlowe, F. W. (2003). A critical period for provisioning by Hadza men: Implications for pair bonding. *Evolution and Human Behavior, 24,* 217–229.

McHenry, H. M. (1992a). Body size and proportions in early hominids. *American Journal of Physical Anthropology, 87,* 407–431.

McHenry, H. M. (1992b). How big were early hominids? *Evolutionary Anthropology, 1,* 15–20.

Miller, G. E. (2000). *The mating mind: How sexual choice shaped the evolution of human nature.* New York: Doubleday.

Moffitt, T. E., Caspi, A., Belsky, J., & Silva, P. A. (1992). Childhood experience and the onset of menarche: A test of a sociobiological model. *Child Development, 63,* 47–58.

Moll, J., Zahn, R., de Oliveira-Souza, R., Krueger, F., & Grafman, J. (2005). The neural basis of human moral cognition. *Nature Reviews: Neuroscience, 6,* 799–809.

Murdock, G. P. (1949). *Social structure.* New York: Macmillan.

Murdock, G. P. (1967). *Ethnographic atlas.* Pittsburgh, PA: University of Pittsburgh Press.

Nowak, M. A., Komarova, N. L., & Niyogi, P. (2001). Evolution of universal grammar. *Science, 291,* 114–118.

Pande, H., Unwin, C., & Haheim, L. L. (1997). Factors associated with the duration of breastfeeding. *Acta Paediatrica, 86,* 173–177.

Pawlowski, B., Lowen, C. B., & Dunbar, R. I. M. (1998). Neocortex size, social skills and mating success in primates. *Behaviour, 135,* 357–368.

Pinker, S. (1994). *The language instinct.* New York: William Morrow.

Plavcan, J. M. (2000). Inferring social behavior from sexual dimorphism in the fossil record. *Journal of Human Evolution, 39,* 327–344.

Plavcan, J. M., Lockwood, C. A., Kimbel, W. H., Lague, M. R., & Harmon, E. H. (2005). Sexual dimorphism in Australopithecus afarensis revisited: How strong is the case for a human-like pattern of dimorphism? *Journal of Human Evolution, 48,* 313–320.

Plavcan, J. M., & Van Schaik, C. P. (1997a). Interpreting hominid behavior on the basis of sexual dimorphism. *Journal of Human Evolution, 32,* 345–374.

Plavcan, J. M., & Van Schaik, C. P. (1997b). Intrasexual competition and body weight dimorphism in anthropoid primates. *American Journal of Physical Anthropology, 103,* 37–68.

Portman, A. (1941). Die Tragzeiten der Primaten und die Dauer der Schwangerschaft beim Menschen: Ein Problem der vergleichenden Biologie. *Revue Suisse de Zoologie, 48,* 511–518.

Quinlan, R. J. (2003). Father-absence, parental care & female reproductive development. *Evolution & Human Behavior, 24,* 367–390.

Quinlan, R. J. (2006). Gender & risk in a matrifocal Caribbean community. *American Anthropologist, 108,* 464–479.

Quinlan, R. J. (2007). Human parental effort and environmental risk. *Proceedings of the Royal Society B: Biological Sciences, 274,* 121–125.

Quinlan, R. J., Quinlan, M. B., & Flinn, M. V. (2003). Parental investment & age at weaning in a Caribbean village. *Evolution and Human Behavior, 24,* 1–17.

Reno, P. L., Meindl, R. S., McCollum, M. A., & Lovejoy, C. O. (2005). The case is unchanged and remains robust: *Australopithecus afarensis* exhibits only moderate skeletal dimorphism. *Journal of Human Evolution, 49,* 279–288.

Roff, D. A. (2002). *Life history evolution.* Sunderland, MA: Sinauer.

Rosenberg, K. (2004). Living longer: Information revolution, population expansion, and modern human origins. *Proceedings of the National Academy of Sciences, 101,* 10847–10848.

Rosenberg, K., & Trevathan, W. (2002). Birth, obstetrics and human evolution. *BJOG: An International Journal of Obstetrics & Gynecology, 109,* 1199–1206.

Roth, G., & Dicke, U. (2005). Evolution of the brain and intelligence. *TRENDS in Cognitive Sciences, 9,* 250–257.

Ruff, C. B. (2002). Variation in human body size and shape. *Annual Review of Anthropology, 31,* 211–232.

Ruff, C. B., Trinkaus, E., Walker, A., & Larsen, C. S. (1993). Postcranial robusticity in Homo. I: Temporal trends and mechanical interpretation. *American Journal of Physical Anthropology, 91,* 21–53.

Sakai, K. L. (2005). Language acquisition and brain development. *Science, 310,* 815–819.

Scheper-Hughes, N. (1992). *Death without weeping: The violence of everyday life in Brazil.* Berkeley: University of California Press.

Sear, R., Mace, R., & McGregor, I. A. (2000). Maternal grandmothers improve the nutritional status and survival of children in rural Gambia. *Proceedings of the Royal Society London B, 267,* 1641–1647.

Shamay-Tsoory, S. G., Tomer, R., & Aharon-Peretz, J. (2005). The neuroanatomical basis of understanding sarcasm and its relationship to social cognition. *Neuropsychology, 19,* 288–300.

Siegal, M., & Varley, R. (2002). Neural systems involved with "Theory of Mind." *Nature Reviews, Neuroscience, 3,* 463–471.

Simons, K., Paternite, C. E., & Shore, C. (2001). Quality of parent/adolescent attachment and aggression in young adolescents. *Journal of Early Adolescence, 21*, 182–203.

Smith, B. H. (1993). The physiological age of KNM-WT 15000. In A. Walker and R. Leakey (Eds.), *The Nariokotome* Homo erectus *skeleton*. Cambridge, MA: Harvard University Press.

Smith, B. H. (1994). Patterns of dental development in homo, Australopithecus, pan, and gorilla. *American Journal of Physical Anthropology, 94*, 307–325.

Smuts, B. B., & Smuts, R. W. (1993). Male aggression and sexual coercion of females in nonhuman primates and other mammals: Evidence and theoretical implications. *Advances in the Study of Behavior, 22*, 1–63.

Stearns, S. C. (1992). *The evolution of life histories*. Oxford: Oxford University Press.

Tomasello, M. (1999). *The cultural origins of human cognition*. Cambridge, MA: Harvard University Press.

Tooby, J., & Cosmides, L. (1992). The psychological foundations of culture. In J. H. Barkow, L. Cosmides, & J. Tooby (Eds.), *The adapted mind* (pp. 19–136). Oxford: Oxford University Press.

Trivers, R. L. (1972). Parental investment and sexual selection. In B. Campbell (Ed.), *Sexual selection and the descent of man* (pp. 136–179). Chicago: Aldine.

Trivers, R. L. (1985). *Social evolution*. Menlo Park, CA: Benjamin/Cummings.

Tulving, E. (2002). Episodic memory: From mind to brain. *Annual Review of Psychology, 53*, 1–25.

Ungar, P., Grine, F. E., Teaford, M. F., & El Zaatari, S. (2006). Dental microwear and diets in early African *Homo*. *Journal of Human Evolution, 50*, 78–95.

West-Eberhard, M. J. (1983). Sexual selection, social competition, and speciation. *Quarterly Review of Biology, 58*, 155–183.

West-Eberhard, M. J. (2003). *Developmental plasticity and evolution*. New York: Oxford University Press.

Whiting, J. W. M., & Whiting, B. B. (1975). Aloofness and intimacy of husbands and wives: A cross-cultural study. *Ethos, 3*, 183–207.

Williams, G. C. (1966). *Adaptation and natural selection*. Princeton: Princeton University Press.

Winterhalder, B., & Leslie, P. (2002). Risk sensitive fertility: The variance compensation hypothesis. *Evolution & Human Behavior, 23*, 59–82.

Wrangham, R. W. (1999). Evolution of coalitionary killing. *Yearbook of Physical Anthropology, 42*, 1–30.

Wrangham, R. W., & Peterson, D. (1996). *Demonic males*. New York: Houghton Mifflin Company.

3 Evolutionary Context of Human Development: The Cooperative Breeding Model

Sarah Blaffer Hrdy

The causal chain of adaptive evolution...begins
with development.

Mary Jane West-Eberhard (2003)

Allow me to briefly summarize my argument at the outset. According to the cooperative breeding hypothesis, allomaternal assistance was essential for child survival during the Pleistocene. This breeding system—quite novel for an ape—permitted hominid females to produce costly offspring without increasing inter-birth intervals, and allowed humans to move into new habitats, eventually expanding out of Africa. Reliance on allomaternal assistance would make maternal commitment more dependent on the mother's perception of probable support from others than is the case in most other primates. One artifact of such conditional maternal investment would be newborns who needed to monitor and engage mothers, as well as older infants and juveniles who benefited from eliciting care and provisioning from a range of caretakers across the prolonged period of dependence characteristic of young in cooperative breeders. Developing in a social context where infants and children more skilled at reading the intentions of others and engaging their solicitude would be more likely to survive and prosper has obvious implications for the evolution of theory of mind and the eagerness human children exhibit for inter-subjective engagement.

MOVING BEYOND BOWLBY

John Bowlby was the first evolutionary psychologist to explore how selection pressures encountered by our Pleistocene ancestors (what he termed "the Environment of Evolutionary Adaptedness," or EEA) shaped the development of human infants. In a now-classic book called *Attachment*, Bowlby (1969) drew on personal and clinical experience with Western childrearing, on such evidence as was then available for hunter–gatherer childrearing, and also for maternal care in primates such as macaques, baboons, and chimps, among whom mothers exhibit continuous and exclusive care. Based on these sources of information, Bowlby assumed that the mother was the primary, typically exclusive, caretaker for human infants in the EEA. In later versions of his book, Bowlby (influenced by Ainsworth and others) mentioned the possibility of multiple caretakers but continued to center his model around a Victorian division of labor within a pair bond where a sexually monandrous mother nurtured offspring provisioned by their father. The last quarter century has produced new evidence from primate sociobiology and from the behavioral ecology of foraging peoples that challenges this exclusive "sex contract" between mother and father as the fundamental economic unit for childrearing among our ancestors and expanded the focus to include assistance from group members other than the genetic parents. In the course of an ongoing—still controversial—paradigm shift within anthropology, the longstanding ideal of an EEA characterized by mother–father childrearing units is being replaced with a model based on cooperative breeding (Hrdy 1999).

WHAT IS MEANT BY "COOPERATIVE BREEDING"?

The Study of Cooperative Breeding

From wild dogs, to elephants, meerkats, marmosets, acorn woodpeckers, and scrub jays, roughly 3% of mammals and between 4 and 17% of bird species (Heinsohn & Double 2004) breed cooperatively. The literature on cooperative breeding in vertebrates is divided between studies of birds, mammals other than primates, and primates (excepting humans). While sometimes appropriate, this taxonomic compartmentalization has hindered synthetic analyses and led to a confusing array of taxonomically specific definitions for cooperative breeding. Here, I use a broad and simple definition: a breeding system in which group members other than the genetic parents (alloparents) help one or both parents care for and provision their offspring. Because we rarely know the genetic identity of fathers, it is often more accurate to specify allomothers, individuals of either sex who are not the mother. Note that an allomother can be male—a male who may or may not be the genetic father. Designating "paternal" assistance can be complicated in the cases of animals such as marmosets or wild dogs, where more than one possible "father" helps, or in species with "multiple paternity" litters, where there may actually be more than one genetic father. In such cases, males with different probabilities of paternity may adjust their level of care according to their past mating history with the mother. For example, male dunnocks calibrate food delivery to nestlings in line with how frequently these males copulated with the mother during the period when she was last fertile (Davies 1992). Male baboons, whose partners have mated polyandrously with multiple males, preferentially intervene on behalf of older infants and juveniles likely to be their own (Buchan, Alberts, Silk, & Altmann 2003).

Theoretical Explanations

At a general level, the altruism of alloparents is explained by Hamilton's rule: The cost of helping should be less than benefits to offspring calibrated in line with the alloparent's degree of relatedness to his or her charge. Hence, alloparents enhance their inclusive fitness by helping kin. Almost certainly, the neural and physiological underpinnings of helpful motivations first evolved in groups of closely related animals. Tendencies that led individuals to invest in unrelated infants at the expense of closely related infants would be selected against. However, there is continuing debate about how important kinship is in *maintaining* dispositions to help once they have evolved. In particular, complex patterns of migration often mean that male and female helpers are not that closely related; yet, with varying levels of commitment, they continue to help.

Cooperative breeding was first studied in social insects and birds, animals without lactation where non-mothers are just as equipped to feed young as mothers are. Struck by how much allomothers were helping in hymenopteran social insects, Hamilton (1964) emphasized the unusually high degree of relatedness between mothers and helpers. His ideas about kin selection have received wide support. For example, cooperatively breeding carrion crows leave their natal groups and then seek out related individuals, preferring to help kin over non-kin. Today most theorists acknowledge that kinship facilitates the evolution of cooperative breeding, even if it is not always essential to maintain helping behaviors once they have evolved. Emlen (1997) has played a major role, emphasizing ecological constraints (such as saturated habitats or predation) that discourage relatives from dispersing. Cooperative breeding is especially likely to evolve where inherited resources are critical for reproduction because maturing animals must queue up. Others emphasize the benefits of philopatry (or remaining in the natal territory). Cockburn (1998) provides the most comprehensive, if aviocentric, review of how helpers might benefit from (1) enhanced production of non-descendant kin; (2) payment of "rent" allowing access to the territory or other group benefits in exchange for being allowed to stay; (3) opportunistic access to mating opportunities; (4) development of the territory or group in ways that enhance future breeding opportunities; (5) social advancement or better opportunities to signal quality to prospective mates; and (6) additional time to mature or to acquire skills within the security of a group.

By such logic, even unrelated allomothers may benefit from caring for infants. Consider the case of help from pre-reproductives whose current breeding opportunities are limited but who also stand to gain from caretaking experience (Fleming 2005; Hrdy 1976). Furthermore, as animals age, and especially as female mammals approach the end of their reproductive careers at menopause, their threshold for helping may decline, while their "donative intent" goes up (see, e.g., Hrdy 1977, Paul 2005). In contrast, when physical reserves are at a low point, or when risks rise high, alloparents with prospects of breeding in the future may become less altruistic (see, e.g., Russell, Sharp, Brotherton, & Clutton-Brock 2003, for meerkats). Yet even helpers with energy to spare, or post-reproductives with little to lose, should prioritize their service depending on degree of relatedness in addition to level of need. The "ideal" allomother's internalized version of Hamilton's rule reads: find infants appealing and help them if you can, so long as cost is not prohibitive and so long as it does not interfere with your own future reproductive career or caring for your own offspring when you have them.

Ecological and Life-History Outcomes

Cooperative breeding systems tend to be flexible and dynamic. Often, there are one or more mated pairs, but depending on circumstances that fluctuate from one habitat to another, and over the course of lifetimes, a breeding female may mate monogamously, polyandrously (i.e., with several males), or polygynously (sharing her mate with other females). Important features of such systems include delayed dispersal by maturing family members or else migration into the group by non-reproducing (or only occasionally reproducing) adults who are nevertheless responsive to maternal and offspring needs.

At a physiological level, there has to be sufficient phenotypic flexibility so individuals can shift between non-reproductive and reproductive roles. At a cognitive and emotional level, there has to be some prior predisposition among alloparents to respond to signs of infant need. That is, the underlying neural circuitry has to be there in both sexes and in both virgin and parous females.

The availability of alloparental assistance diminishes the constraints imposed by "quantity versus quality" life-history tradeoffs. The resulting ecological release permits mothers to produce more, or more closely spaced, offspring, even though the offspring themselves are more costly to produce and rear to independence. With allomaternal assistance, slow-maturing, costly offspring can be produced after short birth intervals without jeopardizing the survival of either the mother or her offspring. Furthermore, reduced opportunity costs from childrearing, along with the benefits of group membership, may actually mean higher probability of maternal survival and hence longer average life spans (see, e.g., Rowley & Russell 1990 for cooperatively breeding birds). Humans, who exhibit the broadest range of mating permutations ever reported, and who also produce some of the costliest infants, have all the earmarks of a species in which maternal reproductive success was correlated with the availability of allomaternal care. Compared to other apes, humans take the longest to mature, yet human infants are born after shorter intervals. (It was this observation that led anthropologists to devise the "sex contract" hypothesis in the first place.) Since provisioning by alloparents buffers immatures from starvation, it allows populations to move into and spread in new habitats where mothers otherwise would not manage to rear surviving young. *Homo erectus*, which evolved in Africa more than 1.8 million years ago and quickly spread into Eurasia and the Near East, exemplifies this pattern.

As early as 1966, Hamilton hypothesized that cooperative breeding would permit slower maturation. Consistent with this speculation, a strong correlation between cooperative breeding and prolonged dependence has been documented in birds. In a sample of 261 species of passerines, 217 never bred cooperatively, 10 did so occasionally, and 34 species were frequent cooperative breeders. The average duration of post-fledging nutritional dependence was significantly longer in cooperative species, and up to twice as long in the obligately cooperative (Langen 2000). Langen attributed these extended periods of nutritional dependence to (1) the reduced cost of parenting produced by a division of labor between helpers who continued to feed youngsters, and mothers who were able to resume breeding; and (2) the fact that provisioned offspring had less incentive to become independent. Logically, these same factors should also pertain in cooperatively breeding mammals. That is, slow maturation combined with short birth intervals would be feasible in cooperatively breeding species such as marmosets and tamarins because allomothers (typically adult males) do so much of the heavy lifting and also help provision infants around the time of weaning. This may explain why, when the much smaller size of babies at birth is taken into account, Callitrichids mature at rates almost as slow as human rates. Nutritional independence is similarly delayed in other cooperatively breeding mammals where immatures rely on special "baby foods" provided by allomothers. These foods include regurgitated meat provided to wolf and wild dog pups. In the case of lions and wild dogs, adults allow weaned but still inexperienced young access at pre-butchered kills, subsidizing long apprenticeships.

Primate Pre-adaptations for Cooperative Breeding, and the Case of Male Primability

The subfamily Callitrichidae provides the "textbook" cases of cooperative breeding among primates, containing species where allomothers *provision* in addition to carry charges. By 2 weeks after offspring are born, male *Calithrix jacchus*—typically former sexual partners of the mother—carry the infants (typically twins) up to 60% of the time. By three weeks, other group members supplement the mother's milk by providing small prey, even though the infant will not be weaned until around 3 months. In rare instances, co-suckling has also been observed when two females were lactating.

The more allomaternal assistance available (especially from males), the higher the mother's reproductive success. *Saquinus oedipus* mothers are so dependent on such help that mothers abandoned their newborns if allomaternal assistance was not forthcoming (Bardi, Petto, & Lee-Parritz 2001). Humans are the only other primates so dependent on alloparental assistance that maternal commitment depends on the mother's perception of social support (Hrdy 1999).

Even though Callitrichidae and humans are the only primates that qualify as full-fledged "cooperative breeders," the order Primate, as a whole, is composed of intensely social species. Many primate attributes predispose group members to respond in ways that promote shared care of the young. Relevant pre-adaptations for cooperative breeding range from a primate-wide tendency to find infants attractive and to protect infants in their group, to strong urges (especially among inexperienced females) to hold or carry babies. Benefits to philopatry can be documented for all primates. These include practical advantages like enhanced knowledge of local resources and protection from predation, and social advantages like support from kin. Not surprisingly, the rule of thumb among primates is that those who *can* remain in their natal troop do so, thereby enjoying the benefits of social support.

Typically, it is those who cannot afford to stay who migrate out. A major incentive for leaving is female reluctance to breed with males likely to be close kin, the relevant cue being familiarity from an early age. Males denied sexual access decamp to find groups of unfamiliar females. In species where males resist migrating and remain near kin (as in chimps), females are pressured to leave rather than breed with fathers or brothers.

For primates able to remain among matrilineal kin in multigenerational groups, there are many benefits, especially for mothers. Enhanced social support brings with it improved vigilance, stress reduction, health, and fitness benefits (e.g., Heinrichs, Baumgartner, Kirschbaum, & Ehlert 2003; Von Holtz 1986; Silk, Alberts, & Altmann 2003) that increase maternal survival chances. Kin support is especially important for primiparas around the time of first births, an especially vulnerable time among primates with universally high mortality rates for firstborn infants. In addition to local social support, proximity of matrilineal kin provides nulliparous daughters greater access to infants and more opportunities to practice and prepare for motherhood (Hrdy 1999, pp. 155–164).

Female apes and Old World monkeys, along with New World monkeys of both sexes, exhibit a "lust" to touch, inspect, or carry newborns. The limiting factor on whether or not allomaternal care occurs is the mother's willingness to allow access. In infant-sharing species like langurs (where in both captivity and the wild, females other than the mother may carry infants up to 50% of daylight hours), mothers freely give up infants to group members, who typically are matrilineal kin. Even though shared care is species-typical, langur infants complain vociferously at being taken from their mother. Babies are accustomed to remaining in body contact with their mother at least half the day and all night, and typically she is the only individual who suckles them. Yet, in spite of frequent transfers to allomothers, infants are unharmed and grow up to be normally functioning adults.

In contrast to langurs, mothers in "continuous care and contact" species like rhesus macaques, savanna baboons, orangutans, gorillas, or chimps completely deny access in the weeks or months after birth. Thus, it is interesting to speculate how differently Attachment Theory might have unfolded if Bowlby had selected langurs rather than rhesus macaques as his "model primates." Like langurs, mothers in just under half of all primate species find some way to alleviate the burden imposed by continuous care. Many prosimian species either leave babies in nests or "park" them in relatively safe hiding places. Many New World monkey species have biparental care with the father helping, or else shared care involving father plus other allomothers. Such shared care varies from nonexclusive, occasional care (e.g., a male baboon sitting close to an offspring he might have sired intervening if protection is needed) to care so costly that those providing it temporarily forego opportunities to breed or forage and lose weight. Among infant-sharing species, shared care frees mothers to forage, with the result that they breed at a faster pace (Mitani and Watts 1997).

Even though the level of shared care varies across species, underlying neural circuitry for responding to infants (especially to their signals of vulnerability and need) are more or less the same. All simian females are attentive to sights and sounds of newborns, and many (especially young females) find newborns magnetically attractive regardless of whether or not they are related to them. By contrast, many male primates (e.g., chimps or langurs) tend to remain aloof from infants, and even in infant-sharing species typically exhibit little interest in holding babies (Hrdy 1976 1999). Such males are quite different from the titi monkeys or marmoset males who are predisposed to caretake and whose top priority it is to hold and carry infants. Yet, even in the species where males do not normally caretake, males can be primed by experiences to do so, although the threshold for responding to infants is set higher than among females (Fleming 2005, Hrdy 1999, pp. 211–214).

The best-studied cases of male primability come from New World monkeys and involve prolactin-mediated systems (Schradin & Anzenberger 1999). The first hint that there was a correlation between prolactin levels and male care came from marmosets. This report was initially met with skepticism, partly because prolactin was viewed as a *maternal* hormone, and also because prolactin is involved in stress responses. However, the discovery was replicated using noninvasive techniques. Subsequently, researchers learned that the rise in prolactin levels was more pronounced among males who had prior caretaking experience (Snowdon 1996). It is noteworthy that it took 2 decades, along with a paradigm shift in the way we think about sex roles, before researchers thought to ask the same questions about human primates. Only then did we learn that men cohabiting with pregnant women and new mothers experience hormonal changes similar to those in cooperatively breeding marmosets. Over the course of a woman's pregnancy, the man's prolactin levels gradually rise. In addition, men exposed to pregnant women and new babies experience a drop in testosterone after birth (Fleming, Corter, Stallings, & Steiner 2002; Storey, Walsh, Quinton, & Wynne-Edwards 2000; see also Grey, Kahlenberg, Barrett, Lipson, & Ellison 2002).

There is little doubt that hormonal changes during pregnancy and lactation are more pronounced in women than in men. Except for species with obligate male care, like titi monkeys, female primates are more sensitive to infant appeals and signals than males are. No one is suggesting that fathers are equivalent to mothers, male caretakers the same as female ones. Physiological and sensory thresholds of the two sexes are so different that experimenters use different scales to measure them. Yet the fact remains: even in animals with low levels of joint caretaking, both sexes can be primed to care. Neither birth, nor even the prospect of giving birth, is a prerequisite for nurturing. Virgin females, or males, can be primed to nurture by prolonged exposure to pregnant mothers and infants. Male predispositions suggest that through evolutionary time primate infants short on care could look equally to males or females for assistance. The necessary wiring for the development, and in some cases the eventual evolution, of male care was perpetually present.

WHY HUMANS MUST HAVE EVOLVED AS COOPERATIVE BREEDERS

Humans are costly to produce, mature slowly, and rarely reach nutritional independence much before age 20. Even with four-year or longer birth intervals, a hunter–gatherer mother would have a new offspring before her last child became self-sufficient. Assuming roughly 13 million calories to rear a child from infancy to nutritional independence, such outlays exceed what a mother by herself could provide (Kaplan, Hill, Lancaster, & Hurtado 2000). Among extant foragers, hunting and/or fishing are important sources of protein but are also risky enterprises. Even when men manage to kill a large animal, meat is typically shared with the group at large rather than channeled to a man's own mate and her offspring. For this reason, Pleistocene mothers relying exclusively on "husbands" were taking a chance (O'Connell Hawkes, Lupo, & Blurton Jones 2002). If fathers died, defected, had little luck hunting, or decided to share what they brought back with the group at large, what kept children from starving? Part of the answer is that many early humans did starve. But which ones survived?

Availability of Allomothers in Pleistocene Societies

Recently, Hawkes, O'Connell, Blurton Jones, Charnov, and Alvarez (1998) focused attention on the role of older matrilineal kin, especially "hardworking" grandmothers studied among Hadza hunter–gatherers in Tanzania. In times of food shortage, children with older matrilineal kin on hand grew better. But as critical as a grandmother (or great aunt) might be, how likely were they to be around? The answer is not knowable. At best, such paleontological and archeological evidence as is available can be used in combination with demographic assumptions derived from extant hunter–gatherers to estimate reasonable demographic profiles for groups under a range of circumstances. Using this methodology, Kurland and Sparks (2003) estimate that, under conditions of low mortality, a 20-year-old primipara would have about a 50% chance of having a 40-year-old mother alive to help her. If higher mortality rates are used, this probability drops to 25%. Under both mortality conditions, the chance of a new mother having a 5-year-older sibling around would be about twice as high as the chance of having a grandmother. The chances of having one or more cousins would be higher still. In other words, mothers would typically be coping with incomplete kinship sets, although deficits in allomaternal assistance could be offset by compensatory behavior on the part of opportunistic strategists (e.g., a grandmother might move to join the daughter who needed her most). The need to expand the number of available "kin" may help explain why classificatory kinship systems are so common and also why foragers place so much stock in trade networks and other reciprocal relationships (Wiessner 2002). Wiessner argues that, in addition to prestige, one reason talented hunters expend so much effort hunting large game and sharing out the meat (which, as Hawkes points out, is not the most efficient way for a father to provision his children) is that the successful hunters exert influence upon the demographic composition and political disposition of their group. By recruiting group members likely to be both efficient providers and/or generous allomothers, a hunter could enhance the survival chances of his kin.

The Debate over Residence Patterns

Demographic reconstructions of Pleistocene family life have long relied on two assumptions about residence patterns. First, it was assumed that early humans lived in "male philopatric" associations. Sons remained near father, brothers, and cousins to form alliances composed of related males who cooperated to protect access to resources (including breeding females) in their local area. Secondly, Murdock (1967) reported that 67% of the world's cultures lived patrilocally, so it was assumed that Pleistocene humans did so as well. Fairly obviously, if women were moving away to live among their husbands' kin, this severely constrained the availability of matrilineal relatives.

However, new data suggest that ape females do not always migrate. Based on molecular data, wild chimp "brotherhoods" may be not much more closely related than females are. Furthermore, longitudinal observations from Gombe reveal that some females manage to remain in their natal territories (Pusey, Williams, & Goodall 1997). In particular, the oldest daughter of a dominant female who finds herself in a good situation may remain to inherit her mother's territory along with her social position, backed up by high-ranking male kin in the area. Females thus privileged reach menarche earlier, breed at shorter intervals, and produce offspring more likely to survive. The new rule of thumb for female chimps can be summarized as "those who can, stay; those who can't, leave" (Hrdy 1999). Furthermore, Alvarez (2004) has painstakingly reexamined the original ethnographies used by Murdock (1967) to classify so many foragers as patrilocal. Murdock's criteria were undeniably precise. For example, a society classified as "ambilocal" (or "bilocal") had to be one where "residence is optionally established with or near the parents of either the husband or the wife…where neither alternative exceeds the other in actual frequency by a ratio greater than two to one." Yet, nowhere in the ethnographies could Alvarez locate the information needed to make such fine-grained determinations. Lacking quantitative data, Murdock assigned societies to residence categories based on his best guess. When Alvarez confined her analysis to only those foraging societies where there was sufficient evidence to classify residence patterns with confidence, only one quarter (12 of 48) were patrilocal. Most were bilocal. Because of bride service (where the new husband hunted on behalf of his wife's family for a time), a daughter was likely to remain near her kin until after she gave birth to her first child. Various other strategic maneuvers (such as older women moving to live near the mothers who most needed them; Marlowe 2005) also served to increase the availability of matrilineal kin, even as harsh demographic realities worked to reduce it.

UNDER PLEISTOCENE CONDITIONS, ALLOMOTHERS WERE *ESSENTIAL* FOR SURVIVAL

Based on my reading of early European family history, mothers with supportive matrilineal kin were less likely to abandon their babies than mothers without (Hrdy 1999). Meanwhile, a vast sociological literature attests to the manifold benefits of extended families and other forms of social support for contemporary mothers and their children (e.g., Olds, Robinson, & O'Brien 2002; Werner 1984). Ethnographers as well have long stressed the usefulness of child minders in non-Western societies (Levine, et al 1996; Tronick, Morelli, & Winn 1987; Weisner & Gallimore 1977). It scarcely comes as news that supportive kin are helpful. What is new is the proposition that in societies with high rates of mortality, children without allomothers might be significantly less likely to survive. That is, allomothers were not just helpful. They were essential for maternal reproductive success. This is the basis for hypothesizing that alloparental assistance must have been integral to human adaptations in the EEA. Nomadic hunter–gatherer mothers would have confronted dilemmas similar to those that working mothers face today, except that given high rates of child mortality, Pleistocene mothers with alloparental assistance would have had children who survived better than those with no such assistance.

Early humans are presumed to have lived at low densities, and the remarkable lack of genetic variation among humans compared to chimps may be due to population crashes and population bottlenecks (although this is not the only interpretation). The most plausible cause for population crashes and local extinctions in widely dispersed populations would be recurring periods of food shortage. Alternative explanations rely on sources of mortality (warfare or disease) that probably only increased after our numbers did, post-Neolithic. Diseases like malaria, cholera, diarrhea, and tuberculosis did not become big killers until after people adopted sedentary lifestyles and lived at higher densities. Based on what we know about primate mortality from food shortage, immatures—especially those just past weaning—are most susceptible. This would be the age group that benefits most from alloparental assistance. Indeed, across traditional societies, evidence now indicates that where child mortality rates are high, alloparents significantly affect their survival.

The Sibling Factor

One reason that the critical role of allomothers was overlooked was that sociologists studied modern, Western populations, where rates of child mortality are typically very low. By the end of the 1980s, however, anthropologists influenced by sociobiological studies of alloparental care in birds and other primates began to ask if allomaternal assistance mattered for human reproductive success in traditional human societies. In a pioneering study, Turke (1988) found a correlation between the availability of allomaternal assistance and increased maternal reproductive success in a matrilineal, matrilocal Ifaluk population living on Truk. On this Pacific island, parents with a daughter to help rear subsequent children had higher reproductive success than parents whose first two children were sons. At about the same time, another sociobiologist, Mark Flinn (1989), reported that Trinidadian mothers in households with non-reproductive helpers—usually daughters—had significantly higher reproductive success than mothers without them. Neither study involved nomadic foragers, and both suffered from small sample sizes. Furthermore, if mothers with helpers had higher reproductive success than mothers without help, how could one be sure that success was due to their help? Perhaps some other factor (like more household resources) encouraged non-reproductive helpers to remain and also enhanced child well being. Nevertheless, this was the beginning.

Accustomed to stratified, patriarchal societies, many of us took for granted that older siblings were a liability who received more parental investment and inherited the bulk of family resources, while younger siblings got short shrift. Indeed, in many Asian societies, a daughter with several older siblings—especially if her family already had older daughters—risked being killed by her parents at birth. We tended to overlook the fact that in less-stratified traditional societies, older siblings can be an asset. For example, among horticulturalists living in the Gambia of West Africa, children with older sisters had significantly higher survival chances than did same-age children without older sisters (Sear, Steel, McGregor, & Mace 2002, p. 58). In situations like Ifaluk, the beneficial effects of siblings depended on daughters being born first. Elsewhere though, the benefits of older siblings did not show up until later in life, when younger sibs themselves reproduced (e.g., Draper & Hames 2000 for !Kung hunter–gatherers in Botswana). Mechanisms behind this correlation are not known. Possibly, adult siblings provide shelter or food in times of crisis, contributing to the survival of nieces and nephews. The point is that help from collateral kin has demographic consequences across the life cycle (Kramer 2005).

Although the lactating mother would typically be the primary caretaker in the first months, the prospect of allomaternal assistance would promote her commitment. Having child minders within easy reach, even inexperienced ones, frees the mother to forage more efficiently. With the approach of weaning, allomothers can offer soft foods to the infant. Experienced grandmothers and great-aunts seem to be especially important for the survival of weaning-age infants, whereas for children whose mother is in poor shape or less than fully committed, allomothers can be critical at any age.

Grandmothers as a Special Class of Allomother

Ever since Hawkes et al. (1998) called attention to how hard and efficiently post-reproductive women foraged among Hadza hunter–gatherers in Tanzania, data have accumulated for a range of societies documenting increased survival for children with older matrilineal kin nearby. Such data are all the more remarkable because the correlation is found over such a broad spectrum of subsistence conditions (see also Paul 2005 for fitness benefits from grandmothers in other primates). Case studies include East African hunter–gatherers; West African horticulturalists (Sear et al. 2002), 18th-century German peasants (Voland & Beise 2002), and rice-growing peasants in 19th-century Tokugawa Japan (Jamison, Cornell, Jamison, & Nakazato 2002). Among patrilocal Bengalis, swidden agriculturalists in northeastern India, grandmothers contribute to shorter birth intervals, whereas among nearby matrilineal Khasi groups, their presence was correlated with increased child survival (see Leonetti, Nath, Hemam, & Neill 2004; Voland, Chasiotis, & Schiefenhoevel 2005, for overview). Particularly detailed demographic data from preindustrial

Finnish and Canadian farmers reveal that the availability of the mother's mother was correlated with her higher fertility and also with having children who were themselves more likely to survive, resulting in the mother's significantly higher lifetime reproductive success (Lahdenpera, Lummaa, Helle, Tremblay, & Russell 2004).

For both German peasants (Voland & Beise 2002) and Gambian horticulturists (Sear et al. 2002), survival advantages from a nearby maternal grandmother showed up around the age of weaning—an especially vulnerable life phase involving emotional stress and the introduction of new foods. The cause is unknown, but the timing points to provisioning by grandmothers. The Gambian population is primarily Muslim, with mothers living patrilocally in their husband's home. At first glance, then, it seems odd that it was the *maternal* grandmother's presence that mattered so much. Noting how common it is for West African mothers to foster babies out at the time of weaning so babies "forget the breast," Sear et al. suggest that the most solicitous caretaker not already living in the household would be—were she still alive, and nearby—the maternal grandmother.

Once allomothers became essential for childrearing, natural selection would have acted on life-history traits that made allomothers more available. These include delayed dispersal, delayed maturity, and longer life spans. In particular, Hawkes et al. (1998) argued that once hominid began to share food, women's long post-menopausal life spans evolved because post-reproductive women helped provision matrilineal kin, favoring the survival of children whose great aunts and grandmothers were genetically prone to longevity. Data from a broad range of societies is now consistent with this hypothesis (see, especially, Lahdenpera et al. 2004), although more work is still needed to explore social mechanisms that prevented post-reproductive group members from becoming a burden (Hrdy 1999, pp. 280–283, and references therein).

How Much Did Fathers Help?

Perhaps the biggest surprise from the Gambia study was how little difference presence of either the father or older brothers made in this population (see also Sugiyama & Chacon 2004). Whereas having an older sister or a maternal grandmother was literally a lifesaver, halving the chances that a Mandinka child in mid-20th-century Gambia would die, the presence of the father had no detectable impact on child survival unless a widowed mother remarried, in which case the presence of a stepfather often meant a diminished survival chance. Yet, in another part of the world, among Ache foragers in South America, death of the father was so lethal to infants' survival prospects that widowed new mothers terminated investment in their newborns (Hill & Hurtado 1996).

Within the order Primate, there is tremendous inter-specific variation in how much fathers care for infants, ranging from a great deal of care among monogamous South American titi monkeys, where males carry infants some 90% of daylight hours, to virtually no direct care among promiscuous chimpanzees, where mothers are exclusive caretakers. Humans stand out for how variable paternal care is within this single primate species. I suspect that the extreme flexibility and variability in human paternal care is in part due to how important alloparental assistance has been in the evolution of our species. When alloparental help is in short supply, fathers are essential. But by the same token, when available, alloparental assistance can compensate for paternal inadequacies. In what are probably fairly typical cases, only one third of children in one group of Hadza hunter–gatherers actually had their genetic father resident in the group (Marlowe 2005, see Chagnon 1992 for similar figures among South American foragers).

Across hunter–gatherer societies, even when fathers are present, there is tremendous variation in the nature of father–child interactions. Among Central African pygmies like the Aka, where men and women are about equally responsible for provisioning, and where fathers spend a lot of time around camp in the vicinity of relatively monandrous wives, fathers are within arm's reach of their babies about half the time and actually hold them 22% of the time. At the other end of the hunter–gatherer continuum of paternal care, !Kung San fathers in the Kalahari held infants only 1.9% of the time (Hewlett 1988; Konner 2005). Furthermore, the concept of fatherhood itself can vary. For example, where male contributions are particularly unpredictable, people have become convinced that more than one man can be the father. Such folk beliefs in "partible paternity" can be documented across broad swaths of South America and are also documented for some foraging and horticultural groups in Africa and Asia. A belief in partible paternity enables mothers who forge polyandrous liaisons to enlist assistance from several "possible fathers," thereby enhancing their survival prospects (Beckerman et al. 1998, Hrdy 1999, chap. "The Optimal Number of Fathers").

The Importance of Real and Perceived Allomaternal Support

Across mammals, the best single predictor of infant survival is maternal commitment. But in humans, this commitment is influenced—at least initially— by the mother's perception of how much pre- and post-partum support she is likely to have from others. The ethnographic and historical record provides many examples of mothers short on allomaternal support who abandon their infants right after birth (Hrdy 1999). Even small increments in social support can enhance maternal responsiveness toward her infant. For example, adolescent U.S. mothers (even when the father remains with them) are more sensitive to their infants' needs and have more securely attached infants if a supportive grandmother is also on hand (Spieker & Bensley 1994). Even minor interventions, such as visiting nurses in the role of "as-if" kin, increase maternal responsiveness and lower the incidence of child abuse in the first 2 years. Benefits from such early interventions remain detectable as much as 15 years later (Olds, Henderson, Chaberlin, & Tatelbaum 1986; Olds et al. 2002].

Social workers and medical personnel have long been aware that both mothers and their children derive emotional and material support from extended, multigenerational families. Even when socioeconomic conditions are held steady, rates of child morbidity and mortality rise with fewer adults in the household (e.g., in single-parent homes; Weitoft, Hjern, Haglund, & Rosén 2003). Allomaternal support is most critical when times are tough or when maternal competence is compromised by immaturity, inexperience, father absence, or resource scarcity. Beneficial effects also extend to socio-cognitive skills. Babies born to unmarried, low-income U.S. teenagers test better on cognitive development if a grandmother is present (Furstenberg 1976). Prospects for children at risk can be improved on a range of measures with the presence of a supportive allomother, who may be a relative (like a grandmother) or an unrelated teacher or mentor (Werner 1984). It is time to consider what prompts such individuals to help.

HAMILTON'S RULE AND THE PROXIMATE CAUSES OF HELPING

Allomaternal Responsiveness

For cooperative breeding to evolve in the first place, group members must be predisposed to respond to signals of infant need. Almost all primates are. Females in particular are attracted to babies and seek to touch, hold, or carry them. Across primates, prior caretaking experience matters for competent parenting. Presumably, such baby "lust" evolved to help insure that pre-reproductives are prepared for parenthood, neurologically primed and also practiced (Fleming 2005). In infant-sharing primates, where females live in matrilineal kin groups, allomaternal assistance keeps the baby safe while the mother is free to forage, contributing to both her fitness and to the inclusive fitness of kin. Males, too, may be attracted to babies, and in some species (like titi monkeys) have an even lower threshold for responding to them than do mothers. To be convinced, one need only watch a male *Callithrix argentata* hovering near his mate at birth, grabbing at the emerging baby, even vying with the mother to eat the placenta. Males primed by prior experience with babies appear especially eager.

In humans, both sexes respond to infantile behaviors like smiling or babbling, and as first noted by Konrad Lorenz, both sexes are attracted by "cuteness" (round heads, small face, big eyes, immature body form, and obvious vulnerability), but there are significant differences in how the sexes respond (Alley 1983). Although both sexes respond to cuteness—and having a younger sibling increased an individual's responsiveness—on average, women were more protective.

Strategic Calibration of Altruism

In many cooperatively breeding mammals, allomothers schedule assistance so as reduce costs to their own fitness. They are most likely to help when they are too young, or too old, to breed themselves, or when for social or ecological reasons breeding would not be practical. Allomothers may be most eager to help when in good condition, but when resources are scarce or when helping would interfere with their own reproduction, they may decline. Simply pretending to help is also an option. For example, in birds, young helpers may ostentatiously carry food to nestlings only to swallow it themselves when parents are not watching (Cockburn 1998, p. 161). There may also be penalties for *not* helping—including reduced parental tolerance for shirking allomothers. Such generalizations apply in spades to humans, where social sanctions operate in many subtle, and not so subtle, ways, and among whom payoffs for generosity and kindness come in many currencies.

IMPLICATIONS OF THE COOPERATIVE BREEDING HYPOTHESIS FOR HUMAN DEVELOPMENT

A heritage of cooperative breeding has profound implications for psychological adaptations across a broad range of life phases. This topic has only begun to be explored. For example, even though human mothers, like other apes, produce singleton young after a long period of gestation, if human mothers had evolved as cooperative breeders, women and their infants would theoretically have been selected to seek and elicit support from a range of individuals. This has repercussions for the psychobiological underpinnings of male–female, female–female, infant–mother, and infant–allomother relationships. Here I focus on the implications for the emotional and cognitive development of infants.

Primates produce costly singleton births. Quality control is built into the process at many levels. Only adequately nourished mothers ovulate, only selected ovulations are fertile, only a single successful sperm is selected, only viable conceptions persist, and so forth. Once they give birth, nonhuman primates are predisposed to carry and care for any infant vigorous enough to catch hold of the mother's fur, reach her nipples, and initiate lactation. Once born, even blind or seriously deformed primate neonates are carried so long as they can cling. Even a stillborn infant may be carried at least for a few hours. In hundreds of thousands of hours of observations, abandonment of full-term infants by their mothers has rarely been observed in wild primates, and mothers in the wild have almost never been observed to deliberately harm their own infants. (Exceptions involve inexperienced primiparae, anxious mothers trying to restrain infants, or mothers who punish offspring they are trying to wean; except in cases of incompetence, such behaviors never result in injury.) Apart from inexperienced primiparae, abandonment occurs only under extreme duress (e.g., mother in very poor condition; infant threatened by infanticidal males). Cooperatively breeding Callitrichids and humans are the only primates to which these generalizations do not apply. In both, maternal commitment is unusually contingent on social circumstances. Like tamarins, women respond to lack of support by failing to commit in the period right after birth, reducing or terminating investment in a newborn by abandoning it, or committing outright infanticide. Furthermore, human mothers are the only primates who have become discriminating about which infants they invest in, using criteria like sex, birth order, birth weight, and other signs of viability.

Selection Pressures on Neonates Produced by Contingent Maternal—and Allomaternal—Commitment

If human mothers are more discriminating about which babies they invest in, neonates that conform to maternal preferences should be more likely to survive. The hypothesis that maternal preferences acted as a selection pressure favoring babies born looking full term and robust may help explain why human infants are born so much fatter at birth than are infants in other primates (Hrdy 1999, chap. 20 and 21). Infants who engage mothers right from birth should also have an advantage over those who do not. Contingent maternal commitment means that, compared to other apes, human infants have a greater need both to appeal to others and to monitor and interpret the moods and intentions of potential caregivers and provisioners so that if a caretaker seems likely to disengage, the infant can rev up efforts to engage her. Unlike other ape neonates, who are exclusively cared for by the mother for the first 3–5 months or longer, infants in hunter–gatherer societies are frequently held by allomothers (Hewlett & Lamb 2005) and as early as 3 months of age, and increasingly through time, are provisioned by allomothers in addition to mothers (e.g., see Eibl-Eibesfeldt 1989 for the ubiquity among foraging peoples of "kiss-feeding," involving transfers of sweetened saliva and premasticated food). More than other apes, hominid infants would have benefited from reading the intentions of allomothers in addition to mothers.

All ape newborns cling, complain when uncomfortable, and signal desperately when separated. We now know that chimp in addition to human newborns seek out faces and initiate contact with others in the period right after birth and are probably more likely to do so when exposed to human allomothers in captivity than when they are cared for only by mothers in the wild (Matsuzawa 2006). Like humans, baby apes may imitate facial expressions in their human allomothers, smile, and laugh (Bard et al. 2005, Matsuzawa 2001, Myowa-Yamakoshi 2006). But whereas chimp infants lose interest in such engagement after the first few months, human babies keep engaging others, improve over time, and become passionately eager for intersubjective engagement (Trevarthen 2005). Furthermore, humans are also endowed with traits not seen in chimps for engaging others. For example, easily visible white sclera surrounding the pupil and iris are present in human newborns right from birth, and these function to highlight the direction of eye gaze in human infants, accentuating their powers of engagement.

All apes maneuver in complex social networks, and immatures depend for survival on prolonged care from their mother and possess neural machinery for monitoring and engaging others (so far well documented only in chimps and humans). Yet, the level of concern with reading the minds and intentions of others appears far greater in humans than in any other ape (Tomasello, Carpenter, Call, Behne, & Moll 2005). Human infants are born with an innate eagerness for intersubjective engagement and innate capacities for reading intentions not found in other apes (Baron-Cohen 1995/2001, Hobson 2004).[1] Given the similarities, why this difference? I hypothesize that the difference is very ancient, far older than language and fully sapient brains, and has to do with the importance of shared care and provisioning in the development and evolution of early hominids (Hrdy 1999, 2005).

---

1. Hauser et al. (2004) report that cooperatively breeding tamarins may be able to gauge another individuals' intentions, and use this information in deciding whether or not to share food. So far this pioneering study stands by itself. We do not yet have the comparative studies which would allow us to say if food sharing and cooperative breeding might predispose primates towards cooperation based on intentions.

SELECTION PRESSURES FROM THE HUMAN
INFANT'S NEED TO ATTRACT ALLOMOTHERS

Any ape baby's primary source of information about his world centers on his mother and her reactions to her world. However, the mother's own commitment level depends on her perception of social support. Furthermore, if humans evolved as cooperative breeders, infants also needed to be sensitive to cues from other members in their immediate community. Such cues, particularly when they inform infants about sources of nurture, inform internal working models about the social world babies have been born into (Bowlby 1969) and provide input for physiological "decisions" as how fast to grow. When infants feel confident of continued succor, they should invest in rapid growth. Alternatively, indifference or neglect might signal a time for the child to shut down growth, conserving resources and increasing the chances of surviving future neglect. This could be one explanation for why neglected children with adequate food nevertheless "fail to thrive."

In other words, human babies are born "connoisseurs" of solicitude. Even with the onset of weaning, early learning biases persist, developing with age and experience. As a baby becomes more discriminating about which caretakers to trust, his ability to predict the behavior of others is further refined and reinforced (Tomasello 1999). Good mind readers become better mind readers (Baron-Cohen 1995/2001). Like some other apes, human infants seek out and engage with eyes, even respond to a direct gaze, and communicate that way. But unlike other apes, who appear to lose interest with time (Myowa-Yamakoshi 2006), humans grow increasingly motivated to read and share mental states over the first months and years of life. By 3–4 months, human infants smile less at adults who avert their gaze, but resume smiling when the adult looks straight at them (Farroni, Csibra, Simion, & Johnson 2002). Evidence from both the field and lab (Myowa-Yamakoshi 2006; Whitten, Horner, & Marshall-Pescini 2003) suggest that chimps are capable of reading intentions and learning through observation and imitation, but by three to four years, humans are more adept at doing so, and more eager to. Children freely imagine what it is like to be someone altogether different, even someone they have never seen, enjoy doing so, and delight in drawing others into this game (Harris, 2000; Trevarthen 2005). This greater interest in an "inter-subjective" understanding of what someone else is trying to do and why (Henninghausen & Lyons-Ruth 2005), coupled with an eagerness to share goals with others, improves human capacities to learn through observation. Thus, a quest for inter-subjective understanding can help explain why humans are especially prone to accumulate and transmit new knowledge (Tomasello 1999). Such mental aptitudes for mind reading are especially valuable for predicting and interpreting the intentions of others, and thus promoting cooperation (Chisholm 2003). But given that our closest ape relations also hunt, use tools, and engage in inter-group aggression, why are humans so much better at cooperation?

HOW SHARED CARE AND PROVISIONING RELATES TO THE QUESTION OF WHY HUMANS ARE SO "HYPER-SOCIAL"

According to proponents of the "Machiavellian intelligence" hypothesis (Byrne & Whitten 1985), reading minds provides a strategic advantage in competitive worlds characterized by shifting alliances. But given that many primates, and all other apes, also live in complexly competitive societies, the need for Machiavellian intelligence fails to explain why humans should be so much better at imagining the intentions of others and moving into their conceptual worlds, than other apes are. Chimps, after all, are at least as dominance-oriented and competitive as humans are, probably more so. So, why should capacities for shared engagement be so much better developed in humans, why should humans (following Tomasello 1999) be so "hyper-social"—and, eventually, so hyper-altruistic (e.g., Fehr & Fischbacher 2003)? What most distinguishes humans from other apes is not so much our competitive heritage as our more cooperative one.

Infants born into cooperative breeding systems depend on a range of caretakers, and maternal commitment itself is contingent on the mother's perception of how much support from allomothers she is likely to have. To prosper in a world with shared care and allomaternal provisioning, infants have to be adept at monitoring caretakers, at reading their moods and intentions and eliciting their solicitude. Chisholm (2003) argues that "theory of mind" reduces the uncertainties youngsters face, helping them predict how others (both mothers and allomothers) are likely to respond. Through practice and conditional rewards, infants get incrementally better at reading intentions and learning to engage caretakers. Infants who spend time a short distance from their mother pay more attention to monitoring faces (Lavelli & Fogel 2002). Similarly, children who grow up tended by older siblings grow up better able to interpret the feelings and intentions of others (Ruffman, Perner, Naito, Parkin, & Clements 1998).

In the case of creatures as intelligent and manipulative as all apes are, precociously expressed abilities to read and interpret the intentions of others continue to develop through the first years of life. There is a ratcheting effect as early efforts develop into sophisticated mind reading (Baron-Cohen 1995/2001, Tomasello 1999, p. 67). Being able to intuit and care about what others are thinking—to cognitively and emotionally put oneself in someone else's shoes and think about what they are thinking, to play with them, learn from them, and share their goals (Trevarthen 2005) has in turn had spectacular repercussions in the evolution of our peculiarly "hyper-social," information-sharing, and culture-transmitting species (Tomasello 1999). The neural underpinnings for mind-reading are laid down in early and later infancy and provide the necessary underpinnings first for empathy, and then for development of full-fledged theory of mind a few years later, usually between ages 4 and 6. Once such traits were expressed in the phenotype, natural selection would have had an opportunity to favor any small changes in genes or gene expression that predispose the organism to develop them (West-Eberhard 2003).

Continuing in this speculative vein, I am struck by other unusual traits that humans share with cooperative breeders. Against all phylogenetic predictions, dogs perform better at extracting information from human social signals than do chimps (with the exception of chimps reared in close contact with humans). In an ingenious set of experiments, Hare, Brown, Williamson, and Tomasello (2003) demonstrated that dogs (and even puppies not yet exposed to humans) were more skillful than were chimps at using human social cues like direction of gaze, finger pointing, and finger tapping to locate containers with hidden food (experimenters controlled for smell). How could this be? Not only do dogs descend from cooperatively breeding wolves—making them, presumably, neurologically equipped to read intentions—but domestic dogs also have a 15,000-year history of co-evolving with humans. In this sense, the social environments of dogs were evolutionarily comparable to those of children. Both depended on tolerance and handouts from larger, food-possessing human allomothers.

Babbling, the repetitive, rhythmical vocalizations long assumed to be uniquely human, represents the strangest of all such convergences. Babbling spontaneously emerges around 7 months, at about the same time that babies begin to grow "milk" teeth, beginning with two tiny incisors at the bottom, then four more on top. This is about the time that babies begin to distinguish familiar people from strangers, and to accept pre-weaning foods. By age 3 or so, there will be 20 sharp little teeth to help babies chew their first solids, mostly soft or mashed foods, or premasticated food. Babbling, as it turns out, is not unique to humans. Something like babbling crops up in Callitrichids, the only primates other than humans (if the hypothesis is correct) to evolve with full-fledged cooperative breeding. In pygmy marmosets, babbling emerges between the first and third weeks, just about the time allomothers take over most of the care (Snowdon 2001). It seems likely that babbling in human babies, like smiling, originated for the same reason that babbling developed in Callitrichids. For babbling (and the rhythmic movements of hands and feet that accompany it in humans) attracts the attention of caregivers and elicits interest, solicitude, and edible tidbits. Even as adult Callitrichids continue to use vocalization as a means of locating and staying in contact with other group members, they engage in far more contact vocalizations than do chimps or other apes—with the exception of humans (Snowdon 2001).

It has long been assumed that infants babble because the practice helps them learn to talk. No doubt it does. But I suspect that babbling evolved before language, and for a different reason. Our ancestors were born clever apes who, because they needed to engage caretakers, babbled at them. The best babblers were the best fed and also learned to talk, thus entering into a world of new possibilities. Of course, long childhoods are critical for such skills to develop, but longer periods of nutritional dependency are predictable corollaries of alloparental provisioning. According to this scenario, opportunities provided by slow development were in place before the evolution of sapient brains. Cooperative breeding had evolved before in many species but never before in a species so clever as an ape.

Dependence on allomaternal assistance produced more contingent maternal commitment and, with it, the need for babies born scanning and monitoring signals of commitment from those around them, equipped from birth and through childhood to engage and elicit investment from mothers and other individuals. Present a talented ape with a long, well-buffered phase in which to develop, and novel co-evolutionary processes are going to be unleashed.

Long Childhoods

To the extent that anthropologists thought about childhood, most viewed it as a unique stage in the life history of human beings that evolved some 2 million years ago to provide extra time for developing large brains and for learning. According to this view, the evolution of childhood and adolescence, the human capacity for symbolic language, and culture are the result of the inclusion of new life stages in human development. From a comparative sociobiological perspective, however, prolonged post-weaning or post-fledging dependence is a predictable corollary of allomaternal provisioning. Even prior to the evolution of big and costly brains and before the need to acquire special cognitive skills for complex tool use, language, and symbolic culture (uniquely human traits that long childhoods supposedly evolved to facilitate), a comparison across species predicts that apes who were cooperative breeders could have afforded to take their time growing up. Other cooperative breeders far less brainy than we are—like crested magpie jays and wolves—also have long "childhoods." I do not think it is a coincidence, the problem-solving and tool-use expertise found in New Caledonian (Chappell & Kacelnik 2002) crop up in taxon with a long history of cooperative breeding.

Conventional explanations for the evolution of sapient brains emphasize the (undeniable) subsistence benefits of tools (Kaplan et al. 2000 and the (also undeniable) social and reproductive benefits of Machiavellian intelligence. But other highly social apes also stand to benefit from tools. Chimps, after all, obtain massive amounts of calories from nuts that they have laboriously learned to crack open using wooden hammers and stone anvils. Chimps, too, would benefit from enhanced learning yet never evolved human-sized brains—why not? Because brains are energetically extremely costly, and delays in maturation are risky (Aiello & Wheeler 1995). How could a chimp that was just a little better at nut cracking gain sufficient reproductive rewards to make delayed maturation and a slightly bigger brain worth it? The slightly dumber nutcracker would still likely outbreed him.

It is difficult to explain why such gifts evolved only in the ape line leading to humans without knowing just what originally distinguished prehominids from other apes. The proposal made here is that the distinguishing condition that set the stage for the evolution of enhanced mind-reading was maternal reliance on allomaternal assistance and, with it, (1) more contingent maternal commitment plus the sociocognitive capacities infants need to engage both mothers and others; and (2) the slow maturation that comes as a corollary of cooperative breeding. If the time until nutritional independence was already delayed, metabolically costly big brains would evolve at a discount. By this logic, long periods of nutritional dependence *preceded* the co-evolutionary processes that selected for bigger and bigger brains and other trademarks of our "hyper-social" species such as language and symbolic thought. Among prehominid creatures who already possessed rudimentary theories of mind, and among whom greater intelligence did not have to compensate its possessors for the entire cost of delayed maturation, even small reproductive payoffs from being smarter would be sufficient to favor bigger brains.

ACKNOWLEDGMENTS

I am indebted to Jim Chisholm, Barry Hewlett, Kristen Hawkes, Mel Konner, and Michael Lamb for discussion over many years of ideas presented at the 92nd Dahlem Workshop, held in Berlin September 28–October 3, 2003. Specific suggestions from Jim Leckman and Karin Grossman at that workshop are gratefully acknowledged. Matthew Gibbons helped revise this chapter for publication here. The original version of this essay was published in *Attachment and Bonding: A New Synthesis*, Dahlem Workshop No. 92, ed. C. S. Carter, L. Ahnert, K. E. Grossmann, S. B. Hrdy, M. E. Lamb, S. W. Porges, and N. Sachser (Cambridge: M.I.T. Press). Permission to reprint here is gratefully acknowledged.

REFERENCES

Aiello, L., & Wheeler, P. (1995). The expensive tissue hypothesis. *Current Anthropology 36*, 199–221.

Alley, T. (1983). Growth-produced changes in body shape and size as determinants of perceived age and adult caregiving. *Child Development, 54*, 241–248.

Alvarez, H. (2004). Residence groups among hunter–gatherers: A view of the claims and evidence for patrilocal bands. In B. Chapais & C. Berman (Eds.), *Kinship and Behavior in Primates* (pp. 400–442). Oxford: Oxford University Press.

Bard, K., Myowa-Yamakoshi, M., Tomonaga, M., Tanaka, M., Quinn, J., Costall, A., et al. (2005). Group differences in the mutual gaze of chimpanzees (Pan troglodytes). *Developmental Psychology, 41*, 616–624.

Bardi, M., Petto, A., & Lee-Parritz, D. (2001). Parental failure in captive cotton-top tamarins (*Saguinus oedipus*). *American Journal of Primatology, 54*, 150–169.

Baron-Cohen, S. (Ed.). (1995/2001). *Mindblindness: An essay on autism and theory of mind*. Cambridge, MA: MIT Press.

Beckerman, S., Lizarralde, R., Ballew, C., Schroeder, S., Fingelton, C., Garrison, A., et al. (1998). The Bari partible paternity project: Preliminary results. *Current Anthropology, 39*, 164–167.

Bowlby, J. (1969). *Attachment and loss: Attachment*. New York: Basic.

Buchan, J. C., Alberts, S. A., Silk, J. B., & Altmann, J. (2003). True paternal care in a multi-male primate society. *Nature, 425*, 179–181.

Byrne, R. W., & Whitten, A. (1985). *Machiavellian intelligence: Social expertise and the evolution of intellect in monkeys, apes and humans*. Oxford: Clarendon.

Chagnon, N. (1992). *Yanomamo: The last days of Eden*. New York: Harcourt Brace & Jovanovich.

Chappell, J., & Kacelnik, A. (2002). Selectivity of tool length by New Caledonian crows. *Animal Cognition, 5*, 71–78.

Chisholm, J. (2003). Uncertainty, contingency and attachment: A life history theory of theory of mind. In K. Sterelny & J. Fitness (Eds.), *From mating to mentality: Evaluating evolutionary psychology* (pp. 125–154). Hove, UK: Psychology Press.

Cockburn, A. (1998). Evolution of helping behavior in cooperatively breeding birds. *Annual Review of Ecol. System, 29*, 141–177.

Davies, N. (1992). Dunnock behaviour and social evolution. Oxford: Oxford University Press.

Draper, P., & Hames, R. (2000). Birth order, sibling investment and fertility among the Ju/'hoansi (!Kung). *Human Nature, 11,* 117–156.

Eibl-Eibesfeldt, I. (1989). *Human ethology* (Pauline Wiessner & Annette Heunemann, Trans.). Hawthorne, NY: Aldine de Gruyter.

Emlen, S. T. (1997). Predicting family dynamics in social vertebrates. In J. R. Krebs & N. B. Davies (Eds.), *Behavioural ecology: An evolutionary approach* (4th ed., pp. 228–253). Oxford: Blackwell.

Farroni, T., Csibra, G., Simion, F., & Johnson, M. (2002). Eye contact detection in humans from birth. *Proceedings of the National Academy of Sciences, USA, 99,* 9602–9605.

Fehr, E., and Fischbacher, U. (2003). The nature of human altruism. *Nature, 425,* 785–791.

Fleming, A.S. (2005). Plasticity of innate behavior: Experiences throughout life affect maternal behavior and its neurobiology. In C. S. Carter; L. Ahnert; K. E. Grossmann; S. B. Hrdy; M. E. Lamb; S. W. Porges; & N. Sachser (Eds.), *Attachment and bonding: A new synthesis* (Dahlem Workshop No. 92) (pp. 137–168). Cambridge: MIT Press.

Fleming, A. S., Corter, C., Stallings, J., & Steiner, M. (2002). Testosterone and prolactin are associated with emotional responses to infant cries in new fathers. *Hormones and Behavior, 42,* 399–413.

Flinn, M. V. (1989). Household composition and female reproductive strategies in a Trinidadian village. In A. E. Rasa, C. Vogel, & E. Voland (Eds.), *The sociobiology of sexual and reproductive strategies* (pp. 206–233). London: Chapman & Hall.

Furstenburg, F. (1976). *Unplanned parenthood: The social consequences of unplanned parenthood.* New York: Free Press.

Grey, P., Kahlenberg, S., Barrett, E., Lipson, S., & Ellison, P. (2002). Marriage and fatherhood are associated with lower testosterone in males. *Evolution and Human Behavior, 23,* 1–9.

Hamilton, W. D. (1964). The genetical evolution of social behaviour. 1 *Journal of Theoretical Biology, 7,* 1–18.

Hamilton, W. D. (1966). The moulding of senescence by natural selection. *Journal of Theoretical Biology, 12,* 12–45.

Hare, B., Brown, M., Williamson, C., & Tomasello, M. (2003). The domestication of social cognition in dogs. *Science, 298,* 1634–1636.

Harris, P. (2000). *The work of the imagination.* Oxford: Blackwell.

Hawkes, K., O'Connell, J. F., Blurton Jones, N. G., Charnov, E. L., & Alvarez, H. (1998). Grandmothering, menopause, and the evolution of human life histories. *Proceedings of the National Academy of Sciences, USA, 95,* 1336–1339.

Heinrichs, M., Baumgartner, T., Kirschbaum, C., & Ehlert, U. (2003). Social support and oxytocin interact to suppress cortisol and subjective responses to psychosocial stress. *Biol. Psychiatry, 54,* 1389–1398.

Heinsohn, R., & Double, M. C. (2004). Cooperate or speciate: New theory for the distribution of passerine birds. *Trends in Ecology and Evolution, 19*, 55–60.

Hennighausen, K., & Lyons-Ruth, K. (2005). Disorganization of attachment strategies in infancy and childhood. In R. F. Tremblay, R. G. Barr, & RdeV. Peters (Eds.). *Enclyclopedia on Early Childhood Development* (online). Montreal, Quebec: Centre of Excellence for early childhood development. Accessed October 1, 2006 at http://www.excellence_earlychildhood.ca/documents/Hennighausen-LyonsRuthANGXP.pdf.

Hewlett, B. (1988). Sexual selection and paternal investment among Aka pgymies. In L. Betzig, M. B. Mulder, & P. Turke (Eds.), *Human Reproductive Behavior* (pp. 263–276). Cambridge: Cambridge University Press.

Hewlett, B., & Lamb, M. (Eds.). (2005). *Hunter–gatherer childhoods: Evolutionary, Developmental and Cultural Perspectives*. Hawthorne, NY: Transaction/Aldine de Gruyter.

Hill, K., & Hurtado, A. (1996). Ache life history: The ecology and demography of a foraging people. Hawthorne, NY: Aldine de Gruyter.

Hobson, P. (2004). *The cradle of thought*. Oxford: Oxford University Press.

Hrdy, S. B. (1976). Care and exploitation of nonhuman primate infants by conspecifics other than the mother. In J. S. Rosenblatt, R. Hinde, E. Shaw, & C. Beer (Eds.) *Advances in the Study of Behavior* (pp. 1–58). New York: Academic Press.

Hrdy, S. B. (1977). *The langurs of Abu: Female and male strategies of reproduction*. Cambridge: Harvard University Press.

Hrdy, S. B. (1999). *Mother Nature: A history of mothers, infants and natural selection*. New York: Pantheon.

Hrdy, S. B. (2005). Comes the child before man. In B. Hewlett & M. Lamb (Eds.), *Hunter Gatherer Childhoods* (pp. 65–101). New Brunswick, NJ: Aldine Transaction.

Jamison, C. S., Cornell, L. L., Jamison, P. L., & Nakazato, H. (2002). Are all grandmothers equal? A review and a preliminary test of the "grandmother hypothesis" in Tokugawa, Japan. *American Journal of Physical Anthropology, 119*, 67–76.

Kaplan, H., Hill, K., Lancaster, J., & Hurtado, A. M. (2000). A theory of human life history evolution: Diet, intelligence and longevity. *Evolutionary Anthropology, 9*, 156–185.

Konner, Melvin. (2005). Hunter–gatherer infancy and childhood: The !Kung and others. In Barry Hewlett and Michael Lamb (Eds.), *Hunter-gatherer childhoods: Evolutionary, developmental and cultural perspectives* (pp. 19–64). New Brunswick, NJ: Aldine Transaction.

Kramer, Karen. (2005). Children help the pace of reproduction: Cooperative breeding in humans. *Evolutionary Anthropology, 14*, 224–237.

Kurland, J., & Sparks, C. (2003, June 6). *Is there a Paleolithic demography? Implications for evolutionary psychology and sociobiology*. Paper presented at the 15th annual meeting of the Human Behavior and Evolution Society, Lincoln, Nebraska.

Lahdenpera, M., Lummaa, V., Helle, S., Tremblay, M., & Russell, A. F. (2004). Fitness benefits of prolonged post-reproductive lifespan in women. *Nature, 428*, 178–181.

Langen, T. A. (2000). Prolonged offspring dependence and cooperative breeding in birds. *Behavioral Ecology, 11*, 367–377.

Lavelli, M. & Fogel, A. (2002). Developmental changes in mother-infant face-to-face communication: Birth to 3 months. *Developmental Psychology, 38*, 288–305.

Leonetti, D., Nath, D. C., Hemam, N. S., & Neill, D. B. (2005). Kinship organization and grandmother's impact on reproductive success among the matrilineal Khasi and patrilineal Bengali of N.E. India. In E. Voland, A. Chasiotis, & W. Schiefenhoevel (Eds.), *Grandmotherhood: The evolutionary significance of the second half of female life* (pp. 194–219). Piscataway, NJ: Rutgers University Press.

Levine, R., Dixon, S., LeVine, S., Richman, A., Leiderman, P. H., Keefer, C. H., & Brazelton, T.B. (1996). Child care and culture: Lessons from Africa. Cambridge: Cambridge University Press.

Marlowe, F. (2005). Who tends Hadza children? In B. Hewlett and M. Lamb (Eds.), *Hunter–Gatherer Childhoods* (pp. 177–190). New Brunswick, NJ: AldineTransaction.

Matsuzawa, T. (director) (2001). *The baby and Ai*. Kyoto, Japan: Primate Research Institute. Distributed by Mico.

Matsuzawa, T. (2006). Evolutionary origins of the human mother–infant relationship. In T. Matsuzawa, M. Tomonaga, & M. Tanaka (Eds.), *Cognitive development in chimpanzees* (pp. 127–141). Berlin: Springer-Verlag.

Mitani, J. C., & Watts, D. (1997). The evolution of non-maternal caretaking among anthropoid primates: Do helpers help? *Behavioral Ecology Sociobiology, 40*, 213–240.

Murdock, G. P. (1967). *Ethnographic Atlas*. Pittsburgh: University of Pittsburgh Press.

Myowa-Yamakoshi, M. (2006). How and when do chimpanzees acquire the ability to imitate. In T. Matsuzawa, M. Tomonaga, & M. Tanaka (Eds.), *Cognitive Development in Chimpanzees* (pp. 214–232). Berlin: Springer-Verlag.

O'Connell, J. F., Hawkes, K., Lupo, K. D., & Blurton Jones, N. G.. (2002). Male strategies and Plio-Pleistocene archeology. *Journal of Human Evolution, 43*, 831–872.

Olds, D., Henderson, C.R., Chaberlin, R., & Tatelbaum, R. (1986). Preventing child abuse and neglect: A randomized trial of nurse home visitation. *Pediatrics, 78*, 65–78.

Olds, D., Robinson, J., O'Brien, R. et al. (2002). Home visiting by paraprofessionals and by nurses: A randomized controlled trial. *Pediatrics, 110*, 486–496.

Paul, A. (2005). Primate predispositions for human grandmaternal behavior. In E. Voland, A. Chasiotis, and W. Schiefenhoevel (Eds.), *Grandmotherhood: The evolutionary significance of the second half of female life* (pp. 21–37). Piscataway, NJ: Rutgers University Press.

Pusey, A., Williams, J., & Goodall, J. (1997). The influence of dominance rank on the reproductive success of female chimpanzees. *Science, 277,* 828–831.

Rowley, I., & Russell, E. (1990). Splendid fairy wrens: Demonstrating the importance of longevity. In P. Stacey & W. Koenig (Eds.), *Cooperative breeding in birds* (pp. 3–30). Cambridge: Cambridge University Press.

Ruffman, T., Perner, J., Naito, M., Parkin, L., & W. Clements. (1998). Older (but not younger) siblings facilitate false belief understanding. *Developmental Psychology, 34,* 161–174.

Russell, A. F., Sharp, L., Brotherton, P., & Clutton-Brock, T. H. (2003). Cost minimization by helpers in cooperative vertebrates. *Proceedings of the National Academy of Sciences, USA, 100,* 3333–3338.

Schradin, C., & Anzenberger, G. (1999). Prolactin, the hormone of paternity. *News in Physiological Sciences, 14,* 221–331.

Sear, R., Steel, F., McGregor, I., & Mace, R. (2002). The effects of kin on child mortality in rural Gambia. *Demography, 39,* 43–63.

Silk, J. B., Alberts, S. C., & Altmann, J. (2003). Social bonds of female baboons enhance infant survival. *Science, 302,* 1231–1234.

Snowdon, C. (1996). Infant care in cooperatively breeding species. *Advances in the Study of Behavior, 25,* 643–689.

Snowdon, C. T. (2001). From primate communication to human language. In F. de Waal (Ed.), *Tree of Origin* (pp. 195–227). Cambridge, MA: Harvard University Press.

Spieker, S. J., & Bensley, L. (1994). The roles of living arrangements and grandmother social Support in adolescent mothering and infant attachment. *Developmental Psychology, 30,* 102–111.

Storey, A., Walsh, C. J., Quinton, R. L., & Wynne-Edwards, K. E. (2000). Hormonal correlates of paternal responsiveness in new and expectant fathers. *Evolution and Human Behavior, 21,* 79–95.

Sugiyama, L. S., & Chacon, R. (2005). Juvenile responses to household ecology among the Yora of Peruvian Amazonia. In B. Hewlett & M. Lamb (Eds). *Hunter-Gatherer Childhoods: Evolutionary, Developmental, and Cultural Perspectives* (pp. 237–226) New York: Transaction.

Tomasello, M. (1999). *The cultural origins of human cognition.* Cambridge, MA: Harvard University Press.

Tomasello, M.; Carpenter, M., Call, J., Behne, T., & Moll, H. (2005). Understanding and sharing intentions: The origins of cultural cognition. *Behavioral and Brain Sciences, 28,* 675–691.

Trevarthen, C. (2005). First things first: infants make good use of the sympathetic rhythm of imitation, without reason or language. *Journal of Child Psychotherapist, 31,* 91–113.

Tronick, E. Z., Morelli, G. A., & Winn, S. A. (1987). Multiple caretaking of Efé (pygmy) infants. *American Anthropologist, 89*, 96–106.

Turke, P. (1988). "Helpers at the nest": Childcare networks on Ifaluk. In L. Betzig, M. Borgherhoff Mulder, & P. Turke (Eds.), *Human Reproductive Behaviour: A Darwinian Perspective* (pp. 173–188). Cambridge: Cambridge University Press.

Voland, E., & Beise, J. (2002). Opposite effects of maternal and paternal grandmothers on infant survival in historical Krummhoern. *Behavioral Ecology and Sociobiology 52*, 435–443.

Voland, E., Chasiotis, A., & W. Schiefenhoevel (Eds.). (2005). *Grandmotherhood: The evolutionary significance of the second half of female life.* Piscataway, NJ: Rutgers University Press.

Von Holst, D. (1986). Psychosocial stress and its pathophysiological effects in tree shrews (*Tupaia belangeri*). In T. H. Schmidt, T. M. Dembroski, and G. Blumchen (Eds.), *Biological and psychological factors in cardiovascular disease* (pp. 476–489). Heidelberg: Springer.

Weisner, T., & Gallimore, R. (1977). My brother's keeper: Child and sibling caretaking. *Current Anthropology, 18*, 169–170.

Weitoft, G. R., Hjern, A., Haglund, B., & Rosén, M. (2003). Mortality, severe morbidity, and injury in children living with single parents in Sweden: A population-based study. *Lancet, 361*, 289–295.

Werner, E. E. (1984). Child care: Kith, kin and hired hands. Baltimore: University Park Press.

West-Eberhard, M. J. (2003). Developmental plasticity and evolution. New York: Oxford University Press.

Whitten, A., Horner, V., & Marshall-Pescini, S. (2003). Cultural anthropology. *Evolutionary Anthropology, 2*, 92–105.

Wiessner, P. (2002). Hunting, healing and *hxaro* exchange: A long-term perspective on !Kung (Ju/'hoansi) large-game hunting. *Evolution and Human Behavior, 23*, 407–436.

PART II

Parent–Child Relationships

4   Life Transitions: Becoming a Parent

Sarah E. Johns and Jay Belsky

INTRODUCTION

The birth of a child is a commonplace event, yet for the two individuals who become parents, it is nothing short of miraculous. This transition to parenthood is a major life event, and both the new mother and father have to adapt to the changes brought about by the responsibility of raising a child. For men and women the challenges of parenthood will differ, and the new parents' relationship will undergo change as the demands of their new roles become apparent (Belsky & Pensky 1988, Roosa 1988). In consequence, becoming a parent, although largely viewed as a positive event, can place huge strains on both a couple's relationship and on individual functioning within that relationship. Having a baby can be extremely stressful, and as with any major life change, it entails some degree of risk, with the challenge of raising children causing new problems or highlighting existing vulnerabilities for both parents (Cowan & Cowan 1995). Parenthood has, therefore, the potential to change both men's and women's feelings about themselves and their relationships as they take on the important role of nurturing their children from birth into adulthood.

This chapter explores the transition to parenthood, in particular asking why this can be difficult, why the experience of having a child is different for men and women, how the timing of the transition can be influenced by family relationships, and how the ease of transition for one generation can influence the timing of the transition in subsequent generations. These subjects have been covered comprehensively by research in the social sciences (primarily psychology) that provides various proximate explanations, but is focused mainly on Western families and seldom coupled with an evolutionary perspective which seeks ultimate explanations of human reproductive patterns and parenting behaviors. In contrast, when evolutionary explanations of human reproductive timing and parenting behavior are sought, research has been undertaken primarily in natural fertility populations in developing countries and has not explored the psychological, or the more proximate, aspects of becoming a parent.

We feel that understanding the transition to parenthood should incorporate an understanding of the differential reproductive strategies, specifically life-history event timings and investment decisions, of both men and women, and that evolutionary-based hypotheses should be used to investigate the tradeoffs between mating and parenting. Here we review the existing literature on the timing and transition to parenthood, place it within an evolutionary framework, and stress areas in which additional research is required to better understand this fundamental aspect of human behavior.

THE TRANSITION TO PARENTHOOD

There is often a decline in marital quality and self-reported marital satisfaction following the birth of a child (Belsky & Pensky 1988; Kanoy, Ulku-Steiner, Cox, & Burchinal 2003; O'Brien & Peyton 2002; Schulz, Cowan, & Cowan 2006; Twenge, Campbell, & Foster 2003), and this decline may begin during pregnancy (Snowden, Schott, Awalt, & Gillis-Knox 1988). Although this transition to parenthood can cause difficulties in well-functioning couples with optimal resources at their disposal, for those with emotional problems or financial difficulties, those who are very young, or those who have a child with a disability, the transition will be even more of a struggle (Cowan & Cowan 1995, Florsheim et al. 2003, Kanoy et al. 2003, Twenge et al. 2003). Mirowsky and Ross (2002, p. 1282) suggest that when economic resources and social support are scarce, "the strains of raising children outweigh the emotional benefits." Individuals who have negative memories of their parents' marriage also have greater difficulty maintaining marital satisfaction in the period following the birth of their own child than do those who report more-positive memories (Belsky & Isabella 1985; Curran, Hazen, Jacobvitz, & Feldman 2005), suggesting that developmental factors may be crucial in some circumstances. Not all families, however, experience extreme difficulties in marital functioning during the transition; indeed, most do not. In one of the first investigations to closely and longitudinally examine individual differences in marital change across the transition to parenthood—from pregnancy to 3 years postpartum—Belsky and Rovine

(1990; Belsky & Kelly 1994) identified distinct groups of families in which patterns of marital change varied. While in this mostly middle- and working-class, white American volunteer sample a small minority of households manifested noteworthy declines in marital quality, the large majority of couples had only modest declines in their marital quality. Moreover, not only did some families not change at all, but a small minority actually showed improvements. More recently, O'Brien and Peyton (2002) have also documented that even though, *on average*, marital quality declines somewhat across the transition to parenthood, this central tendency masks notable variation in response to the arrival and rearing of a first child.

Although the transition to parenthood affects marital functioning and the satisfaction of many couples, becoming a parent has different and independent effects on men and women. From pregnancy onward, the transition to parenthood is often thought of, or described as, a natural process for women (Berg & Dahlberg 2001), but the ease of the new mother's transition is dependent on many factors. Without appropriate support, problems can arise during the transitional period that may have serious consequences for the mother, her children, and the functioning of the family unit. Violation of individual expectations of the transition to parenthood has greater and more serious consequences for women than it does for men (Belsky 1985; Belsky, Spanier, & Rovine 1983; Kach & McGhee1982). Incidences of self-reported depression and distress during the first year postpartum have been found to be higher in new mothers when compared to new fathers (Matthey, Barnett, Ungerer, & Waters 2000), and psychological disturbances are more likely to develop in the first year of motherhood than at any other time (Nicolson 1998). Women have also been found to change in their psychological attachment orientation, demonstrating increased anxiety about the level of their partner's love, commitment, and support 6 months postpartum if they believe their spouse to be unsupportive and angry during the prenatal period (Simpson, Rholes, Campbell, & Wilson 2003). Such emotional and psychological distress will put the newborn infant at risk, as depressed mothers substantially reduce their level of maternal care and investment (see Belsky & Jaffee 2006 for review), and can even affect child survival (Hagen 1999).

In a Western context, where many women are active in the labor market, there may be difficulties adapting to parenthood that occur when mothers have little choice but to be apart from their young children (Hyde, Essex, Clark, & Klein 2001). Women who work and are part of a dual-earning couple find the transition to parenthood more stressful than do their husbands (Hyde, Klein, Essex, & Clark 1995; Lewis & Cooper 1988). Taking a short maternity leave (of fewer than 12 weeks) is associated with increased levels of maternal depression, with women reporting negative impacts on both their self-esteem and their marriage (Feldman, Sussman, & Zigler 2004).

This may be especially true when a speedy return to employment coincides with other factors, such as being dissatisfied with available child care (Hyde et al. 2001). Wider societal support for new mothers in the form of shorter work hours and increased childcare quality have been found to improve women's functioning at work when they do return (Feldman, Masalha, & Nadam 2001). In addition, Belsky and Kelly (1994) contend that the transition is harder for modern parents as there is far less consensus regarding traditional male and female roles within the home (e.g., breadwinner and homemaker). Because of this social shift, conflicts are now more likely to arise over the equitable distribution of household and childcare tasks as household roles are not clearly defined and expectations of each parent by the other are no longer transparent (Helms-Erikson 2001; Kluwer, Heesink, & Van De Vliert 2002).

An early transition to parenthood (during adolescence) in a Western context may also have extensive consequences for the young mother (Florsheim et al. 2003; Woodward, Fergusson, & Horwood 2006). For example, decreased educational attainment and lowered employment opportunities have often been cited as two of the major consequences of an adolescent's decision to have a baby (Furstenberg 1976; Hudson & Ineichen 1991; Klepinger, Lundberg, & Plotnick 1995; Menken 1972; Miller 2000). Younger mothers are more likely to be the sole or primary caregiver to their children when compared to young fathers (Woodward et al. 2006), and women who bear their first child at an early age tend to give birth to their subsequent children more rapidly than those who postpone childbearing (Card & Wise 1978; Langfield & Pasley 1997; Millman & Hendershot 1980; Mott 1986; Wellings, Wadsworth, Johnson, Field, & MacDowell 1999). Closely spaced children may put extra strain on a mother and increase her risk of depression and malaise (Thorpe, Golding, MacGillivray, & Greenwood, 1991).

For men, in contrast to women, the difficulties associated with the transition to parenthood appear primarily to affect their childrearing skills and practices rather than their emotional functioning. They are less prone than their partners to suffer from anxiety, depression, and fatigue, and are not as likely to experience a profound, all-consuming, intense emotional attachment to their new child (Belsky & Kelly 1994). However, there is evidence to suggest that the security and quality of a man's spousal relationship before becoming a father has a large influence on how easily he adjusts to his new role (Florsheim et al. 2003).

The quality of a father's relationship with his children depends on his relationship with his partner (Florsheim et al. 2003), with fathers who perceive that their marriage has deteriorated since the birth of their child being more negative and intrusive in their parenting behaviors (Belsky, Youngblade, Rovine, & Volling 1991b; Belsky & Jaffee 2006). Furthermore, men who have access to greater economic and social resources and who are psychologically healthier have more positive, harmonious interactions with their children compared to men who score poorly on these measures (Woodworth, Belsky, & Crnic 1996). Families headed by fathers who are insecure in their state of mind regarding attachment (to their own parents) have more marital problems prenatally and more negative interactions at 24 months after the birth of the first child (Paley et al. 2005), and men are at greater risk of clinical depression and experiencing marital strain if their partners suffer postpartum depression (Stuchbery, Matthey, & Barnett 1998). Cowan and Cowan (1992) have also reported that when men feel unready for fatherhood but agree to the pregnancy to maintain the relationship, the relationship is likely to break down before the child's fifth birthday. Poor or absent paternal support may have serious effects for children unlucky enough to be born to fathers who do not cope, or who refuse to cope, with their paternal role.

The difficulties associated with becoming a parent have been explored predominantly in a modern, Western setting. Some authors claim that "the high rates of misery experienced by new mothers in contemporary Western society are socially and culturally induced" (Barclay & Kent 1998, p. 4), with women suffering most where social recognition of the transition to motherhood and postnatal aid and support are lacking, such as in the United States (Stern & Kruckman 1983). Women in the West tend to have reduced kin support and may suffer social isolation during maternity leave. They are expected to care independently for their new baby before they have recovered from the birth, which may have been handled in an insensitive and overly clinical manner, and they live in a social structure that does not provide adequate remuneration or support during parental leave from economic responsibilities (as reviewed by Hayes, Roberts, & Davare 2000). In addition, lack of support by the father of the child, marital problems, and extreme forms of pre-pregnancy and prenatal spousal abuse have been found to correlate with increased rates of maternal postpartum depression (Hagen 1999, Records & Rice 2005).

Among new mothers from some non-Western societies or traditional cultures, the incidence of postpartum depression has been found to be lower (although is not entirely absent; Bashiri & Spielvogel 1999). In a cultural context where grandmothers or grandmothers-in-law provide a portion of postpartum support and help the new mother in her transition to parenthood (Halbreich & Karkun 2006), or where obstetric and family rituals specifically celebrating childbirth exist (Cox 1988), it is likely that a new mother will be better able to cope with maternity. Comparable work examining new fathers and their difficulties in the transition to fatherhood in non-Western settings is, unfortunately, lacking.

Summary

Together, these findings, such as they are, suggest that men and women are affected by the transition to parenthood in very different ways. Psychological studies have revealed that women find becoming a parent more difficult than do men and that these difficulties are often related to the disproportionate childrearing burdens they bear and to the level of support that a woman perceives she is receiving from the father of the child. Lack of additional parenting support from extended family may create further problems for new mothers, especially in Western contexts. Women also find the transition problematic when they are expected to choose between their children and economic opportunities (lack of childcare, inflexible working hours, etc.). Men, however, find the transition more difficult when they feel forced into having a child and when there are problems in their spousal/partner relationship. Lack of resources can cause problems for both men and women. The psychological and marital difficulties that appear to be associated with becoming a parent have been explored primarily in Western, modern societies. The transition is suggested to be more difficult in this socio-cultural setting, although this is based on little more than supposition, as there is little comparative data on the psychology of new parenthood in traditional cultures or developing countries, other than that specifically related to postpartum depression.

AN EVOLUTIONARY APPROACH

The existing literature on the transition to parenthood raises important questions about how men and women cope when they become parents and what they expect from one another; questions that are fundamentally related to investment in the child and conflicts over the relative levels of paternal and maternal investment, and potentially, the balance between present investment and future reproduction. When both parents continue to care for their young after birth, as is predominantly the case in humans, conflicts over the amount of investment provided by each parent are likely to occur (Wedell, Kvarnemo, Lessells, & Tregenza 2006). In the majority of Western, socially (and often serially) monogamous families, mothers provide more direct care to their children than do fathers (Yeung, Sandberg, Davis-Kean, & Hofferth 2001), and the amount and type of childrearing undertaken by each parent can become a major source of disagreement (Belsky & Kelly 1994), one that may be specific to male–female relationships. Women in lesbian relationships, for example, have reported that they receive more support in child rearing from their female partners than their heterosexual friends do from their husbands (Ross 2005; Ross, Steele, & Sapiro 2005); as with heterosexual couples, this support protects against relationship conflict (Goldberg & Sayer 2006).

Conflicts over investment in children are not solely confined to socially monogamous partnerships. Such conflicts can also arise in polygamous family situations, between the husband and one of his wives, or between co-wives who will be competing with one another to ensure that their children are favored and cared for by their father. Among the Dogon of Mali, for example, Strassmann (1997) found that childhood mortality increased with number of resident co-wives (Strassmann 1997), suggesting resources critical to child survival are limited, and conditions necessary for competition between wives may exist.

To understand why there are conflicts over investment, sex differences in levels of investment, and why men and women are affected differently by having children, it may be useful to explore the transition to parenthood using an evolutionary framework, drawing particularly on that provided by life-history theory. This body of theory offers evolutionary explanations for the scheduling of fertility, mortality, and growth during an organism's life cycle (Hill & Kaplan 1999) and is relevant to understanding human parenting behaviors because it has the capacity to explain how, under given life circumstances, individuals optimally partition their time and energy into childbearing and childrearing. Empirical research into life-history strategies among humans is a relatively new approach (Voland 1998), but a number of studies have examined whether or not life-history theory predicts the life-event timings of particular human populations (Hill & Hurtado 1996; Kaplan, Lancaster, Bock, & Johnson 1995; Mace 1996; Marlowe 1999; Strassmann & Gillespie 2002; Waynforth, Hurtado, & Hill 1998). Relevant life-history traits, known to vary between individuals, are life span, reproductive rate, age at sexual maturity and first reproduction, length of the gestational period, size at birth, number of offspring, and investment in offspring (Stearns 1992). The patterning of these variables describes an individual's reproductive strategy, and it is likely that differences between male and female strategies influence how individuals respond to parenthood. Understanding these reproductive strategies may provide explanations as to why having children can cause conflicts within a marriage and why there are sex-specific differences in the transition to parenthood.

Life-History Tradeoffs

Energy allocated to somatic effort (maintenance and growth), and possibly in humans extrasomatic effort such as the accrual of wealth and education (Voland 1998), reduces the amount of energy that can be made available for reproductive effort, forcing a tradeoff between these outcomes. Furthermore, somatic maintenance and growth are investments in future reproduction, as the size and health of an individual affects the probability that it will survive for future reproduction and governs the amount of energy it will be able to transform into reproductive effort (Kaplan, Hill, Lancaster, & Hurtado 2000). These energy-allocation decisions will affect the total number of descendants an organism will leave (Hill & Kaplan 1999).

The effort allocated by an individual to reproduction can be subdivided into two components, mating effort and parenting effort, and a tradeoff exists between them. Mating effort refers to the investment put into trying to find and keep a sexual partner (Rowe, Vazsonyi, & Figueredo 1997), whereas parenting effort refers to the amount of care and investment that is given to offspring (Voland 1998). Parental investment usually occurs at the expense of both somatic effort and mating effort. This is especially true in humans, where infants are extremely helpless at birth and have an extensive period of juvenile dependence, therefore requiring a considerable degree of parental care to survive. As a result, parents have to decide, based on their current circumstances, whether to invest in themselves, their current offspring, or mating and the possibility of future offspring (Hagen 1999).

In terms of the investment required by each parent to ensure offspring survival, having children is much more costly for women than it is for men. This mirrors the situation found in nearly all female mammals that have internal gestation and a period of necessary postpartum lactation and suckling (Clutton-Brock 1989). As Troisi asserts (2001, p. 446), "at every stage of the process of reproduction (fertilisation, pregnancy, lactation, rearing), the difference between male and female parental investment increases." The extended period of care required by human infants places additional time and energy demands on mothers that will constrain their future reproductive potential. Such demands may be especially costly if mothers lack support in parenting.

Importance of Additional Help in Raising Children

For a woman to be reproductively successful—that is, for her children to survive infancy and childhood, and for them to maintain good health and well-being throughout their juvenile period—it is ideal that she have additional parental support. Hrdy (1999) contends, in fact, that humans are a cooperative breeding species. Support serves to reduce mothers' own parenting effort, allowing her to partition any remaining resources (time, energy, nutrients, etc.) into either having more children (mating effort) or somatic (and extrasomatic) maintenance. This support typically comes from her own close kin or the child's father. Support, particularly from kin, is thought to be extremely important for improving infant survival and maternal ability to care for more than one child at a time. For example, mothers who abuse their children tend to have weak kin networks (Albarracin, Repetto, & Albarracin 1997), and young mothers who receive postpartum assistance from their mothers show fewer depressive symptoms (Quinlivan, Luehr, & Evans 2004). A woman's own mother, the child's grandmother, may be particularly important for child survival, especially in unstable environments where resources are scarce. Hawkes, O'Connell, and Blurton Jones (1997) have suggested that women who have assistance from their own mother in childrearing, and who become pregnant with a subsequent child, can wean their first child knowing that it will be looked after by an experienced family member. This creates an opportunity for grandmothers to increase their daughter's, and hence their own, reproductive success by investing in grandchildren. This hypothesis is strongly supported by empirical research (see Beise 2002; Gibson & Mace 2005; Leonetti & Nath 2004; Sear, Mace, & McGregor 2000; Sear, Steele, McGregor, & Mace 2002; Voland & Beise 2002); the presence of maternal grandmothers enhances child survival.

The majority of empirical studies that have investigated the relative contributions of different types of kin to child survival and well-being have, however, primarily analyzed data from natural fertility and natural mortality populations, so little is known about which types of kin support are the most critical in post-demographic transition societies. In these modern societies, where socially monogamous families are the norm, there is an increased role for fathers in raising their children and offering their wife co-parental support. When extended families are geographically separated from the new mothers, as is often the case in the West (Hayes et al. 2000), fathers may be replacing support that would be provided by other types of kin. Problems and conflict within a spousal relationship will therefore greatly affect both the amount of assistance that a woman receives and her perception of her partner's investment in their children. It is in circumstances when adequate childcare is compromised because of societal and economic demands, and when women are not coping psychologically, emotionally, and physically in their new maternal role, that fathers and their support and care giving may become especially important.

Paternal care in humans appears to be facultative, usually occurring under conditions of high paternity certainty, when particular social and ecological factors reduce male mating opportunities, and when the costs of reproducing with additional women outweigh those of providing paternal investment. It also is of primary importance when socio-ecological conditions dictate that it is necessary for offspring survival (for a thorough review, see Geary 2000). Low levels of paternal investment have been shown to be related to many negative social and emotional outcomes among those who have lived or grown up under such conditions in modern, Western societies (O'Connor, Thorpe, Dunn, & Golding 1999; Pfiffner, McBurnett, & Rathouz 2001; Spruijt, DeGoede, & Vandervalk 2001). Children of divorced parents tend to do less well in school and have been found to be less helpful (Barber 1998), and older children are more likely to drop out of school if their family becomes fragmented (McLanahan 1985). Women with divorced parents also appear to be more insecure in their adult relationships (Barber 1998). Children born into families where a biological father is not present, or where paternity is not acknowledged, have been found to be at higher risk of childhood maltreatment and death (see Berger 2004; Daly & Wilson 1985, 1988; Gaudino, Jenkins, & Rochat 1999), to die in unintentional accidents (Tooley, Karakis, Stokes, & Ozanne-Smith 2006), and to have increased odds of being a low-birth-weight infant (McIntosh, Roumayah, & Bottoms 1995; Oakley 1985, 1988). Similar findings have been found for hunter–gatherer groups (Hill & Hurtado 1996) and historical populations (Voland 1988). Being a single mother or raising children in the presence of an unrelated male can, therefore, be very costly in terms of offspring health and life expectancy.

Although Hawkes et al. (1997) have suggested that women (primarily in a hunter–gatherer context) are not as reliant on male provisioning in raising children as was once thought (e.g., Lovejoy 1981), the evidence is plentiful that, in some socio-ecological circumstances at least, fathers do matter and their support with childrearing is crucial. A father's support is known to be of central importance for a woman's transition to parenthood in Western societies (Feldman et al. 2004), where it reduces the chance of the new mother experiencing postpartum depression (Campbell, Cohn, Flanagan, Popper, & Meyers 1992). Mothers who perceive that they do not have this support (and who may not have access to other avenues of assistance) may therefore find the transition to parenthood more difficult because of the increased effort and investment required to produce viable offspring.

Timing of Parenthood

The impact of varying levels of support may be felt beyond the individual's transition to parenthood. The amount and type of parental investment that a child receives appears to affect the timing and ease of the child's own experiences of becoming a parent, with timing itself being an important factor in the psychological impact of the transition. Marriage breakdown in one generation may affect the reproductive timings of the subsequent generation, with children who have been raised in dysfunctional or non-nuclear families, or without a father present, being more likely to reach puberty, have sex, and reproduce at a younger age (for thorough reviews, see Ellis 2004; Kim, Smith, & Palermiti 1997; Miller, Benson, & Galbraith 2001; Quinlan, 2003). The family or home environment is thought to be an especially important influence on life-history events (Belsky 1997, 2006; Belsky, Steinberg, & Draper 1991a; Chisholm 1993, 1999; Draper & Harpending 1982; Voland 1998). For example, research has linked early age at menarche to general family conflict (Moffitt, Caspi, Belsky, & Silva 1992), and has shown that individuals with divorced parents are more likely to have sex at a younger age and with a greater number of partners (Jónsson, Mjardvik, Olafsdóttir, & Grétarsson 2000), while father absenteeism and unpredictable social environments were found to increase the likelihood of individuals following high mating-effort reproductive strategies (Bereczkei & Csanaky 1996).

The timing of life-history events is affected not only by family fragmentation and father absenteeism but by the level of parental supportiveness, the amount of affection, and the type of relationship that a girl has with her parents, especially her father (Belsky 2007, Belsky et al. 1991a). For example, strained relations with parents lowered the age at which girls reached menarche (Ellis & Garber 2000; Ellis, McFadyen-Ketchum, Dodge, Pettit, & Bates 1999), and girls who were more psychologically distanced from their fathers also reached puberty at an earlier age (Steinberg 1988). Johns (2003) found that women who thought poorly of their fathers, who reported stressful childhoods, and who were not living with both parents at puberty had increased odds of motherhood during their teenage years, while Landy, Schubert, Cleland, Clark, and Montgomery (1983) found that pregnant teenagers had poorer relationships with their fathers than a group of non-pregnant controls. Adolescents with one or both parents absent from their lives were more likely to become parents as teenagers (Kiernan & Hobcraft 1997; Wellings et al. 1999), while women who grew up in non-intact families were also significantly more likely to enter cohabiting or married relationships at earlier ages than were their peers (Kiernan & Hobcraft 1997) and to have a child before marriage (Garfinkel & McLanahan 1986, Wu & Martinson 1993).

These trends are not found only in the West. They have been described in developing countries, such as Ecuador, where pregnant teenagers were found less often to be living with their biological parents (Guijarro et al. 1999), and South Africa where pregnant teenagers were more likely to come from homes where the mother was head of the household, indicating the absence of a father (Craig & Richter-Strydom 1983).

Although becoming a mother at a young age is generally regarded as an undesirable occurrence that results from ignorance and immoral behavior, it may be more useful to regard it as the product of an evolved reproductive strategy, an adaptive response to living in an unstable family or wider environment where a secure future is not guaranteed (Barrett, Dunbar, & Lycett 2002; Belsky 2007; Belsky et al. 1991a; Chisholm 1993, 1999; Johns 2003; Lancaster 1994; Low, Simon, & Anderson 2002). Father absenteeism, fragmented families, and poor familial relationships, themselves possible outcomes of a poor transition to parenthood, are cues to an adolescent regarding the future stability and predictability of her social environment. Under such conditions, high mating effort and a discounting of the future in favor of reproducing as early as possible may be advantageous once a particular level of somatic maturity has been reached (cf. Chisholm 1993, 1999), a strategy that should at least ensure the birth of one child in a potentially unstable environment. Examples of this approach can be seen in the work of Geronimus (1987, 1992, 1996), who argues that becoming a teenage mother is a strategy undertaken by women who do not see long-term futures for themselves. An empirical study of a contemporary British sample also supports this position (Johns 2003).

It appears that children who are insecurely attached to their parents and have poor relationships with them may be unconsciously pursuing a reproductive strategy that is dependent on early puberty—or early reproduction—and this may, in the future, affect their ability to form secure adult relationships (Surbey 1998). This may also have direct bearing on these children's ability to maintain marital satisfaction and cope with the demands of parenthood (Belsky & Isabella 1985, Curran et al. 2005), leading to difficulties in the transition to parenthood that span the generations.

CONCLUSIONS

Life-history theory provides a means of understanding the variation between individuals in their timing of, and transition to, parenthood. It has the potential to explain why women and men differ in their experiences and why kin support may be important for an easy transition. For women, having children is especially demanding, and support is required to reduce the intensity of the childrearing burden; without it, a woman may struggle to function well as a mother. Where kin support is reduced, the importance of the father in family life will increase, perhaps with his becoming the partner's sole system of support. In circumstances where paternal investment is required but where the father has emotional or psychological issues, pursues additional mating opportunities, doubts the paternity of his child, or simply feels pushed into becoming a father, the woman may find herself unable to parent effectively or cope with her own transition to parenthood.

Coupling an evolutionary approach with the known literature concerning the consequences of becoming a parent provides us with a theoretical framework that generates testable hypotheses about the evolution of human parenting behaviors that should apply across cultures, once variation in local socio-ecology is considered. Testing these hypotheses requires cross-cultural empirical research that considers the psychological dimension of the transition to parenthood in the context of reproductive strategies. For example, more comparative research is needed in traditional societies to explore whether some of the difficulties associated with the transition to parenthood in the West are due to a social environment that is evolutionarily novel. To date, most studies examine either the psychological dimension, typically in Western cultures, or reproductive strategies and life-history event timings in non-Western cultures. Integrating the two, and constructing a broad cross-cultural perspective, will be critical before any definite conclusions can be drawn.

REFERENCES

Albarracin, D., Repetto, M. J., & Albarracin, M. (1997). Social support in child abuse and neglect: Support functions, sources, and contexts. *Child Abuse & Neglect, 21*, 607–615.

Barber, N. (1998). Sex differences in disposition towards kin, security of adult attachment, and sociosexuality as a function of parental divorce. *Evolution and Human Behavior, 19*, 125–132.

Barclay, L., & Kent, D. (1998). Recent immigration and the misery of motherhood: A discussion of pertinent issues. *Midwifery, 14*, 4–9.

Barrett, L., Dunbar, R., & Lycett, J. (2002). *Human Evolutionary Psychology.* Basingstoke, England: Palgrave.

Bashiri, N., & Spielvogel, A. M. (1999). Postpartum depression: A cross-cultural perspective. *Primary Care Update for OB/GYNS, 6*, 82–87.

Beise, J. (2002). A multilevel event history analysis of the effects of grandmothers on child mortality in a historical German population, Krummhörn, Ostfriesland, 1720–1874. *Demographic Research, 7*, 469–498.

Belsky, J. (1985). Exploring individual differences in marital change across the transition to parenthood: The role of violated expectations. *Journal of Marriage and the Family, 47*, 1037–1044.

Belsky, J. (1997). Attachment, mating, and parenting: An evolutionary interpretation. *Human Nature, 8*, 361–381.

Belsky, J. (2007). Childhood experiences and reproductive strategies. In R. Dunbar & L. Barrett (Eds.), *Oxford Handbook of Evolutionary Psychology* (pp. 237–254). Oxford: Oxford University Press.

Belsky, J., & Isabella, R. (1985). Marital and parent–child relationships in family of origin and marital change following the birth of a baby: A retrospective analysis. *Child Development, 56*, 342–349.

Belsky, J., & Jaffee, S. (2006). The multiple determinants of parenting. In D. Cicchetti & D. Cohen (Eds.), *Developmental Psychopathology* (2nd ed.): Vol. 3. *Risk, disorder and adaptation* (pp. 38–85). New York: Wiley.

Belsky, J., & Kelly, J. (1994). *The transition to parenthood: How a first child changes a marriage.* London: Vermilion.

Belsky, J., & Pensky, E. (1988) Marital change across the transition to parenthood. *Marriage and Family Review, 12,* 133–156.

Belsky, J., & Rovine, M. (1990). Patterns of marital change across the transition to parenthood: Pregnancy to three years postpartum. *Journal of Marriage and the Family, 52,* 5–19.

Belsky, J., Spanier, G. B., & Rovine, M. (1983). Stability and change in marriage across the transition to parenthood. *Journal of Marriage and the Family, 45,* 567–577.

Belsky, J., Steinberg, L., & Draper, P. (1991a). Childhood experience, interpersonal development, and reproductive strategy: An evolutionary theory of socialization. *Child Development, 62,* 647–670.

Belsky, J., Youngblade, L., Rovine, M., & Volling, B. (1991b). Patterns of marital change and parent–child interaction. *Journal of Marriage and the Family, 53,* 487–498.

Bereczkei, T., & Csanaky, A. (1996). Evolutionary pathway of child development: Lifestyles of adolescents and adults from father-absent families. *Human Nature, 7,* 257–280.

Berg, M., & Dahlberg, K. (2001). Swedish midwives' care of women who are at high obstetric risk or who have obstetric complications. *Midwifery, 17,* 259–266.

Berger, L. M. (2004). Income, family structure, and child maltreatment risk. *Children and Youth Services Review, 26,* 725–748.

Campbell, S. B., Cohn, J. F., Flanagan, C., Popper, S., & Meyers, T. (1992). Course and correlates of postpartum depression during the transition to parenthood. *Development and Psychopathology, 4,* 29–47.

Card, J. J., & Wise, L. L. (1978). Teenage mothers and teenage fathers: The impact of early childbearing on the parents' personal and professional lives. *Family Planning Perspectives, 10,* 199–205.

Chisholm, J. S. (1993). Death, hope and sex: Life-history theory and the development of reproductive strategies. *Current Anthropology, 34,* 1–24.

Chisholm, J. S. (1999). *Death, hope and sex: Steps to an evolutionary ecology of mind and morality.* Cambridge: Cambridge University Press.

Clutton-Brock, T. H. (1989). Mammalian mating systems. *Proceedings of the Royal Society of London, Series B—Biological Science, 236,* 339–372.

Cowan, C. P., & Cowan, P. A. (1992). *When partners become parents: The big life change for couples.* New York: Basic Books.

Cowan, C. P., & Cowan, P. A. (1995). Interventions to ease the transition to parenthood: Why they are needed and what they can do. *Family Relations, 44,* 412–423.

Cox, J. L. (1988). Childbirth as a life event: Sociocultural aspects of postnatal depression. *Acta Psychiatrica Scandinavica, 78,* 75–83.

Craig, A. P., & Richter-Strydom, L. M. (1983). Unplanned pregnancies among urban Zulu school children: A summary of the salient results of a preliminary investigation. *Journal of Social Psychology, 121,* 239–246.

Curran, M., Hazen, N., Jacobvitz, D., & Feldman, A. (2005). Representations of early family relationships predict marital maintenance during the transition to parenthood. *Journal of Family Psychology, 19,* 189–197.

Daly, M., & Wilson, M. (1985). Child abuse and other risks of not living with both parents. *Ethology and Sociobiology, 6,* 197–210.

Daly, M., & Wilson, M. (1988). *Homicide.* New York: Aldine de Gruyter.

Draper, P., & Harpending, H. (1982). Father absence and reproductive strategy: An evolutionary perspective. *Journal of Anthropological Research, 38,* 255–273.

Ellis, B. J. (2004). Timing of pubertal maturation in girls. *Psychological Bulletin, 130,* 920–958.

Ellis, B. J., & Garber, J. (2000). Psychosocial antecedents of variation in girl's pubertal timing: Maternal depression, stepfather presence, and marital and family stress. *Child Development, 71,* 485–501.

Ellis, B. J., McFadyen-Ketchum, S., Dodge, K. A., Pettit, G. S., & Bates, J. E. (1999). Quality of early family relationships and individual differences in the timing of pubertal maturation in girls: A longitudinal test of an evolutionary model. *Journal of Personality and Social Psychology, 77,* 387–401.

Feldman, R., Masalha, S., & Nadam, R. (2001). Cultural perspective on work and family: Dual-earner Israeli-Jewish and Arab families at the transition to parenthood. *Journal of Family Psychology, 15,* 492–509.

Feldman, R., Sussman, A. L., & Zigler, E. (2004). Parental leave and work adaptation at the transition to parenthood: Individual, marital, and social correlates. *Journal of Applied Developmental Psychology, 25,* 459–479.

Florsheim, P., Sumida, S., McCann, C., Winstanley, M., Fukui, R., Seefeldt, T., et al. (2003). The transition to parenthood among young African American and Latino couples. *Journal of Family Psychology, 17,* 65–79.

Furstenberg, F. F., Jr. (1976). The social consequences of teenage parenthood. *Family Planning Perspectives, 8,* 148–151, 155–164.

Garfinkel, I., & McLanahan, S. S. (1986). *Single mothers and their children: A new American dilemma.* Washington, DC: Urban Institute.

Gaudino J. A., Jr., Jenkins, B., & Rochat, R. W. (1999). No fathers' names: A risk factor for infant mortality in the State of Georgia, USA. *Social Science & Medicine, 48,* 253–265.

Geary, D. C. (2000). Evolution and proximate expression of human paternal investment. *Psychological Bulletin, 126,* 55–77.

Geronimus, A. T. (1987). On teenage childbearing and neonatal mortality in the United States. *Population and Development Review, 13,* 245–279.

Geronimus, A. T. (1992). Teenage childbearing and social disadvantage: Unprotected discourse. *Family Relations, 41,* 244–248.

Geronimus, A. T. (1996). What teen mothers know. *Human Nature, 7,* 323–352.

Gibson, M. A., & Mace, R. (2005). Helpful grandmothers in rural Ethiopia: A study of the effect of kin on child survival and growth. *Evolution and Human Behavior, 26,* 469–482.

Goldberg, A.E., & Sayer, A. (2006). Lesbian couples' relationship quality across the transition to parenthood. *Journal of Marriage and the Family, 68,* 87–100.

Guijarro, S., Naranjo, J., Padilla, M., Gutiérez, R., Lammers, C., & Blum, R. W. (1999). Family risk factors associated with adolescent pregnancy: Study of a group of adolescent girls and their families in Ecuador. *The Journal of Adolescent Health, 25,* 166–172.

Hagen, E. H. (1999). The functions of postpartum depression. *Evolution and Human Behavior, 20,* 325–359.

Halbreich, U., & Karkun, S. (2006). Cross-cultural and social diversity of prevalence of postpartum depression and depressive symptoms. *Journal of Affective Disorders, 91,* 97–111.

Hawkes, K., O'Connell, J. F., & Blurton Jones, N. G. (1997). Hadza women's time allocation, offspring provisioning, and the evolution of long post-menopausal life spans. *Current Anthropology, 38,* 551–577.

Hayes, M. J., Roberts, S., & Davare, A. (2000). Erratum: Transactional conflict between psychobiology and culture in the etiology of postpartum depression. *Medical Hypotheses, 55,* 266–276.

Helms-Erikson, H. (2001). Marital quality ten years after the transition to parenthood: Implications of the timing of parenthood and the division of labor. *Journal of Marriage and the Family, 63,* 1099–1110.

Hill, K., & Hurtado, M. (1996). *Aché life history: The ecology and demography of a foraging people.* New York: Aldine de Gruyter.

Hill, K., & Kaplan, H. (1999). Life history traits in humans: Theory and empirical studies. *Annual Review of Anthropology, 28,* 397–430.

Hrdy, S. B. (1999). *Mother Nature: A history of mothers, infants and natural selection.* New York: Ballantine.

Hudson, F., & Ineichen, B. (1991). *Taking it lying down: Sexuality and teenage motherhood.* London: Macmillan.

Hyde, J. S., Essex, M. J., Clark, R., & Klein, M. H. (2001). Maternity leave, women's employment and marital incompatibility. *Journal of Family Psychology, 15,* 476–491.

Hyde, J. S., Klein, M. H., Essex, M. J., & Clark, R. (1995). Maternity leave and women's mental health. *Psychology of Women Quarterly, 19,* 257–285.

Johns, S. E. (2003). *Environmental risk and the evolutionary psychology of teenage motherhood.* Unpublished doctoral dissertation, University of Bristol, England.

Jónsson, F. H., Mjardvik, U., Olafsdóttir, G., & Grétarsson, S. J. (2000). Parental divorce: Long-term effects on mental health, family relations and adult sexual behavior. *Scandinavian Journal of Psychology, 41,* 101–105.

Kach, J. A., & McGhee, P. E. (1982). Adjustment of early parenthood: The role of accuracy of preparenthood experiences. *Journal of Family Issues,* 3, 375–388.

Kanoy, K., Ulku-Steiner, B., Cox, M., & Burchinal, M. (2003). Marital relationship and individual psychological characteristics that predict physical punishment of children. *Journal of Family Psychology, 17,* 20–28.

Kaplan, H., Hill, K., Lancaster, J., & Hurtado, A. M. (2000). A theory of human life history evolution: Diet, intelligence and longevity. *Evolutionary Anthropology, 9,* 156–185.

Kaplan, H. S., Lancaster, J. B., Bock, J. A., & Johnson, S. E. (1995). Does observed fertility maximize fitness among New Mexican men: A test of an optimality model and a new theory of parental investment in the embodied capital of offspring. *Human Nature, 6,* 325–360.

Kiernan, K. E., & Hobcraft, J. (1997). Parental divorce during childhood: Age at first intercourse, partnership and parenthood. *Population Studies, 51,* 41–55.

Kim, K., Smith, P. K., & Palermiti, A. (1997). Conflict in childhood and reproductive development. *Evolution and Human Behavior, 18,* 109–142.

Klepinger, D. H., Lundberg, S., & Plotnick, R. D. (1995). Adolescent fertility and the educational attainment of young women. *Family Planning Perspectives, 27,* 23–28.

Kluwer, E. S., Heesink, J. A., & Van De Vliert, E. (2002). The division of labor across the transition to parenthood: A justice perspective. *Journal of Marriage and the Family, 64,* 930–943.

Lancaster, J. B. (1994). Human sexuality, life histories, and evolutionary ecology. In A. S. Rossi (Ed.), *Sexuality across the life course* (pp. 39–62). Chicago: University of Chicago Press.

Landy, S., Schubert, J., Cleland, J. F., Clark, C., & Montgomery, J. S. (1983). Teenage pregnancy: Family syndrome. *Adolescence, 18,* 679–694.

Langfield, P. A., & Pasley, K. (1997). Understanding stress associated with adolescent pregnancy and early childbearing. In S. A. Wolchik & I. N. Sandler (Eds.), *Handbook of children's coping: Linking theory and intervention. Issues in clinical child psychology* (pp. 245–271). New York: Plenum Press.

Leonetti, D. L., & Nath, D. C. (2004). Do women really need marital partners for support of their reproductive success? The case of the matrilineal Khasi of NE India. *Research in Economic Anthropology, 23,* 151–174.

Lewis, S. N. C., & Cooper, C. L. (1988). The transition to parenthood in dual-earner couples. *Psychological Medicine, 18,* 477–486.

Lovejoy, C. O. (1981). The origin of man. *Science, 211,* 341–350.

Low, B. S., Simon, C. P., & Anderson, K. G. (2002). An evolutionary ecological perspective on demographic transitions: Modeling multiple currencies. *American Journal of Human Biology, 14,* 149–167.

Mace, R. (1996). Biased parental investment and reproductive success in Gabbra pastoralists. *Behavioral Ecology and Sociobiolgy, 38,* 75–81.

Marlowe, F. (1999). Male care and mating effort among Hadza foragers. *Behavioral Ecology and Sociobiology, 46,* 57–64.

Matthey, S., Barnett, B., Ungerer, J., & Waters, B. (2000). Paternal and maternal depressed mood during the transition to parenthood. *Journal of Affective Disorders, 60,* 75–85.

McIntosh, L. J., Roumayah, N. E., & Bottoms, S. F. (1995). Perinatal outcome of broken marriage in the inner city. *Obstetrics & Gynecology, 85,* 233–236.

McLanahan, S. S. (1985). Family structure and the reproduction of poverty. *American Journal of Sociology, 90,* 873–901.

Menken, J. (1972). The health and social consequences of teenage childbearing. *Family Planning Perspectives, 4,* 45–53.

Miller, B. C., Benson, B., & Galbraith, K. A. (2001). Family relationships and adolescent pregnancy risk: A research synthesis. *Developmental Review, 21,* 1–38.

Miller, F. C. (2000). Impact of adolescent pregnancy as we approach the new millennium. *Journal of Pediatric and Adolescent Gynecology, 13,* 5–8.

Millman, S. R., & Hendershot, G. E. (1980). Early fertility and lifetime fertility. *Family Planning Perspectives, 12,* 139–140, 145–149.

Mirowsky, J., & Ross, C. E. (2002). Depression, parenthood, and age at first birth. *Social Science & Medicine, 54,* 1281–1298.

Moffitt, T. E., Caspi, A., Belsky, J., & Silva, P. A. (1992). Childhood experience and the onset of menarche: A test of the sociobiological model. *Child Development, 63,* 47–58.

Mott, F. L. (1986). The pace of repeated childbearing among young American mothers. *Family Planning Perspectives, 18,* 5–7, 9–12.

Nicolson, P. (1998). *Postnatal depression: Psychology, science and the transition to motherhood.* London: Routledge.

Oakley, A. (1985). Social support in pregnancy: The "soft" way to increase birthweight? *Social Science and Medicine, 21,* 1259–1268.

Oakley, A. (1988). Is social support good for the health of mothers and babies? *Journal of Reproductive and Infant Psychology, 6,* 3–21.

O'Brien, M., & Peyton, V. (2002). Parenting attitudes and marital intimacy: A longitudinal analysis. *Journal of Family Psychology, 16,* 118–127.

O'Connor, T. G., Thorpe, K., Dunn, J., & Golding, J. (1999). Parental divorce and adjustment in adulthood: Findings from a community sample. *Journal of Child Psychology and Psychiatry, 40,* 777–789.

Paley, B., Cox, M. J., Kanoy, K. W., Harter, K. S. M., Burchinal, M., & Margand, N. A. (2005). Adult attachment and marital interaction as predictors of whole family interactions during the transition to parenthood. *Journal of Family Psychology, 19,* 420–429.

Pfiffner, L. J., McBurnett, K., & Rathouz, P. J. (2001). Father absence, and familial antisocial characteristics. *Journal of Abnormal Child Psychology, 29,* 357–367.

Quinlan, R. J. (2003). Father absence, parental care, and female reproductive development. *Evolution and Human Behavior, 24,* 376–390.

Quinlivan, J. A., Luehr, B., & Evans, S. F. (2004). Teenage mother's predictions of their support levels before and actual support levels after having a child. *Journal of Pediatric and Adolescent Gynecology, 17,* 273–278.

Records, K., & Rice, M. (2005). A comparative study of postpartum depression of abused and non-abused women. *Archives of Psychiatric Nursing, 19*, 281–290.

Roosa, M. W. (1988). The effect of age in the transition to parenthood: Are delayed childbearers a unique group? *Family Relations, 37*, 322–327.

Ross, L. E. (2005). Perinatal mental health in lesbian mothers: A review of potential risk and protective factors. *Women & Health, 41*, 113–128.

Ross, L. E., Steele, L., & Sapiro, B. (2005). Perceptions of predisposing and protective factors for perinatal depression in same-sex parents. *Journal of Midwifery & Women's Health, 50*, e65–e70.Rowe, D. C., Vazsonyi, A. T., & Figueredo, A. J. (1997). Mating-effort in adolescence: A conditional or alternative strategy. *Personality and Individual Differences, 23*, 105–115.

Schulz, M. S., Cowan, C. P., & Cowan P. A. (2006). Promoting healthy beginnings: A randomized controlled trial of a preventive intervention to preserve marital quality during the transition to parenthood. *Journal of Consulting and Clinical Psychology, 74*, 20–31.

Sear, R., Mace, R., & McGregor, I. A. (2000). Maternal grandmothers improve nutritional status and survival of children in rural Gambia. *Proceedings of the Royal Society of London, Series B—Biological Science, 267*, 1641–1647.

Sear, R., Steele, F., McGregor, I. A., & Mace, R. (2002). The effects of kin on child mortality in rural Gambia. *Demography, 39*, 43–63.

Simpson, J. A., Steven Rhodes, W., Campbell, L., & Wilson, C. L. (2003). Changes in attachment orientations across the transition to parenthood. *Journal of Experimental Social Psychology, 39*, 317–331.

Snowden, L. R., Schott, T. L., Awalt, S. J., & Gillis-Knox, J. (1988). Marital satisfaction in pregnancy: Stability and change. *Journal of Marriage and the Family, 50*, 325–333.

Spruijt, E., DeGoede, M., & Vandervalk, I. (2001). The well-being of youngsters coming from six different family types. *Patient Education and Counseling, 45*, 285–294.

Stearns, S. C. (1992). *The Evolution of Life Histories*. Oxford: Oxford University Press.

Steinberg, L. (1988). Reciprocal relation between parent–child distance and pubertal maturation. *Developmental Psychology, 13*, 122–128.

Stern, G., & Kruckman, L. (1983). Multi-disciplinary perspectives on postpartum depression: An anthropological critique. *Social Science & Medicine, 17*, 1027–1041.

Strassmann, B. I. (1997). Polygyny as a risk factor for child mortality among the Dogon. *Current Anthropology, 38*, 688–695.

Strassmann, B. I., & Gillespie, B. (2002). Life history theory, fertility and reproductive success in humans. *Proceedings of the Royal Society of London, Series B—Biological Sciences, 269*, 553–562.

Stuchbery, M., Matthey, S., & Barnett, B. (1998). Postnatal depression and social supports in Vietnamese, Arabic and Anglo-Celtic mothers. *Social Psychiatry and Psychiatric Epidemiology, 33*, 483–490.

Surbey, M. K. (1998). Parent and offspring strategies in the transition to adolescence. *Human Nature, 9*, 67–94.

Thorpe, K., Golding, J., MacGillivray, I., & Greenwood, R. (1991). Comparison of prevalence of depression in mothers of twins and mothers of singletons. *British Medical Journal, 302*, 875–878.

Tooley, G. A., Karakis, M., Stokes, M., & Ozanne-Smith, J. (2006). Generalising the Cinderella Effect to unintentional childhood fatalities. *Evolution and Human Behavior, 27*, 224–230.

Troisi, A. (2001). Gender differences in vulnerability to social stress: A Darwinian perspective. *Physiology and Behavior, 73*, 443–449.

Twenge, J. M., Campbell, W. K., & Foster, C. A. (2003). Parenthood and marital satisfaction: A meta-analytic review. *Journal of Marriage and the Family, 65*, 574–583.

Voland, E. (1988). Differential infant and child mortality in evolutionary perspective: Data from 17th- to 19th-century Ostfriesland. In L. Betzig, M. Borgerhoff Mulder, & P. Turke (Eds.), *Human Reproductive Behavior* (pp. 253–261). Cambridge: Cambridge University Press.

Voland, E. (1998). Evolutionary ecology of human reproduction. *Annual Review of Anthropology, 27*, 347–374.

Voland, E., & Beise, J. (2002). Opposite effects of maternal and paternal grandmothers on infant survival in historical Krummhörn. *Behavioural Ecology & Sociobiology, 52*, 435–443.

Waynforth, D., Hurtado, A. M., & Hill, K. (1998). Environmentally contingent reproductive strategies in Mayan and Ache males. *Evolution and Human Behavior, 19*, 369–385.

Wedell, N., Kvarnemo, C., Lessells, C. K. M., & Tregenza, T. (2006). Sexual conflict and life histories. *Animal Behaviour, 71*, 999–1011.

Wellings, K., Wadsworth, J., Johnson, A., Field, J., & MacDowell, W. (1999). Teenage Fertility and Life Chances. *Reviews of Reproduction, 4*, 184–190.

Woodward, L. J., Fergusson, D. M., & Horwood, L. J. (2006). Gender differences in the transition to early parenthood. *Development and Psychopathology, 18*, 275–294.

Woodworth, S., Belsky, J., & Crnic, K. (1996). The determinants of fathering during the child's second and third years of life: A developmental analysis. *Journal of Marriage and the Family, 58*, 679–692.

Wu, L. L., & Martinson, B. C. (1993). Family structure and the risk of a premarital birth. *American Sociological Review, 58*, 210–232.

Yeung, W. J., Sandberg, J. F., Davis-Kean, P. E., & Hofferth, S. L. (2001). Children's time with fathers in intact families. *Journal of Marriage and the Family, 63*, 136–154.

5   Maternal Investment

Heidi Keller and Athanasios Chasiotis

Evolutionary theory defines the maximization of genetic reproductive success as the ultimate goal of human life strategies. Individuals need to select the behavioral alternatives that promise highest reproductive outcomes in a particular ecological situation. Since the perspective on evolution as a gene-distributing process implies mortality of individuals, the time range for these reproductive "decisions" is restricted. Therefore, optimal decision sequences have been selected. Thus, the reproductive individual is not the evolutionary "end product," but the species-specific pattern of the lifespan consisting of infancy, childhood, adolescence, adulthood, and old age (Keller 2000, Keller & Chasiotis, in press). Human development is different from that of all other primates in quantitative terms because it is slow and extended, and also in qualitative terms, in that infancy is followed by a childhood phase and adolescence with a rapid growth spurt before adulthood (Bjorklund, Yunger, & Pellegrini 2002). The temporal structure of growth, survival, and reproduction concerns decisions about the allocation of usually restricted resources. Resources can be placed into growth and development or into reproduction; they can be physical (e.g., food), social (e.g., mating), or emotional (e.g., parental care; Keller & Chasiotis 2006). From an evolutionary perspective, it is unimportant whether or not these decisions are deliberate and intentional, are guided by maturational processes, or are intuitively shaped because they are assumed to be in the service of gene-egoistic purposes in any case.

According to this evolutionary perspective, humans are unusual primates because their reproductive behavior of mating and parenting has some unique features: the lowest birth rate, the longest pregnancy, and the longest childhood among primates. Especially the extended childhood, which is adaptive for preparing the offspring for the social complexity of larger groups (e.g., Dunbar 1995), necessitates an amount of parental investment that was unknown in primate societies (Trivers 1972, 1974). *Parental investment* can be defined as any parental effort with respect to a child that increases the parental inclusive fitness (for a discussion of inclusive fitness, see Hamilton, 1964) while reducing alternative possibilities of investments in other born or unborn children at the same time (Keller 2000). Infantile helplessness (altriacility) is regarded as a prerequisite for socialization to reproductively more successful adults, referred to as the better-adult hypothesis (Alexander 1988). Therefore, parenting behavior is of key importance for reproductive success (Bogin 1997; Chasiotis & Keller 1993, 1995; Keller 2000). Due to sexual selection (Darwin 1871), the investment of men and women is not equal; for most mammals, investment in an offspring is substantially greater for females than for males (Clutton-Brock & Vincent 1991), with conception and gestation occurring inside the female, and the mother providing the majority of postnatal nutrition.

Parental investment can occur in different modes, time, energy, life risks, and styles of parenting. It can be directed at very different developmental phases of the offspring, like gamete production, prenatal development, and postnatal development. Although men also show significant paternal investment (see chap. 6, this volume), the remainder of this chapter is devoted to the discussion of human maternal investment. In this chapter, we concentrate on the postnatal maternal investment. Moreover, we concentrate primarily on the phase of infancy, that is, the first two years of an infant's life because this time span is crucial for investment decisions with respect to the survival of the child. Moreover, it constitutes a brain-imprint period with consequences for psychological development and thus adaptation (Keller 2007).

In order to understand the evolutionary basis of maternal investment, we can look at our primate relatives from two perspectives, homology and analogy. Homology integrates us in the array of other primate species, all descending from a creature like a modern ape; understanding other primates will help us understand our ancestors with respect to shared phenomena like hunting, tool use, and even lethal aggression and maternal investment (cf. Goodall 1986). The problem with ape "models," however, is that we do not know which one (chimpanzees, bonobos, gorillas, or orangutans) to choose because there is a great variety in behavioral adaptations and social organization: all modern apes live in forests, but hominids moved out of the forest and have many features that may not be like those of our common ancestor (Kappeler & Pereira 2003, Kappeler & van Schaik 2004).

Analogy, on the other hand, can demonstrate similarities in evolution between primates and humans because we are very similar to other primates in morphology, physiology, and behavior. Comparative analyses allow us to deduce rules or patterns of adaptation, for example, concerning the effect of contact comfort on development (Harlow 1958), or the relationship between social organization and sexual dimorphism (Bradley et al., 2005, Chapman & Pavelka 2005, Schülke 2005). Thus, analogy by comparison is more powerful than homology because it may generate general principles about how evolution shapes behavior, social organization, and mating and parenting strategies in particular ecologies.

From a comparative perspective, it is important to stress that the outstanding feature of primate social organization is that all primates live in groups, whereas most mammals live alone, where males and females meet only briefly, and females raise their offspring alone (e.g., only 10% of mammals bond in pairs, Kappeler & van Schaik 2004). Moreover, there is a major sex difference: Competition for food is particularly important for female primates because their nutritional status affects their reproductive parameters like the ability to conceive, become pregnant, and lactate. Male reproduction, on the other hand, is more influenced by access to females than by nutrition. Another way to put it is that the female primate's socioecology (i.e., the ecological forces that shape the size and structure of social groups) is shaped by natural selection, whereas that of male primates is mainly shaped by sexual selection: females go where the food is, and males go where females are.

A consequence of this line of reasoning is that mating effort in female primates can be seen as being part of their maternal investment: whereas the reproductive benefits of primate males to engage in mating effort, that is, to have multiple mates, are quite straightforward, reasons for female promiscuity are less obvious because they are directly linked to the consequences of mating, namely maternity. These hidden benefits of female promiscuity were and often still are underestimated or even not considered at all (Hrdy 1999). One important reason is the danger of infanticide by unrelated males. Since infanticide is a major cause of infant mortality in primates, and fathers or adult males present at conception defend infants in 65% of the observed cases (cf. Kappeler & van Schaik 2004), females try to develop relationships with protective and dominant males, while trying at the same time to confuse males about paternity by mating with multiple males when they are not likely to conceive (Hrdy 1999; see also Kappeler & van Schaik 2004). Finally, women can also benefit from promiscuous behavior: besides direct benefits like food, gifts, or protection, there are genetic benefits for their offspring, including "good genes" or the lack of "bad" ones (deleterious mutations) and genes to diversify the brood and to help the mother establish a hedging reproductive strategy (cf. Jennions & Petrie 2000; see also Gangestad 2006). This represents the double strategy of female reproductive investment: acquiring and keeping male investment and improving the genetic quality of their offspring. In the concluding part of this chapter, we will come back to this intricate relationship of male mating effort and maternal investment.

FEMALE PREPAREDNESS FOR CHILDCARE

Mothers are especially prepared to care for their children. This is related to two facts: in humans, as in all mammals, maternity is always certain, whereas paternity never is (Kappeler & van Schaik 2004), and women are the more highly investing sex. In the following, the major dimensions of maternal preparedness will be summarized.

Breastfeeding

Mothers are prepared to nurture their infants with breast milk, which is optimally adapted to infant's needs and protects the infant from infections through immunoactive substances (Liepke et al. 2002). Breastfeeding acts as natural contraception, delaying the onset of ovulation (Stern, Konner, Herman, & Reichlin 1986). The composition of human breast milk, low in fat and very low in protein (Lawrence 1994), implies that infants are supposed to be frequently nursed and therefore in close to their mothers.

In traditional cultural environments, weaning age averages between 2 and 4 years (Dettwyler 1995; Nelson, Schiefenhövel, & Haimerl 2000; Yovsi 2003), so that during that first developmental phase, mothers are necessarily the primary caregivers. This imperative is reflected in the fact that women in all cultures and over historical times care for and interact with their small children substantially more than do fathers or other male relatives (Eibl-Eibesfeldt 1989; Whiting & Whiting 1975). In the classical Whiting and Whiting six-cultures study, children were 3 to 12 times more frequently in the presence of their mothers than of their fathers (Whiting & Whiting 1975). Even in societies with an unusual amount of paternal childcare, like the Aka pygmies, mothers spent substantially more time with their infants than did fathers and other caretakers (e.g., Hewlett 1991). In a study assessing the social experiences of Cameroonian Nso and Indian Gujarati village babies, the compiled experience of other caregivers could, in most cases, not match the presence of mothers (Keller et al. 2007).

Maternal Personality

It is assumed that human psychologies evolved in the environment of evolutionary adaptedness. The EEA is constituted by the Pleistocene hunter-gatherer way of living. Although the ecology of living has dramatically changed since then, there are still biases that underlie the behavior of modern city dwellers. This does not imply, however, that there was one adaptive psychology in the EEA, nor that there is a deterministic influence on today's psychological functioning. Modern women and their ancestors preferred and prefer intelligent and successful men to father their children (Buss 1989). Women who have a higher education and economic potential than their husbands are still rare exceptions.

Bjorklund and Pellegrini (2002; see also Bjorklund & Kipp 1996) argue that it is in women's reproductive interest to have greater control over their sexual arousal. Because of the higher maternal investment, it is valuable to check the potential partner out before consenting to sex. Accordingly, there is empirical evidence that women are able to control their emotional expressions much better than men despite their greater emotional expressivity (Bjorklund & Kipp 1996, Cole 1986, Saarni 1984). Women are more compliant from early childhood than are men in terms of following instructions, delaying gratifications, and resisting temptations (Bjorklund & Kipp 1996; Kochanska, Forman, Aksan, & Dunbar 2005).

Maternal Parenting Styles

Here we address parenting styles, which apply to caregivers irrespective of age or sex (for a discussion of gender-independent caregiving motivation, see Chasiotis, Hofer, & Campos 2007). Nevertheless, we discuss the maternal perspective only. Maternal investment cannot be described only quantitatively, in terms of how much and how long, but also differs qualitatively to shape the psychology of the offspring to become competent in a particular environment. The resulting psychological differences express specific emphases on the basic personality dimensions of autonomy and relatedness as major avenues to place the self within the social environment (Keller 2007). Accordingly, we characterize the psychology, which emphasizes relatedness over autonomy, as "relational psychology," and the psychology that emphasizes autonomy over relatedness as "autonomous psychology." Both are briefly characterized below.

A relational psychology views the individual as defined through membership in a social system, mainly the family; harmonious relationships, acceptance of hierarchy (mainly age- and gender-based), cooperation, and conformity are hallmarks of development. Relational psychology prioritizes the perception of a fluidly defined and contextually based individual as an interrelated co-agent with others (Greenfield, Keller, Fuligni, & Maynard 2003; Keller 2003). A relational psychology is adapted to rural subsistence-based modes of living.

The psychology that is assumed to be adapted to the urban educated socioeconomic environment can be described in terms of autonomy (Kağitçibaşi 1996; Keller 2003; Markus & Kitayama 1991). An autonomous psychology denotes an individual who is self-contained, competitive, separate, unique, self-reliant, assertive, and having an inner sense of owning opinions. An autonomous psychology focuses on mental states and personal qualities supporting self-enhancement, self-expression, and self-maximization. The self is defined as "essentialist," which means it has a timeless core identity that also does not change across situations (Flores, Teuchner, & Chandler 2004).

Different parenting styles support these different psychologies differentially from birth onward. Neurophysiological research has indicated that the newborn period can be characterized as a brain-imprint period. Accordingly, the neonatal environment, which is primarily social, has major and lasting consequences (Storfer 1999). It can be assumed that the prevalent social experiences are represented in perceptual and motor schemas that form the early memory structure of the self. The exposure to particular parenting experiences thus can be regarded as wiring the neonatal brain (Siegel 1999).

The component model of parenting postulates a phylogenetically evolved universal repertoire of parenting systems that are individually modulated by interactional mechanisms (Keller 2000, 2007). The parenting systems are defined by particular parenting behaviors, the interactional mechanisms shape the mode and style of these behaviors. "Primary care," "body contact," "body stimulation," "object stimulation," "face-to-face exchange," and the "narrative envelope" are each considered to form systems of functionally related behaviors. Yet, the expressions of these behaviors can differ substantially because the interactional mechanisms fine-grain the interactional style. The interactional mechanisms basically comprise the mode of attention (exclusive or shared), contingency in terms of prompt reactivity, and emotional warmth. The interactional mechanisms can address positive or negative infant signals within the different parenting systems (Keller 2002). An evolutionary account suggests that there are alternative strategies to recurrent problems that our ancestors faced throughout evolution (Bjorklund 1997). Thus, parenting systems and also interactional mechanisms are considered basically independent of each other (Keller 2007) to allow alternative strategies through different combinations. These contextually informed alliances are adaptive for particular environmental demands and facilitate the acquisition of an adaptive contextually based psychology.

It has been repeatedly documented that relational psychology is supported with a proximal style of parenting during the first year of life. A proximal style of parenting consists primarily of body contact and body stimulation, with a low elaborative verbal environment (Keller 2007). Body contact is constituted by close bodily proximity, carrying, and cosleeping. In various traditional environments—the "back and hip cultures"—infants (LeVine 1990) are carried on the bodies of their mothers or other caregivers for a substantial part of the day. For example, Aka Pygmy mothers carry their infants for about eight hours a day (Hewlett 1991; cf., also, for the !Kung, Barr, Konner, Bakeman, & Adamson 1991), the South American Ache infants spend about 93% of their daylight time in tactile contact with mainly the mother (Hill & Hurtado 1996).

The psychological function of body contact is mainly the experience of emotional warmth, which is associated with social cohesion (MacDonald 1992) and feelings of relatedness and belongingness (e.g., Mize & Pettit 1997). Warmth contributes to the child's willingness to embrace parental messages and values (Kochanska & Thompson 1997, Maccoby 1984), preparing the individual for a life based on harmony, and respects hierarchy among family members or the primary social group (cf. Keller, Lohaus, Völker, Cappenberg, & Chasiotis 1999). Yet, parental care in terms of body contact allows continued participation in subsistence labor (e.g., through farming, fetching water, cooking, etc.), although carrying a child might compete for a mother's time with other resource-producing activities (Hill & Hurtado 1996).

Also, body stimulation is based on body communication but as an exclusive dyadic activity. Mothers stimulate their infants by providing them with motorically challenging experiences through touch and movement. The array ranges from lifting the whole baby up and down in an upright position, among West African caregivers, to gently exercising the infant's arms or legs, among German caregivers (Keller, Yovsi, & Voelker 2002). Body stimulation can be related functionally to motor development. The motor precocity of the African infant (Geber & Dean 1959, Super 1976) has been interpreted as a consequence of these early stimulation patterns (Bril 1989). Also, Indian baby bathing and massaging have been demonstrated as accelerating developmental progress (Landers 1989, Walsh Escarce 1989). The psychological function of body stimulation might generally consist of intensifying body perception and, thus, the emergence of a body self is promoted. Body stimulation might further enhance somatic development, for example, in order to prepare an organism for early reproduction.

The verbal environment is skeletal, repetitive, and low-elaborative (Fivush & Fromhoff 1988). It is characterized by commands and instructions, with the mother taking a leading role in conversations. A high value is placed on social context, moral rectitude, and behavioral consequences (Wang, Leichtman, & Davies 2000). Emotions tend to be viewed as disruptive and are expected to be controlled (Bond 1991, Chao 1995). The repetitive style has been identified as characteristic for an interdependent sociocultural orientation (Keller, Kärtner, Borke, J., Yovsi, & Kleis 2005).

An autonomous psychology, on the other hand, is supported by a distal style of parenting. Distal parenting during infancy consists primarily of face-to-face contact, object stimulation, and an elaborative, embellished verbal environment.

Face-to-face exchange is characterized by mutual eye contact and the frequent use of language (Keller 2007). The parental investment into the face-to-face system consists mainly in the exclusive devotion of time and attention to dyadic behavioral exchange. Face-to-face exchange follows the rules of pseudo dialogues, providing the infant with the experience of contingency perception. Through the prompt (contingent) responses of parents to infant communicative signals, the infant can perceive him- or herself as the cause of the parental action. Thus, the infant is informed about his or her uniqueness and self-efficacy. Also, positive emotions are communicated in face-to-face situations (Keller et al. 1999). The object-stimulation system is aimed at linking the infant to the nonsocial world of objects and the physical environment in general. Early object stimulation is pervasive in the urban educated middle class. The psychological function of early object stimulation consists in nurturing the cognitive system and disengaging the infant from the dependency of social relationships at the same time.

The elaborative and conversation-eliciting style is characterized by frequent questions, elaborations, and the tendency to integrate the child's input so that an equal conversational pattern emerges (Reese, Haden, & Fivush 1993). The narrations are rich, embellished, and detailed. The focus is on personal attributes, preferences, and judgments. Emotions are often regarded as a direct expression of the self and an affirmation of the importance of the individual (Markus & Kitayama 1994). The elaborated style has been identified as characteristic for an independent sociocultural orientation (Fiske, Kitayama, Markus, & Nisbett 1998; Markus & Kitayama 1994; see also Chasiotis, Bender, Kiessling, & Hofer in press). The prevalence of the distal face-to-face parenting system is especially salient in contexts where a separated agency has to meet the demands of self-contained and competitive social relationships.

Evolutionary theorists have argued that it is highly unlikely that only one adaptive pattern of parent–child relationships evolved in the Environment of Evolutionary Adaptedness (Belsky 1999). The component model of parenting therefore allows the evolutionary account of functional analyses of parenting behaviors (Buss, Haselton, Shackelford, Bleske, & Wakefield 1998). Nevertheless, taking care of children is an ongoing process of negotiation between one's own and one's children's needs, which operates on a conscious and also on an unintentional, subliminal level. Evolutionary theory has captured this conflict in the theory of parent–child conflict (Trivers 1974) and the conception of differential parental investment.

DIFFERENTIAL MATERNAL INVESTMENT

It is a universal phenomenon that parents treat their children differently and allocate resources according to the parental condition and the children's promising reproductive value in a particular socio-ecological environment. This notion still evokes protest from individuals who believe in human behavior and action as completely intentional and consciously controlled. However, there is substantial evidence about differential investment across cultures and historical epochs because the reproductive interests of parents and infants differ (Voland 1998, Voland & Stephan 2000).

Parent–Child Conflict

Parental investment benefits parental fitness. However, investment decisions reflect cost–benefit calculations that may or may not be in the interest of the offspring. Therefore, Trivers (1974) proposed that any offspring interest would be to exploit the parental resource as much as possible to maximize the child's own fitness. Mothers and fathers, however, also have to take their own growth and development and that of other offspring or genetic relatives into their calculations. One major issue of parent–child conflict is the time parents invest in a particular child. Weaning is an excellent example of this conflict, since children rarely comply with their mother's intent to wean them. Weaning is regarded as a critical life event for the infant that is sometimes accompanied by harsh maternal measures to achieve it. Cameroonian Nso mothers, for instance, put hot pepper or caterpillars on their breasts in order to frighten their children so that they do not want to breastfeed any longer (Yovsi 2003, Yovsi & Keller 2003).

Mother–child conflict can result in infanticide. Especially in circumstances of scarcity of resources and extreme poverty, mothers may "decide" to abort or kill an infant (Daly & Wilson 1988, Hrdy 1999). The ethologist Wulf Schiefenhövel (e.g., 1988) has reported that Eipo mothers in West New Guinea give birth alone outside the woman's house. The woman decides whether or not to bring the infant to the village or leave it in the bush, wrapped with branches and leaves. These decisions are obviously working as birth control, since the small valley can nourish only a limited number of people. These decisions are also driven by the infant's signs of liveliness. One infant who was destined to die was unwrapped by his mother and taken to the other women when a little foot started kicking through the package. A similar line of argument and evidence is presented by Nancy Scheper-Hughes (1995), who observed mother–infant relations among recent rural migrants in a shantytown in Brazil. The unusually high infant-mortality rate during the first year of life was seemingly accepted by the mothers because these infants were seen as too weak to survive the adverse circumstances of extreme poverty with the consequence of malnutrition and ever-present diseases. This judgment resulted in detachment of the mother from the infant, to "let it go." Nancy Scheper-Hughes (1995) saved the life of an extremely malnourished 1-year-old boy whose mother was ready to let him go because she assumed that he "wanted" to die. When he survived, his mother took good care of him, and they developed a good relationship. Also, here, as in the Eipo case that Schiefenhövel observed, the signs of life and health highly influenced maternal acceptance and care.

There are numerous other examples, like the fact that name-giving ceremonies are only held with children who are at least a year old, when it is probable that the infant will survive, or the fact that, in conditions of adversity, mother care and mother love start only when the infant has evidenced its ability to survive and thus have potential to contribute to the mother's genetic fitness (cf. Bjorklund & Pellegrini 2002, Chisholm 1999).

CHILDREN'S CONDITION

It is obvious that children need to elicit care because they cannot survive on their own. Therefore, they have to attract and maintain the attention and the motivation of their social environment to care for them. Morphologically, they enact the "babyness" (*Kindchenschema*), that Konrad Lorenz (e.g., 1969) first described. Babyness is characterized by a head that is large, compared to the rest of the body; a round face; big eyes; and a prominent forehead. It has been demonstrated in different species that these features block aggression and elicit positive emotions and protective motivation. Infants express attachment behaviors from birth onward. They communicate distress and cry, and they also communicate positive emotions when they gaze, smile, and vocalize. These behaviors generally elicit empathy from parents and other caregivers the motivation to care for an infant (see also Chasiotis, Hofer, & Campos 2007).

As mothers have to decide where to allocate their investment, infants strive to get better at eliciting care "by more cleverly molding parents' (and others') behavior...in their favor. Those best at molding their parents...would tend to elicit more and longer parental investment, thereby acquiring the material and socioemotional security that by all accounts fosters survival, growth and development, and long-term reproductive success" (Chisholm, Burbank, Coall, & Gemmiti 2005, p. 89).

Child's Health

The child's health is a major indicator of future reproductive success. The "healthy-baby-hypothesis" (Mann 1992) indicates that mothers allocate their resources to the children according to their health status. There is remarkable evidence from traditional societies, as we have outlined earlier, that sickly infants do not receive proper care. Today, women in industrialized and post-industrialized societies have much more support, including governmental assistance, than did their ancestors and contemporary women in traditional societies to raise weak children. Nevertheless, the evolutionary heritage also biases modern women to differentiate their investments according to the expected reproductive value of their children. Daly and Wilson (1988) have summarized convincing evidence that children with mental retardation or other congenital defects have a 2- to 10-times-higher rate of abuse than do healthy children. Mann (1992) demonstrated that mothers of premature and low-birth-weight twins in the United States demonstrated more positive be-havior in terms of playing, kissing, holding, and soothing the healthier of the twins, even though the weaker twin was more responsive to the mother.

Child's Age

One major tradeoff for reproductive success exists between investing in older versus younger offspring. Older children have higher reproductive value be-cause of their demonstrable success in survival, growth, and development, and are likely to survive even if investment is reduced. Younger children and newborns, on the other hand, have lower reproductive value because of high rates of mortality, and have little chance of survival without continual care and attention. The optimal solution will depend, at least in part, on the relationship between allocation and fitness returns. During limited periods of resource stress, parents may favor investing in infants because older children can buffer short-term deficits in parental care. Conversely, longer periods of stress may incline parents to invest in older children because infants are un-likely to survive in any case. Daly and Wilson (1984, 1988) tested this latter proposition by looking at rates of child abuse and homicide committed by parents relative to the age of the child. They found that infants (who have lower intrinsic reproductive value) were far more likely than older children to be killed by parents, a pattern that differed markedly from child homicides committed by non-parents, even after accounting for rates of child exposure to parents versus non-parents.

Child Gender

Mothers (in addition to fathers) should invest more in the offspring whose sex is less costly and/or provides higher fitness returns. Parents may realize higher fitness payoffs by investing in girls instead of boys, or vice versa (Trivers & Willard 1973). In many species, including humans, male reproduction is both more variable in outcome than for women, and often incurs more costs from intrasexual competition for mates. Men with access to considerable resources can attract multiple mates and potentially sire hundreds of offspring, whereas men with few resources may be unable to attract a mate and consequently sire no offspring. Women, on the other hand, are limited to a dozen or so offspring, but are very unlikely to go childless—sperm is cheap. Parents with fewer resources may take the safer bet and invest in daughters, whereas parents with substantial resources may choose to invest more in sons. To give but a few examples of the many studies examining sex-biased parenting in humans, Borgerhoff Mulder (1998) found that poor Kipsigis families showed a greater concern for their daughters' education than did rich families. Gaulin and Robbins (1991) measured maternal investment (e.g., birth weight, birth interval, and lactational commitment) among a sample of approximately 900 U.S. mothers. Maternal condition was assessed by income and by the presence or absence of a co-resident man. Some measures of investment showed marked and significant sex-by-condition interactions of the type and in the direction predicted by Trivers and Willard (1973), and none showed significant effects in the opposite direction.

THE MATERNAL CONDITION

In the following paragraphs, maternal conditions crucial for reproductive tradeoffs will be discussed.

Maternal Age

The age of a woman indicates how many opportunities exist for giving birth to further children. Therefore, younger women can be more selective with the allocation of investment than can older women. There is an abundance of research literature demonstrating that children of younger mothers run more physical and emotional risks than do children of older mothers. Daly and Wilson (1988) have demonstrated with homicide rates in Canada between 1974 and 1983 that teenage mothers were more likely to kill their infants than were mothers older than 20. An analysis of abuse and neglect of children (George & Lee 1997) revealed that there are 110 reported incidents of abuse and neglect per 1,000 teen mothers, as compared 51 incidents per 1,000 mothers older than 20 years. Similarly, rates of foster-care placement are significantly higher for children whose mothers are under 18. Children born to teen mothers suffer from higher rates of low birth weight and related health problems. The proportion of babies with low birth weights born to teens is 21% higher than the proportion for mothers age 20–24 (Flanagan, Coll, Andreozzi, & Riggs 1995). Low birth weight raises the probabilities of infant death, blindness, deafness, chronic respiratory problems, mental retardation, mental illness, and cerebral palsy. In addition, low birth weight doubles the chances that a child will later be diagnosed as having dyslexia, hyperactivity, or another disability.

Children of teen mothers not only have poorer health conditions with higher risks but also receive less medical care and treatment. In his or her first 14 years, the average child of a teen mother visits a physician and other medical providers an average of 3.8 times per year, compared with 4.3 times for a child of older childbearers (Flanagan, Coll, Andreozzi, & Riggs 1995).

Social Support

Mothers need support in order to raise their children. Cross-culturally, support comes mostly from female relatives and from peer women or, more rarely, from fathers (Hrdy 1999). There is evidence that children who did not receive any paternal investment have a higher risk of neglect or even death in diverse cultural contexts (Daly & Wilson 1984). Even if there is no direct contact, the paternal support of the mother is crucial for the survival of the offspring (Hill & Hurtado 1996). From an evolutionary perspective, grandparents should be interested to contribute to the survival of their grandchildren because it contributes to their own genetic fitness (Voland, Chasiotis, & Schiefenhövel 2005). Voland and Beise (2002) addressed the differential effect of paternal and maternal grandmothers on the survival of their grandchildren. Based on the analysis of historical church documents, these authors found that the survival chance of grandchildren was higher if the maternal grandmother was alive. With only the maternal grandmother alive, fewer grandchildren died than when both grandmothers were alive. Even more important, more than twice as many newborns died if the paternal grandmother lived in the same community with her son's family compared to her not being present in the community. These results impressively document that maternal and paternal grandmothers entertain different relationships with their grandchildren, with dramatically different consequences. Voland and Beise (2002) refer to paternal insecurity in explaining grandmaternal inequalities. They also focus on the work load that is expected of the young mother in support of the paternal family which can result in detrimental effects on pregnancy and children's health which are accepted due to the young age of the women.

Not only grandmothers but also siblings and other caretakers are crucial for child survival. Allomothers are not just helpful—the children in the EEA would not have survived without them (Hrdy 2005; Voland, Chasiotis, & Schiefenhövel 2005).

CONCLUSION AND OUTLOOK

In the remainder of this chapter, we return to the comparative perspective outlined in the introduction to link ecological nutritional resources, female intrasexual competition, and intersexual social behavior to human maternal investment (Kappeler & van Schaik 2004, 2005). In a simplified description of this model, the distribution of resources ultimately affects the form of social organization as described below.

The distribution of food in dispersed, low-value patches leads to scramble competition, that is, if food is distributed evenly, food items are not worth fighting over and there is no direct competition for food. This leads to low dominance and unstable hierarchies and more social egalitarianism and may also lead to ecologically imposed monogamy with comparatively higher paternal investment (cf. Alexander 1979). Clumped and valuable patches, on the other hand, where resources are scarce and valuable and therefore worth fighting for, lead to contests for access to particular resources. In a competition, males can monopolize females by occupying valuable patches that, in turn, can lead to dominance hierarchies and unequal social organizations. If rank affects access to resources, and a dominant male can monopolize them, females try to benefit from help from allies and develop kinship alliances and remain with kin ("female philopatry"), while males disperse to prevent inbreeding (cf. Silk, Alberts, & Altmann 2003). This comparative socio-ecological model works quite well for primates by showing intraspecies variations according to ecological constraints (e.g., Ramnagar langurs show dominance hierarchies and female philopatry in clumped patches; Kanha langurs from the same species show female dispersal and poorly developed hierarchies, cf. Kappeler & van Schaik 2005).

Although there are obvious complications to disentangle the ecological and social complexities in human mating systems (cf. Low 2003), this comparative model could be fruitful in investigating the human primate, too, because, as Chris Knight (2006, personal communication) puts it: "There's no gene for polygyny, there's only a gene for digestion: the digestive system determines the mating system." Extrapolating this reasoning to humans, Knight (1998; see also Knight & Power 2005) speculates about how male mating and parenting effort is linked to maternal investment. Accordingly, also in humans, maternal investment depends on ecology, while paternal investment depends on the sexual autonomy of the woman. This female ability of trading sexual accessibility for male provision can be seen as a special form of intersexual cooperation (Noe 2005a, 2005b).

Generally, the mating market of possible male cooperative partners will determine female choice and behavior (cf. Noe 2005a, 2005b): Although trading sex for food or other forms of cooperation within a reproductive unit pays in raising offspring, defection pays even more when the partner still cooperates. This danger of being defected in the reproductive cooperating game is higher for female primates because they are the higher-investing sex ("Concorde fallacy," cf. Dawkins 1976). Key and Aiello (2001) argue that, in humans, where female reproductive costs are also much higher than the male costs, intersexual cooperation occurs only if women can punish uncooperative men. But how could they be punished? Their answer is: by female sexual withdrawal ("sex strike"). A popular hypothesis in this context is that women solved their problems by ceasing to restrict sexual activity to the period around ovulation ("sham oestrus," Hill 1982). This concealment of ovulation is another sign of the female strategy of keeping a caretaker and thus increasing paternal investment in their offspring. By withholding information about their true periods of fertility, women kept their mate(s) sexually interested. Additionally, endocrinological synchronization of the female cycles helped minimize female competition while maximizing male competition. Because females synchronized their cycles, a dominant male simply would not have the time to service all fertile females. This, in turn, would give more males a chance to procreate and increase their incentive to stay. According to this line of argument, hominid mothers were trying to avoid monopolization by dominant males and were driven to meet the costs of rapid encephalization and infant altriciality by making use of all available males through kin-coalitions of females and collective withdrawal of sexual access. Thus, concealed ovulation, continuous sexual receptivity, and synchronization of cycles in women could have evolved as ways to encourage men to stick around and compete for them (Douglas 2001). And ultimately, as Power (1999) argues, women did not need to synchronize their cycles to benefit from menstrual coalitions; they perhaps had only to fake the signs.

According to this "sham menstruation theory" (Knight 1991; Power 1999; Power & Aiello 1997), women took collective action to deal with the threat of young, menstruating women's attracting male attention by signaling their fertility. This collective action might have taken the form of synchronizing their cycles not only endocrinologically, but also symbolically by painting their bodies with red ochre, suggesting that cosmetics are the roots of human culture (i.e. symbolic art) and religion (e.g., lipsticks made of red ochre are the earliest human artifact recently found in South Africa, dating to at least 70,000 or perhaps even 130,000 years ago, cf. Douglas 2001, Watts 1999).

The strength of this Darwinian view on human maternal investment is that it links evolved female reproductive interests and the dynamics of social groups with the emergence of symbolic culture. Moreover, it sheds a new light on the old anthropological matrilinearity–patrilinearity controversy and the evolutionary significance of female post-reproductive lifespan (Knight & Power 2005; Voland, Chasiotis, & Schiefenhövel 2005). Integrating the just-developed arguments from evolutionary comparative primatology and evolutionary anthropology, monogamy and the nuclear family were probably not the basis of early human society, but descent through women could have preceded patrilineal inheritance (Knight & Power 2005). The description of Morgan (1877) about the transition from "mother-right" to patriliny, resting on the isolation of women from one another and the sex division of labor with the dawning of agriculture, leading to the male opportunity to accumulate heritable wealth, fits with the abundant evidence for the significance of matrilineal bonds in primates and the primate model of a transformation from the dispersed patches of the hunter–gatherers to the clutchy patches of agriculture just described (cf. Knight & Power 2005). Also, Hrdy's account (1999, 2005) of the paternity confusing tactics of the unchaste woman, and the "showing off" hypothesis by Hawkes (1991)—where men are not trading provisioning for pair-bonds and paternity certainty but for access to females—fit into this picture. Furthermore, the importance of female reliable food provisioning within kin, found in the same culture of the Hadza (cf. Hawkes, O'Connell, & Blurton Jones 1997), is another indicator of our possible evolutionary heritage of hominid matrilinearity. In the view of Knight and Power (2005), the evolution of female menopause is also evidence for ancestral female philopatry because it features matrilineal cooperation by matrilocal residence patterns (for an overview, see Voland, Chasiotis, & Schiefenhövel 2005). Instead of assuming cooperation between the sexes, kinship systems can likewise be viewed as variable outcomes to intersexual conflicts, with factors like paternity certainty and heritable wealth altering the tradeoffs (Holden, Sear, & Mace 2003; Knight & Power 2005). Thus, instead of generalizing college campus lifestyles (Ellis & Symons 1990) from U.S. contemporary samples or post-agricultural societies (Buss 1989; Schmitt

2005), additional cross-cultural comparisons with more-diverse, preferably hunter–gatherer, samples are needed to get a more complete picture of the evolutionary origins and contextual variation of maternal investment.

References

Alexander, R. D. (1979). *Darwinism and human affairs*. Seattle: University of Washington Press.

Alexander, R. D. (1988). Evolutionary approaches to human behavior: What does the future hold? In L. Betzig, M. Bogerhoff Mulder & P. Turke (Eds.), *Human reproductive behaviour: A Darwinian perspective* (pp. 317–341). Cambridge: Cambridge University Press.

Barr, R. G., Konner, M., Bakeman, R., & Adamson, L. (1991). Crying in !Kung San infants. A test of the cultural specificity hypothesis, *Developmental Medicine and Child Neurology, 33*, 601–610.

Belsky, J. (1999). Interactional and contextual determinants of attachment security. In J. Cassidy & P. R. Shaver (Eds.), *Handbook of attachment: Theory, research, and clinical applications* (pp. 249–264). New York: Guilford Press.

Bjorklund, D. F. (1997). In search of a metatheory for cognitive development (or, Piaget is dead and I don't feel so good myself). *Child Development, 68*, 142–146.

Bjorklund, D. F., & Kipp, K. (1996). Parental investment theory and gender differences in the evolution of inhibition mechanisms. *Psychological Bulletin, 120*, 163–188.

Bjorklund, D. F., & Pellegrini, A. D. (2002). *The origins of human nature: Evolutionary developmental psychology*. Washington, DC: American Psychological Association.

Bjorklund, D. F., Yunger, J. L., & Pellegrini, A. D. (2002). The evolution of parenting and evolutionary approaches to childrearing. In M. Bornstein (Ed.), *Handbook of parenting* (2nd ed.): *Vol. 1: The biology of parenting* (pp. 3–30). Mahwah, NJ: Erlbaum.

Bogin, B. (1997). Evolutionary hypotheses for human childhood. *Yearbook of Physical Anthropology, 40*, 63–89.

Bond, M. H. (1991). *Beyond the Chinese face*. Hong Kong: Oxford University Press.

Borgerhoff Mulder, M. (1998). Brothers and sisters: How sibling interactions affect optimal parental allocations. *Human Nature, 9*, 119–162.

Bradley, B. J., Robbins, M. M., Williamson, E. A., Steklis, H. D., Steklis, N. G., Eckhardt, et al. (2005). Mountain gorilla tug-of-war: Silverbacks have limited control over reproduction in multimale groups. *Proceedings of the National Academy of Science, 102*, 9418–9423.

Bril, B. (1989). Die kulturvergleichende Perspektive: Entwicklung und Kultur [The cross-cultural perspective: Development and culture]. In H. Keller

(Ed.), *Handbuch der Kleinkindforschung* [Handbook of Infancy Research] (1st ed., pp. 71–88). Heidelberg: Springer.

Buss, D. M. (1989). Sex differences in human mate preferences: Evolutionary hypotheses tested in 37 cultures. *Behavioral and Brain Sciences, 12*, 1–49.

Buss, D. M., Haselton, M. G., Shackelford, T. K., Bleske, A. L., & Wakefield, J. C. (1998). Adaptations, exaptations, and sprandels. *American Psychologist, 53*, 533–548.

Chao, R. K. (1995). Chinese and European American cultural models of the self reflected in mothers' childrearing beliefs, *Ethos, 23*, 328–354.

Chapman, C. A., & Pavelka, M. (2005). Group size in folivorous primates: Ecological constraints and the influence of social factors. *Primates, 46*, 1–9.

Chasiotis, A., & Keller, H. (1993). Die menschliche Kindheit und die Kindheit der Menschheit: Die ersten Lebensjahre aus evolutionsbiologischer Perspektive [Human childhood and childhood of humankind: The first years of life from an evolutionary perspective]. In E. Voland (Ed.), *Evolution und Anpassung: Warum die Vergangenheit die Gegenwart erklärt* (pp. 190–209). Stuttgart: Hirzel Verlag.

Chasiotis, A., & Keller, H. (1995). Kulturvergleichende Entwicklungspsychologie und evolutionäre Sozialisationsforschung [Cross cultural developmental psychology and evolutionary socialization research]. In G. Trommsdorff (Ed.), *Kindheit und Jugend in verschiedenen Kulturen. Entwicklung und Sozialisation in kulturvergleichender Sicht* (pp. 21–42). München: Juventa Verlag.

Chasiotis, A., Bender, M., Kiessling, F., & Hofer, J. (in press). The emergence of the independent self: Autobiographical memory as a mediator of false belief understanding and motive orientation in Cameroonian and German preschoolers. *Journal of Cross-Cultural Psychology.*

Chasiotis, A., Hofer, J., & Campos, D. (2006). When does liking children lead to parenthood? Younger siblings, implicit prosocial power motivation, and explicit love for children predict parenthood across cultures. *Journal of Cultural and Evolutionary Psychology, 4*, 95–123.

Chisholm, J. (1999). *Death, hope, and sex.* Cambridge: Cambridge University Press.

Chisholm, J. S., Burbank, V. K., Coall, D. A., & Gemmiti, F. (2005). Early stress: perspectives from developmental evolutionary ecology. In B. Ellis & D. Bjorklund (Eds.), *Origins of the social mind* (pp. 76–107). New York: Guilford Press.

Clutton-Brock, T. H., & Vincent, A. C. J. (1991). Sexual selection and the potential reproductive rates of males and females. *Nature, 351*, 58–60.

Cole, P. M. (1986). Children's spontaneous control of facial expression. *Child Development, 57*, 1309–1321.

Daly, M., & Wilson, M. (1984). A sociobiological analysis of human infanticide. In G. Hausfater & S. Hrdy (Eds.), *Infanticide: Comparative and evolutionary perspectives* (pp. 487–502). Hawthorne, NY: Aldine.

Daly, M., & Wilson, M. (1988). *Homicide.* Hawthorne, NY: Aldine.

Darwin, C. (1871). *The descent of man*. London: John Murray.

Dawkins, R. (1976). *The selfish gene*. Oxford: Oxford University Press.

Dettwyler, K. A. (1995). A time to wean. In P. Stuart-Macadam & K. Dettwyler (Eds.), *Breastfeeding: Biocultural perspectives* (pp. 39–73). Hawthorne, NY: Aldine de Gruyter.

Douglas, K. (2001). Painted ladies. *New Scientist, 2312*, 42–45.

Dunbar, R. I. M. (1995). Neocortex size and group size in primates: A test of the hypothesis. *Journal of Human Evolution, 28*, 287–296.

Eibl-Eibesfeldt, I. (1989). *Human ethology*. New York: Aldine de Gruyter.

Ellis, B. J., and Symons, D. (1990). Sex differences in sexual fantasy: An evolutionary psychological approach. *The Journal of Sex Research, 27*, 527–555.

Fiske, A. P., Kitayama, S., Markus, H. R., & Nisbett, R. E. (1998). The cultural matrix of social psychology. In D. Gilbert, S. Fiske, & G. Lindzey (Eds.), *The handbook of social psychology* (4th ed., Vol. 4, pp. 915–981). Boston: McGraw-Hill.

Fivush, R., & Fromhoff, F. (1988). Style and structure in mother–child conversations about the past. *Discourse Process, 11*, 337–355.

Flanagan, P., Coll, C., Andreozzi, L., & Riggs, S. (1995). Predicting maltreatment of children of teen mothers. *Pediatrics & Adolescent Medicine, 149*, 451–455.

Flores, J. P., Teuchner, U. C., & Chandler, M. J. (2004, May). *Telling selves in time: Aboriginal and non-aboriginal accounts of identity*. Paper presented at the University of Saskatchewan, Saskatoon, Canada.

Gangestad, S. (2006, September 28–30). *Trans-cultural patterns and sex differences in human mating behaviour*. Paper presented at the international conference Transcultural Universals II: Sexuality, Reproduction, and Kinship at the Hanse Institute for Advanced Studies (HWK), Delmenhorst, Germany.

Gaulin, S. J. C., & Robbins, C. J. (1991). Trivers–Willard effect in contemporary North American society. *American Journal of Physical Anthropology, 85*, 61–69.

Geber, M., & Dean, R. (1959). The state of development of newborn African children. *Lancet, 1*, 1215.

George, R. M., & Lee, B. J. (1997). Abuse and neglect of the children. In R. Maynard (Ed.), *Kids having kids* (pp. 205–230). Washington, DC: The Urban Institute Press.

Goodall, J. (1986). *The chimpanzees of Gombe*. Cambridge, MA: Belknap.

Greenfield, P. M., Keller, H., Fuligni, A., & Maynard, A. (2003). Cultural pathways through universal development. In *Annual Review of Psychology, 54*, 461–490.

Hamilton, W. (1964). The genetical evolution of social behaviour (I + II). *Journal of Theoretical Biology, 7*, 1–52.

Harlow, H. F. (1958). The nature of love. In *American Psychologist, 13*, 673–685.

Hawkes, K. (1991). Showing off: Tests of an hypothesis about men's foraging goals. *Ethology and Sociobiology, 12,* 29–54.

Hawkes, K., O'Connell, J. F., & Blurton Jones, N. G. (1997). Hadza women's time allocation, offspring provisioning, and the evolution of long post-menopausal life spans. *Current Anthropology, 38,* 551–557.

Hewlett, B. S. (1991). *Intimate fathers: The nature and context of Aka Pygmy paternal infant care.* Ann Arbor: University of Michigan Press.

Hill, K. (1982). Hunting and human evolution. *Journal of Human Evolution, 11,* 521–544.

Hill, K., & Hurtado, A. M. (1996). Ache life history: The ecology and demography of a foraging people. New York: Walter de Gruyter.

Holden, C. J., Sear, R., and Mace, R. (2003). Matriliny as daughter-biased investment. *Evolution and Human Behavior, 24,* 99–112.

Hrdy, S. B. (1999). *Mother nature: A history of mothers, infants, and natural selection.* New York: Pantheon.

Hrdy, S. B. (2005). Cooperative breeders with an ace in the hole. In E. Voland, Chasiotis, & Schiefenhövel (Eds.) *Grandmotherhood: The evolutionary significance of the second half of female life* (pp. 295–317). New Brunswick, NJ: Rutgers University Press.

Jennions, M. D., & Petrie, M. (2000). Why do females mate multiply? A review of genetic benefits. *Biological Reviews of the Cambridge Philosophical Society, 75,* 21–64.

Kağıtçıbaşi, C. (1996). The autonomous-relational self: a new synthesis. *European Psychologist, 1,* 180–186.

Kappeler, P. M., & Pereira, M. E. (Eds.) (2003). *Primate Life History and Socioecology.* Chicago: University of Chicago Press.

Kappeler, P. M., van Schaik, C. P. (Eds.) (2004). *Sexual Selection in Primates: New and comparative perspectives.* Cambridge: Cambridge University Press.

Kappeler, P. M., & van Schaik, C. P. (Eds.) (2005). *Cooperation in Primates and Humans: Mechanisms and evolution.* Heidelberg, Germany: Springer.

Keller, H. (2000). Human parent–child relationships from an evolutionary perspective. [Special issue titled Evolutionary psychology: Potential and limits of a Darwinian framework for the behavioral sciences]. *American Behavioral Scientist, 43,* 957–969.

Keller, H. (2002). Development as the interface between biology and culture: A conceptualization of early ontogenetic experiences. In H. Keller, Y. Poortinga, & A. Schoelmerich (Eds.), *Between culture and biology* (pp. 215–240). Cambridge: Cambridge University Press.

Keller, H. (2003). Socialization for competence: Cultural models of infancy. *Human Development, 46,* 288–311.

Keller, H. (2007). *Cultures of infancy.* Mahwah, NJ: Erlbaum.

Keller, H., Abels, M., Borke, J., Lamm, B., Lo, W., Su, Y., et al. (2007). Socialization environments of Chinese and Euro-American middle-class babies: Parenting behaviors, verbal discourses and ethnotheories. *Journal of Cross-Cultural Psychology, 31,* 210–217.

Keller, H., & Chasiotis, A. (2006). Evolutionary perspectives on social engagement. In P. J. Marshall & N. A. Fox (Eds.), *The development of social engagement: Neurobiological perspectives* (pp. 275–303). Oxford: Oxford University Press.

Keller, H., & Chasiotis, A. (in press). Entwicklung im Spannungsfeld zwischen Natur und Kultur [Development in the stress field between nature and culture]. In H.M. Hasselhorn & R. Silbereisen (Eds.), *Enzyklopädie Psychologie, Serie V: Entwicklung, Band 4: Psychologie des Säuglings- und Kindesalter* [Encyclopedia Psychology, Series V: Development, Vol. 4: Psychology of Babyhood and childhood].

Keller, H., Kärtner, J., Borke, J., Yovsi, R. D., & Kleis, A. (2005). Parenting styles and the development of the categorical self: A longitudinal study on mirror self recognition in Cameroonian Nso farming and German families. *International Journal of Behavioral Development, 29,* 496–504.

Keller, H., Lohaus, A., Völker, S., Cappenberg, M., & Chasiotis, A. (1999). Temporal contingency as an independent component of parenting behavior. *Child Development, 70,* 474–485.

Keller, H., Yovsi, R. D., & Voelker, S. (2002). The role of motor stimulation in parental ethnotheories: The case of Cameroonian Nso and German women. *Journal of Cross-Cultural Psychology, 33,* 398–414.

Key, C. A., & Aiello, L. C. (2001). A prisoner's dilemma model of the evolution of paternal care. *Folia Primatologica, 71,* 77–92.

Knight, C. (1991). *Blood relations.* London: Yale University Press.

Knight, C. (1998). Ritual/speech coevolution: A solution to the problem of deception. In J. Hurford, M. Studdert-Kennedy, & C. Knight (Eds.), *Approaches to the evolution of language: Social and cognitive bases* (pp. 68–91). Cambridge: Cambridge University Press.

Knight, C., and Power, C. (2005). Grandmothers, politics, and getting back to science. In E. Voland, A.Chasiotis, & F. Schiefenhövel (Eds.) *Grandmotherhood: The evolutionary significance of the second half of female life* (pp. 81–98). New Jersey: Rutgers University Press.

Kochanska, G., Forman, D. R., Aksan, N., & Dunbar, S. B. (2005). Pathways to conscience: Early mother–child mutually responsive orientation and children's moral emotion, conduct, and cognition. *Journal of Child Psychology and Psychiatry, 46,* 19–34.

Kochanska, G., & Thompson, R. A. (1997). The emergence and development of conscience in toddlerhood and early childhood. In J. Grusec & L. Kuczynski (Eds.), *Parenting and children's internalization of values: A handbook of contemporary theory* (pp. 53–77). New York: Wiley.

Landers, C. (1989). A psychobiological study of infant development in South India. In J. Nugent, B. Lester, & T, Brazelton (Eds.), *The cultural context of infancy* (pp. 169–207). Norwood, NJ: Ablex.

Lawrence, R. A. (1994). *Breastfeeding: A guide for the medical profession* (4th ed.). St. Louis: Mosby.

LeVine, R. A. (1990). Infant environments in psychoanalysis. A cross-cultural view. In J. Stigler, R. Shweder, & G. Herdt (Eds.), *Cultural psychology: Essays on comparative human development* (pp. 454–474). Cambridge: Cambridge University Press.

Liepke, C., Adermann, K., Raida, M., Mägert, H.-J., Forssmann, W.-G., and Zucht, H.-D. (2002). Human milk provides peptides highly stimulating the growth of bifidobacteria. *European Journal of Biochemistry, 269*, 712–718.

Lorenz, K. (1969). Innate bases of learning. In K. Pribram (Ed.), *On the biology of learning* (pp. 13–93). New York: Harcourt.

Low, B. (2003). Ecological and social complexities in human monogamy. In U. Reichard & C. Boesch (Eds.), *Monogamy: Mating strategies and partnerships in birds, humans, and other mammals* (pp. 161–176). Cambridge: Cambridge University Press.

Maccoby, E. E. (1984). Middle childhood in the context of the family. In W. A. Collins (Ed.), *Development during middle childhood: The years from 6–10* (pp. 184–239). Washington, DC: National Academy Press.

MacDonald, K. B. (1992). Warmth as a developmental construct: An evolutionary analysis. *Child Development 63*, 753–773.

Mann, J. (1992). Nurturance or negligence: Maternal psychology and behavioral preference among preterm twins. In J. Barkow, L. Cosmides, & J. Tooby (Eds.), *The adapted mind: Evolutionary psychology and the generation of culture* (pp. 367–390). New York: Oxford University Press.

Markus, H. R., & Kitayama, S. (1991). Culture and the self: Implications for cognition, emotion and motivation. *Psychological Review, 98*, 224–253.

Markus, H. R., & Kitayama, S. (1994). The cultural construction of self and emotion. Implications for social behavior. In S. Kitayama & H.R. Markus (Eds.), *Emotion and Culture: Empirical studies of mutual influence* (pp. 89–130). Washington D.C.: American Psychological Association.

Mize, J., & Pettit, G. S. (1997). Mothers' social coaching, mother–child relationships style and children's peer competence: Is the medium the message? *Child Development, 68*, 312–332.

Morgan, L. H. (1877). *Ancient society.* London: MacMillan.

Nelson, E. A. S., Schiefenhövel, W., & Haimerl, F. (2000). Child care practices in nonindustrialized societies. *Pediatrics, 105*, e75 .

Noe, R. (2005a). Digging for the roots of trading. In P. Kappeler & C. van Schaik (Eds.), *Cooperation in Primates and Humans: Mechanisms and evolution* (pp. 223–251). Heidelberg: Springer.

Noe, R. (2005b). Cooperation experiments: Coordination through communication versus acting apart together. *Animal Behaviour, 71*, 1–18.

Power, C. (1999). Beauty magic: The origins of Art. In R. Dunbar, C. Knight, & C. Power (Eds.), *The evolution of culture* (pp. 92–112), Edinburgh: Edinburgh University Press.

Power, C., and Aiello, L. C. (1997). Female proto-symbolic strategies. In L. Hager (Ed.), *Woman in human evolution* (pp. 153–171). New York: Routledge.

Reese, E., Haden, C. A., & Fivush, R. (1993). Mother–child conversations about the past: Relationships of style and memory over time. *Cognitive Development, 8,* 403–430.

Saarni, C. (1984). An observational study of children's attempts to monitor their expressive behavior. *Child Development, 55,* 1504–1513.

Scheper-Hughes, N. (1995). *Death without weeping.* Berkeley: University of California Press.

Schiefenhövel, W. (1988). *Geburtsverhalten und reproduktiver Strategien der Eipo. Ergebnisse humanethologischer und ethnomedizinischer Untersuchungen im zentralen Bergland von Irian Jaya (West-Neuguinea), Indonesien* (Birth behavior and reproduktive strategies of the Eipo–results of humanethologischer and ethnomedizinischer investigations in the central mountain country of Irian Jaya [west new Guinea], Indonesia). Berlin: Reimer.

Schmitt, D. (2005). Sociosexuality from Argentina to Zimbabwe: A 48-nation study of sex, culture, and strategies of human mating. *Behavioral and Brain Sciences, 28,* 247–311.

Schülke, O. (2005). Evolution of pair-living in Phaner furcifer. *International Journal of Primatology, 26,* 903–919.

Siegel, D. J. (1999). *The developing mind: Toward a neurobiology of interpersonal experience.* New York: Guilford Press.

Silk, J. B., Alberts, S. C., & Altmann, J. (2003). Social bonds of female baboons enhance infant survival. *Science, 302,* 1231–1234.

Stern, J. M., Konner, M., Herman, T. N., & Reichlin, S. (1986). Nursing behaviour, prolactin and postpartum amenorrhea during prolonged lactation in American and !Kung mothers. *Clinical Endocrinology, 25,* 247–258.

Storfer, M. (1999). Myopia, intelligence, and the expanding human neocortex: Behavioral influences and evolutionary implications. *International Journal of Neuroscience, 98,* 153–276.

Super, C. M. (1976). Environmental effects on motor development: A case of African infant precocity. *Developmental Medicine and Child Neurology, 18,* 561–567.

Trivers, R. L. (1972). Parental investment and sexual selection. In B. G. Campbell (Ed.), *Sexual selection and the descent of man: 1871–1971* (pp. 136–179). Chicago: Aldine de Gruyter.

Trivers, R. L. (1974). Parent–offspring conflict. *American Zoologist, 14,* 249–264.

Trivers, R. L., & Willard, D. (1973). Natural selection of parental ability to vary the sex ratio of offspring. *Science, 179,* 90–92.

Voland, E. (1998). Evolutionary ecology of human reproduction. *Annual Review of Anthropology, 27,* 347–374.

Voland, E., & Beise, J. (2002). Opposite effects of maternal and paternal grandmothers on infant survival in 558 historical Krummhörn. *Behavioral Ecology and Sociobiology, 52,* 435–443.

Voland, E., Chasiotis, A., and Schiefenhövel, W. (2005). Grandmotherhood: An overview of three related fields of research on the evolutionary significance of postgenerative female life. In E. Voland, A. Chasiotis, & W. Schiefenhövel (Eds.) *Grandmotherhood: The evolutionary significance of the second half of female life* (pp. 1–17). New Brunswick, NJ: Rutgers University Press.

Voland, E., & Stephan, P. (2000). The hate that love generated: Sexually selected neglect of one's offspring in humans. In C. van Schaik & C. Jason (Eds.), *Infanticide by males and its implications* (pp. 447–465). Cambridge: Cambridge University Press.

Walsh Escarce, M. E. (1989). A cross-cultural study of Nepalese neonatal behavior. In J. Nugent, B. Lester, & T. Brazelton (Eds.), *The cultural context of infancy, Vol. 1: Biology, culture, and infant development* (pp. 65–86). Norwood, NJ: Ablex.

Wang, Q., Leichtman, M. D., & Davies, K. I. (2000). Sharing memories and telling stories: American and Chinese mothers and their three-year-olds. *Memory, 8*(3), 159–177.

Watts, I. (1999). The origin of symbolic culture. In R. Dunbar, C. Knight, & C. Power (Eds.), *The evolution of culture* (pp. 113–146). Edinburgh: Edinburgh University Press.

Whiting, B. B., & Whiting, J. W. M. (1975). *Children of six cultures: A psychocultural analysis.* Cambridge, MA: Harvard University Press.

Yovsi, R. D. (2003). *An investigation of breastfeeding and mother–infant interactions in the face of cultural taboos and belief systems: The case of Nso and Fulani mothers and their infants of 3–5 months of age in Mbvem, Subdivision of the North-west province of Cameroon.* Münster: Lit.

Yovsi, R. D., & Keller, H. (2003). Breastfeeding: An adaptive process. *Ethos, 31*, 147–171.

6 Evolution of Fatherhood

David C. Geary

There is considerable discussion in academic, political, and social circles about the role of fathers in the family and in society in general (Cherlin 2005, Geary & Flinn 2001, Hewlett 1992, Tamis-LeMonda & Cabrera 1999). Much of the discussion centers on the importance of fathers for the health and development of their children, differences in the parenting contributions made by mothers and fathers, and often on how to increase the participation of fathers in the family (Booth & Crouter 1998, Silverstein & Auerbach 1999). The discussions rarely address the deeper question: Why is fatherhood found at all in humans? This question is central to our understanding of men and families, because human fathers are a scientific riddle. This is because men's parenting is highly unusual when placed in the context of little, if any, male parenting in at least 95% of other mammalian species (Clutton-Brock 1989), including the two species most closely related to humans, that is, chimpanzees (*Pan troglodytes*) and bonobos (*Pan paniscus*). In this chapter, I attempt to explain some aspects of this riddle and, in doing so, hope to provide a wider perspective on human fatherhood, its evolution, and its expression in various social and cultural contexts (see also Geary 2000, 2005). In the first section, I focus on the cross-species patterns of male parenting or paternal investment and the implications for understanding the conditions that promote the evolution and proximate expression of this form of parenting. In the second section, I use the basic patterns described in the first section to analyze the evolution and expression of men's parenting.

MALE PARENTING IN NONHUMAN SPECIES

Male parenting has to be considered in the wider context of the costs-benefits of parenting in general, whether provided by the mother or the father. For many species, there is little investment in offspring by either parent. For species in which investment does occur, it is always at some cost to the parent, including increased risk of illness and premature death (Clutton-Brock 1991, Trivers 1974). Given these costs, parenting can evolve only if there are considerable benefits to offspring and thus considerable reproductive benefits to the parent providing the investment. These benefits are well documented in species in which parenting is found. In these species, parenting is generally associated with lower offspring mortality due to protection from predators and conspecifics (i.e., member of the same species) and parental provisioning (Clutton-Brock 1991). The result is offspring that develop into healthier adults that in turn are better able to compete for mates and that produce larger and healthier offspring themselves (e.g., Clutton-Brock, Albon, & Guinness 1988). In short, in species in which it is found, parents pay the cost of investing in offspring, because these offspring are more likely to survive and reproduce than are offspring that receive reduced or no direct parental investment.

Paternal Investment

Evolution

Although rare in mammals, male protection or provisioning of offspring is found in most species of bird, and in some species of fish and insect (Perrone & Zaret 1979; Thornhill 1976; Wolf, Ketterson, & Nolan 1988). Determining the costs-benefits that influence the expression of this male parenting is complicated by the evolutionary history of the species, as well as by whether paternal investment is obligate or is facultatively expressed (Arnold & Owens 2002; Clutton-Brock 1991; Fishman, Stone, & Lotem 2003). Obligate investment means that male care is absolutely necessary for the survival of his offspring, and thus evolution favors males that always invest in offspring. One potential result is that males could show high levels of parental investment, even if conditions change and the investment is no longer critical to offspring survival (Westneat & Sherman 1993).

For many species, including humans, male parenting is facultatively expressed; that is, it is not always necessary for offspring survival and, thus, the quantity and quality of this investment varies with social and ecological conditions (Westneat & Sherman 1993). Across species, the facultative expression of male parenting varies with the influence of this investment on offspring survival prospects and quality; the degree of paternity certainty or risk of being cuckolded (i.e., raising the offspring of another male) by his partner; and, the extent to which parenting restricts opportunities to mate with multiple females (Birkhead & Møller 1996, Møller & Cuervo 2000, Perrone & Zaret 1979, Trivers 1972). These tradeoffs suggest that the evolution of facultative male parenting was driven by balancing the benefits to offspring survival and later competitiveness with the risks of cuckoldry and the costs of lost mating opportunities.

Costs-Benefits

Evidence for the just noted tradeoffs in the costs-benefits of male parenting can be found in species in which this parenting occurs and when males vary this investment with cuckoldry risk and mating opportunities lost. For instance, male parenting in fish species is typically associated with external fertilization and male defense of nesting sites to exclude competitors (Perrone & Zaret 1979). Under these conditions, paternal certainty is high because males directly fertilize eggs after the female deposits them. Males are also able to fertilize the eggs of more than one female, and thus investment does not reduce mating opportunities. In contrast, male parenting is rare in fish species with internal fertilization, presumably because paternity is not certain and because males can abandon females after fertilization and avoid the cost of investment.

Although male parenting is uncommon in fish with internal fertilization, it does occur in most species of bird and a few mammals (Dunbar 1995, Mock & Fujioka 1990). Across and within these species, the degree of paternal involvement again varies with the potential benefits to offspring, cuckoldry risks or paternity certainty, and availability of other mates. The benefit to offspring has been demonstrated by removing fathers from nests, which results in lower offspring survival rates, and from naturalistic studies that have documented reduced paternal investment following partner infidelity and a corresponding increase in offspring mortality (Arnqvist & Kirkpatrick 2005). In an analysis across 31 bird species, Møller (2000) determined that 34% of the variability in offspring survival was due to paternal investment.

Given the risks of male abandonment or reduction in parental investment, it is not surprising that cuckoldry rates are very low in species in which male investment is obligate (Birkhead & Møller 1996). For species in which male investment is not obligate, cuckoldry rates appear to vary with male quality. In some species, females paired with low-quality males will sometimes risk loss of male investment and copulate with healthier males (Møller & Tegelström 1997). One potential benefit is that the offspring sired by healthier males, and in at least one species their grand-offspring, may be healthier and suffer less mortality (e.g., J. M. Reid et al. 2005; Saino, Møller, & Bolzern 1995), but the strength of this benefit is currently debated (Arnqvist & Kirkpatrick 2005; Westneat & Sherman 2003). In any event, cuckoldry risks are more consistently related to reductions in male provisioning and protection of offspring (Arnqvist & Kirkpatrick 2005). Although the strength of the relation between cuckoldry risk and male parenting is mixed (Dixon, Ross, O'Malley, & Burke 1994; Kempenaers, Lanctot, & Robertson 1998; Sheldon, Räsänen, & Dias 1997), some of the inconsistencies may be related to the ability of males to detect their partner's extra-pair copulations or risks of extra-pair paternity of offspring (Neff & Sherman 2002).

As an example, Neff (2003) studied the relation between mate protection of eggs and paternity certainty in the bluegill sunfish (*Lepomis macrochirus*). In this species, there are different types of males, some dads and others cads. Parental males defend a territory, then externally fertilize and fan and protect eggs. One type of cad or cuckolder male hides behind rocks or plants and attempts to sneak into the nest to fertilize the eggs. Before the eggs hatch, threats to paternity can thus be determined by the presence or absence of cuckolder males. After the eggs hatch, parental males can determine paternity based on olfactory cues from fry urine. If parental males have evolved to vary their investment in offspring with the probability that the offspring are theirs, then these males are predicted to reduce fanning and protecting of eggs if cuckolder males are present. This is exactly what happened. Moreover, once the fry hatched and parental males could determine paternity, they protected them only if they had fathered them, whether or not cuckolder males were present before the fry hatched. This and other well-controlled studies (Arnqvist & Kirkpatrick 2005, Ewen & Armstrong 2000) suggest that when males detect risks to paternity, they reduce their level of paternal investment, often in direct relation to the magnitude of the risk (Møller 2000). However, provisioning and protecting offspring is not always parental investment, as these behaviors are sometimes related to mating effort, that is, specifically, to obtain sexual access to the offspring's mother (Rohwer, Herron, & Daly 1999; Smuts & Gubernick 1992).

In any case, paternity certainty and an improvement in the survival rate of his offspring are not sufficient for the evolution or facultative expression of paternal investment. The benefits of paternal investment must also be greater than the benefits of siring offspring with more than one female (Dunbar 1995). For most species of mammal, female investment through postpartum suckling is sufficient for offspring survival and development, and dominant males are able to reproductively monopolize the majority of these females (Andersson 1994). Under these conditions, it is in males' reproductive best interest to compete for mates rather than to parent. Nevertheless, social monogamy and high levels of paternal investment are found in some mammals, mostly carnivores and some primates (Mock & Fujioka 1990; van Schaik & Kappeler 2003). In these species, males are able to contribute to the direct care or protection of offspring and often have better reproductive options with such a strategy than by engaging in intense competition for mates.

For instance, male parenting is common in canids, such as coyotes (*Canis latrens*), who tend to have large litters (Asa & Valdespino 1998). Large litter sizes, prolonged offspring dependency, and the ability of the male to provide food during this dependency result in *canid* males being able to sire more offspring with a monogamous, high parental investment strategy than with a polygynous strategy. Paternal investment might also evolve if females are ecologically dispersed and thus males do not have the opportunity to pursue multiple mating partners, as with callitrichid monkeys, such as marmosets (*Callithrix*) (Dunbar 1995). In these species, paternal investment is related to male–female joint defense of a defined territory, which limits the male's ability to expand his territory to include other females; female-on-female aggression that prevents males from forming harems; concealed ovulation, which prolongs the pairs' relationship to ensure conception; and, females' often have twins, which increases the benefits of paternal care. Additional examples and extended discussion of monogamy in mammals and birds can be found in Reichard and Boesch (2003).

HUMAN FATHERHOOD

As noted, humans are among the 5% of mammalian species in which males invest in the well-being of their offspring, although this investment is facul-tatively expressed (Geary 2000). To understand the evolution and proximate expression of men's parenting, it is necessary to consider the relation between this investment and the just described factors related to male parenting in other species, that is, benefits to offspring, cuckoldry risk, and lost mating opportunity. I address the former issue in the first section and the two latter issues in the second. In the third section, I outline the conditions associated with the facultative expression of men's parental investment, and in the final section, I discuss the potential evolutionary history of this investment.

Children's Well-being

The evolution and maintenance of men's parenting could occur only if the added benefits—above and beyond those resulting from the mother's parenting—to children were substantial. As with other species, the most obvious benefits would be better health and reduced mortality. For a highly social and slow-developing species, men's parenting might also enable children to better acquire social and culturally important competencies that will contribute to their reproductive competitiveness in adulthood (Geary & Flinn 2001).

Physical Well-being

In traditional and developing societies and in the historical record, there is a consistent relation between men's investment and children's mortality rates, but disentangling the direct effect of paternal investment from potential confounds is difficult. This is because healthier and culturally successful men are typically paired with healthier and culturally successful women (Blurton Jones, Hawkes, & O'Connell 1997), and thus the higher survival rates of their children cannot be attributed solely to men's parenting. Moreover, men's parenting may at times be part of mating effort and is thus not paternal investment per se (Borgerhoff Mulder 2000, Marlowe 2000).

Nevertheless, men's providing care, food, and other resources is associated with lower infant- and child-mortality risks and generally better physical health of children in most traditional societies today and during the preindustrial era of Western societies. Among the hunter-gatherer Ache (Paraguay), about 1 out of 3 children die before reaching the age of 15, with highly significant differences in mortality rates for father-present and father-absent children (Hill & Hurtado 1996). Father absence triples the probability of death due to illness and doubles the risk of the child being killed by other Ache. Overall, father absence at any point prior to the child's 15th birthday is associated with a mortality rate of more than 45%, as compared to a mortality rate of about 20% for children whose father resides with them until their 15th birthday. In developing countries today, there is a consistent relation between marital status and infant- and child-mortality rates, with the lowest rates for children living with both biological parents, and higher rates for single, divorced, and widowed women (United Nations 1985).

The same pattern is found in the historical record of preindustrial and industrializing Europe and the United States (Herlihy 1965; Klindworth & Voland 1995; Morrison, Kirshner, & Molho 1977; Schultz 1991). In an analysis of demographic records from 18th-century Berlin, Schultz found a strong correlation ($r = .74$) between socioeconomic status (SES, a composite of income, educational level, and father's occupational status) and infant- and child-mortality rates. In 19th-century Sweden, infant-mortality rates were 1.5 to 3 times higher for children born to unmarried mothers than for children born to married couples (Brändström 1997). An analysis of mortality risks in early twentieth-century England and Wales suggested that "a child's chance of survival was strongly conditioned by ... what job its father did" (A. Reid 1997, p. 151). Children of professional fathers had a 54% lower mortality rate than did children whose fathers were unskilled laborers. Even when SES, environment (urban vs. agricultural setting), maternal age, and other factors were controlled, infants and young children of working mothers had a 34% higher mortality rate than did children whose mothers did not work. This is because women married to men with a sufficient income often stayed home to breastfeed, which significantly lowered infant mortality (Rollet 1997).

The best evidence for a direct effect of father's investment on child health is found with studies of changes within families. These studies control for maternal and child characteristics and reveal increased infant- and child-mortality rates following paternal death in developing nations today and in the historical record (Klindworth & Voland 1995; Kok, van Poppel, & Kruse 1997; United Nations 1985).

Social Well-being and Competitiveness

In addition to improving the health of their children, men's parenting may also provide a number of social competitive advantages to children, that is, its evolution may have been influenced in part by the effect of this parenting on their children's ability to later compete for resources in adulthood (Davis & Daly 1997; Geary 2002; Geary & Flinn 2001). If this is the case, then paternal investment should improve social competitiveness, and even though the men would have a smaller number of children, the children's social competitiveness should result in reproductive advantages for these men.

In industrial societies, one trait associated with social competitiveness is educational achievement, which is related to a combination of heritable individual differences in cognitive ability and to home environment (Cleveland, Jacobson, Lipinski, & Rowe 2000). In these societies, paternal investment, including income provided to the family, and direct care, is correlated with better academic skills in children and higher SES when these children reach adulthood (Kaplan, Lancaster, & Anderson 1998; Pleck 1997). However, a causal relation between men's investment and these outcomes has not been firmly established (Parke & Buriel 1998). Indirect, genetic influences—more-able fathers have more-able and thus more-competitive children—cannot be ruled out, nor can the effects of mate choices. With respect to the latter, high-investing men tend to marry women who are more competent, intelligent, and better educated and thus more effective parents than are women married to lower-investing men (Luster & Okagaki 1993). Indeed, the strength of the relation between father characteristics and child outcomes is reduced considerably once maternal characteristics are controlled (Amato 1998). Nonetheless, it does appear that the father's investment of time (e.g., helping with homework) and income (e.g., for tutoring or college) is associated with children's upward social mobility, even when maternal characteristics (e.g., years of education) are controlled for (Amato 1998; Kaplan, Lancaster, Bock, & Johnson 1995; Kaplan et al. 1998).

Moreover, withdrawal or reduction of paternal investment, as often happens following divorce, is associated with costs to children's later social success. But again, causal relations are difficult to determine. Although many differences comparing children from divorced and intact families can be traced to differences in family functioning before the divorce (Cherlin et al. 1991, Furstenberg & Teitler 1994), some differences remain after controlling for pre-divorce levels of family conflict and other confounding variables. Following divorce, there are small-to-moderate increases in aggressive and noncompliant behaviors in boys, and an earlier onset of sexual activity and lower long-term educational achievement for both sexes (Amato & Keith 1991; Belsky, Steinberg, & Draper 1991; Ellis et al. 2003; Florsheim, Tolan, & Gorman-Smith 1998).

Father's play and social engagement may also contribute to the social competencies of their children (Parke 1995; Pleck 1997). Men's involvement in play is associated with children's skill at regulating their emotional states and with their later social competence. For instance, children who have fathers who regularly engage them in physical play are more likely to be socially popular than are children who do not regularly engage in this type of play (Carson, Burks, & Parke 1993). Qualitative features of fathers' relationships with their children, such as positive emotional tone of the interactions, are also associated with greater social and academic competencies in children (Parke & Buriel 1998) and with fewer behavioral (e.g., aggression) and psychological (e.g., depression) difficulties (Florsheim et al. 1998; Pleck 1997).

Girls who have a warm relationship with their father and whose father is highly invested in the family experience menarche later than do girls living in father-absent homes or with an emotionally distant father (Ellis 2004; Ellis, McFadyen-Ketchum, Dodge, Pettit, & Bates 1999). In contrast, high familial stress, presence of a stepfather or mother's boyfriend, and sexual abuse contribute to early sexual maturation in girls and, in some cases, earlier sexual activity (Ellis & Garber 2000; Vigil, Geary, & Byrd-Craven 2005). Age of sexual maturation and initiation of sexual activity is important because delaying these developmental milestones provides girls with a greater opportunity to acquire additional social-competitive competencies (e.g., more education), and thus greater ability to compete socially in adulthood and eventually invest in their children (Geary & Flinn 2001, Vigil & Geary

2006). The traits that may be fostered by a warm relationship with the father may also contribute to the development of competencies that support high cooperation with a spouse and thus high paternal investment in their children (MacDonald 1992).

Cuckoldry Risks and Mating Opportunity

As with other species, men's parenting comes at a cost, in terms of risk of cuckoldry and lost mating opportunity (see Platek & Shackelford 2006). If there has been an evolutionary history of male parenting in humans, comparatively high levels of paternity certainty (i.e., low risk of cuckoldry) and restricted mating opportunities are predicted (Geary 2000). This is not to say that men are never cuckolded or never seek additional mates; they sometimes are and do. Rather, women are predicted to risk cuckoldry, that is, risk partner aggression and abandonment, only when his contributions to the family are small or when he is in poor physical and thus presumably genetic health (e.g., Daly & Wilson 1985; Daly, Wilson, & Weghorst 1982; Flinn 1992; Shackelford & Larsen 1997). I address the issues related to paternity certainty and reliance on paternity cues in the first section. In the second section, I address the issue of women's sexuality and men's mating opportunities.

Paternity

Paternity certainty. There have been no large-scale studies of cuckoldry, or nonpaternity, using representative samples, and thus definitive conclusions cannot be drawn regarding the overall certainty of paternity. Estimates of the frequency of nonpaternity range from about 1% to more than 30% of children (Anderson 2006; Bellis & Baker 1990; Bellis, Hughes, Hughs, & Ashton 2005; Flinn 1988; Gaulin, McBurney, & Brakeman-Wartell 1997; McBurney, Simon, Gaulin, & Geliebter 2002). In a meta-analysis, Anderson reported that when the father suspected he had been cuckolded, nonpaternity is found in about 30% of the cases. When the father is confident of paternity, nonpaternity is found for about 2% of their children. In another meta-analysis, Bellis et al. found the median non-paternity rate to be about 4%. One of the more intriguing examples of cuckoldry is the occasional finding of twins who have been sired by two different men (e.g., Lebeau-Le Guiner, Guidet, Bompoil, Marka & Pascal 2003). In any case, nonpaternity varies considerably across social and economic contexts. Sasse, Muller, Chakraborty, and Ott (1994) reported that nonpaternity rates were 1% in Switzerland, but others have reported rates greater than 20% in low socioeconomic settings

(Cerda-Flores, Baron, Marty-Gonzalez, Rivas, & Chakraborty 1999; Potthoff & Whittinghill 1965).

The other side of these nonpaternity estimates is a high degree of paternity certainty. In our two closest relatives, chimpanzees and bonobos, paternity is uncertain because females mate with multiple males. In this circumstance, little if any male parenting is predicted to evolve, and little is found (Whitten 1987). Overall, human paternity certainty is likely to be greater than 90% and possibly as high as 95%. When there are large deviations from these percentages, it appears to be in situations with low levels of male parenting or low male quality, as is found in other species with the facultative expression of paternal investment, variation in male quality, and female benefits to cuckoldry (Møller & Cuervo 2000).

Paternity Cues. Even though paternity certainty is high for human fathers, it is never 100%. Given this and the high and prolonged costs of parental care, men are predicted to have evolved biases that orient them to cues to the paternity of the children in which they are investing, much like those found for bluegill sunfish. Moreover, women are predicted to bias the use of these same cues as a means of maintaining paternal investment, especially in situations in which paternity is ambiguous (Daly & Wilson 1982; McLain, Setters, Moulton, & Pratt 2000; Pagel 1997). Of particular importance is men's sensitivity to cues of resemblance to their putative children and the corresponding prediction that they will invest more heavily in children they perceive as resembling themselves. These predictions are not related to step-parenting or adoption, because in these situations the man knows he is not the biological father and is providing some investment for other reasons, primarily to maintain a relationship with the children's mother (Anderson, Kaplan, Lam, & Lancaster 1999; Anderson, Kaplan, & Lancaster 1999; Flinn 1992).

Several studies suggest that fathers, more so than mothers, do indeed bias their investment in children based on their perceived resemblance to the child (Apicella & Marlowe 2004; Burch & Gallup 2000; Platek, Burch, Panyavin, Wasserman, & Gallup 2002; Platek et al. 2004), although results are mixed as to whether infants and young children do in fact resemble fathers more than mothers (Christenfeld & Hill 1995, McLain et al. 2000). There is also evidence that men who are not yet fathers show the same preference. In one study, Platek et al. (2002) morphed digital photographs of men and women to create the face of a preschool child that resembled them. Participants were then presented with a set of five morphed photos of children (the self morph was in half of these sets) and asked to choose the child whom they were more likely to adopt, find most attractive, be most likely to spend time with, and invest other resources on. Men were significantly more likely than were women to indicate that they would invest in their self-morph. DeBruine (2004), however, found this effect in both men and women. As a follow-up and to address DeBruine's failure to find a sex difference, Platek et al. (2004) replicated their original sex difference finding and, in a brain-imaging study, showed different patterns of brain activation in men and women when they evaluated children that resembled themselves and children that did not. Men's activation patterns suggested attentional focus, active evaluation of the self-morph, and inhibition of potentially negative affect.

If men are sensitive to paternity cues, regardless of cuckoldry risk, and their investment is beneficial to children, as it is, then women are predicted to have an evolved bias to manipulate information regarding paternity (Pagel 1997). In a study of spontaneous interactions in maternity wards in the United States, Daly and Wilson (1982) found that mothers stated the newborn resembled the father more than the newborn resembled her, but fathers were more skeptical of this resemblance. Follow-up studies confirmed the pattern in Canada and Mexico and suggested it extends to maternal kin (Daly & Wilson 1982, McLain et al. 2000, Regalski & Gaulin 1993). Men are thus biased to invest in children whom they perceive as resembling themselves, and women and their kin are biased such that they are much more likely to provide social cues suggesting greater paternal than maternal resemblance to children; in other words, women and their kin either implicitly or explicitly attempt to manipulate social information in ways that would result in increased paternal investment.

Women's Sexuality

Because women and their children benefit from men's parental investment, evolution will favor women with behavioral and other traits that will increase the likelihood men will invest in these children. These would include traits that resulted in, or at least suggested, high levels of paternity certainty, and also traits that reduced the primary cost of paternal investment, lost mating opportunities. There are, in fact, several features of women's sexuality consistent with these predictions, including concealed ovulation, women's aversion to casual sex, and pair bonding (Geary 1998, Miller & Fishkin 1997, Oliver & Hyde 1993). To ensure conception, concealed ovulation requires men to maintain a longer relationship with women than is found in most other primates (Dunbar 1995), but this, in and of itself, is not sufficient to ensure paternal investment. If other proximate mechanisms were not operating, such as pair bonding (Miller & Fishkin 1997), then once physical signs of pregnancy were evident, men could easily abandon women. Concealed ovulation and the associated period of extended sexual activity may in fact be one mechanism that fosters pair bonding and continued paternal investment (MacDonald 1992).

Women's aversion to casual sex greatly restricts men's mating opportunities (Buss & Schmitt 1993) and, through this, lowers the opportunity cost of parenting. It is not that women have somehow colluded to restrict men's mating opportunities. Rather, female choosiness is found in all species in which females invest more in parenting than males do (Andersson 1994; Darwin, 1871), and one result is that many males have fewer mating opportunities than they would prefer (Symons 1979). Men are, however, highly variable in this regard, with many men biased toward monogamous relationships and others toward polygynous relationships (Miller & Fishkin 1997). Nonetheless, any evolved tendency toward monogamy on the part of men was potentially predated by restricted mating opportunities, as found in monogamous primates (Dunbar 1995).

When and Where Do Men Parent?

The evolution of the facultative expression of men's parental care is predicted to have involved the same cost-benefit tradeoffs described in the Male Parenting in Nonhuman Species section. These involve the benefits to children's survival prospects and later social competitiveness and the man's paternity certainty, as these are balanced against the cost of lost mating opportunities. The when and where of men's actual investments in a family and children are thus predicted to vary with the benefits this investment provides to children, and the quality of the relationship with his wife. The latter is important because this is likely to be a paternity cue and reflects women's efforts to maintain men's investment in the family. Men's tendency to invest in children or not also appears to be influenced by their experiences while growing up and by social and cultural influences on mating opportunities. Of course, many of these effects are also influenced by genes and hormones, as I discuss in the first section. In the second section, I discuss the family and background correlates of men's parenting, and in the third section I focus on wider cultural and social influences on this parenting.

Genetic and Hormonal Correlates

In addition to social and ecological context, sex differences and within-sex variation in parenting are associated with hormones and other biological mechanisms (Wynne-Edwards 2001). The expression of these hormones and, through this, parental behavior can be influenced by individual differences in genes (Schneider et al. 2003; Young, Roger, Waymire, MacGregor & Insel 1999) or by social context (Storey, Walsh, Quinton, & Wynne-Edwards 2000). For both mothers and fathers, high levels of the stress hormone cortisol are correlated with the attentive and sensitive parenting of newborns (Corter & Fleming 1995; Stallings, Fleming, Corter, Worthman, & Steiner 2001), although there are other hormonal correlates that differ across mothers and fathers (Fleming, Ruble, Krieger, & Wong 1997; S. E. Taylor et al. 2000). Expectant fathers who respond to infant distress cues (e.g., crying) with concern and a desire to comfort the infant have higher prolactin levels and lower testosterone levels than do other men (Storey et al. 2000). It is not yet fully understood whether these differences cause more attentive parenting by fathers, change in response to exposure to their children, or both.

In any case, it is clear that individual differences in the quality of maternal and paternal care are related, in part, to genetic differences. In a study of twins, Pérusse, Neale, Heath, and Eaves (1994) found evidence for modest genetic contributions to two features of parental investment, care (e.g., sensitivity to emotional state), and protection (e.g., keeping the child close). Genetic models explained 18% to 25% of the individual differences on these dimensions of men's parenting and 23% to 39% of the individual differences in women's parenting. At the same time, this study also suggested that unique environmental effects—experiences unique to each person—account for the majority of the variation in paternal and maternal care and protection. A similar study found that parental reports of positive support (e.g., affection, encouragement) of their children were moderately heritable, although separate estimates were not provided for mothers and fathers (Losoya, Callor, Rowe, & Goldsmith 1997).

These results are interesting but in need of replication with other measures of parental investment. Moreover, the findings might not reflect genetic influences on paternal investment per se but rather heritable personality factors that are not directly related to the evolution of paternal care but nonetheless influence parenting. Of particular importance are heritable personality factors, such as conscientiousness, associated with the stability of long-term relationships, especially with one's spouse; and factors, such as irritability, that would affect responsiveness to children (Graziano & Eisenberg 1997; Jockin, McGue, & Lykken 1996; Rowe 2002). Still, it is likely that individual differences in both fathers' and mothers' investment in children reflect some degree of heritable variability in the hormonal systems associated with parenting behavior, although whether or not these hormonal differences are expressed may depend on experience.

Social Correlates

The most consistently found predictor of men's engagement with their children and satisfaction with parenting is the quality of the spousal relationship (Amato & Keith 1991; Belsky, Gilstrap, & Rovine 1984; Cox, Owen,

Lewis, & Henderson 1989; Davies & Cummings 1994; Feldman, Nash, & Aschenbrenner 1983; Howes & Markman 1989). Marital conflict, in contrast, often results in men's withdrawal from children and spouses (Christensen & Heavey 1990), although this is sometimes more pronounced for daughters than for sons (Kerig, Cowan, & Cowan 1993). The bottom line is that men in satisfying spousal relationships show higher levels of investment in their children than other men do. It follows from this that women's efforts to maintain an intimate and cooperative spousal relationship is a strategy, though not necessarily conscious, to induce and maintain paternal investment. It is also possible that men biased toward paternal investment are more cooperative and prone to monogamy, and thus less likely to incite conflict with their wives than are other men, or that the relation between marital satisfaction and paternal investment reflects genetic and not social effects. Most likely it is a combination of heritable biases and reactivity to marital dynamics that influence paternal investment, but definitive answers must await research designs that assess social and genetic factors and their interaction (Parke & Buriel 1998).

Developmental Correlates

Certain childhood experiences have been proposed as influencing if men will be biased to invest in parenting or in mating as adults (Belsky et al. 1991; Chisholm 1993; Miller & Fishkin 1997). Local mortality risks and low resource availability, in particular, are hypothesized to be associated with this bias. When mortality risks are high or resources are scarce, investment in more, rather than fewer, offspring is assumed to ensure that at least some will survive to adulthood. Specifically, Belsky et al. and Chisholm argued that mortality risks and low resource availability influence the nature of parent–child relationships. In risky, low-resource environments, the psychological and physiological stressors on parents are high, resulting in less-attentive and more-conflicted parent–child relationships. The prediction is that these relationships will be associated with a later tendency to form unstable relationships that focus on mating rather than parenting. In less-risky, high-resource environments, parent–child relationships are warmer and reflect higher levels of investment by both parents (MacDonald 1992). The prediction is that these relationships will be associated with a tendency to later form stable, high-parental-investment relationships.

Aspects of the model have been supported in several studies. As an example, Wilson and Daly (1997) found age of first reproduction, number of children birthed per woman, mortality risks, and local resource availability to be interrelated in modern-day Chicago. With few resources in the local environment, men compete intensely for resource control. The result is higher premature-death rates and an average lifespan of 54 years, as compared to 77 years in the most affluent neighborhoods. Shorter life spans are associated with earlier age of first reproduction for both men and women, and nearly twice as many children birthed per woman, comparing the least and most affluent neighborhoods. In other words, the early and frequent reproduction of women and men in these contexts, and low levels of maternal and often no paternal investment might be, at least in part, a facultative response to high mortality risks (see also Geary 2002; Korpelainen 2000). Other studies are, however, inconsistent with the psychosocial stress model. For Ache and Mayan men, Waynforth, Hurtado, and Hill (1998, p. 383) found that "measures of family stress and violence were unsuccessful in predicting age at first reproduction, and none of the psychosocial stress indicators predicted lifetime number of partners." Father absence was related to less "willingness to pay time and opportunity costs to maintain a sexual relationship" (Waynforth et al. 1998, p. 383), although this could easily reflect genetic and not psychosocial effects. Other studies of human populations and of other species suggest low resource availability, and other stressors are associated with delayed, not early, reproduction (Krebs & Davies 1993).

Vigil and Geary (2006) approached parental investment in terms of the ability of parents to add to children's social competitiveness before these children reach adulthood (see also Geary 2002; Geary & Flinn 2001). In this view, children and parents are predicted to be sensitive to children's social competitiveness vis-à-vis the children's peer group, as this is the most likely representation of the social competition the children will face in adulthood. Peer relations and wider community conditions suggest men's investment should increase with increases in the level of competition their children will face as adults. To test this hypothesis, 623 low-income women reported on various reproductive milestones—including ages at menarche, first sexual intercourse, and first childbirth—indicators of social competitiveness (e.g., years of education), community background (e.g., wealth of community), and family history, including amount of time spent with their father. There was a counterintuitive relation between time spent with their father, the community's background, and reproductive delay, that is, delaying having their first child to get a better education. It appeared that fathers invested the most time in their daughters when they lived in wealthier and highly competitive communities, that is, when their daughters required additional investment to keep them competitive with their peer group.

A similar pattern was reported by Harris and Marmer (1996). They found that the often-reported positive correlation between warm father–child relations and children's long-term economic and educational success is stronger in wealthier families, and concluded that "the positive effect of father's behavioral involvement ... [is] less effective for children who experience long -term poverty" (Harris & Marmer 1996, p. 632). These results, and those of Vigil and Geary (2006), suggest that fathers may vary their investment in response to what their children need to be socially competitive in their peer group, or at least in their perceived peer group.

Men's Parenting Across Cultures and Social Circumstances

Across cultures, there are differences in men's relative emphasis on investing their time and other resources in parenting or in finding multiple mates. Draper and Harpending (1988) described this variation, in terms of human cultures, as tending to be father-absent or father-present. I provide a brief contrast of father-absent and father-present societies in the first section and discuss how men's reproductive biases vary with the social circumstances that influence mating opportunities in the second.

Father-Absent and Father-Present Cultures

In father-absent societies, spousal relationships tend to be aloof, paternal investment is inconsistent, and polygynous marriages are allowed and pursued by many men. A correlate of polygyny is an increase in male-on-male aggression and thus more local warfare and male social displays (Draper & Harpending 1988, Hewlett 1988, Konner 2005, Whiting & Whiting 1975). These conditions "are particularly prevalent in so-called middle-range societies, i.e., those where agriculture is practiced at a very low level" (Draper & Harpending 1988, p. 349), and in resource-rich ecologies. In the latter, women can often provide for their children without the direct contribution of the father (Draper 1989), although fathers often control the land and other resources women use to feed their children (Borgerhoff Mulder 2000). In these societies, wealthy men often invest resources or social power in attempting to secure additional wives, often to their reproductive advantage (Chagnon 1988) and often at a risk of increased child mortality and thus a large cost to individual wives (Marlowe 2000).

Father-present societies are common in harsh ecologies and in industrial societies (Draper & Harpending 1988). These societies are characterized by ecologically or socially imposed monogamy (Flinn & Low 1986). In harsh ecologies, most men are unable to acquire the resources (e.g., meat) needed to support more than one wife and family, and thus their parental investment is functionally obligate. In other words, in these difficult conditions, children's survival is often dependent on heavy investment by both parents. In Western and some other industrial societies, men's ability to mate polygynously is limited by legal and moral prohibitions against these marriages, combined with women's preference for monogamy (Geary 1998). One result is a relative shift in men's efforts from mating to parenting.

Social Circumstances

Independent of cultural rules for marriage, mating opportunities vary with the ratio of reproductive-age men to reproductive-age women in the local social group, which is called the operational sex ratio (OSR). In human populations, the OSR is influenced by sex differences in birth rates, death rates, and migration patterns. In industrial societies, the population growth rate is particularly important because expanding populations yield an "oversupply" of women. This is because women prefer slightly older marriage partners (Kenrick & Keefe 1992). With an expanding population, the younger generation of women compete for marriage partners among a smaller cohort of older men.

In historical periods in which there is an oversupply of women, as from 1965 through the 1970s in the United States, men are better able to pursue their reproductive preferences. These periods are generally characterized by liberal sexual mores, high divorce rates, an increase in the number of out-of-wedlock births and the number of families headed by single women, an increase in women's participation in the workforce, and lower levels of men's parenting (Guttentag & Secord 1983). These patterns emerge because men are able to express their preference for a variety of sexual partners and relatively low levels of paternal investment (Pedersen, 1991), although some men remain monogamous (Miller & Fishkin 1997). When there is an oversupply of men (Guttentag & Secord 1983), women are better able to enforce their preference for a monogamous, high-investment spouse. These historical periods are generally characterized by an increase in the level of commitment of men to marriage, as indexed by declining divorce rates and greater levels of paternal investment.

Hurtado and Hill (1992) reported a similar pattern among the Ache and Hiwi (hunter-gatherers in southwestern Venezuela). In the Ache, there are more reproductive-age women than men (OSR of 1.3), whereas in the Hiwi there are more reproductive-age men than women (OSR of .78). These differences "in levels of mating opportunities between the Ache and the Hiwi occur alongside marked contrasts in marital stability. Whereas serial monogamy and extramarital promiscuity are very common among the Ache, stable lifetime monogamous unions with almost no extramarital copulation is the normative mating pattern among the Hiwi" (Hurtado & Hill 1992, p. 40). These patterns are found despite high infant- and child-mortality risks associated with paternal abandonment with the Ache and low risks with the Hiwi, suggesting some men are willing to risk the lives of some of their children to pursue a polygynous reproductive strategy.

Evolutionary History

The evolutionary history of men's parental behavior has almost certainly been influenced by the same cost-benefit tradeoffs associated with paternal investment in other species, but reconstructions of the history of these tradeoffs are never certain. The possibilities can, nevertheless, be guided by comparative analyses of evolutionarily related species. A common approach is to use patterns among our two closest relatives, chimpanzees and bonobos. However, for a variety of reasons discussed elsewhere (Geary 2006; Geary & Flinn 2001), Flinn and I have argued that if our ancestors were like chimpanzees or bonobos, multiple changes in male (e.g., increase in parenting) and female (e.g., emergence of concealed ovulation) reproductive behavior would have had to occur to create the current human reproductive pattern. In contrast, we proposed that the reproductive behaviors of our ancestors might have been more similar to that of our distant cousin, the gorilla (*Gorilla gorilla*). This is because moving from a gorilla-like pattern to the current human pattern would require fewer evolutionary changes than would be necessary to move from a chimpanzee- or bonobo-like pattern to the modal human pattern.

The typical social organization of gorillas is often described as isolated single-male harems, which typically include one reproductive male, two to four females, and their offspring (Fossey 1984, Stewart & Harcourt 1987, A. B. Taylor 1997). However, there is considerable variation in this social structure, even in the most isolated groups of mountain gorillas (*Gorilla gorilla beringei*); Robbins (1999) found that 40% of these groups included several, often related, males (e.g., brothers or father-sons). Groups of lowland gorillas (*Gorilla gorilla gorilla*) also maintain a harem structure but, in contrast to mountain gorillas, are less socially isolated. Several families will occupy the same geographical region, and encounters between groups are often friendly, especially among the males (Bradley et al. 2004). With the exception of strong male coalitions, the family groupings among these gorillas are very similar to the embedding of polygynous and monogamous families in human male kinship groups that is found in most traditional societies (Pasternak, Ember, & Ember 1997).

Moreover, the dynamics that emerge within families of lowland gorillas is similar to that found in human families. Unlike the multiple matings of female chimpanzees (during estrous) and bonobos, and a corresponding low level of paternity certainty (de Waal & Lanting 1997, Goodall 1986), adult male and female gorillas often form long-term social relationships. DNA fingerprinting indicates that male gorillas show high levels of paternity certainty (> 95%; Bradley et al. 2004), and behavioral observation has revealed high levels of affiliation with their offspring. As Whitten (1987) observed, "Associated males hold, cuddle, nuzzle, examine, and groom infants, and infants turn to these males in times of distress" (p. 346). Unlike female chimpanzees and bonobos, female gorillas do not typically have conspicuous sexual swellings and primarily solicit copulations behaviorally (Stewart & Harcourt 1987). The gorilla-like pattern of female sexual solicitation is more similar to the current human pattern (e.g., concealed ovulation) than is the pattern of female solicitation in chimpanzees or bonobos.

Other similarities between the human family and men's parenting and the social and reproductive relationships found among gorillas are presented elsewhere (Geary 2006; Geary & Flinn 2001). My point is that if this hypothesis is correct, then a family structure that includes mothers and fathers and high levels of paternal investment has been part of our evolutionary history for millions years (see also Lovejoy 1981).

CONCLUSION

Cultural debates regarding men's contributions to families and their children and the occasional rancor over the unequal contributions of men and women to parenting (Cherlin 2005, Silverstein & Auerbach 1999) belie a deeper and rarely considered scientific riddle; specifically, on the basis of little or no male parenting in nearly all other mammalian species and among our two closest living relatives (Clutton-Brock 1989, Whitten 1987), it is a scientific curiosity that men invest in families and children at all (Geary 2000). To understand how men's parenting evolved and how it is maintained in the here and now, we must consider the factors related to the evolution and expression of male parenting across other species. These factors involve tradeoffs that balance the benefits of male protection and provisioning to the health and later competitiveness of his offspring, weighed against the risk of cuckoldry and the cost of lost mating opportunities. Of course, it is likely that male parenting would benefit offspring even in species where this parenting does not occur. However, in these species, males that compete for access to mates out-reproduce any parental fathers, and thus any tendency toward the latter does not evolve (Andersson 1994).

Men's parenting is consistent with the same cost-benefit tradeoffs in other species in which paternal investment is found. In traditional and developing societies today and in the historical record, men's investment in families substantively reduced children's morality risks and improved their physical health and development (e.g., Morrison et al. 1977, Schultz 1991, United Nations 1985). In these societies and in Western societies today, men's investment often facilitates their children's ability to acquire the skills needed to compete in adulthood (Kaplan et al. 1998, Vigil & Geary 2006). Children who become successful adults are able to better care for and thus lower the mortality risks and enhance the later competitiveness of men's grandchildren. Men also benefit because of comparatively high levels of paternity certainty, although cuckoldry does occur and men and women show evidence of corresponding adaptations (e.g., Platek & Shackelford 2006). Women's reluctance to engage in casual sex greatly reduces men's mating opportunities, and in so doing, lowers the opportunity cost of paternal investment.

Even with an evolved bias to invest in children, there is considerable variation among men as to when and with whom they will invest in a family. The influences on the expression of men's parental behaviors are multifaceted and range from the genes that influence the expression of parenting-related hormones to the quality of the marital relationships to cultural mores regarding marriage practices (e.g., whether or not polygyny is allowed; Belsky et al. 1984, Flinn & Low 1986, Guttentag & Secord 1983, Storey et al. 2000). A comparative and evolutionary perspective on men's parenting provides a broader perspective for understanding these patterns and allows us to more fully understand when, where, and with whom men will invest in families.

References

Amato, P. R. (1998). More than money? Men's contributions to their children's lives. In A. Booth & A. C. Crouter (Eds.), *Men in families: When do they get involved? What difference does it make?* (pp. 241–278). Mahwah, NJ: Erlbaum.

Amato, P. R., & Keith, B. (1991). Parental divorce and the well-being of children: A meta-analysis. *Psychological Bulletin, 110,* 26–46.

Anderson, K. G. (2006). How well does paternity confidence match actual paternity? *Current Anthropology, 47,* 513–520.

Anderson, K. G., Kaplan, H., Lam, D., & Lancaster, J. (1999). Paternal care by genetic fathers and stepfathers II: Reports from Xhosa high school students. *Evolution and Human Behavior, 20,* 433–451.

Anderson, K. G., Kaplan, H., & Lancaster, J. (1999). Paternal care by genetic fathers and stepfathers I: Reports from Albuquerque men. *Evolution and Human Behavior, 20,* 405–431.

Andersson, M. (1994). *Sexual selection*. Princeton, NJ: Princeton University Press.

Apicella, C. L., & Marlowe, F. W. (2004). Perceived mate fidelity and paternal resemblance predict men's investment in children. *Evolution and Human Behavior, 25,* 371–378.

Arnold, K. E., & Owens, I. P. F. (2002). Extra-pair paternity and egg dumping in birds: Life history, parental care and the risk of retaliation. *Proceedings of the Royal Society of London B, 269,* 1263–1269.

Arnqvist, G., & Kirkpatrick, M. (2005). The evolution of infidelity in socially monogamous passerines: The strength of direct and indirect selection on extrapair copulation behavior in females. *American Naturalist, 165,* S26–S37.

Asa, C. S., & Valdespino, C. (1998). Canid reproductive biology: An integration of proximate mechanisms and ultimate causes. *American Zoologist, 38,* 251–259.

Bellis, M. A., & Baker, R. R. (1990). Do females promote sperm competition? Data for humans. *Animal Behaviour, 40,* 997–999.

Bellis, M. A., Hughs, K., Hughs, S., & Ashton, J. R. (2005). Measuring paternal discrepancy and its public health consequences. *Journal of Epidemiology and Community Health, 59,* 749–754.

Belsky, J., Gilstrap, B., & Rovine, M. (1984). The Pennsylvania infant and family development project, I: Stability and change in mother–infant and father–infant interaction in a family setting at one, three, and nine months. *Child Development, 55,* 692–705.

Belsky, J., Steinberg, L., & Draper, P. (1991). Childhood experience, interpersonal development, and reproductive strategy: An evolutionary theory of socialization. *Child Development, 62,* 647–670.

Birkhead, T. R., & Møller, A. P. (1996). Monogamy and sperm competition in birds. In J. M. Black (Ed.), *Partnerships in birds: The study of monogamy* (pp. 323–343). New York: Oxford University Press.

Blurton Jones, N. G., Hawkes, K., & O'Connell, J. F. (1997). Why do Hadza children forage? In N. L. Segal, G. E. Weisfeld, & C. C. Weisfeld (Eds.), *Uniting psychology and biology: Integrative perspectives on human development* (pp. 279–313). Washington, DC: American Psychological Association.

Booth, A., & Crouter, A. C. (Eds.) (1998). *Men in families: When do they get involved? What difference does it make?* Mahwah, NJ: Erlbaum.

Borgerhoff Mulder, M. (2000). Optimizing offspring: The quantity–quality tradeoff in agropastoral Kipsigis. *Evolution and Human Behavior, 21,* 391–410.

Bradley, B. J., Doran-Sheehy, D. M., Lukas, D., Boesch, C., & Vigilant, L. (2004). Dispersed male networks in Western gorillas. *Current Biology, 14,* 510–513.

Brändström, A. (1997). Life histories of lone parents and illegitimate children in nineteenth-century Sweden. In C. A. Corsini & P. P. Viazzo (Eds.), *The decline of infant and child mortality* (pp. 173–191). Hague, Netherlands: Martinus Nijhoff Publishers.

Burch, R. L., & Gallup, G. G., Jr. (2000). Perceptions of paternal resemblance predict family violence. *Evolution and Human Behavior, 21,* 429–435.

Buss, D. M., & Schmitt, D. P. (1993). Sexual strategies theory: An evolutionary perspective on human mating. *Psychological Review, 100,* 204–232.

Carson, J., Burks, V., & Parke, R. D. (1993). Parent–child physical play: Determinants and consequences. In K. MacDonald (Ed.), *Parent–child play: Descriptions & implications* (pp. 197–220). Albany: State University of New York Press.

Cerda-Flores, R. M., Baron, S. A., Marty-Gonzalez, L. F., Rivas, F., & Chakraborty, R. (1999). Estimation of nonpaternity in the Mexican population of Nuevo Leon: A validation study with blood group markers. *American Journal of Physical Anthropology, 109,* 281–293.

Chagnon, N. A. (1988). Life histories, blood revenge, and warfare in a tribal population. *Science, 239,* 985–992.

Cherlin, A. J. (2005). American marriage in the early twenty-first century. *The Future of Children, 15,* 33–55.

Cherlin, A. J., Furstenberg, F. F. Jr., Chase-Lansdale, P. L., Kiernan, K. E., Robins, P. K., Morrison, D. R., et al. (1991). Longitudinal studies of effects of divorce on children in Great Britain and the United States. *Science, 252,* 1386–1389.

Chisholm, J. S. (1993). Death, hope, and sex: Life-history theory and the development of reproductive strategies. *Current Anthropology, 34,* 1–24.

Christenfeld, N. J. S., & Hill, E. A. (1995). Whose baby are you? *Nature, 378,* 669.

Christensen, A., & Heavey, C. L. (1990). Gender and social structure in the demand/withdraw pattern of marital conflict. *Journal of Personality and Social Psychology, 59,* 73–81.

Cleveland, H. H., Jacobson, K. C., Lipinski, J. J., & Rowe, D. C. (2000). Genetic and shared environmental contributions to the relationship between the home environment and child and adolescent achievement. *Intelligence, 28,* 69–86.

Clutton-Brock, T. H. (1989). Mammalian mating systems. *Proceedings of the Royal Society of London B, 236,* 339–372.

Clutton-Brock, T. H. (1991). *The evolution of parental care.* Princeton, NJ: Princeton University Press.

Clutton-Brock, T. H., Albon, S. D., & Guinness, F. E. (1988). Reproductive success in male and female red deer. In T. H. Clutton-Brock (Ed.), *Reproductive success: Studies of individual variation in contrasting breeding systems* (pp. 325–343). Chicago: University of Chicago Press.

Corter, C. M., & Fleming, A. S. (1995). Psychobiology of maternal behavior in human beings. In M. H. Bornstein (Ed.), *Handbook of parenting, Vol. 2: Biology and ecology of parenting* (pp. 87–116). Mahwah, NJ: Erlbaum.

Cox, M. J., Owen, M. T., Lewis, J. M., & Henderson, V. K. (1989). Marriage, adult adjustment, and early parenting. *Child Development, 60,* 1015–1024.

Daly, M., & Wilson, M. (1982). Whom are newborn babies said to resemble? *Ethology and Sociobiology, 3,* 69–78.

Daly, M., & Wilson, M. I. (1985). Child abuse and other risks of not living with both parents. *Ethology and Sociobiology, 6,* 155–176.

Daly, M., Wilson, M., & Weghorst, S. J. (1982). Male sexual jealousy. *Ethology and Sociobiology, 3,* 11–27.

Darwin, C. (1871). *The descent of man, and selection in relation to sex.* London: John Murray.

Davies, P. T., & Cummings, E. M. (1994). Marital conflict and child adjustment: An emotional security hypothesis. *Psychological Bulletin, 116,* 387–411.

Davis, J. N., & Daly, M. (1997). Evolutionary theory and the human family. *Quarterly Review of Biology, 72,* 407–435.

de Waal, F., & Lanting, F. (1997). *Bonobo: The forgotten ape.* Berkeley: University of California Press.

DeBruine, L. M. (2004). Resemblance to self increases the appeal of child faces in both men and women. *Evolution and Human Behavior, 25,* 142–154.

Dixon, A., Ross, D., O'Malley, S. L. C., & Burke, T. (1994). Paternal investment inversely related to degree of extra-pair paternity in the reed bunting. *Nature, 371,* 698–700.

Draper, P. (1989). African marriage systems: Perspectives from evolutionary ecology. *Ethology and Sociobiology, 10,* 145–169.

Draper, P., & Harpending, H. (1988). A sociobiological perspective on the development of human reproductive strategies. In K. B. MacDonald (Ed.), *Sociobiological perspectives on human development* (pp. 340–372). New York: Springer-Verlag.

Dunbar, R. I. M. (1995). The mating system of callitrichid primates: I. Conditions for the coevolution of pair bonding and twinning. *Animal Behaviour, 50,* 1057–1070.

Ellis, B. J. (2004). Timing of pubertal maturation in girls: An integrated life history approach. *Psychological Bulletin, 130,* 920–958.

Ellis, B. J., Bates, J. E., Dodge, K. A., Fergusson, D. M., Horwood, J. L., Pettit, et al. (2003). Does father absence place daughters at special risk for early sexual activity and teenage pregnancy? *Child Development, 74,* 801–821.

Ellis, B. J., & Garber, J. (2000). Psychosocial antecedents of variation in girls' pubertal timing: Maternal depression, stepfather presence, and marital and family stress. *Child Development, 71,* 485–501.

Ellis, B. J., McFadyen-Ketchum, S., Dodge, K. A., Pettit, G. S., & Bates, J. E. (1999). Quality of early family relationships and individual differences in the timing of pubertal maturation in girls: A longitudinal test of an evolutionary model. *Journal of Personality and Social Psychology, 77,* 387–401.

Ewen, J. G., & Armstrong, D. P. (2000). Male provisioning is negatively correlated with attempted extrapair copulation in the stitchbird (or *hihi*). *Animal Behaviour, 60*, 429–433.

Feldman, S. S., Nash, S. C., & Aschenbrenner, B. G. (1983). Antecedents of fathering. *Child Development, 54*, 1628–1636.

Fishman, M. A., Stone, L., & Lotem, A. (2003). Fertility assurance through extrapair fertilizations and male paternity defense. *Journal of Theoretical Biology, 221*, 103–114.

Fleming, A. S., Ruble, D., Krieger, H., & Wong, P. Y. (1997). Hormonal and experiential correlates of maternal responsiveness during pregnancy and the puerperium in human mothers. *Hormones and Behavior, 31*, 145–158.

Flinn, M. V. (1988). Mate guarding in a Caribbean village. *Ethology and Sociobiology, 9*, 1–28.

Flinn, M. V. (1992). Paternal care in a Caribbean village. In B. S. Hewlett (Ed.), *Father–child relations: Cultural and biosocial contexts* (pp. 57–84). New York: Aldine de Gruyter.

Flinn, M. V., & Low, B. S. (1986). Resource distribution, social competition, and mating patterns in human societies. In D. I. Rubenstein & R. W. Wrangham (Eds.), *Ecological aspects of social evolution: Birds and mammals* (pp. 217–243). Princeton, NJ: Princeton University Press.

Florsheim, P., Tolan, P., & Gorman-Smith, D. (1998). Family relationships, parenting practices, the availability of male family members, and the behavior of inner-city boys in single-mother and two-parent families. *Child Development, 69*, 1437–1447.

Fossey, D. (1984). *Gorillas in the mist*. Boston: Houghton Mifflin Co.

Furstenberg, F. F., Jr., & Teitler, J. O. (1994). Reconsidering the effects of marital disruption. *Journal of Family Issues, 15*, 173–190.

Gaulin, S. J. C., McBurney, D. H., & Brakeman-Wartell, S. L. (1997). Matrilateral biases in the investment of aunts and uncles: A consequence and measure of paternity uncertainty. *Human Nature, 8*, 139–151.

Geary, D. C. (1998). *Male, female: The evolution of human sex differences*. Washington, DC: American Psychological Association.

Geary, D. C. (2000). Evolution and proximate expression of human paternal investment. *Psychological Bulletin, 126*, 55–77.

Geary, D. C. (2002). Sexual selection and human life history. In R. Kail (Ed.), *Advances in child development and behavior* (Vol. 30, pp. 41–101). San Diego: Academic Press.

Geary, D. C. (2005). Evolution of paternal investment. In D. M. Buss (Ed.), *The evolutionary psychology handbook* (pp. 483–505). Hoboken, NJ: John Wiley & Sons.

Geary, D. C. (2006). Coevolution of paternal investment and cuckoldry in humans. In T. K. Shackelford & S. Platek (Eds.), *Female infidelity and paternal uncertainty* (pp. 14–34). New York: Cambridge University Press.

Geary, D. C., & Flinn, M. V. (2001). Evolution of human parental behavior and the human family. *Parenting: Science and Practice, 1*, 5–61.

Goodall, J. (1986). *The chimpanzees of Gombe: Patterns of behavior*. Cambridge, MA: Belknap Press.

Graziano, W. G., & Eisenberg, N. (1997). Agreeableness: A dimension of personality. In R. Hogan, J. Johnson, & S. Briggs (Eds.), *Handbook of personality psychology* (pp. 795–824). San Diego: Academic Press.

Guttentag, M., & Secord, P. (1983). *Too many women?* Beverly Hills: Sage.

Harris, K. M., & Marmer, J. K. (1996). Poverty, paternal involvement, and adolescent well-being. *Journal of Family Issues, 17*, 614–640.

Herlihy, D. (1965). Population, plague and social change in rural Pistoia, 1201–1430. *The Economic History Review, 18*, 225–244.

Hewlett, B. S. (1988). Sexual selection and paternal investment among Aka pygmies. In L. Betzig, M. Borgerhoff Mulder, & P. Turke (Eds.), *Human reproductive behaviour: A Darwinian perspective* (pp. 263–276). Cambridge, England: Cambridge University Press.

Hewlett, B. S. (Ed.) (1992). *Father–child relations: Cultural and biosocial contexts*. New York: Aldine de Gruyter.

Hill, K., & Hurtado, A. M. (1996). *Ache life history: The ecology and demography of a foraging people*. New York: Aldine de Gruyter.

Howes, P., & Markman, H. J. (1989). Marital quality and child functioning: A longitudinal investigation. *Child Development, 60*, 1044–1051.

Hurtado, A. M., & Hill, K. R. (1992). Paternal effect on offspring survivorship among Ache and Hiwi hunter–gatherers: Implications for modeling pair-bond stability. In B. S. Hewlett (Ed.), *Father–child relations: Cultural and biosocial contexts* (pp. 31–55). New York: Aldine de Gruyter.

Jockin, V., McGue, M., & Lykken, D. T. (1996). Personality and divorce: A genetic analysis. *Journal of Personality and Social Psychology, 71*, 288–299.

Kaplan, H. S., Lancaster, J. B., & Anderson, K. G. (1998). Human parental investment and fertility: The life histories of men in Albuquerque. In A. Booth & A. C. Crouter (Eds.), *Men in families: When do they get involved? What difference does it make?* (pp. 55–109). Mahwah, NJ: Erlbaum.

Kaplan, H. S., Lancaster, J. B., Bock, J. A., & Johnson, S. E. (1995). Does observed fertility maximize fitness among New Mexican men? A test of an optimality model and a new theory of parental investment in the embodied capital of offspring. *Human Nature, 6*, 325–360.

Kempenaers, B., Lanctot, R. B., & Robertson, R. J. (1998). Certainty of paternity and paternal investment in eastern bluebirds and tree swallows. *Animal Behaviour, 55*, 845–860.

Kenrick, D. T., & Keefe, R. C. (1992). Age preferences in mates reflect sex differences in human reproductive strategies. *Behavioral and Brain Sciences, 15*, 75–133.

Kerig, P. K., Cowan, P. A., & Cowan, C. P. (1993). Marital quality and gender differences in parent–child interaction. *Developmental Psychology, 29*, 931–939.

Klindworth, H., & Voland, E. (1995). How did the Krummhörn elite males achieve above-average reproductive success? *Human Nature, 6,* 221–240.

Kok, J., van Poppel, F., & Kruse, E. (1997). Mortality among illegitimate children in mid-nineteenth-century the Hague. In C. A. Corsini & P. P. Viazzo (Eds.), *The decline of infant and child mortality* (pp. 193–211). The Hague, Netherlands: Martinus Nijhoff Publishers.

Konner, M. (2005). Hunter–gather infancy and childhood: The !Kung and others. In B. S. Hewlett & M. E. Lamb (Eds.), *Hunter–gatherer childhoods: Evolutionary, developmental, & cultural perspectives* (pp. 19–64). New Brunswick, NJ: AldineTransaction.

Korpelainen, H. (2000). Fitness, reproduction and longevity among European aristocratic and rural Finnish families in the 1700s and 1800s. Proceedings of the Royal Society London, B267, 1765–1770.

Krebs, J. R., & Davies, N. B. (1993). *An introduction to behavioural ecology* (3rd ed.). Oxford, England: Blackwell Science.

Lebeau-Le Guiner, S., Guidet, F., Bompoil, T., Marka, C., & Pascal, O. (2003). Two fathers for twin sisters. *International Congress Series, 1239,* 933–937.

Losoya, S. H., Callor, S., Rowe, D. C., & Goldsmith, H. H. (1997). Origins of familial similarity in parenting: A study of twins and adoptive siblings. *Developmental Psychology, 33,* 1012–1023.

Lovejoy, C. O. (1981). The origin of man. *Science, 211,* 341–350.

Luster, T., & Okagaki, L. (1993). Multiple influences on parenting: Ecological and life-course perspectives. In T. Luster & L. Okagaki (Eds.), *Parenting: An ecological perspective* (pp. 227–250). Hillsdale, NJ: Erlbaum.

MacDonald, K. (1992). Warmth as a developmental construct: An evolutionary analysis. *Child Development, 63,* 753–773.

Marlowe, F (2000). Paternal investment and the human mating system. *Behavioural Processes, 51,* 45–61.

McBurney, D. H., Simon, J., Gaulin, S. J. C., & Geliebter, A. (2002). Matrilateral biases in the investment of aunts and uncles: Replication in a population presumed to have high paternity certainty. *Human Nature, 13,* 391–402.

McLain, D. K., Setters, D., Moulton, M. P., & Pratt, A. E. (2000). Ascription of resemblance of newborns by parents and nonrelatives. *Evolution and Human Behavior, 21,* 11–23.

Miller, L. C., & Fishkin, S. A. (1997). On the dynamics of human bonding and reproductive success: Seeking windows on the adapted-for-human-environmental interface. In J. A. Simpson & D. T. Kenrick (Eds.), *Evolutionary social psychology* (pp. 197–235). Mahwah, NJ: Erlbaum.

Mock, D. W., & Fujioka, M. (1990). Monogamy and long-term pair bonding in vertebrates. *Trends in Ecology & Evolution, 5,* 39–43.

Møller, A. P. (2000). Male parental care, female reproductive success, and extrapair paternity. *Behavioral Ecology, 11,* 161–168.

Møller, A. P., & Cuervo, J. J. (2000). The evolution of paternity and paternal care. *Behavioral Ecology, 11,* 472–485.

Møller, A. P., & Tegelström, H. (1997). Extra-pair paternity and tail ornamentation in the barn swallow *Hirundo rustica*. *Behavioral Ecology and Sociobiology, 41*, 353–360.

Morrison, A. S., Kirshner, J., & Molho, A. (1977). Life cycle events in 15th-century Florence: Records of the *Monte Delle Doti*. *American Journal of Epidemiology, 106*, 487–492.

Neff, B. D. (2003). Decisions about parental care in response to perceived paternity. *Nature, 422*, 716–719.

Neff, B. D., & Sherman, P. W. (2002). Decision making and recognition mechanisms. *Proceedings of the Royal Society of London B, 269*, 1435–1441.

Oliver, M. B., & Hyde, J. S. (1993). Gender differences in sexuality: A meta-analysis. *Psychological Bulletin, 114*, 29–51.

Pagel, M. (1997). Desperately concealing father: A theory of parent–infant resemblance. *Animal Behaviour, 53*, 973–981.

Parke, R. D. (1995). Fathers and families. In M. H. Bornstein (Ed.), *Handbook of parenting: Vol. 3: Status and social conditions of parenting* (pp. 27–63). Mahwah, NJ: Erlbaum.

Parke, R. D., & Buriel, R. (1998). Socialization in the family: Ethnic and ecological perspectives. In W. Damon & E. Eisenberg (Eds.), *Handbook of child psychology* (5th ed., Vol. 3, pp. 463–552). New York: John Wiley & Sons.

Pasternak, B., Ember, C. R., & Ember, M. (1997). *Sex, gender, and kinship: A cross-cultural perspective*. Upper Saddle River, NJ: Prentice-Hall.

Pedersen, F. A. (1991). Secular trends in human sex ratios: Their influence on individual and family behavior. *Human Nature, 2*, 271–291.

Perrone, M., Jr., & Zaret, T. M. (1979). Parental care patterns of fishes. *American Naturalist, 113*, 351–361.

Pérusse, D., Neale, M. C., Heath, A. C., & Eaves, L. J. (1994). Human parental behavior: Evidence for genetic influence and potential implication for gene–culture transmission. *Behavior Genetics, 24*, 327–335.

Platek, S. M., Burch, R. L., Panyavin, I. S., Wasserman, B. H., & Gallup, G. G., Jr. (2002). Reactions to children's face resemblance affects males more than females. *Evolution and Human Behavior, 23*, 159–166.

Platek, S. M., Raines, D. M., Gallup, G. G., Jr., Mohamed, F. B., Thomson, J. W., Myers, et al. (2004). Reactions to children's faces: Males are more affected by resemblance than females are, and so are their brains. *Evolution and Human Behavior, 25*, 394–405.

Platek, S. M., & Shackelford, T. K. (Eds.) (2006). *Female infidelity and paternal uncertainty*. Cambridge: Cambridge University Press.

Pleck, J. H. (1997). Paternal involvement: Levels, sources, and consequences. In M. E. Lamb (Ed.), *The role of the father in child development* (3rd ed., pp. 66–103). New York: John Wiley & Sons.

Potthoff, R. F., & Whittinghill, M. (1965). Maximum-likelihood estimation of the proportion of nonpaternity. *American Journal of Human Genetics, 17*, 480–494.

Regalski, J. M., & Gaulin, S. J. C. (1993). Whom are Mexican infants said to resemble? Monitoring and fostering paternal confidence in the Yucatan. *Ethology and Sociobiology, 14*, 97–113.

Reichard, U. H., & Boesch, C. (Eds.) (2003). *Monogamy: Mating strategies in birds, humans and other mammals.* Cambridge, England: Cambridge University Press.

Reid, A. (1997). Locality or class? Spatial and social differentials in infant and child mortality in England and Wales, 1895–1911. In C. A. Corsini & P. P. Viazzo (Eds.), *The decline of infant and child mortality* (pp. 129–154). The Hague, Netherlands: Martinus Nijhoff Publishers.

Reid, J. M., Arcese, P., Cassidy, A. L. E. V., Hiebert, S. M., Smith, J. N. M., Stoddard, P., et al. (2005). Fitness correlates of song repertoire in free-living song sparrows (*Melospiza melodia*). *American Naturalist, 165*, 299–310.

Robbins, M. M. (1999). Male mating patterns in wild multimale mountain gorilla groups. *Animal Behaviour, 57*, 1013–1020.

Rohwer, S., Herron, J. C., & Daly, M. (1999). Stepparental behavior as mating effort in birds and other animals. *Evolution and Human Behavior, 20*, 367–390.

Rollet, C. (1997). Childhood mortality in high-risk groups: Some methodological reflections based on French experience.In C. A. Corsini & P. P. Viazzo (Eds.), *The decline of infant and child mortality* (pp. 213–225). The Hague, Netherlands: Martinus Nijhoff.

Rowe, D. C. (2002). What twin and adoption studies reveal about parenting. In J. G. Borkowski, S. L. Ramey, & M. Bristol-Power (Eds.), *Parenting and the child's world: Influences on academic, intellectual, and social–emotional development* (pp. 21–34). Mahwah, NJ: Erlbaum.

Saino, N., Møller, A. P., & Bolzern, A. M. (1995). Testosterone effects on the immune system and parasite infestations in the barn swallow (*Hirundo rustica*): An experimental test of the immunocompetence hypothesis. *Behavioral Ecology, 6*, 397–404.

Sasse, G., Muller, H., Chakraborty, R., & Ott, J. (1994). Estimating the frequency of nonpaternity in Switzerland. *Human Heredity, 44*, 337–343.

Schneider, J. S., Stone, M. K., Wynne-Edwards, K. E., Horton, T. H., Lydon, J., O'Malley, B., et al. (2003). Progesterone receptors mediate male aggression toward infants. *Proceedings of the National Academy of Sciences USA, 100*, 2951–2956.

Schultz, H. (1991). Social differences in mortality in the eighteenth century: An analysis of Berlin church registers. *International Review of Social History, 36*, 232–248.

Shackelford, T. K., & Larsen, R. J. (1997). Facial asymmetry as an indicator of psychological, emotional, and physiological distress. *Journal of Personality and Social Psychology, 72*, 456–466.

Sheldon, B. C., Räsänen, K., & Dias, P. C. (1997). Certainty of paternity and paternal effort in the collared flycatcher. *Behavioral Ecology, 8*, 421–428.

Silverstein, L. B., & Auerbach, C. F. (1999). Deconstructing the essential father. *American Psychologist, 54*, 397–407.

Smuts, B., & Gubernick, D. J. (1992). Male–infant relationships in nonhuman primates: Paternal investment or mating effort? In B. S. Hewlett (Ed.), *Father–child relations: Cultural and biosocial contexts* (pp. 1–30). New York: Aldine de Gruyter.

Stallings, J., Fleming, A. S., Corter, C., Worthman, C., & Steiner, M. (2001). The effects of infant cries and odors on sympathy, cortisol, and autonomic responses in new mothers and non-postpartum women. *Parenting: Science and Practice, 1*, 71–100.

Stewart, K. J., & Harcourt, A. H. (1987). Gorillas: Variation in female relationships. In B. B. Smuts, D. L. Cheney, R. M. Seyfarth, R. W. Wrangham, & T. T. Struhsaker (Eds.), *Primate societies* (pp. 155–164). Chicago: University of Chicago Press.

Storey, A. E., Walsh, C. J., Quinton, R. L., & Wynne-Edwards, K. E. (2000). Hormonal correlates of paternal responsiveness in new and expectant fathers. *Evolution and Human Behavior, 21*, 79–95.

Symons, D. (1979). *The evolution of human sexuality*. New York: Oxford University Press.

Tamis-LeMonda, C. S., & Cabrera, N. (1999). *Perspectives on father involvement: Research and policy* (Social Policy Report, Vol. 13, No. 2). Ann Arbor, MI: Society for Research in Child Development.

Taylor, A. B. (1997). Relative growth, ontogeny, and sexual dimorphism in Gorilla (*Gorilla gorilla gorilla* and *G. g. beringei*): Evolutionary and ecological considerations. *American Journal of Primatology, 43*, 1–31.

Taylor, S. E., Klein, L. C., Lewis, B. P., Gruenewald, T. L., Gurung, R. A. R., & Updegraff, J. A. (2000). Biobehavioral responses to stress in females: Tend-and-befriend, not fight-or-flight. *Psychological Review, 107*, 411–429.

Thornhill, R. (1976). Sexual selection and paternal investment in insects. *American Naturalist, 110*, 153–163.

Trivers, R. L. (1972). Parental investment and sexual selection. In B. Campbell (Ed.), *Sexual selection and the descent of man 1871–1971* (pp. 136–179). Chicago: Aldine Publishing.

Trivers, R. L. (1974). Parent–offspring conflict. *American Zoologist, 14*, 249–264.

United Nations (1985). *Socio-economic differentials in child mortality in developing countries*. New York: United Nations.

van Schaik, C. P., & Kappeler, P. M. (2003). The evolution of social monogamy in primates. In U. H. Reichard & C. Boesch (Eds.), *Monogamy: Mating strategies in birds, humans and other mammals* (pp. 59–80). Cambridge, England: Cambridge University Press.

Vigil, J. M., & Geary, D. C. (2006). Family and community background and variation in women's life history development. *Journal of Family Psychology, 20*. 597–604.

Vigil, J. M., Geary, D. C., & Byrd-Craven, J. (2005). A life history assessment of early childhood sexual abuse in women. *Developmental Psychology, 41*, 553–561.

Waynforth, D., Hurtado, A. M., & Hill, K. (1998). Environmentally contingent reproductive strategies in Mayan and Ache males. *Evolution and Human Behavior, 19*, 369–385.

Westneat, D. F., & Sherman, P. W. (1993). Parentage and the evolution of parental behavior. *Behavioral Ecology, 4*, 66–77.

Westneat, D. F., & Sherman, P. W. (2003). Extra-pair paternity in birds: Causes, correlates, and conflict. *Annual Review of Ecology, Evolution, & Systematics, 34*, 365–396.

Whiting, B. B., & Whiting, J. W. M. (1975). *Children of six cultures: A psychocultural analysis*. Cambridge: Harvard University Press.

Whitten, P. L. (1987). Infants and adult males. In B. B. Smuts, D. L. Cheney, R. M. Seyfarth, R. W. Wrangham, & T. T. Struhsaker (Eds.), *Primate societies* (pp. 343–357). Chicago: University of Chicago Press.

Wilson, M., & Daly, M. (1997). Life expectancy, economic inequality, homicide, and reproductive timing in Chicago neighbourhoods. *British Medical Journal, 314*, 1271–1274.

Wolf, L., Ketterson, E. D., & Nolan, V., Jr. (1988). Paternal influence on growth and survival of dark-eyed junco young: Do parental males benefit? *Animal Behaviour, 36*, 1601–1618.

Wynne-Edwards, K. E. (2001). Hormonal changes in mammalian fathers. *Hormones and Behavior, 40*, 139–145.

Young, L. J., Nilsen, R., Waymire, K. G., MacGregor, G. R. & Insel, T. R. (1999). Increased affiliative response to vasopressin in mice expressing the V1a receptor from a monogamous vole. *Nature, 400*, 766–768.

7 Parent–Offspring Conflict

Catherine A. Salmon

At first glance, the relationship between parent and child seems to begin in perfect harmony. The image of parents' devotion to their infant is one that has been depicted in art for thousands of years. It often seems like a sharp contrast to the modern image of the typical adolescent–parent relationship, usually portrayed as full of strife. But is either really accurate? What factors shape the degree of conflict between parent and child? And are there particular stages in the life of a child or a parent that attenuate or exaggerate the degree of conflict? An evolutionary perspective on the family provides useful insights.

PARENT–OFFSPRING CONFLICT THEORY

From a genetic standpoint, our children are all-important. They are our genetic passport into the future. So one might, on the surface, predict that parents would never come into conflict with their children; they would sacrifice all for their well-being. And under some circumstances, parents do just that, giving their time and resources to better equip their own children to be successful and have children of their own.

But conflicts do occur for various reasons, a primary one being that parental best interests and the best interests of any particular child may not exactly coincide. From the parental perspective, each child is equally genetically related to them by the degree 0.5 (i.e., they share 50% of their genes, on average). But among a sibship of children, each child is related to any sibling by 0.5 but to themselves by 1.0 (the special case of identical twins, siblings related by 1.0, is discussed in a later chapter). As a result, children might be expected to care more about themselves than about their siblings, whereas parents might care equally about their children and invest accordingly. Such differing opinions about the allocation of resources among siblings are a primary source of parent–child conflict. Who has not heard themselves or heard stories about children accusing a parent of loving another child more than them or treating another child better? "Sally got a bigger piece of cake; not fair!" "You love Billy best!" This often spills into conflict between the siblings, either verbal or physical. And yet, the early stages of parent–child conflict are set and played out even before birth.

MATERNAL–FETAL CONFLICT

Although the majority of paternal investment in children occurs after the child is born, mothers begin to invest long before birth. For 9 months, the mother's body will provide all the nutrients for the baby's development in addition to a safe environment in which to grow. At this stage, it would appear that the fetus and mother have identical interests, the safety and growth of the fetus. But their genetic interests are not identical. Because the fetus is more closely related to itself than to either its mother or any future siblings, pregnancy becomes a sensitive balance between the developing fetus's attempts to secure as large a share of maternal resources as possible and the mother's attempts to preserve some resources for herself and future offspring. Fetal genes will be selected to increase the transfer of nutrients to the fetus, whereas maternal genes will be selected to limit any transfers that would be in excess of the optimum, from the mother's perspective. Often, this balancing act results in a variety of unpleasant symptoms for the mother and occasionally generates serious pregnancy complications. Haig (1993, 1998) has analyzed pregnancy complications from a maternal–fetus conflict perspective, suggesting that such conflicts are responsible for some puzzling aspects of pregnancy and its complications.

One of these complications involves gestational diabetes. Pregnancy alters the regulation of maternal blood-glucose levels, with fasting blood-sugar levels falling during early pregnancy and then stabilizing at a new lower level at the end of the first trimester and remaining there until the baby is born (Lind & Aspillaga 1988). However, fasting insulin levels remain the same during the first two trimesters, rising in the third along with the growth of the fetus. For a non-pregnant woman, blood-glucose levels rise after a meal but rapidly return to fasting levels in response to insulin release. For a woman in the later stages of pregnancy, maternal blood glucose and insulin both reach higher levels and remain elevated for a longer duration. This occurs because the placental hormone, human placental lactogen (hPL) acts on maternal prolactin receptors to increase maternal resistance to insulin. If there is no opposition, hPL will maintain higher blood-glucose levels for longer periods after eating. However, this usually is opposed by increased maternal production of insulin. So, in the third trimester, the same meal will produce an exaggerated insulin response, which is less effective at reducing blood-glucose levels (Buchanan, Metzger, Freinkel, & Bergman 1990; Catalano, Tyzbir, Roman, Amini, & Sims 1991).

This occurs because the mother is attempting to restrict fetal access to blood glucose. Haig (1993) thought to ask two important questions: "Why should a mother restrict fetal access to glucose, and why should she increase her production of insulin at the same time as she is becoming resistant to its effects?" The partial answer is that if fetal demands for glucose go unopposed, the fetus may remove more glucose from maternal blood than is in the mother's interests to give up. For most of our evolutionary history, food was not in abundant supply, and so from both the fetus's and the mother's perspectives, resources are in high demand. After each meal, there is conflict over the share of blood glucose each will receive, and the longer the mother takes to reduce blood-sugar levels, the greater the share obtained by the fetus. Thus, the insulin resistance of late pregnancy is caused by placental hormones increasing blood-glucose levels and a corresponding increased production of insulin by the mother (Haig 1993). For pregnant women (without preexisting diabetes), the birth weight of the child has been positively correlated with maternal glucose levels two hours after a meal (Tallarigo et al. 1986). But the benefit of increased maternal glucose levels for the fetus can be gained at some cost to the mother's health. If blood-glucose levels remain elevated, gestational diabetes can develop. This condition occurs when the mother is unable to increase her insulin production sufficiently to match the insulin resistance that developed during the pregnancy.

Another arena in which maternal–fetal conflict occurs is maternal blood pressure. Blood pressure can be thought of in terms of two components, the cardiac output (or flow rate) and resistance, which is influenced by the size of the structures the blood flows through. During pregnancy, the fetus depends on the mother's circulatory system for all its needs. Conflict can arise over the relative flow of blood to the uteroplacental circulation (from which the fetus obtains its nutrients) versus the nonplacental remainder. Theoretically, the fetus can increase its share of the cardiac output by decreasing resistance in the uteroplacental circulatory subsystem or by increasing resistance in the nonplacental subsystem. The mother can reduce the fetal share of the output by doing the opposite, increasing uteroplacental resistance or decreasing nonplacental resistance (Haig 1993). As a result, placental factors will act to increase maternal blood pressure, and maternal factors will act to decrease maternal blood pressure.

A fetus benefits from increases in maternal blood pressure. And, in fact, gestational hypertension typically results in a positive fetal outcome. Hypertensive pregnancies have lower perinatal mortality than normotensive pregnancies (Symonds 1980). For white American women, birth weight is correlated positively with maternal blood pressure for mothers with low pre-pregnancy weight and low weight gain during pregnancy (Naeye 1981). And studies suggest that chronic hypertension is associated with higher birth weights, and chronic hypotension is associated with lower birth weights (Ng and Walters, 1992; Salafia, Xenophon, Vintzileos, Lerer, & Silberman 1990). However, there are risks associated with pregnancy-induced hypertension when it is extreme and occurs along with proteinuria (excessive protein in maternal urine). This condition is called preeclampsia and can result in maternal and fetal death.

WEANING CONFLICT

The dispute over weaning in mammals is a clear example of parent–offspring conflict. Parents are selected to continue to invest in their offspring up to the point at which the cost, in terms of reduced reproductive success (the more parents invest in current offspring, the less they have to invest in future offspring), outweighs the benefits of increased survival for the current offspring. In other words, as soon as the costs begin to exceed the benefits ($B/C < 1$, where B = benefit of parental actions to an offspring's survival and C = cost to the parents' ability to invest in other offspring), parents should stop investing in the current offspring and start to work on the next (Trivers 1974). One can imagine a dog with a litter of puppies. From the mother's perspective, at a certain point, it is time to stop nursing. The puppies rarely agree at first, and they often have to be physically dislodged from the mother, sometimes being dragged, unwilling to relinquish the teat, as the mother gets up and moves away.

At this point, an offspring would prefer investment continue, being more closely related to itself than to any future siblings; it has been selected to demand investment until the cost-benefit ratio drops below 0.5. After that point, continued demands for investment would lead to a reduction in indirect fitness because the parent would produce fewer siblings with whom the offspring would share genes. In other words, we expect the mother to encourage altruistic acts among offspring when the benefits to one offspring are greater than the costs to another (Hrdy 1999). In turn, we expect that the offspring forced to give up benefits will agree only if the benefits to its current or future sibling are twice the costs to itself. An offspring will be expected to stop attempting to extract more from its mother when the costs to the mother (in terms of her survival or ability to invest in future or other offspring) are more than twice the benefits that the offspring receives from the investment.

In this type of conflict, children are at a disadvantage. They are smaller and, to a certain extent, at the mercy of their parents. Physical force is not going to be a typical strategy of offspring to coerce more parental investment. The image of a mare kicking at her colt to get him to stop trying to nurse demonstrates the futility of children's trying to force parental cooperation. The tactics children use are quite different, temper tantrums being one example of behavior designed to manipulate parents into acquiescing to the child's will. In general, when parental investment is threatened, perhaps by the birth of a new sibling, children will often try to exaggerate their own need, acting younger (wanting to nurse and engaging in behaviors they had previously abandoned) or pretending distress to receive more parental care. This has been documented in other primates, such as chimpanzees (Hrdy 1999), and is familiar to anyone who has witnessed the behavior of young children who are either being weaned or dealing with a new baby in the family.

ADOLESCENT CONFLICT

Adolescence is often viewed as a time of conflict between parent and child. As children mature sexually and begin to form a sense of who they are, they remain socially dependent on their parents. For a minority of parents and their children, the conflict can be significantly stressful (Steinberg & Morris 2001), but for most, the conflict is relatively mild. One U.S. Gallup poll (Carroll 2002) reported that, according to the teenagers themselves, 97% of teenagers got along either fairly well or very well with their parents. Hardly the level of angst often portrayed in the media.

A typical conflict of the teenage years is unsurprising from an evolutionary perspective. Children are the vehicles of their parents' fitness and, as a result, parents have a keen interest in their children's reproductive activities and, in particular, their choice of a long-term mate or sexual partner. In societies with formally arranged marriages, parents have a significant amount of control over their child's mating partner. In societies in which people are, in principle, free to choose as mates whomever they want, parents still show a keen interest and express their approval or disapproval of these choices. In a sense, they have their own genetic interests at heart, although these interests may often coincide with those of their children.

FACTORS INFLUENCING PARENTAL INVESTMENT IN CHILDREN

Many factors can influence the amount of investment parents channel to any particular child. These factors tend to exacerbate, at times, the level of conflict between parent and child. In general, they fall into three categories: factors that influence the costs of investment to parents, factors that influence the benefits of such investments to parents, and the relatedness between parent and child.

Costs to Parents

Factors that influence the costs of investment to parents include parental age, the number of children they already have, and their own access to resources. With increasing parental age, the fitness value of any offspring of any given age and quality increases relative to the parents' residual reproductive value (or expected future reproductive value) (Fisher 1930). For any species in which expected future reproduction is a declining function of parental age, older parents will have been selected to invest more in offspring than will younger parents (Pugesek 1995, Salmon & Daly 1998, Voland & Gabler 1994). Evidence from many species suggests that this is the case (Clark, Moghaddas, & Galef 2002; Clutton-Brock 1984). There are also relevant human data. Studies of infanticide, for example, indicate that the age of the mother is a significant factor in the likelihood of her perpetrating infanticide. Young women—those likely to have many future opportunities to reproduce—might be expected to be more willing to sacrifice a current child. Women close to the end of their reproductive years who pass up the opportunity to have a baby may never have that chance again. As the likelihood of future reproduction decreases, the cost of delaying childbirth becomes expensive from a fitness perspective. As a result, we expect natural selection to favor older women who invest immediately and to a significant extent in children rather than delaying investment. The dramatic decrease observed cross-culturally in the rate of maternally perpetrated infanticide as a function of maternal age is a reflection of the change over time of the weight the maternal psyche places on a current offspring versus possible future offspring (Daly & Wilson 1995; Lee & George 1999; Overpeck, Brenner, Trumble, Trifiletti, & Berendes 1998).

The number of children parents have at any one time also is expected to have an impact on parental investment (and levels of conflict). Parental investment is a limited resource (whether measured in food, time, money, or other resources) that must be allocated among offspring, and most parental resources will be in shorter supply when there are multiple children (not necessarily all the same age) at the same time. More children means fewer resources for any individual child. This is one reason that existing children are often so resistant to adding another child to the household, not being keen on sharing their parents with a sibling. Michalski addresses sibling relationships in his chapter in this volume, but it is clear that not only do parent and child disagree at times over the allocation of resources among siblings (Kennedy 1989, Salmon & Daly 1998) but also that sibling conflict is a reflection of these disagreements and conflicts.

The amount of resources available to parents is also expected to have an impact on parental investment. When resources are scarce or difficult to acquire, any parental investment is more costly from the parental perspective, as opposed to when resources are easy to acquire. Modeling studies of parental investment in the Western bluebird (Davis & Todd 1999; Davis, Todd, & Bullock 1999) demonstrated that the success of various parental decision-making rules depends on the amount of resources available to parents. The fewer resources parents have available, the more biased they should be in their investments. Parents with few resources ought to invest more in a single child, ignoring the others, giving at least that one child a decent chance at success. As resources become more abundant, more-egalitarian strategies are best, from the parental perspective. In other words, the degree to which parents divide current investment unequally among their children may be a function of the amount of resources available to them.

Benefits to Parents

Two factors that influence the benefits to parents of parental investment are the age of the child and the child's expected future prospects. In terms of the age of the child, we expect a greater fitness payoff from investing in older children. An individual's expected contribution to parental fitness is mainly in his or her reproductive value or expected future reproduction. This quantity increases with age until puberty, making an older, immature offspring more valuable from the parental perspective than a younger one (Montgomerie & Weatherhead 1988). This increase is due primarily to the degree of childhood mortality in developing societies. The average teenager has a higher reproductive value than the average infant because some infants do not survive to their teenage years. Surviving to puberty was more difficult over most of human evolutionary history, when rates of infant mortality were higher. But it is also true that, on average, the older a particular child gets, the less valuable parental investment, especially certain kinds of investment, will be in terms of the child's ability to use it when compared to its utility to other, younger children. A great deal of parental investment is critical to the survival and reproductive future of young children.

Parents respond to the changing needs and abilities of their children. Infants require more time, perhaps teenagers more money. But when times are very tough, and one child must be sacrificed so that others can be saved, it is a cross-cultural universal that the youngest is the likeliest victim (Daly & Wilson 1984). Studies of Canadian homicides also suggest a greater valuation of older children. Daly and Wilson (1988) have studied familial homicide for more than 20 years. When they examined the risk of homicide of a child by a genetic parent in relation to the child's age, infants were at a much higher risk of being killed than any other group of children. After 1 year of age, the rates drop dramatically until they reach close to zero at 17 years of age. Lest the reader supposes this is because it is easier to kill a baby than a teenager, consider this: The risk of a child being killed by a non-relative shows a rather different pattern, with 1 year olds more likely to be killed than infants, and teenagers the most likely to be killed.

A child's future prospects will also be expected to play a role in the benefit to parents of parental investment. The survival and reproductive success of the child are factors that define the benefit to parents. If it were unlikely that there would be a fitness return on investment, natural selection would be unlikely to favor mechanisms that direct investment toward such a child. Like age, the child's expected future prospects are related to his or her ability to convert parental investment into fitness. As a result, we expect parental solicitude to be sensitive to cues of child "quality" or ability to convert parental care into future reproductive success. For example, children who are disabled in some way, all else equal, are likely to have lesser future reproductive success than children who are healthy (Daly & Wilson 1984).

Poor infant quality affects parental investment. Children born with a severe physical deformity are more likely than non-deformed infants to be the victims of infanticide, especially in societies where institutional care of the disabled is not available (Daly & Wilson 1984, 1988). Hill and Ball (1996) examined the ethnographic literature for the reasons given cross-culturally for infanticide. Most involved abnormal circumstances surrounding the birth, but they noted that many of the characteristics were associated with conditions that increase infant or childhood morbidity. The increased level of care such children require for a lower evolutionary payoff (they are less likely to reproduce even if they do survive) means that parents are better off if they terminate investment early and begin to invest in a new child. Even in North America, children with physical disabilities are at greater risk of abuse and more likely to suffer injuries that require a hospital visit at the hands of their parents than are healthy children (Daly & Wilson 1984).

Abuse, neglect, and filicide are not the only phenomena that reveal the importance of a child's future prospects as predictors of parental investment. Trivers and Willard (1973) argued that when one sex has a greater variance in lifetime reproductive success than the other and when parents (particularly mothers) vary in their physical condition or access to resources in a way that influences children's success, differences in preferences for children of one or the other sex are likely to evolve. If male reproductive success depends on the individual's condition, mothers in good condition who are able to invest heavily will be able to influence the reproductive success of their sons more successfully than will mothers in poor condition. They should prefer to have sons, or to invest more in their sons than in their daughters (Bercovitch, Widdig, & Nurnberg 2000; Trivers & Willard 1973). Mothers in poor condition should prefer daughters because daughters are less of a reproductive risk (women have lower variance in reproductive success than do men). This is known as the Trivers–Willard effect, and it has been demonstrated in non-human species such as horses (Cameron & Linklater 2000) and other ungulates (Sheldon & West 2004).

In humans, several studies have demonstrated the Trivers–Willard effect (Gaulin & Robbins 1991, Hopcroft 2005, Kanazawa 2005), but others have found no evidence for sex-biased investment (Freese & Powell 1999; Keller, Nesse, & Hofferth 2001; Sieff 1990). Dickemann's (1979) review of infanticide in the Indian caste system reveals that infanticide was common in high-caste families before the 20th century. The victims were overwhelmingly female. The problem was that there were very few marriage options for high-caste daughters because they could marry only within their own caste, not into a lower one. For high-caste families, investment in sons (who could marry women from their own or lower castes) paid larger dividends in terms of grandchildren. As a result, parents biased their investment heavily toward boys (Gupta 1987). At the lower end of the social scale, the tendency for men to marry down meant daughters out-reproduced sons, and low-caste parents biased their investment toward daughters. This can be seen in a much lower rate of female infanticide among the lower castes. Studies in the United States (Gaulin & Robbins 1991) and Kenya (Cronk 1989) indicate that female infants from low-income families are nursed more than are infant boys.

Bereczkei and Dunbar's (1997, 2002) studies of Hungarian Gypsy populations are informative. When compared to native Hungarians, Gypsies have many more daughters than sons. Like the lower caste Indians, the Gypsies are low in social status. Gypsy women, like their low-caste Indian counterparts, are much more likely to marry up the social scale than are men, and typically out-reproduce their Gypsy brothers. In the process, they also tend to have healthier babies than do those Gypsy women who marry within their own group. Like the low-caste Indians, Gypsy parents invest more heavily in their daughters than in their sons. Bereczkei and Dunbar (1997) also found that compared to native Hungarians, Gypsy women spent more time nursing their firstborn daughters than nursing their sons, and provided more education for their daughters than for their sons (their education was not free and came at a significant cost to the parents).

But there are times when investment may favor sons over daughters. In societies where the possession of resources has a significant impact on male reproductive success (such as in India), a preference for sons, or for investing heavily in them, will be seen among the affluent. This was also the case in 18th-century northern German villages (Voland 1998) and has been noted in the records of probated wills among Canadians living in British Columbia (Smith, Kish, & Crawford 1987).

Relatedness

From a genetic perspective, the degree of relatedness will influence investment. Three factors that influence relatedness in a parent–child context are paternity certainty, stepparenting, and adoption.

Paternity certainty is one of several reasons women typically invest more in parenting than do men. From a genetic perspective, men should invest only if they are sure the child is their own. For human (and other mammalian) females with internal fertilization and gestation, maternity has never been in doubt. Men do not have that degree of certainty ("Momma's baby, Papa's maybe") and therefore should be alert to cues of paternity, tending to invest only when such cues are present. This is well documented in birds (Green 2002, Osorio-Beristain & Drummond 2001), and there are numerous studies that suggest that paternity uncertainty has an impact on human paternal investment. Daly and Wilson's (1982) study of the comments made by Canadian parents and grandparents after the birth of a child suggests that mothers and maternal grandparents make many more comments about paternal resemblance in the baby's face than about any maternal resemblance. Similar results were found in a Mexican replication of the Daly and Wilson study (Regalski & Gaulin 1993). Maternal kin seem to go out of their way to present the image of the baby as a little version of the father—especially if the "father" is around to hear these comments.

Stepparenting influences relatedness in that the stepparent is not genetically related to any of his or her stepchildren. In this case, paternity (or maternity) or the lack of it is clear, and we would predict that mechanisms that motivate the allocation of parental investment will be sensitive to whether or not a child is a person's genetic child, with the result that resources are directed away from stepchildren and toward genetic children. This can also cause conflict between parents over the allocation of resources. For example, a woman with children from both a previous union and a current union is equally related to all her children and might desire to allocate her investment equally, whereas her partner might desire to allocate resources preferentially toward the children that are the product of their union only and not her previous one (Hofferth & Anderson 2003). In turn, siblings who are stepsiblings are related through one parent, not two, and thus will be expected to value themselves even higher in relation to their stepsiblings than they do in relation to their genetic siblings, increasing the degree of conflict they experience over parental resources.

Daly and Wilson (1984, 1988, 2001) have spent many years studying the dynamics of discriminative parental solicitude, often focusing on stepparenting in humans. If we view parental care along a continuum, self-sacrifice might be found at one end (parents who sacrifice not only their own wants but in some cases their health and even their lives), whereas at the other end are acts that inflict costs on the child, including child neglect, abuse, and homicide. Inclusive fitness theory would suggest that genetic relatedness to a child is one predictor of the willingness to invest. The less genetically related the adult is to the child, the lower the likelihood of investment and the higher the risk of infanticide. Daly and Wilson tested this proposal in their study (Daly & Wilson 1988) of child abuse in Hamilton, Ontario. The results indicated that children living with one genetic parent and one stepparent are about 40 times more likely to be physically abused than are children living with both genetic parents. This occurs even when controlling for poverty and socioeconomic status. It is necessary to control for these because poverty and socioeconomic status are associated with higher rates of child abuse.

A similar pattern is seen in cases of children killed by a parent. The perpetration rates of infanticide are far higher for stepparents than for genetic parents, and the risk is highest for the very young, especially those under 2 years of age. Daly and Wilson (1988) found that the risk of a preschool-aged child being killed ranged from 40 to 100 times higher for stepchildren than for children living with two genetic parents. In many cases, it is not so much that the stepparent actively desires to kill the child but that he or she is not as careful or caring as a genetic parent might be, and so often the child dies from indifference or intolerance rather than specific enmity. And, of course, not all stepparents are dangerous to their stepchildren; many are very good and caring parents. But even many of those good stepparents report that their affection for their stepchildren is not as great as that for their own biological children (Ganong & Coleman 1986, Hobart 1988; 1989).

A less extreme example of discriminative parental solicitude involves the degree of investment, rather than the decision to maintain or terminate investment. Stepfathers invest fewer financial resources in their stepchildren than in their biological children. In a study of Albuquerque, New Mexico, men, Anderson, Kaplan, and Lancaster (1999) reported that genetic children were 5.5 times more likely to receive money for college than were stepchildren. In fact, genetic children received, on average, $15,500 more for college and had 65% more of their college expenses paid for than did stepchildren. Some researchers have also proposed that when stepparental investment is seen, it may reflect mating effort on the part of men (intended to make themselves more attractive to their new mate) rather than parental effort per se (Anderson et al. 1999; Hofferth & Anderson 2003; Rohwer, Herron, & Daly 1999).

Adoption also changes the degree of relatedness, and it can do so to varying degrees. The adoption of related children changes relatedness but does not eliminate it. When unrelated children are adopted, there is no genetic relatedness at all. With one's own children, relatedness is 0.5. The adoption of other genetically related kin (e.g., niece, cousin's child) would entail a lesser degree of relatedness, but there would still be some genetic common interest. As a result, we would expect a lesser degree of parental investment in adopted related children than in their own genetic children (Silk 1980). But from this perspective, we expect little to no parental investment in an unrelated adopted child because there is no genetic link. With stepparent situations, at least one parent is the genetic parent; in unrelated adoptive situations, there is no genetic parent present.

It seems unlikely, however, that the adoption of unrelated individuals has occurred with any significant frequency over most of our evolutionary history. Non-human primates, who often live in kin groups like humans do, tend not to adopt orphaned young (Silk 1990). In most species, especially in ones where parents come into contact with many young to whom they are not related, such as in colonially nesting birds (Medvin & Beecher 1986) or bats (McCracken 1993), parents recognize their own offspring. In species in which parents are solitary or their offspring tend to remain in the nest or den where they are born (e.g., some cliff-nesting birds) (Medvin, Stoddard, & Beecher 1993), parental recognition is less accurate (for example, a bird might feed any baby bird that was in its nest), and accidental adoptions occur, in which the adopted bird is treated as if it is the genetic offspring of the parent (Knudsen & Evans 1986, Medvin, Stoddard, & Beecher 1993).

The majority of information about historical accounts of human adoption and adoption practices in traditional societies has focused on the adoption of genetically related individuals. Individuals who cannot have their own genetic children sometimes adopt a sibling's child when that sibling has an excess of children (Pennington & Harpending 1993, Silk 1980, 1987).

Stack's (1974) study of an urban black community indicated that most of the fostered children were with their mother's genetic kin, typically older sisters, aunts, or grandmothers. There is no theoretical reason to expect a mechanism designed specifically to deal with the adoption of genetically unrelated individuals because the historical evidence suggests it rarely occurred. It may be that in our current human environment, strong parental and cultural desires lead some individuals to adopt unrelated children. Indeed, the relationship between adopted children and parents in the modern Western world typically functions in the same way as that between genetic parents and children, particularly when the adoption is of infants. In such cases, the majority of parent–child relations mimic those of a biological parent–child unit in that, other than childbirth and breastfeeding, the early care and rearing are similar to that of a biological child. It would be interesting to compare the bonding process for adoptive mothers and fathers. Is it easier for adoptive fathers because they have always had to learn that a child is their own than for mothers, who are missing the pregnancy and birthing that is part of the natural process? Greater levels of conflict are more often found when the child is adopted at an older age (Barth & Berry 1988, Stolley 1993). Such children may have suffered from abuse, neglect, and abandonment and have difficulty accepting or trusting their new parental figures. The new parents may also experience difficulty supporting and bonding to their new children; in some cases this is exacerbated by the special needs of some of these children (Groze 1986). More evolutionarily informed studies of the dynamics of adoption might help identify the factors that assist in easing or exacerbating the conflicts experienced in the adoption of unrelated children, such as resemblance, "quality" of the child, and so on.

CONCLUSIONS

Many aspects of the relationship between parent and child show remarkable consistency throughout history and between cultures. As a result, we expect psychological mechanisms to have evolved that are designed to manage these relationships, mechanisms that are sensitive to the many social and ecological variables that influence such relationships, including the various costs and benefits of investment from both parents' and children's perspectives. Although parent and child have shared genetic interests, they are not identical interests, and this fact can lead to various forms of conflict from maternal–fetal, to weaning, to conflicts over which child gets what, to conflicts over friends and sex. The better we understand the psychology behind such conflicts, the better able we will be to understand not only our own behavior but that of our children.

REFERENCES

Anderson, J. G., Kaplan, H. S., & Lancaster, J. B. (1999). Paternal care by genetic fathers and stepfathers I: Reports from Albuquerque men. *Evolution and Human Behaviour, 20,* 405–431.

Barth, R. P., & Berry, M. (1988). *Adoption and disruption: rates, risks, and responses.* Hawthorne, NY: Aldine de Gruyter.

Bercovitch, F. B., Widdig, A., & Nurnberg, P. (2000). Maternal investment in rhesus Macaques (*Macaca mulatto*): reproductive costs and consequences on raising sons. *Behavioral Ecology and Sociobiology, 48,* 1–11.

Bereczkei, T., & Dunbar, R. I. M. (1997). Female-biased reproductive strategies in a Hungarian Gypsy population. *Proceedings of the Royal Society, London, B, 264,* 17–22.

Bereczkei, T., & Dunbar, R. I. M. (2002). Helping-at-the-nest and sex-biased parental investment in a Hungarian Gypsy population. *Current Anthropology, 43,* 804–809.

Buchanan, T. A., Metzger, B. E., Freinkel, N., & Bergman, R.N. (1990). Insulin sensitivity and B-cell responsiveness to glucose during late pregnancy in lean and moderately obese women with normal glucose tolerance or mild gestational diabetes. *American Journal of Obstetrics and Gynecology, 162,* 1008–1014.

Cameron, E. Z., & Linklater, W. L. (2000). Individual mares bias investment in sons and daughters in relation to their condition. *Animal Behaviour, 60,* 359–367.

Carroll, J. (2002, March 12). Parent/teen relations: Where's the grief? *Gallup Tuesday Briefing.* Available from http://www.gallup.com.

Catalano, P. M., Tyzbir, E. D., Roman, N. M., Amini, S. B., & Sims, A. H. (1991). Longitudinal changes in insulin release and insulin resistance in nonobese pregnant women. *American Journal of Obstetrics and Gynecology, 165,* 1667–1672.

Clark, M. M., Moghaddas, M., & Galef, B. G., Jr., (2002). Age at first mating affects parental effort and fecundity of female Mongolian gerbils. *Animal Behaviour, 63,* 1129–1134.

Clutton-Brock, T. H. (1984). Reproductive effort and terminal investment in iteroparous animals. *American Naturalist, 123,* 25–35.

Cronk, L. (1989). Low socioeconomic status and female-based parental investment: The Mokogodo example. *American Anthropologist, 91,* 414–429.

Daly, M., & Wilson, M. (1982). Whom are newborn babies said to resemble? *Ethology and Sociobiology, 3,* 69–210.

Daly, M., & Wilson, M. (1984). A sociobiological analysis of human infanticide. In G. Hausfater & S. B. Hrdy (Eds.). *Infanticide: Comparative and evolutionary perspectives* (pp. 487–502). Hawthorne, NY: Aldine.

Daly, M., & Wilson, M. (1988). *Homicide.* Hawthorne, NY: Aldine.

Daly, M., & Wilson, M. (1995). Discriminative parental solicitude and the relevance Of evolutionary models to the analysis of motivational systems.

In M. Gazzaniga (Ed.), *The cognitive neurosciences* (pp. 1269–1286). Cambridge, MA: MIT Press.

Daly, M., & Wilson, M. (2001). An assessment of some proposed exceptions to the phenomenon of nepotistic discrimination against stepchildren. *Ann. Zool. Fennici, 38,* 287–296.

Davis, J. N. & Todd, P. M. (1999). Parental investment by decision rules. In G. Gigerenzer, P. M. Todd, & The ABC Research Group (Eds.). *Simple heuristics that make us smart* (pp. 309–324). New York: Oxford University Press.

Davis, J. N., Todd, P. M., & Bullock, S. (1999). Environment quality predicts parental provisioning decisions. *Proceedings of the Royal Society of London B, 266,* 1791–1797.

Dickemann, M. (1979). Female infanticide, reproductive strategies, and social stratification: a preliminary model. In N. A. Chagnon & W. Irons (Eds.). *Evolutionary biology and human social behavior* (pp. 321–367). North Scituate, MA: Duxbury Press.

Fisher, R. A. (1930). *The genetical theory of natural selection.* Oxford: Clarendon Press.

Freese, J., & Powell, B. (1999). Sociobiology, status, and parental investment in sons and daughters: Testing the Trivers–Willard Hypothesis. *American Journal of Sociology, 106,* 1704–1743.

Ganong, L. H., & Coleman, M. (1986). Stepchildren's perceptions of their parents. *Journal of Genetic Psychology, 148,* 5–17.

Gaulin, S. J. C., & Robbins, C. J. (1991). Trivers–Willard effect in contemporary North American society. *American Journal of Physical Anthropology, 85,* 61–69.

Green, D. J. (2002). Pair bond duration influences paternal provisioning and the primary sex ratio of brown thornbill broods. *Animal Behaviour, 64,* 791–800.

Groze, V. (1986). Special needs adoption. *Child and Youth Services Review, 8,* 363–373.

Gupta, D. (1987). Selective discrimination against female children in rural Punjab. *Population and Development Review, 13,* 77–100.

Haig, D. (1993) Genetic conflicts in human pregnancy. *The Quarterly Review of Biology, 68,* 495–532.

Haig, D. (1998). Genetic conflicts of pregnancy and childhood. In S. C. Stearns (Ed.), *Evolution in health and disease,* (pp. 77–90). Oxford: Oxford University Press.

Hill, C. M., & Ball, H. L. (1996). Abnormal births and other "ill omens": The adaptive case of infanticide. *Human Nature, 7,* 381–401.

Hobart, C. (1988). Perceptions of parent–child relationships in nuclear and remarried Families. *Family Relations, 37,* 175–182.

Hobart, C. (1989). Experiences of remarried families. *Journal of Divorce, 13,* 121–144.

Hofferth, S., & Anderson, K. G. (2003). Are all dads equal? Biology versus marriage as basis for paternal investment. *Journal of Marriage and Family, 65,* 213–232.

Hopcroft, R. L. (2005). Parental status and differential investment in sons and daughters: Trivers–Willard revisited. *Social Forces, 83,* 1111–1136.

Hrdy, S. B. (1999). *Mother nature: A history of mothers, infants and natural selection.* New York: Pantheon.

Kanazawa, S. (2005). Big and Tall Parents Have More Sons: Further Generalizations of the Trivers-Willard Hypothesis. *Journal of Theoretical Biology.* 235, 583–590.

Keller, M. C., Nesse, R. M., & Hofferth, S. (2001). The Trivers–Willard hypothesis of parental investment: No effect in the contemporary United States. *Evolution and Human Behavior, 22,* 343–366.

Kennedy, G. E. (1989) Middleborns' perceptions of family relationships. *Psychological Reports, 64,* 755–760.

Knudsen, B., & Evans, R. M. (1986). Parent–young recognition in herring gulls (*Larus argentatus*). *Animal Behaviour, 34,* 77–80.

Lee, B. J., & George, R. M. (1999). Poverty, early childbearing and child maltreatment: A multinomial analysis. *Children and Youth Services Review, 21,* 755–780.

Lind, T., & Aspillaga, M. (1988). Metabolic changes during normal and diabetic pregnancy. In E. A. Reece & D. R. Coustan (Eds.), *Diabetes mellitus in* pregnancy: Principles and practice (pp. 75–102). New York: Churchill Livingstone.

McCracken, G. F. (1993). Locational memory and female-pup reunions in Mexican free-tailed bat maternity colonies. Animal Behaviour, 45, 811–813.

Medvin, M. B., & Beecher, M. D. (1986). Parent–offspring recognition in the barn swallow (*Hirundo rustica*). *Animal Behaviour, 34,* 1627–1639.

Medvin, M. B., Stoddard, P. K., & Beecher, M. D. (1993). Signals for parent–offspring recognition: A comparative analysis of the begging calls of cliff swallows and barn swallows. *Animal Behaviour, 45,* 841–850.

Montgomerie, R. D., & Weatherhead, P. J. (1988). Risks and rewards of nest defense by parent birds. *Quarterly Review of Biology, 63,* 167–187.

Naeye, R. L. (1981). Maternal blood pressure and fetal growth. *American Journal of Obstetrics and Gynecology, 141,* 780–787.

Ng, P. H., & Walters, W. A. W. (1992). The effects of chronic maternal hypertension during pregnancy. *Australian and New Zealand Journal of Obstetrics and Gynecology, 32,* 14–16.

Osorio-Beristain, M., & Drummond, H. (2001). Male boobies expel eggs when paternity is in doubt. *Behavioral Ecology, 12,* 16–21.

Overpeck, M. D., Brenner, R. A., Trumble, A. C., Trifiletti, L. B., & Berendes, H. W. (1998). Risk factors for infant homicide in the United States. *New England Journal of Medicine, 339,* 1211–1216.

Pennington, R., & Harpending, H. (1993). *The structure of an African pastoralist community: Demography, history, and ecology of the Ngamiland Herero.* Oxford: Oxford University Press.

Pugesek, B. H. (1995). Offspring growth in the California gull: Reproductive effort and Parental experience hypotheses. *Animal Behavior, 49,* 641–647.

Regalski, J. M., & Gaulin, S. J. C. (1993). Whom are Mexican infants said to resemble? Monitoring and fostering paternal confidence in the Yucatan. *Ethology and Sociobiology, 14,* 97–113.

Rohwer, S., Herron, J. C., & Daly, M. (1999). Stepparental behavior as mating effort in birds and other animals. *Evolution and Human Behavior, 20,* 367–390.

Salafia, C. M., Xenophon, J., Vintzileos, A. M., Lerer, T., & Silberman, L. (1990). Fetal growth and placental pathology in maternal hypertensive diseases. *Clinical and Experimental Hypertension, 9,* 27–41.

Salmon, C. A., & Daly, M. (1998). Birth order and familial sentiment: Middleborns are different. *Evolution and Human Behavior, 19,* 299–312.

Sheldon, B. C., & West, S. A. (2004). Maternal dominance, maternal condition, and offspring sex in ungulate mammals. *American Naturalist, 163,* 40–54.

Sieff, D. F. (1990). Explaining biased gender ratios in human populations. *Current Anthropology, 31,* 25–48.

Silk, J. B. (1980). Adoption and kinship in Oceania. *American Anthropologist, 82,* 799–820.

Silk, J. B. (1987). Adoption among the Inuit. *Ethos, 15,* 320–330.

Silk, J. B. (1990). Which humans adopt adaptively and why does it matter? *Ethology and Sociobiology, 11,* 425–426.

Smith, M. S., Kish, B. J., & Crawford, C. B. (1987). Inheritance of wealth and human kin investment. *Ethology and Sociobiology, 8,* 171–182.

Stack, C. B. (1974). *All our kin.* New York: Harper & Row.

Steinberg, L., & Morris, A.S. (2001). Adolescent development. *Annual Review of Psychology, 52,* 83–110.

Stolley, K. S. (1993). Statistics on adoption in the United States. *The Future of Children: Adoption, 3,* 26–42.

Symonds, E. M. (1980). Aetiology of pre-eclampsia: A review. *Journal of the Royal Society of Medicine, 73,* 871–875.

Tallarigo, L., Giampietro, O., Penno, G., Miccoli, R., Gregori, G., & Navalesi, R. (1986). Relation of glucose tolerance to complications of pregnancy in nondiabetic women. *New England Journal of Medicine, 316,* 1343–1346.

Trivers, R. L. (1974). Parent–offspring conflict. *American Zoologist, 14,* 249–264.

Trivers, R. L., & Willard, D. (1973). Natural selection of parental ability to vary the Sex-ratio of offspring. *Science, 179,* 90–92.

Voland, E. (1998). Evolutionary ecology of human reproduction. *Annual Review of Anthropology, 27,* 347–374.

Voland, E., & Gabler, S. (1994). Differential twin mortality indicates a correlation between age and parental effort in humans. *Naturwissenschaften, 81,* 224–225.

8 Birth Order

Frank J. Sulloway

Sibling competition is a common occurrence in the animal world and occasionally ends in siblicide. Birth order often affects the outcome of such struggles because it is a proxy for differences in age, size, power, and access to scarce resources. Among humans, ordinal position is associated with disparities in parental investment, which can lead to differences in behavior, health, and mortality. In addition, siblings in our own species typically occupy disparate niches within the family system and, in mutual competition, generally use different tactics based on age, size, and sex. These alternative strategies and life experiences have effects on personality and also foster differences in attitudes, motivations, and sentiments about the family.

Birth order has long been an important factor in certain social customs and life experiences. These include choice of professions, opportunities for reproduction, emigration decisions, inheritance practices, and rules of royal succession. Ordinal position has also played a role in some social and political transformations. Although a substantial literature has documented a wide variety of birth order effects in health, intellectual performance, and behavior, the magnitude of these effects, and the nature of the domains in which they express themselves, remain sources of scholarly contention. Within the family, the role of birth order appears to be considerable in the expression of personality, social attitudes, and family sentiments. By contrast, in nonfamilial contexts, these effects are more muted. Moreover, the expression of birth-order effects is often dependent, outside the family milieu, on whether or not certain attitudes and sentiments about the family are tapped in ways that make them salient.

SOURCES OF SIBLING COMPETITION

On average, siblings with the same parents share half their genes. As a consequence, most siblings are twice as related to themselves as they are to one another. Based on this genetic insight, William Hamilton (1964a, 1964b) realized that siblings should compete for scarce resources whenever the gain from doing so is more than half the cost to another sibling. From this cost–benefit perspective, sibling competition and parent–child competition are opposite sides of the same biological coin. Whereas siblings, on average, are only half related to one another, they are fully related to themselves. Parents, however, are equally related to all their biological children. Because of these disparities in biological relatedness, parents will sometimes invest in future children at the expense of current children, a decision that the current children will generally resist.

Weaning conflicts provide a good example of such disputes (Trivers 1974), as do intrauterine conflicts between mother and fetus (Haig 1993). Several life-threatening disorders of pregnancy, including gestational diabetes and preeclampsia, arise as a result of the fetus's efforts to increase the blood supply to the placenta at the expense of the optimal physical condition of the mother. A related set of findings is associated with genetic imprinting (Haig 2004). It is generally in the interests of paternal genes to maximize the mother's contribution to offspring because the mother's future offspring may not be by the same father. Depending on whether or not they are inherited from the mother or the father, the genes that control fetal growth and development may express themselves differently. For example, some paternal genes promote greater fetal size, whereas the same genes, when inherited from the mother, counteract this tendency.

Sibling competition has long been documented among insects, fish, amphibians, birds, and animals (Mock 2004, Mock & Parker 1997). Even plants sometimes exhibit sibling competition. The Indian black plum (*Syzygium cuminii*) produces multiple seeds from the same fruit, which are all botanical siblings. The first of these seeds to be fertilized secretes a "death chemical" that destroys its sibling rivals (Krishnamurthy, Shaanker, & Ganeshaiah 1997). Sibling competition is especially common among birds of prey and among seabirds, and often leads to siblicide. Typically the victim is the youngest member of the brood. Parents make no effort to intervene in such instances, as it is not in their genetic interests to do so.

In some species, particularly birds of prey, siblicide is obligate, meaning that it occurs independently of environmental conditions. In other species, siblicide is facultative, meaning that its occurrence depends on the abundance of food resources available to parents. Among blue-footed boobies (*Sula nebouxii*), siblicide occurs only when the body weight of the elder chick drops to 80% of normal (Drummond & García-Chevelas 1989). In times of plenty, blue-footed boobies are able to successfully fledge as many as three chicks.

Some passerine bird species regulate parental investment and sibling competition by hormonal means. Female canaries (*Serinus canaria*) lace each successive egg with greater amounts of testosterone. This hormone accelerates neural development and also makes the younger chicks more pugnacious, increasing their ability to compete successfully with their older nest mates (Schwabl 1996; Schwabl, Mock, & Gieg 1997). Depending on the presence of parasitic mites in the nest, female house finches (*Carpodacus mexicanus*) regulate the birth order of their chicks by sex (Badyaev, Hamstra, Oh, & Acevedo Seaman 2006). Male chicks suffer greater mortality from nest mites than do female chicks. In response to mite infestations, breeding females shield their male offspring from parasitism by laying male eggs later than female eggs. Greater allocation of maternal steroids to male eggs accelerates development within the egg, which further reduces exposure to nest mites by allowing males to fledge sooner.

SOCIAL AND ECONOMIC ASPECTS

Like the offspring of other primates, children are heavily dependent on parental investment. For this reason, parental decisions about how to allocate resources among children play an important role in human development. Before the 19th century, childhood illnesses killed half of all children. Parental discrimination by sex and by birth order often determined who lived and who died (Boone 1986; Voland 1988, 1990).

Having survived the most serious illnesses of infancy and early childhood, older children were generally better Darwinian prospects for transmitting their own, and their parents', genes to the next generation. Accordingly, in the premodern period, parents appear to have systematically favored eldest children. As an example, infanticide is widely practiced in traditional societies, but it is invariably the newborn that is killed, not an older infant who is close in age (Daly & Wilson 1988). In non-Western societies, anthropologists have noted that firstborns are generally favored over their younger siblings in a variety of ways—for example, by being given more elaborate birth ceremonies, and by having authority over their siblings in adulthood (Rosenblatt & Skoogberg 1974). Firstborns are also more likely than laterborns to receive the same name as a parent, a practice that is associated with greater parental investment (MacAndrew, King, & Honoroff 2002).

Inheritance customs and practices are sometimes influenced by birth order. Several different systems have been observed. These include primogeniture (leaving all parental property to the firstborn or to the eldest male), secundogeniture (leaving everything to the secondborn or to the second son), and ultimogeniture (leaving everything to the lastborn or to the youngest son). Local economic and geographical circumstances generally dictate which practice is followed (Hrdy & Judge 1993). For example, primogeniture is frequently practiced when land is a limited resource. By leaving everything to the eldest child or son, parents avoid subdividing the family estate. Ultimogeniture is typically practiced when death taxes represent a heavy burden on estates. Leaving everything to the youngest child or son maximizes the interval before successive taxations. An equal inheritance of parental property has generally been favored in environments where risk taking and skill are associated with economic success. In Renaissance Venice, where fortunes were favored by ability in speculative commerce, parents typically divided their states equally among their children, increasing the chances that multiple children would succeed and that the family name would be perpetuated (Herlihy 1977).

Parental investment according to ordinal position has long been a factor in the professional opportunities and marriage prospects that were available to offspring. Among the nobility in medieval Portugal, birth order had "a catastrophic effect" on the probability of marriage (Boone 1986, p. 869). Compared with their younger siblings, firstborns were nearly four times more likely to marry and to leave children of their own. Because they were frequently unable to marry, laterborns were significantly more likely to have children out of wedlock. Given that landless younger sons represented a threat to political stability, they were systematically sent to faraway lands, such as India, where they participated in military campaigns and often died in battle or from diseases. Some historians have argued that the Crusades were in part a response to the constant political threat posed by these landless younger sons (Duby 1977).

SIBLING DIFFERENCES

Despite the fact that siblings typically share half their genes, parents are frequently struck by how different their children actually are. Studies of twins raised together and apart have shown that about 40% of the variance in personality is genetic in origin, about 35% is explained by the nonshared environment, and only about 5% is attributable to the environment that siblings share as they are growing up within the same family. The remaining 20% of the variance in personality test scores is attributable to errors of measurement (Loehlin 1992, Plomin & Daniels 1987).

These findings have led some commentators to argue that the family has little influence on children (Harris 1998, Pinker 2002). This conclusion, however, is something of an exaggeration and also fails to appreciate the true nature of family dynamics. To begin with, measurement errors cause a systematic underestimation of the role of the shared family environment. In addition, the role of the family environment is much larger, statistically, than most people realize based on estimates of influence couched as "variance explained." For technical reasons that have to do with the squaring of numbers less than 1.0 to obtain "variance" statistics, small amounts of variance generally represent much more substantial effects than most people realize (Rosenthal & Rosnow 1991, Rosnow & Rosenthal 2003). For example, one of the largest known sources of individual differences in personality is gender, which on average explains 2% of the variance in specific personality traits (Feingold 1994, Hyde 2005). In a medical context, 2% of the variance is equivalent to a drug that increases the odds of surviving a deadly disease by 76%—hardly a negligible effect. New drugs designed to cure potentially fatal illnesses are generally considered newsworthy when they explain just 1% of the variance in treatment outcomes. (A drug that explains 1% of the variance in treatment outcomes is equivalent to a 22% increase in the cure rate and a 49% increase in the odds of being cured.) One of the great triumphs of modern medicine—the Salk vaccine for polio—accounts for only 1/10th of 1% of the variance in post-vaccination outcomes, or about 1/50th of the variance that is associated with the shared family environment and its effects on personality. Expressed in these terms, the shared family environment appears to play a reasonably important role in personality development. By explaining as much as 5% of the variance in personality, this influence is equivalent to a child's having twice the likelihood of being in the top half of the population distribution on a given personality trait—such as being self-disciplined—compared with a child who has not been exposed to the same shared family influence.

The big surprise from behavioral genetics research is the substantial role played by the nonshared environment, which is seven times more influential than the shared environment. One response to these unexpected findings has been to conclude that personality is primarily shaped by peer groups, outside the family of origin (Harris 1998). Although Harris, following Rowe (1994), is fully justified in highlighting the importance of nonshared experiences in personality development, this viewpoint has led to the misleading conclusion that the family itself is relatively unimportant in this process. The family, however, is substantially a nonshared environment, and the bulk of its influence is therefore specific to each child. For example, the same event, such as the death of a grandparent or other family member, occurs when siblings are of different ages and hence is experienced somewhat dissimilarly. Likewise, because offspring are genetically different, they often react disparately to the same behavioral responses from other family members. When such differences in behavior are manifested by parents, children are particularly sensitive to them (Dunn & Plomin 1990). Seen from this perspective, the most important conclusion from research in behavioral genetics is not that the family exerts little influence on personality but rather that it does so in a considerably different manner than was previously thought, namely, through the nonshared family environment. Expressed in another way, families exert their greatest influence by making children different, not similar.

PSYCHOLOGICAL MECHANISMS

Birth order is one influence among many that helps explain the effects of the nonshared family environment. At least five separate processes are associated with birth order within a family dynamics model: (1) differences in parental investment; (2) sibling dominance hierarchies; (3) niche specialization; (4) deidentification, or the tendency for siblings to strive to be different from one another; and (5) sibling stereotypes.

Parental Investment

Typically, differences in parental investment cause quadratic or U-shaped distributions in resources, with middleborns receiving fewer resources than firstborns or lastborns. Such U-shaped distributions result in part from what has been termed the "equity heuristic" and its counterintuitive consequences (Hertwig, Davis, & Sulloway 2002). The equity heuristic is a variant of resource-dilution theories and refers to the tendency for parents, in modern societies where resources are relatively abundant, to treat their children equally. Unlike middleborns, firstborns and lastborns experience a period in which they are the only children living at home. As a consequence, the cumulative investment they receive from parents is greater than that allotted to middleborns, who generally obtain an equal share of resources divided among all the children who are present within the home. When a particular parental resource is allocated in childhood, such as financial resources for vaccinations, the equity heuristic predicts linear birth order trends in which firstborns are favored over their younger siblings. This is because younger children cannot equalize the acquisition of such resources at a later age, when older siblings have finally left the home, given that these resources are no longer developmentally relevant.

In contrast to middleborns, lastborns benefit from another tendency in parental investment. As mothers reach the end of the reproductive careers, youngest children increasingly become the last child they will ever bear. Under such circumstances, it is adaptive for parents to invest greater resources in youngest children, especially during the vulnerable stages of infancy and early childhood, because these offspring cannot be replaced (Rohde et al. 2003, Salmon & Daly 1998). The tendency for parents to favor lastborns augments the typical U-shaped distributions that result from parents' allocating resources according to the equity heuristic. In short, the only way for parents to be truly equitable to offspring on a cumulative basis is for them to systematically favor middleborns—something that other offspring would not readily tolerate.

A variety of studies underscore these theoretical perspectives on birth order and parental investment. In one noteworthy study, Lindert (1977) tracked the total number of childcare hours devoted by parents to their children up to the age of 18. In families with two or more children, middleborns typically received 10% less childcare than did firstborns or lastborns. In a study of 1,903 children living in the Philippines, Horton (1988) found that laterborns received less nourishment than firstborns, as assessed by children's height and weight. Other studies have shown that the likelihood of being vaccinated declines by 20–30% with each successive child within the family (Hertwig et al. 2002). Such differences in nourishment and healthcare appear to be directly related to mortality. In a study of 14,192 Swedish children, third- and fourthborns were 2.1 times more likely than firstborns to die before the age of 10 (Modin 2002).

Sibling Dominance Hierarchies

Siblings create dominance hierarchies based on age, size, and power. Both physically and verbally, firstborns can easily intimidate their younger brothers and sisters. As a result, they usually exert dominance over their siblings. Several aspects of personality and behavior, as expressed within the family, reflect these differences in position within sibling dominance hierarchies (see below, under Behavior and Personality).

Family Niches

Sibling differences arise in part because of the different roles that children adopt within the family system. These differing roles are fostered by genetic disparities, and also by differences in sex and birth order. The resulting diversification of family roles exemplifies Darwin's (1859) famous "principle of divergence." As with competing species in nature, role specialization among children leads to a division of labor and reduces competition. Specialization also makes it harder for parents to compare the abilities of one child against those of another (which generally benefits younger and less-experienced offspring). Darwin's principle of divergence is one of the most important principles of evolutionary biology; it explains the phenomenon of "adaptive radiation" among closely related species, as with his famous Galápagos finches (Grant 1999; Kleindorfer, Chapman, Winkler, & Sulloway 2006). Ordinal position within the family is directly relevant to this process of sibling diversification because birth rank is inextricably linked with age and hence with opportunities for children to engage in age-specific tasks. Because of their greater age, for example, first-borns tend to occupy the niche of a surrogate parent, leading them to develop a sense of parent-like responsibility and to emulate other adult behaviors.

Deidentification

Siblings often strive to differentiate themselves from one another, a process that has been called "deidentification" (Schachter, Gilutz, Shore, & Adler 1978). This process extends to patterns of identification with, and attachment to, parents. If one child prefers one parent, for example, another child will often identify more closely with the other parent (Rohde et al. 2003, Schachter 1982). Such patterns of deidentification are expected to produce zigzag trends because each child seeks to maximize the process of differentiation from his or her closest siblings in age (Skinner 1992).

Birth-order Stereotypes

Stereotypes associated with ordinal position appear to reinforce, and perhaps to foster, some of the behavioral differences observed among siblings. Stereotypes generally build upon real differences that are widely observed and culturally sanctioned. Such stereotypes are well documented in the literature on birth order (Baskett 1985, Musun-Miller 1993, Nyman 1995). It is generally believed, for example, that firstborns tend to be more intellectually oriented than their younger siblings, are more conscientious in their work habits and studies, and attain higher levels of professional status in life. These stereotypes correspond closely with observed differences by birth order (Herrera, Zajonc, Wieczorkowska, & Cichomski 2003).

BEHAVIOR AND PERSONALITY

More than 2,000 publications have dealt with birth order and its effects on human behavior and intellectual performance. Unfortunately, most of these studies are not controlled for differences in important background influences, such as social class and family size. As Ernst and Angst (1983) have noted, lower-class families are biased for large sibships. Hence, a study that is not controlled for social class or sibship size and that reports a birth-order difference for some attribute may simply have detected a spurious cross-correlation with socioeconomic or other background factors. Nevertheless, when well-controlled studies are examined and subjected to meta-analysis—a technique for amalgamating study results to reduce statistical error—modest but consistent trends do emerge in birth-order research (Sulloway 1995, 2000, 2002b).

Personality, and much of human behavior more generally, can be usefully classified in terms of five dimensions—often called the "Big Five" (Costa & McCrae 1992, McCrae & John 1992). Within this five-factor model of personality, the salient dimensions are conscientiousness, agreeableness, extraversion, openness to experience, and neuroticism. When assessed in terms of these five dimensions, the cumulative research on birth order and personality is reasonably consistent with predictions based on a family-dynamics model.

In within-family studies (which need to be distinguished methodologically from between-family studies), firstborns generally score higher in most aspects of conscientiousness. Firstborns are rated by both parents and siblings as being more self-disciplined, organized, and deliberate than their younger brothers and sisters. They are also considered the "achievers" of the family (Healey & Ellis, 2007; Paulhus, Trapnell, & Chen 1999; Plowman 2005; Sulloway 1996, 1999, 2001). These consistent findings strongly suggest that firstborns experience a different family environment than do laterborns. For example, firstborns often occupy the role of a surrogate parent, a family niche that tends to ingratiate them with parents as the "responsible" child. Owing to their relative immaturity, laterborns are generally unsuited for the role of a surrogate parent and must seek parental favor by other means—for instance, through athletic ability or by developing other latent abilities.

Again, in within-family studies, laterborns score higher than firstborns on most aspects of agreeableness (Paulhus et al. 1999; Sulloway 1999, 2001). Firstborns can readily avail themselves of greater physical size to achieve dominance over their younger siblings. By contrast, laterborns tend to employ low-power strategies to obtain what they want. These strategies include pleading, bargaining, and, when all else fails, appealing to parents for protection and assistance. The unusual status of middleborns—sandwiched as they are between firstborns, who have greater status and physical power, and lastborns, who are protected by parents—may explain why middleborns are typically rated higher than their siblings on most measures of agreeableness.

On the Big Five dimensions of extraversion, there are distinctly hetero-geneous results by birth order (Sulloway 2001). Firstborns are rated as being more dominant and assertive than laterborns. By contrast, laterborns are rated as being more fun-loving, affectionate, and drawn to risk taking and excitement. More often than their elder siblings, laterborns also seem to use humor as a strategy and sometimes cultivate the role of family comedian.

The attributes of openness to experience, like those of extraversion, exhibit a high degree of heterogeneity, or diversity, in within-family studies. First-borns score higher on those measures of this personality dimension that tap intelligence and intellectual orientation. Laterborns score higher on those measures that tap imagination, attraction to novelty, and rejection of tradi-tion. When asked in one study to list various "unconventional" aspects of their lives, laterborns offered significantly more examples of such behaviors and interests, as evaluated by two independent judges (Sulloway 2001). Sim-ilarly, Paulhus et al. (1999) found that laterborns were twice as likely as first-borns to describe themselves as "the rebel" of the family. Rohde et al. (2003) obtained a nearly identical odds ratio (1.8:1) in another within-family study that included samples from Israel, Norway, Russia, and Spain. In a study involving participants from Australia, Healey and Ellis (2007) found that laterborns were more "rebellious," "nonconformist," and "open to experience" ($r = .19$, which translates to an odds ratio of 1.8 to 1).

Differences in neuroticism by ordinal position tend to be small. This is expected because many neurotic traits do not appear to be adaptive in the context of a family-dynamics model of personality, and most birth-order dif-ferences are expected to serve adaptive functions, either in mutual sibling competition or in optimizing parental investment. One consistent finding, however, is noteworthy: laterborns—particularly middle children—display lower self-esteem than other siblings (Kidwell 1982). This finding may relate to observed birth-order differences in parental investment.

Most birth-order effects appear to be environmental in origin. This con-clusion follows from the fact that there are no genes for being a firstborn or a laterborn. Nevertheless, the intrauterine environment is known to foster at least one birth-order difference. Among brothers, later birth order is cor-related with an increased tendency toward homosexuality (Blanchard 2004). This well-replicated finding is consistent with the hypothesis that, during pregnancy, some mothers develop antibodies to antigens of the male-specific histocompatibility complex. These antibodies appear to interfere with the masculinization of successive fetuses, causing laterborns to exhibit a 33% increase in homosexuality for each older brother present in the family.

In assessing birth-order differences in human behavior, it is important to distinguish between functional and biological birth order. A large gap in age between a firstborn and an immediately younger sibling can create functional "only children" of both siblings. Only children need to be distinguished psychologically from children of other birth orders. They represent a controlled experiment in birth-order research because they experience childhood without the effects of either sibling rivalry or sibling dominance hierarchies. For this reason, only children tend to be intermediate between firstborns and laterborns on most aspects of personality. Because they have no siblings and tend to identify closely with their parents, only children do resemble firstborns in attributes that are related to conscientiousness, including the attainment of high levels of intellectual achievement. Some of the distinguishing features of only children, such as greater educational attainment, also relate to the economic benefits of growing up in small families.

Because age spacing mediates the effects of birth order, these effects vary considerably in their degree of expression. In general, an age gap of 2 to 4 years produces the largest birth-order effects. In a carefully designed study that controlled for social class, sibship size, and other variables, Helen Koch (1955, 1956) documented numerous moderating effects on personality and intellectual performance that were related to age separation, sex, and sex of sibling. These effects, which often involved two- and three-way interactions, underscore some of the ways in which the family environment is not shared by siblings.

CRITICAL METHODOLOGICAL ISSUES

Birth-order differences in personality and behavior are most prevalent in studies in which parents evaluate their own children, or siblings rate one another (Ernst & Angst 1983; Healey & Ellis, 2007; Paulhus et al. 1999; Sulloway 1999, 2001, 2002b). In this class of studies, birth order explains 1–2% of the variance in individual dimensions of the five-factor model of personality.

Within-family studies of birth order and personality may overestimate effect sizes for some traits and behaviors. For example, within-family studies appear to involve "contrast effects" or a tendency for parents and children to magnify true differences in rendering such comparisons (Saudino 1997). For some attributes, within-family studies may also confuse differences in personality with differences in family roles. Firstborns, for example, may be rated as being more "conscientious" than their younger siblings because the role of a surrogate parent generally falls to them, together with the behavioral attributes that go with this "responsible" role.

A particularly important question involves the manifestation of birth-order effects outside the family. When subjects taking standard personality tests are asked to rate themselves without reference to a sibling, birth-order effects are usually small and often not significant (Ernst &

Angst 1983; Harris 1998; Jefferson, Herbst, & McCrae 1998; Parker 1998). Such findings may be contrasted, however, with the modest but consistent differences by birth order that are obtained when spouses and roommates evaluate one another, and also the differences found in studies involving real-life behaviors as opposed to self-ratings of personality (Sulloway 2001, 2002b). In these types of studies, birth-order effects are about one-third to one-half the magnitude typically reported in within-family studies. Even more noteworthy is the fact that birth-order effects documented in extrafamilial studies correlate strongly (r = .65) with effects for the same traits reported using direct sibling comparisons. This meta-analytic finding suggests a high degree of continuity in behavior, even if the magnitude of such effects is generally reduced in nonfamilial settings.

A few examples of such consistent behavioral continuity may be cited here. Firstborns are typically overrepresented on standard measures of social and intellectual achievement, such as being world leaders, being listed in *Who's Who*, and receiving prestigious awards for their scientific or literary accomplishments (Altus 1966, Clark & Rice 1982, Sulloway 1996). In adulthood, firstborns also score slightly higher than laterborns on standard intelligence tests—IQ declines about 1 point with each successive birth rank in the family (Belmont & Marolla 1973). These differences in intellectual performance appear to reflect a dilution of parental resources associated with increased family size. As new children are added to the family, parents have less time and financial resources to devote to each child. In addition, each successive newborn dilutes the family's average intellectual environment, causing a reduction in IQ among children raised in large families (Zajonc 1976, Zajonc & Mullally 1997).

Differences in intellectual performance by birth order do not always show up in carefully designed studies involving siblings from the same family. These null findings have led some researchers to dismiss the importance of birth order (Wichman, Rodgers, & MacCallum 2006). Such null results, however, are generally confined to studies of young children, before the developmental effects of birth order have fully manifested themselves. According to Zajonc's (1976) "confluence model" of intellectual performance, when children are at the same age, laterborns actually experience a richer intellectual environment than do their elder siblings because the presence of elder siblings helps enrich that environment. Firstborns, however, steadily benefit from being able to teach what they know to younger siblings and from aspiring to fulfill parental expectations, such as doing well at school. The net result of these contrasting influences is that firstborns begin to score higher than their younger siblings by the time they reach adolescence (Zajonc & Sulloway in press).

Another behavioral domain in which birth-order effects have been documented in nonfamilial studies involves risk taking and excitement seeking, which are closely related to the Big Five dimension of extraversion. In one well-designed study of Columbia University students (N = 1,967), laterborns were 1.6 times more likely than firstborns to participate in dangerous sports such as rugby, football, and soccer (Nisbett 1968). These findings may also reflect a tendency for laterborns to avoid athletic competition with accomplished older siblings who had already adopted safer sports such as swimming, tennis, and basketball.

Birth-order differences in risk taking have been documented in several other behavioral domains. In a historical study of scientists and explorers, Sulloway (1996) found that laterborns were significantly more likely than firstborns to travel to remote parts of the globe, where they ran a greater risk of dying from accidents or contracting life-threatening diseases. Such was the fate of Alfred Russel Wallace, who codiscovered the theory of natural selection while recovering from a malarial fit in faraway Malaysia. Charles Darwin risked death several times during the *Beagle* voyage. He may also have acquired a debilitating parasitic disease during his 5-year voyage around the world.

In the course of history, laterborns have generally been more likely than firstborns to challenge the status quo (Sulloway 1996). During the Protestant Reformation, younger siblings were more supportive than their elder siblings of calls for church reforms, including the abolition of celibacy among priests and nuns. This particular policy directly benefited younger siblings, who were systematically shunted into the clergy under the reigning system of primogeniture and hence were less likely to marry and have children of their own (Boone 1986). Leading Protestants also proclaimed the principle of primogeniture to be "unchristian" and urged political rulers to let their sons share in royal succession through partible inheritance of principalities.

Throughout Western history, many political revolutions have been championed by younger siblings, including such political leaders as Georges-Jacques Danton, Vladimir Lenin, Leon Trotsky, Fidel Castro, and Ho Chi Minh (Boone 1986; Sulloway 1996, 2000, 2002a). There is also evidence that middleborn revolutionaries differ from other political radicals in preferring nonviolent means of political transformation, which accords with within-family findings about birth-order differences in agreeableness. During the French Revolution, for example, middleborn deputies to the National Convention were more likely than their colleagues to oppose the extreme measures that led to the Reign of Terror.

Within the field of science, radical revolutions have generally been led and supported by laterborns (Sulloway 1996, 2000; Numbers 1998).

"Radical" revolutions may be defined as those having important religious or political implications, engendering widespread public debate outside the scientific community, and/or taking many years to resolve. The most notable leaders of radical scientific revolutions have included Nicholas Copernicus (the youngest of four children), Francis Bacon (the youngest of eight), René Descartes (the youngest of three), Charles Darwin and Alfred Russel Wallace (both the fifth of six), and Werner Heisenberg (the middle of three).

Firstborn scientists have also led a variety of important conceptual revolutions. These particular scientific transformations have tended to be more technical and less ideologically charged than the kinds of radical revolutions endorsed by laterborn scientists such as Copernicus and Darwin. Famous firstborn revolutionaries include Johannes Kepler, Galileo, William Harvey, Isaac Newton, Antoine Lavoisier, Charles Lyell, and Albert Einstein. Many firstborn revolutionaries have benefited from other influences that are known to promote openness to experience. Compared with firstborn scientists who have opposed new scientific ideas, those firstborns who have led revolutions have tended to be significantly younger, to be more socially liberal, and to have experienced higher levels of conflict with one or both parents. Independently of birth order, these three influences are substantial predictors of support for radical revolutions.

Although the role of birth order in radical revolutions may have drawn some of its strength from the prior practice of primogeniture, contemporary evidence has confirmed historical findings. In a study of middle-aged Canadian subjects, Salmon and Daly (1998) asked: "Do you think that you are open to new and radical ideas (such as cold fusion)?" Controlled for age, sex, and sibship size, laterborns were 2.3 times more likely than firstborns to claim that they would be open to such novel ideas. In a study that was controlled for sibship size, Zweigenhaft and Von Ammon (2000) found that laterborns were 2.2 times more likely than firstborns to undergo multiple arrests at a strike for better working conditions at a Kmart in Greensboro, North Carolina.

In contrast to these supporting studies, Freese, Powell, and Steelman (1999) analyzed social and political attitudes among subjects included in the General Social Survey. They found only 3 significant differences out of 33 measures. In addition, all 3 findings were opposite to the direction predicted. In spite of such inconsistent findings, a meta-analysis of 20 studies of social attitudes that are controlled for sibship size (at a minimum) reveals a modest but consistent trend for laterborns to endorse the liberal or radical alternative ($r = .09$, $N = 11,240$). It is also noteworthy that when these 20 studies were independently rated on a scale of personal and emotional involvement, the reported effect sizes were significantly larger for studies that entailed a high degree of involvement, such as real-life episodes of conflict, as opposed to responses on paper-and-pencil tests (Sulloway 2001).

SITUATION-SPECIFIC BEHAVIOR

Although much of personality is consistent from one situation to another, a substantial part of human behavior is sensitive to behavioral contexts and hence is consistent only within the same contexts (Cervone & Shoda 1999). The collective literature on birth order and human behavior accords with this situational perspective: such differences express themselves in their fullest form only when situations trigger responses that draw on patterns of behavior learned within the family.

Only a few studies have specifically sought to test the role of situation-specific tendencies as they relate to birth order. One example is provided by Salmon (1998), who played an electronically recorded campaign speech to 112 university students. In an effort to evoke latent family sentiments, Salmon created one version of the speech containing political appeals to "brothers," "sisters," and "brethren." A second version of the speech replaced these family-related references with appeals to "friends." Salmon predicted that firstborns and lastborns, who typically receive greater parental investment, would prefer the political speech containing family-related language, whereas middleborns were expected to favor the version containing references to friends. These predictions were confirmed. In another study, Salmon and Daly (1998) found that middleborns were significantly underrepresented in a sample of 236 adult genealogical researchers. In addition, these two researchers found that middleborns were less likely than other children to name a parent as the person to whom they were closest, and were less likely to seek comfort from a parent during times of emotional upset. These findings have been replicated by Rohde et al. (2003).

Such studies strongly suggest that birth-order effects indeed manifest themselves outside the family milieu when the behavioral context provides a direct tie with latent familial sentiments or patterns of identification. In this connection, it would be helpful to know more about childhood preferences for certain family niches and how these preferences influence the roles people adopt as adults within the new families they create for themselves. We also need to know more about the specific psychological processes that are involved when behaviors learned within the family express themselves in other nonfamilial contexts. Recent research on the relational nature of the self, together with social–cognitive models of transference, may help fill this gap (Chen, Boucher, & Tapias 2006).

EVOLUTIONARY ASPECTS OF FAMILY DYNAMICS

Ordinal position is just one influence among many that contributes to family dynamics and its influence on human development. In attempting to elucidate the multiple sources of the nonshared family environment, behavioral scientists continue to face a considerable challenge. Given the substantial role played by genetic factors, behavioral genetics models have become an important methodological tool in studies of human development. Such models, however, do not directly analyze the nonshared environment. Rather, they infer its influence from the statistical variance that remains unexplained after assessing the influence of shared genes and shared environments. A major challenge for the future is to begin to disentangle the relative contribution of the nonshared family environment from the overall nonshared environment (McGuire 2001; Plomin, Asbury, & Dunn 2001; Turkheimer 2004; Turkheimer & Waldron 2000). Given the amount of time that children spend interacting with their parents and siblings, it would not be surprising if a substantial portion of the variance in behavior that is attributable to the nonshared environment owes its origins to within-family differences. A reasonable estimate is that the family may explain a third to a half of this variance, or about 12 to 18% of the overall variance in human personality. Combined with the influence of the shared family environment, which explains another 5% of the variance, an effect of this magnitude would be at least eight times greater than that represented by gender differences. It would also be equivalent to an influence that, at a minimum, quadruples one's likelihood of developing a particular personality trait.

From a Darwinian perspective on human behavior, it should come as no surprise that behavioral dispositions first acquired within the family are expressed only conditionally in adulthood. Human behavior and personality exemplify a host of cumulative adaptations to life as it is experienced within, and later beyond, the family of origin. Over the millennia, natural selection has fine-tuned such context-sensitive responses to the adaptive problems people face. As adults, we do not treat strangers or friends in the same way that we treat family members. Strategies for getting along with other family members that we originally learned as children provide a behavioral toolkit that we continually modify and update as we interact with other people over our lifespan. We draw from this evolving toolkit as needed but only when specific behavioral responses are appropriate to the situation.

In spite of the many questions that remain about the role of birth order and family dynamics in human development, one general conclusion bears special emphasis. The origins of personality, social attitudes, and behavior— and their evolving expressions in the course of human development—are more complex than most researchers believed just a few decades ago. Individual influences, such as birth order and gender, appear to play more restrictive roles than was once thought, and the roles they do play are more nuanced. Nevertheless, within this revised and increasingly interactionist perspective on human development, an evolutionary approach continues to identify birth order and sibling competition as fruitful subjects for future research.

References

Altus, W. D. (1966). Birth order and its sequelae. *Science, 151,* 44–49.

Badyaev, A., Hamstra, T. L., Oh, K. P., & Acevedo Seaman, D. A. (2006). Sex-biased maternal effects reduce ectoparasite-induced mortality in a passerine bird. *Proceedings of the National Academy of Sciences, 103,* 14,406–14,411.

Baskett, L. M. (1985). Sibling status: Adult expectations. *Developmental Psychology, 21,* 441–45.

Belmont, L., & Marolla, F. A. (1973). Birth order, family size, and intelligence. *Science, 182,* 1096–1101.

Blanchard, R. (2004). Quantitative and theoretical analyses of the relation between older brothers and homosexuality in men. *Journal of Theoretical Biology, 230,* 173–187.

Boone, J. L. (1986). Parental investment and elite family structure in preindustrial states: A case study of late medieval-early modern Portuguese genealogies. *American Anthropologist, 88,* 859–878.

Cervone, D., & Shoda, Y. (1999). *The coherence of personality: Social–cognitive bases of consistency, variability, and organization.* New York: Guilford.

Chen, S., Boucher, H. C., and Tapias, M. P. (2006). The relational self revealed: Integrative conceptualization and implications for interpersonal life. *Psychological Bulletin, 132,* 151–179.

Clark, R. D., & Rice, G. A. (1982). Family constellations and eminence: The birth orders of Nobel Prize winners. *The Journal of Psychology, 110,* 281–287.

Costa, P. T., Jr., & McCrae, R. R. (1992). *NEO PI–R professional manual.* Odessa, FL.: Psychological Assessment Resources.

Daly, M., & Wilson, M. (1988). *Homicide.* Hawthorne, NY: Aldine de Gruyter.

Darwin, C. R. (1859). *On the origin of species by means of natural selection.* London: John Murray.

Drummond, H., & García-Chevelas, C. (1989). Food shortage influences sibling aggression in the blue-footed booby. *Animal Behavior, 37,* 806–818.

Duby, G. (1977). *The chivalrous society* (Cynthia Poston, Trans.). Berkeley: University of California Press.

Dunn, J., & Plomin, R. (1990). *Separate lives: Why siblings are so different.* New York: Basic Books.

Ernst, C., and Angst, J. (1983). *Birth order: Its influence on personality.* New York: Springer-Verlag.

Feingold, A. (1994). Gender differences in personality: A meta-analysis. *Psychological Bulletin, 116,* 429–456.

Freese, J., Powell, B., and Steelman, L. C. (1999). Rebel without a cause or effect: Birth order and social attitudes. *American Sociological Review, 64,* 207–231.

Grant, P. R. (1999). *Ecology and evolution of Darwin's finches.* Princeton, NJ: Princeton University Press.

Haig, D. (1993). Genetic conflicts in human pregnancy. *Quarterly Review of Biology, 68,* 495–532.

Haig, D. (2004). Genomic imprinting and kinship: How good is the evidence? *Annual Review of Genetics, 38,* 553–585.

Hamilton, W. (1964a). The genetical evolution of social behavior. I. *Journal of Theoretical Biology, 7,* 1–16.

Hamilton, W. (1964b). The genetical evolution of social behavior. II. *Journal of Theoretical Biology, 7,* 17–32.

Harris, J. R. (1998). *The nurture assumption: Why children turn out the way they do.* New York: Free Press.

Healey, M. D., & Ellis, B. J. (2007). Birth order, conscientiousness, and openness to experience: Tests of the family-niche model of personality using a within-family methodology. *Evolution and Human Behavior,* 28, 55–59.

Herlihy, D. (1977). Family and property in Renaissance Florence. In D. Herlihy & A. L. Udovitch (Eds.), *The Medieval City* (pp. 3–24). New Haven, CT: Yale University Press.

Herrera, N., Zajonc, R. B., Wieczorkowska, G., & Cichomski, B. (2003). Beliefs about birth rank and their reflections in reality. *Journal of Personality and Social Psychology, 85,* 142–150.

Hertwig, R., Davis, J., & Sulloway, F. J. (2002). Parental investment: How an equity motive can produce inequality. *Psychological Bulletin, 128,* 728–745.

Horton, S. (1988). Birth order and child nutritional status: Evidence from the Philippines. *Economic Development and Cultural Change, 36,* 341–354.

Hrdy, S.B., & Judge, D. (1993). Darwin and the puzzle of primogeniture. *Human Nature,* 4, 1-45.

Hyde, J. S. (2005). The gender similarities hypothesis. *American Psychologist,* 60, 581–592.

Jefferson, T., J., Herbst, J. H. &, McCrae, R. R. (1998). Associations between birth order and personality traits: Evidence from self-reports and observer ratings. *Journal of Research on Personality, 32,* 498–508.

Kidwell, J. S. (1982). The neglected birth order: Middleborns. *Journal of Marriage and the Family, 44,* 225–235.

Kleindorfer, S., Chapman, T. W., Winkler, H., & Sulloway, F. J. (2006). Adaptive divergence in continuous populations of Darwin's Small Ground Finch (*Geospiza fuliginosa*). *Evolutionary Ecology Research, 8,* 357–372.

Koch, H. (1955). Some personality correlates of sex, sibling position, and sex of sibling among five- and six-year-old children. *Genetic Psychology Monographs, 52,* 3–50.

Koch, H. (1956). Attitudes of young children toward their peers as related to certain characteristics of their siblings. *Psychological Monographs, 70,* 1–41.

Krishnamurthy, K. S., Shaanker, R. U., & Ganeshaiah, K. N. (1997). Seed abortion in an animal dispersed species, *Syzygium cuminii* (L.) Skeels (Myrtaceae): The chemical basis. *Current Science, 73,* 869–873.

Lindert, P. H. (1977). Sibling position and achievement. *The Journal of Human Resources, 12,* 198–219.

Loehlin, John C. (1992). *Genes and environment in personality development.* Newbury Park, CA: Sage Publications.

MacAndrew, F. T., King, J. C., & Honoroff, L. R. (2002). A sociobiological analysis of namesaking patterns in 322 American families. *Journal of Applied Social Psychology, 32,* 851–864.

McCrae, R. R., & John, O. P. (1992). An introduction to the five-factor model and its applications. *Journal of Personality, 60,* 175–215.

McGuire, S. (2001). Nonshared environment research: What is it and where is it going? *Marriage & Family Review, 33,* 31–56.

Mock, D. W. (2004). *More than kin and less than kind: The evolution of family conflict.* Cambridge, MA: Harvard University Press.

Mock, D. W., & Parker, G. A. (1997). *The evolution of sibling rivalry.* Oxford, England: Oxford University Press.

Modin, B. (2002). Birth order and mortality: A life-long follow-up of 14,200 boys and girls born in early 20th century Sweden. *Social Science & Medicine, 54,* 1051–1064.

Musun-Miller, L. (1993). Sibling status effects: Parents' perceptions of their own children. *The Journal of Genetic Psychology, 154,* 189–198.

Nisbett, R. E. (1968). Birth order and participation in dangerous sports. *Journal of Personality and Social Psychology, 8,* 351–353.

Numbers, R. L. (1998). *Darwinism comes to America.* Cambridge, MA: Harvard University Press.

Nyman, L. (1995). The identification of birth order personality attributes. *The Journal of Psychology, 129,* 51–59.

Parker, W. D. (1998). Birth order effects in the academically talented. *Gifted Child Quarterly, 42,* 29–36.

Paulhus, D. L., Trapnell, P. D., & Chen, D. (1999). Birth order and personality within families. *Psychological Science, 10,* 482–488.

Pinker, S. (2002). *The blank slate: The modern denial of human nature.* New York: Viking.

Plomin, R., Asbury, K., & Dunn, J. (2001). Why are children in the same family so different? Nonshared environment a decade later. *Canadian Journal of Psychiatry, 46,* 225–233.

Plomin, R., & Daniels, D. (1987). Why are children in the same family so different from one another? *Behavioral and Brain Sciences, 10,* 1–60.

Plowman, I. C. (2005). *Birth-order, motives, occupational role choice and organizational innovation: An evolutionary perspective.* Unpublished doctoral dissertation, University of Queensland, Australia.

Rohde, P. A., Atzwanger, K., Butovskaya, M., Lampert, A., Mysterud, I., Sanchez-Andres, A., & Sulloway, F. J. (2003). Perceived parental favoritism, closeness to kin, and the rebel of the family: The effects of birth order and sex. *Evolution and Human Behavior, 24,* 261–276.

Rosenblatt, P. C., & Skoogberg, E. L. (1974). Birth order in cross-cultural perspective. *Developmental Psychology, 10,* 48–54.

Rosenthal, R., & Rosnow, R. (1991). *Essentials of behavioral research: Methods and data analysis* (2nd ed.). New York: McGraw Hill.

Rosnow, R. L., & Rosenthal, R. (2003). Effect sizes for experimenting psychologists. *Canadian Journal of Experimental Psychology, 57,* 221–237.

Rowe, D. C. (1994). *The limits of family influence: Genes, experience, and behavior.* New York: Guildford Press.

Salmon, C. A. (1998). The evocative nature of kin terminology in political rhetoric. *Politics and the Life Sciences, 17,* 51–57.

Salmon, C. A., & Daly, M. (1998). Birth order and familial sentiment: Middleborns are different. *Human Behavior and Evolution, 19,* 299–312.

Saudino, K. J. (1997). Moving beyond the heritability question: New directions in behavioral genetic studies of personality. *Current Directions in Psychological Science, 6,* 86–90.

Schachter, F. F. (1982). Sibling deidentification and split-parent identifications: A family tetrad. In M. E. Lamb & B. Sutton-Smith (Eds.), *Sibling relationships: Their nature and significance across the lifespan* (pp. 123–152). Hillsdale, NJ: Lawrence Erlbaum.

Schachter, F. F., Gilutz, G., Shore, E., & Adler, M. (1978). Sibling deidentification judged by mothers: Cross-validation and developmental studies. *Child Development, 49,* 543–546.

Schwabl, H. (1996). Environment modifies the testosterone levels of a female bird and its eggs. *Journal of Experimental Zoology, 276,* 157–163.

Schwabl, H., Mock, D. W., & Gieg, J. A. (1997). A hormonal mechanism for parental favouritism. *Nature, 386,* 231.

Skinner, G. W. (1992). Seek a loyal subject in a filial son: Family roots of political orientation in Chinese society. In *Family process and political process in modern Chinese history* (pp. 943–993). Taipei, Republic of China: Chiang Ching-kuo Foundation for International Scholarly Exchange.

Sulloway, F. J. (1995). Birth order and evolutionary psychology: A meta-analytic overview. *Psychological Inquiry, 6,* 75–80.

Sulloway, F. J. (1996). *Born to rebel: Birth order, family dynamics, and creative lives*. New York: Pantheon.

Sulloway, F. J. (1999). Birth order. In Mark A. Runco & Steven Pritzker (Eds.), *Encyclopedia of Creativity* (Vol. 1, pp. 189–202). San Diego: Academic Press.

Sulloway, F. J. (2000). "Born to rebel" and its critics. *Politics and the Life Sciences, 19*, 181–202.

Sulloway, F. J. (2001). Birth order, sibling competition, and human behavior. In H. R. Holcomb III (Ed.), *Conceptual challenges in evolutionary psychology: Innovative research strategies* (pp. 39–83). Boston: Kluwer Academic Publishers.

Sulloway, F. J. (2002a). *Biographical data on political activists*. Retrieved October 1, 2006 from http://www.sulloway.org/politics.html.

Sulloway, F. J. (2002b). *Technical report on a vote-counting meta-analysis of the birth-order literature (1940–1999)*. Retrieved October 1, 2006 from http://www.sulloway.org/metaanalysis.html.

Trivers, R. L. (1974). Parent–offspring conflict. *American Zoologist, 14*, 249–264.

Turkheimer, E. (2004). Spinach and ice cream: Why social science is so difficult. In L. F. DiLalla (Ed.), *Behavior genetics principles: Perspectives in development, personality, and psychopathology* (pp. 161–189). Washington, DC: American Psychological Association.

Turkheimer, E., & Waldron, M. (2000). Nonshared environment: A theoretical, methodological, and quantitative review. *Psychological Bulletin, 126*, 78–108.

Voland, E. (1988). Differential infant and child mortality in evolutionary perspective: Data from the late 17th to 19th century Ostfriesland (Germany). In L. Betzig, M. Bergerhoff Mulder, & P. Turke (Eds.), *Human reproduction behaviour: A Darwinian perspective* (pp. 253–262). Cambridge, England: Cambridge University Press.

Voland, E. (1990). Differential reproductive success within the Krummhorn population (Germany, 18th and 19th centuries). *Behavioral Ecology and Sociobiology, 26*, 54–72.

Wichman, A. L., Rodgers, J. L., & MacCallum, R. C. (2006). A multilevel approach to the relationship between birth order and intelligence. *Personality and Social Psychology Bulletin, 32*, 117–127.

Zajonc, R. B. (1976). Family configuration and intelligence. *Science, 192*, 227–236.

Zajonc, R. B., & Mullally, P. R. (1997). Birth order: Reconciling conflicting effects. *American Psychologist, 52*, 685–699.

Zajonc, R. B., & Sulloway, F. J. (in press). The confluence model: Birth order as a within-family or between-family dynamic? *Personality and Social Psychology Bulletin*.

Zweigenhaft, R. L., & Von Ammon, J. (2000). Birth order and civil disobedience: A test of Sulloway's "born to rebel" hypothesis. *Journal of Social Psychology, 140*, 624–627.

PART III

Other Family Relationships

9 Evolutionary Perspectives on Sibling Relationships

Richard L. Michalski and Harald A. Euler

The sibships into which we are born are crucial
social environments, with associated opportunities,
costs and "niches," and it would be remarkable if
our evolved social psyches did not contain features
adapted to the peculiarities of sibling relationship.
Martin Daly, Catherine Salmon, & Margo Wilson
(1997, p. 276)

OVERVIEW

The quote above highlights crisply the focus of this chapter. Sibling relationships are unique. They are the longest lasting human social relationship,
and exceed, on average, the length of relationships with parents, mates, and
children. Reports of sibling relationships and, in particular, their potential for
strife and fratricide are features of mythology (e.g., Dardanus) and of biblical
accounts (e.g., Cain and Abel). These tales suggest that sibling relationships
have been the fodder of disputes and gossip throughout written history and
probably throughout human evolutionary history. Sibling relationships gal-
vanize our interests when used to explain why our personalities have been

shaped as they have been. Many humans delight in the disclosure of the sibling status of potential mates and friends who seem to then "know" them better based on features of the sibling relationship such as the sex composition of sibships and their birth order. The powerful underlying evolved psychological mechanisms activated in the contexts of sibling relationships are revealed in the attempts often made by parents to foster closeness between their children. Parents often attempt to groom young children for the arrival of a younger sibling. Consumer evidence of these manipulative parental mechanisms is revealed in the books available to parents to educate them on aiding their oldest child's adjustment to the arrival of a younger sibling. There are also children's books available that can be used to suit the fitness interests of parents by enticing children into the role of helpful, older siblings who are not jealous over the investment demands of newborns (Sears, Sears, & Kelly 2001). Put simply, these books would have no market if it were not for the evolved psychological mechanisms triggered in the minds of children that attempt to counteract the diversion of parental resources to siblings. As we will discuss in this chapter, the most powerful guidance available to unmask this psychology is offered by evolutionary theories, including inclusive fitness theory (Hamilton 1964), parental-investment theory (Trivers 1972), and parent–offspring conflict theory (Trivers 1974).

Sibling relationships differ according to types of siblings, namely full siblings, half-siblings, stepsiblings, adoptive siblings, fictive siblings, or siblings-in-law. Full siblings are two individuals who share the same two biological parents. Half-siblings are two individuals who share only one biological parent. Stepsiblings share no biological parent but are linked as a result of the marriage of the biological parent of one child to the biological parent of their other child. Adoptive siblings are two individuals, one or both of whom are legally adopted by two parents. Fictive siblings are two individuals who are genetically unrelated but who are given the status of siblings. Siblings-in-law are labels for relationships between individuals who, by virtue of the establishment of long-term pair bonds to one of the categories of siblings listed above, are considered siblings. Siblings-in-law have different distinctions across cultures, but these categories, broadly defined, can be the spouse of one's sibling, the sibling of one's spouse, or the spouse of one's spouse's sibling.

The literature on sibling relationships is fairly disjointed, with little emphasis placed on integrating these separate areas of research. Typical areas of study on sibling relationships include sibling relationships in childhood, sibling relationships in adulthood, studies on differences between siblings, sibling violence and abuse, and altruism toward siblings, to name just a few. Few researchers operate within an overarching framework from which to understand the nature of various sibling relationships and how these relationships change across the lifespan. We propose that more earnest attempts need to be made to incorporate explicit evolutionary accounts of sibling relationships to propel future research in the area of sibling relationships in an integrated way. Research that does purport to use an integrated, overarching framework (e.g., family systems theory), we believe, falls short in its attempts to understand *why* unique features of the sibling relationship exist. Relatively recent writings on sibling relationships often fail to mention evolution or to highlight any of the research done by evolutionary psychologists on the topic of sibling relationships (see, for example, Cicirelli 1995). In short, the most revealing research on the nature of sibling relationships has yet to be done because the most powerful tool available to social scientists has not been fully brought to bear on the topic—Darwin's theory of evolution by natural selection.

A BRIEF PRIMER ON EVOLUTIONARY PSYCHOLOGY

Researchers guided by an evolutionary perspective are unified in their belief that the psychological mechanisms have evolved via processes of natural selection and sexual selection (Darwin 1859, 1871). Selection produces evolved psychological mechanisms that function to take in relatively narrow slices of environmental input and generate output correlated with reproductive and survival success in ancestral environments. The behavioral expression of modern humans represents the interaction of modern environmental input with evolved psychological mechanisms. This interaction between environments and evolved psychological mechanisms has spurred researchers working from an evolutionary perspective to examine the impact of siblings on various psychological outputs.

Siblings, having been recurrent features of ancestral social environments, may have posed adaptive problems that led to the development of psychological mechanisms that counteract the adaptive problems posed by siblings. We propose (1) that sibling relationships may contribute to the development of certain classes of psychological mechanisms, including, for example, personality and sexual strategies, (2) that sibling relationships may have forged specific, evolved psychological mechanisms triggered only by the presence of siblings, and (3) that the activation of these evolved psychological mechanisms are unique to specific adaptive problems confronted at certain points throughout development. There were several influential theories that equipped evolutionary scientists with the tools necessary to begin to tackle the study of sibling relationships.

Hamilton's (1964) inclusive fitness theory is one of these influential theories. Inclusive fitness theory states that natural selection favored not only those traits that promoted individual survival or reproductive success but also those traits that increased the chances that other related family members, who share copies of genes, would reach reproductive age and produce children. Not all ancestral humans, however, shared the same assurance of relatedness to other family members. Ancestral women could place their long-term partners at risk of investing resources in a rival's offspring by cuckolding their long-term partners. Inclusive fitness theory also sheds light on the interconnectedness of parental psychology and sibling psychology. Siblings also benefited from greater paternity certainty by virtue of fitness advantages accrued through investments in siblings with whom more-certain genetic relatedness were shared. We find that, as the study of parental psychology progresses, these insights illuminate features of sibling relationships that were darkened prior to this research.

Parental-investment theory was another influential theory that led to a deeper appreciation of parental investment as limited and partitionable (Trivers 1972). For nearly a century after the original publication of Darwin's theory of sexual selection, the focus was placed on biological sex as the driving force behind sexual selection. Parental-investment theory forced evolutionary biologists and, later, evolutionary psychologists to reformulate the impact of biological sex on sexual selection. Trivers's theory proposes that it is not biological sex that drives sexual selection but differences in the *minimum* obligatory parental investment. Parental investment is defined as any investment that a parent makes in its offspring that increases that offspring's chances of survival at the expense of the parent's ability to invest in additional or future offspring. Parental investment in one sibling therefore forecloses investment in other siblings.

Among humans, women make the larger investment in their offspring compared to men (see Hrdy, this volume). Female sex cells are larger and metabolically more costly than male sex cells to produce. Additionally, fertilization occurs within females. As a result, women bear the costs of gestating offspring for about nine months, going through the process and historical risks of childbirth, and nursing an offspring for several years. A man's minimum obligatory investment can end with the act of sexual intercourse. Because the costs associated with parental investment are not isomorphic between the sexes, a suite of psychological mechanisms are proposed to exist in women that are not expected to exist in men. Following impregnation, a woman's reproductive opportunities are more constrained by the investment that must be made during pregnancy. A man's reproductive opportunities are not constrained in similar fashion, making a man's reproductive potential considerably larger than the woman's reproductive potential.

Cross-culturally, men invest substantially less than women in their offspring (see Geary, this volume). Even in cultures with relatively high paternal investment, maternal investment dwarfs the investments made by fathers. This asymmetry between the sexes sets the stage for a host of potential, evolved psychological mechanisms to deal with social dilemmas posed by other family members—including siblings.

In sexually reproducing species, parents and their offspring are genetically related, on average, by 50%. Offspring, in contrast, are 100 percent related to themselves. This difference resulted in selection pressures on offspring and on parents in ancestral environments over the allocation of parental resources. This insight was developed in parent–offspring conflict theory (Trivers 1974; see Salmon, this volume). Parent–offspring conflict theory predicts that offspring covet more resources from parents than parents are willing to give. A key prediction of this theory is that parents will encourage offspring to value their siblings more than siblings will be inclined to value each other. Siblings are primary competitors over parental resources, and mechanisms have been selected in offspring that increase investment in themselves relative to their siblings. This leads to clear implications for the literature on birth order (see Sulloway, this volume). Birth order, a proxy for age, size, and status differences between siblings, may be predictably related to advantages that siblings have in securing resources from parents. First-borns, being older and larger than their laterborn siblings early in life, may have been in a better position to compete for access to resources. This is the theoretical engine behind much of the evolutionarily informed research on differences between siblings based on birth order.

COMPETITIVENESS

Siblings are each other's main competitors over parental resources. The ways in which siblings compete with each other over those resources are beginning to be unveiled. One method by which children attempt to distort parental perceptions of need was identified by Dunn and Kenrick (1982), who report that older siblings often "regress" to earlier developmental stages upon the birth of a younger sibling. This tactic of regressing may have functioned in ancestral environments as a way in which children, who have a more impoverished arsenal of competitive tactics, signal to parents their need for a greater proportion of parental resources. Children also may "compete" with siblings who have not yet been conceived as a means of staving off the introduction of a competitor over parental resources. For example, future research may reveal psychological tactics in children that result in reduced maternal or paternal sexual interests.

Siblings are competitors over parental resources throughout their lives and upon the death of one or both parents. Although speculative, younger siblings may stand to gain more parental resources when an older, perhaps parentally favored, sibling dies. This may be particularly true for men. Because men's reproductive variance is greater than women's, selection has created in men psychological adaptations that create more-intense competitions with others over access to resources that men can translate into reproductive opportunities. The inclination of men to enter into competition, especially with other men, is evident in childhood and is so pervasive that it also appears early in life as competition with siblings.

Siblings may have evolved psychological adaptations that function to channel investment in them at the expense of their siblings. Siblings also may have psychological adaptations that function to channel parental resources toward their children at the expense of their sibling's children (see Euler & Michalski, this volume). Parents may attempt to cultivate grandparent–grandchild relationships for their children in a way that they do not for their nieces and nephews. Within the parental psychological arsenal of tactics of resource extraction may be attempts to present their parents with pictures of grandchildren, attempts to get the grandchildren to spend more time with their grandparents, and attempts to "talk up" the accomplishments of their children. Although this hypothesis has, to our knowledge, never been tested, mothers *and* fathers may be more likely to attempt to get their children to spend time with the most investing grandparent (the maternal grandmother). To date, there exists no study that has examined the ways in which parents attempt to distort the attitudes of their parents and their children in ways that foster grandparental investment. It is possible as well that grief intensity over the death of a grandparent acts as a gauge of relational closeness and as a manifestation of sibling competition. If grief is more intense among closer individuals, then grief may signal to others (siblings) the deservingness of grandparental resources after their death. In this way, future researchers may examine grief over the loss of a loved one as one strategy for extracting a larger portion of the deceased's resources. We eagerly await these future studies.

SIBLING CONFLICTS: FULL SIBLINGS, STEPSIBLINGS, AND HALF-SIBLINGS

Research on how sibling relationships vary as a function of genetic relatedness has not been central. We expect mechanisms that easily distinguish categories of siblings, like those listed in the beginning of the chapter, to exist in the minds of humans. Additionally, we expect mechanisms to exist that subtly distinguish full siblings based on signals of genetic relatedness between them. Full siblings are *putative* full siblings, and psychological mechanisms may ignite conflict with siblings under certain circumstances when triggered by cues of less-certain genetic relationships between them. Female infidelity may have placed children at risk of investing in half-siblings instead of full siblings. We expect selection to have crafted, in the minds of humans, psychological mechanisms that help identify kin based on characteristics that may signal a genetic relationship. In siblings, these psychological adaptations may become activated based on actual or perceived psychological similarity, actual or perceived physical similarity, parental attempts to manipulate perceptions of psychological or physical similarity, presence of the same putative father, and/or features of maternal behavior to which siblings may be sensitive (e.g., favoritism).

A particularly powerful study on the ability of human sibling psychology to trump cultural attempts to obliterate siblings' preferences was made by Jankowiak and Diderich (2000). These researchers examined sibling solidarity among full and half-siblings in a Mormon fundamentalist polygamous community in the western United States. Based on the ideology of this religious group, siblings are not differentiated along full sibling and half-sibling lines and are consequently instructed to not differentiate between these two types of siblings. The logic of inclusive fitness theory predicts that sibling solidarity will be strongly crafted by the genetic relationship between two individuals, with full siblings expressing more solidarity to each other than will be expressed between half-siblings. But, despite ideological claims to the contrary, more solidarity was expressed with full siblings than with half-siblings, as shown in monetary gifts, requests to babysit, feelings of closeness, favoritism, and attendance at birthday and wedding celebrations.

Using a sample of several hundred young adults, we examined whether the conflict reported between full siblings, half-siblings, and stepsiblings changes over time. We collected reports from several hundred young adults on conflict they experienced with their sibling while they were growing up and the current conflict they experience with their siblings. Results from these analyses reveal a main effect of sibling type, with siblings reporting the most conflict with their full siblings with whom they are in the most direct competition over parental resources. We also found a significant interaction between sibling type and time. For both full siblings and half siblings, there are more reports of sibling conflict while they were growing up relative to current conflict. In contrast, reports of conflict with stepsiblings did not decrease from childhood to young adulthood. These findings highlight future directions for research on sibling conflicts throughout the lifespan. Elucidating the types of sibling conflicts that change over the lifespan presents an additional area in which to focus future work.

There seems to exist no inventory to assess the types of conflict that siblings experienced while they were growing up. Although it was possible in the above study to identify overall trends in conflict, the kinds of conflicts that riddle sibling relationships could not be identified. To follow up on this study, we asked college students to list acts of aggression their siblings had made against them while growing up. This study resulted in the development of an inventory (Michalski & Shackelford 2007). Aggressive tactics ranged from verbal insults and destruction of property to threats of death and actual physical violence. The kind of sibling aggression differed between girls and boys, with siblings being more likely to insult a sister's features of physical attractiveness (e.g., calling a sibling fat) and siblings more likely to insult a brother's intelligence (e.g., calling a sibling stupid)—features linked to sex-specific, reproductively relevant characteristics. Participants indicated they were insulted by claims they were unrelated to the family (e.g., telling a sibling he or she was adopted). Apparently, a popular tactic includes derogating a sibling by saying he or she has no genetic relationship with others "in the family." This tactic would emerge only if siblings were sensitive to the extent to which they are related to others in the family because of the consequences of *not* being related to kin in ancestral environments. Another tactic that emerged was to claim that a sibling did not look like a father (Daly & Wilson 1982). Not one participant mentioned the tactic of claiming that a sibling did not look like the mother. The prospect of a more-detailed picture of the impact of an evolutionary history of sibling relationships on competitiveness and the conflict that emerges from this competitiveness seems bright. Although childhood conflict often is reflected in pleasant memories shared by adult siblings, for others, these conflicts can become lethal.

SIBLICIDE

Siblicide—the killing of one sibling by another—is rare relative to other types of homicide. Underwood and Patch (1999) report that, of 65,390 total homicides coded in the Supplementary Homicide Reports (SHRs) of the Federal Bureau of Investigation (FBI) for the years 1993 through 1995, only 572 (0.9%) were cases in which the offender and victim were siblings. But despite this rarity, violence between siblings is the most frequent form of intra-familial non-lethal violence (Wiehe 1997). The study of siblicide, we believe, can provide insight into sibling relationships and non-lethal sibling conflict.

An evolutionary perspective has been applied to the study of homicide (Daly & Wilson 1988), and to siblicide, in particular (Daly, Wilson, Salmon, Hiraiwa-Hasegawa, & Hasegawa 2001; Russell, Michalski, Shackelford, & Weekes-Shackelford 2007; Sulloway 1996). Daly et al. found that older siblings are more likely to kill younger siblings earlier in life and that younger siblings are more likely to kill older siblings later in life. Previous research on siblicide from an evolutionary perspective failed to differentiate siblicides perpetrated against siblings of varying genetic relationships. Genetic relatedness may be an important moderator of conflict and homicide among family members, including siblings (Daly & Wilson 1988, Daly et al. 2001, Russell et al. 2007).

Russell et al. (2007) conducted the first investigation of siblicide as a function of the genetic relatedness between the victim and the offender. Using the Chicago Homicide Database (CHD) for the years 1965 through 1994, the researchers found that a greater proportion of siblicides of full siblings were single-victim siblicides, relative to the proportion of siblicides of half-siblings and stepsiblings. Russell et al. also found that a greater proportion of siblicides of half-siblings and stepsiblings were perpetrated through beatings, relative to the proportion of siblicides of full siblings. The patterns of results were as predicted but did not reach statistical significance owing, perhaps, to small sample sizes.

As an extension of Russell et al. (2007), Michalski, Russell, Shackelford, and Weekes-Shackelford (2007) examined siblicides perpetrated by siblings-in-law to yield data distinguishing full, genetic siblings from unrelated siblings in a historical homicide database from Chicago spanning the years 1870 to 1930. Siblings may be less likely to kill a full sibling, for example, because the evolutionary "fitness" costs associated with the death of a full sibling, with whom the perpetrator shares 50% of his or her genes, are higher than the fitness costs associated with the death of a sibling-in-law, with whom the perpetrator shares 0% of his or her genes. Siblicides between siblings-in-law may be more likely than those between full siblings to include more than one victim because siblings-in-law may be more likely to commit siblicide during a moment of intense bitterness and resentment—emotions that may co-occur with greater behavioral disorganization and spontaneity (Weekes-Shackelford & Shackelford 2004). Full siblings, on the other hand, may single out one particular sibling—perhaps that sibling perceived by the offender to be the recipient of a greater share of parental investment.

Parental investment in siblings-in-law may be viewed by a sibling as "wasted" investment. Such a "misdirected" investment may lead to feelings of jealousy and indignation toward siblings-in-law that are not present to the same degree toward full siblings. Michalski, Russell, et al. (2007) tested whether a greater proportion of siblicides of siblings-in-law will be perpetrated via beatings, relative to the proportion of siblicides of full siblings, and found that the results were in the predicted direction but were not statistically significantly.

Because a greater evolutionary "fitness" cost is associated with the death of a full sibling, relative to the death of a sibling-in-law, deliberate and intentional siblicides may be more frequent among siblings-in-law than among full siblings. Michalski, Russell, et al. (2007) found that accidental siblicides were more common between full siblings than between siblings-in-law, who may be more inclined toward purposeful and contemplated siblicides. Future breakthroughs on siblicide research await but must rely on larger, national databases that code for the genetic relatedness of victim and offender. Such databases are, unfortunately, currently lacking.

PARENTAL FAVORITISM

Parents are not expected to invest in offspring equally because the genetic interests of parents and their children are not identical (Daly & Wilson 1987; Hertwig, Davis, & Sulloway 2002; Trivers 1974). Parental genetic interests translate into "strategies" that reflect evolved psychological mechanisms designed to increase fitness by channeling investment to children who were likely to yield the greatest reproductive returns in ancestral environments (Hamilton 1964). Recent work suggests that perceived parental favoritism may be contingent on the birth order of children (Hertwig et al. 2002, Rohde et al. 2003, Salmon 2003, Sulloway, 2001).

Michalski, Shackelford, and Salmon (2007) tested several predictions about perceptions of parental favoritism. Previous research reveals a bias of paternal investment in daughters and a bias of maternal investment in sons (Salmon 2003). This pattern of investment may be understood by appreciating the role of relational uncertainty. Relational uncertainty refers to the probability that a genetic relationship between two kin could have been severed by cuckoldry (Euler & Weitzel 1996, Hartung 1985, Michalski & Shackelford 2005). Grandfathers faced the adaptive problem of relational uncertainty at higher rates than did grandmothers because paternal and maternal grandfathers averaged more potential links of cuckoldry between themselves and their grandchildren than did maternal and paternal grandmothers. Grandfathers would have benefited by investing more heavily in daughters than in sons because they could have been more certain that each unit of investment in a daughter would go toward aiding her children. The predicted pattern of greater investment in daughters than in sons may not be exclusive to periods when grandchildren through daughters are present. An ontogenetic history of increased investment in daughters relative to sons may result in prolonged investment biases throughout a daughter's life. Grandmothers' investments are not expected to favor one particular sex over the other, all else being equal. Grandmothers may channel more investment in daughters because of greater certainty that the investment will be directed toward grandchildren who have a higher probability of being genetically related. On the other hand, grandmothers may channel more investment in sons because that investment, relative to an equal investment in daughters, may be more directly related to additional mating opportunities for their sons, relative to such opportunities for daughters, especially when resources are abundant (Trivers & Willard 1973). Paternity uncertainty coupled with relational uncertainty suggests a paternal bias toward investing in daughters rather than investing in sons—a finding documented by Michalski et al. (2007).

The investment costs incurred by parents in ancestral environments are likely to have been higher for mothers than for fathers (Hrdy 1999). Psychological mechanisms in women motivating investment in children, therefore, were likely to have been a special target of selective processes. One stable feature of ancestral environments that may have prompted increased investment was the presence of a mate who is unrelated to her children. Daughters react more negatively than do sons in mother–stepfather families because of the stepfather's disruption of the tie established between mother and daughter (Bray 1999). Mothers may appear to favor daughters in this context because of this disruption, to compensate for this loss of emotional closeness. An alternative explanation of mother's favoritism toward daughters centers on the unique risks that daughters in blended families incur. Female sexual abuse perpetrated by a stepfather is higher than abuse by a biological father (Russell 1984, Wilson & Daly 1987). As a result of this risk, mothers may invest more heavily in daughters than in sons in the presence of a stepfather. Such a conditional strategy may be an attempt by mothers to reduce the risk of sexual abuse that girls suffer in such a condition. A similar pattern is not expected to emerge for fathers because their current partners do not pose an equivalent risk that mothers' partners pose to stepdaughters. Previous favoritism by a mother in sons may shift to favoritism toward daughters when a stepfather or mother's partner is present. Michalski et al. (2007) found that daughters are perceived as favored by mothers in blended families. This finding, to our knowledge, represents the first hint of a strategy of thwarting the sexual interests of stepfathers in stepdaughters.

Theoretical models and evidence collected to test those models reveal a preference for both mothers and fathers to invest disproportionately in genetically related children compared to genetically unrelated children (e.g., Anderson, Kaplan, & Lancaster 1999; Daly & Wilson 1987). Among blended families, it is likely that both mothers and fathers will be perceived as favoring genetically related children over stepchildren. Michalski et al. (2007) found that adult children perceive parents as favoring genetic children over stepchildren.

Parental psychological mechanisms may be sensitive to the reproductive "value" that children offer (Daly & Wilson 1987). This value may be assessed by parents through three broad classes of child characteristics: the probability that a child will survive to reproductive maturity and reproduce, the value of investment in one child relative to others, and the parent's probability of future reproduction. Firstborn children, on average, are highest in reproductive value because they have survived for a greater period of time and are closer to reproductive maturity than their younger siblings (Salmon 2005). One unit of investment is, on average, more valuable to lastborns because they are more vulnerable than older siblings. This reasoning has led researchers to predict a pattern of parental investment that favors firstborns and lastborns over middleborns, with associated psychological and behavioral ramifications for expressions of family solidarity (Salmon 1999, Salmon & Daly 1998), personality (Michalski & Shackelford 2002a, Sulloway 1996), and sexual strategies (Michalski & Shackelford 2002b, Salmon 2003). Previous research has shown that children nominate birth order as a determinate of parental favoritism (Zervas & Sherman 1994). Using data collected from several countries, for example, Rohde et al. (2003) found that (1) parents are reported as favoring lastborn children more often than firstborn children and (2) lastborns are more likely to indicate that they are favorites relative to parallel reports by firstborns and middleborns. Michalski et al. (2007) investigated separately whether or not reports of maternal and paternal favoritism by firstborns, middleborns, and lastborns corroborate these findings. The results revealed a pattern of perceiving both mothers and fathers as favoring firstborn and lastborn siblings at the expense of middleborn siblings.

SEXUAL AND EMOTIONAL JEALOUSY

Research documents a sex difference in the psychological weighting of aspects of a partner's infidelity: Men report greater upset than do women in response to a partner's sexual infidelity, and women report greater upset than do men in response to a partner's emotional infidelity (for review, see Buss 2003). An opportunity to unpack two competing predictions of how this sex difference in jealousy is generated is offered by the opportunity to examine jealousy over an in-law's infidelities. Men and women report greater upset over a daughter-in-law's sexual infidelity and over a son-in-law's emotional infidelity (Fenigstein & Peltz 2002; Shackelford, Michalski, & Schmitt 2004). These researchers argued that when the adaptive problem is a child's partner's infidelities, it is the sex of the child that determines whether a sexual infidelity or emotional infidelity is likely to lead to greater reproductive costs. By virtue of shared genes, in turn, greater reproductive costs for a child translate to greater reproductive costs for the parents. Michalski, Shackelford, and Salmon (2007) extended these findings to sibling relationships, finding that men and women are more upset over a sister's partner's emotional infidelity and are more upset over a brother's partner's sexual infidelity. Highlighting the importance of appreciating the need for relevant triggers for psychological adaptations, the researchers found this effect only among older participants. Among older participants who are more likely to actually have nieces and nephews, the costs of a sister's partner's emotional infidelity, as a cue to his diversion of resources away from a sister, are more damaging because of this greater probability of the presence of nieces and nephews.

In a follow-up study and methodological extension of this study, Michalski (2007) examined upset over a sibling's infidelity rather than upset over a sibling's partner's infidelity (N = 769). Participants were asked to report distress over a brother's and a sister's imagined infidelities when both had occurred. Preliminary analyses of the reports suggest different patterns of results than was revealed by Michalski et al. (2007). Michalski (2007) found that men and women are more upset over a sister's sexual infidelity than her emotional infidelity and that this effect is more dramatic for brothers than for sisters. A similar finding emerged in response to a brother's infidelity. A sex difference emerged only in response to a brother's infidelities—female participants reporting greater upset over a brother's infidelities than male participants reported. When comparing upset over a sister's infidelities and a brother's infidelities, participants were more upset over a sister's sexual infidelity than a brother's sexual infidelity and were more upset over a sister's emotional infidelity than a brother's emotional infidelity.

RELATIONSHIPS WITH SIBLINGS-IN-LAW

Very little research exists to understand features of the relationships between siblings-in-law with no known research that differentiates the three types of siblings-in-law mentioned in the beginning of this chapter. As such, we know little about the nature of conflicts or the satisfaction between siblings-in-law. Conflict with siblings-in-law appears to become particularly salient during times when desire for shares of inheritance from deceased parents arise (Horsley 1996). Siblings-in-law may play a role in provoking mates to negotiate for larger shares of parental resources. The conditions under which siblings-in-law may become more vocal in their desire for a greater share have not yet been studied. It is possible that (1) the mates of female siblings may be more vocal than the mates of male siblings in securing parental resources and (2) the mates of younger siblings, relative to older siblings, may be more vocal in the need to secure a larger share of parental resources. The mates of younger siblings may attempt to undo parental favoring of older siblings on the younger sibling's behalf. The mates of female siblings may be more vocal because of their greater competitiveness over resources relative to the competitiveness of the mates of male siblings.

The relationship between siblings-in-law may be sex-specific and focused on the reproductively relevant resources offered by siblings-in-law to a sibling. We predict that men and women will report their relationships with brothers-in-law as closer and less contentious when the brother-in-law exhibits characteristics linked with the mate preferences of the sister (e.g., access to resources, emotional fidelity). Conversely, we predict that men and women will report their relationships with sisters-in-law closer and less contentious when the sister-in-law exhibits characteristics linked with the mate preferences of the brother (e.g., youthfulness, sexual fidelity).

Among heterosexual, same-sex siblings, there is a potential for sexual attraction to develop between siblings-in-law. We are not aware of any data that indicate how prevalent attraction between siblings-in-law is, but we speculate that same-sex siblings may nevertheless reveal features of the potential for such sexual relationships to emerge, including increased mate retention. Future research in this area may follow from an appreciation of the underlying mating psychologies of men and women. For example, men and women might report interactions between their spouses and opposite-sex siblings-in-law as more distressing than interactions with same-sex siblings-in-law.

Research documents that men, more than women, place greater emphasis on youthfulness in evaluating a prospective mate (Buss 2003). This sex difference in mate preferences leads to the prediction that among siblings, older brothers may be more likely to view as attractive (and consequently attempt to poach) the mates of younger brothers because younger brothers will be mated to younger women than will older brothers. Women may then be more upset over interactions between their spouse and a younger brother's spouse than an older brother's spouse. Men may be more upset over interactions between their spouse and an older sister's spouse than a younger sister's spouse. Support for such predictions awaits future empirical scrutiny, but we expect such effects to emerge consistent with the nature of sibling relationships and of sex-differentiated mating psychology. With respect to "lover's triangle" homicides, we expect older men to kill younger siblings-in-law more often than older siblings-in-law because of their greater interest, on average, in slightly younger partners. We expect younger women to kill older siblings-in-law more often than younger siblings-in-law because of their greater interest in slightly older partners. In short, research in the area of relationships with siblings-in-law is wide open with a multitude of opportunities to study the nature of sibling-in-law relationships.

BIRTH ORDER AND PERSONALITY: FUTURE DIRECTIONS WITH DYNAMICAL SYSTEMS

There is a long history of research on the relationships between birth order and personality, scattered across the social and behavioral sciences (see Sulloway 1996, for a review). Sulloway organized this literature and conducted a meta-analysis of these relationships. Following current and historical work in the field of personality, personality characteristics were organized into five major dimensions: extraversion, agreeableness, conscientiousness, emotional stability, and openness to experience (Norman 1963).

Parents generally invest more in firstborn children than in laterborn children (see Sulloway 1996, for a review). According to Sulloway, differential parental investment motivates differences in the strategies that children in the same family use to solicit parental investment. To solicit parental investment, firstborns display beliefs, attitudes, and personality characteristics that mirror parental beliefs, attitudes, and personality characteristics—Sulloway refers to this mirroring as "upholding the parental status quo." Laterborns use a strategy of investment solicitation that differs from that used by firstborns. According to Sulloway, laterborns develop beliefs, attitudes, and personality characteristics that differ from those of firstborns and of parents. Sulloway hypothesized and found that firstborn status correlates positively with extraversion, conscientiousness, and neuroticism. Sulloway also hypothesized and found that firstborn status correlates negatively with agreeableness and openness to experience.

Several recent and reputable studies have failed to replicate Sulloway's findings (Beer & Horn 2000; Freese, Powell, & Steelman 1999; Jefferson, Herbst, & McCrae 1998; Michalski & Shackelford 2002a). The inconsistent history of findings between the relationships between birth order and personality present a challenge to evolutionary accounts of sibling differences based on birth order. Harris (1998) has commented on the mercurial nature of birth order effects in personality. Her argument is that siblings have no evolutionary, relevant reason to maintain a suite of personality characteristics forged from differing family patterns in the home to relationships outside it. The evolutionary logic behind this argument suggests that siblings who moderated personality characteristics relative to each other and continued to carry those characteristics with them throughout their life would have been out-reproduced by ancestral siblings who moderated personality characteristics to the environments in which they might have found themselves in the future. This argument suggests that personality is domain-specific in nature and has the possibility to change over time.

Researchers have typically examined mean differences among firstborns and laterborns. It is possible that the mean levels of personality dimensions mask revealing features of the dynamics of personality systems that can change over time through interactions with others (Mischel & Shoda 1995). The possibility that birth order does not predict mean differences in personality but rather predicts *changes* in how the cognitive structures of personality systems react to various environmental cues remains unexplored. To assess the potential for change in personality characteristics over time, it may become necessary to invoke theoretical and methodological tools developed in dynamical social psychology (for a more complete discussion of dynamical social psychology, see Nowak & Vallacher 1998).

Nowak and Vallacher (1998) stated that to understand a complex system, it is necessary to examine how that system changes over time. Nowak, Vallacher, and Zochowski (2002) describe two types of synchronization: positive, whereby behaviors of one person induce similar behaviors in another, and, negative, wherein one person's feelings or behaviors result in the opposite feelings or behaviors in another. Synchronization refers to the temporal similarity in thoughts, actions, or behaviors between two people. Nowak, Vallacher, and Zochowski (2002) assume that individuals set their internal (personality) states through synchronization with others as a result of ontogenetic social interactions. These interactions result in stable attractor states corresponding to specific psychology dimensions. The sibling environment may be one such set of ontogenetic social interactions that results in different personality "landscapes" for firstborns and laterborns. We expect firstborns and laterborns to have similar depths of attractor states (personality traits). This similar depth in the personality landscapes of firstborns and laterborns may result in the findings revealed in the literature of few mean personality differences between siblings based on birth order. A difference, however, may exist in the shape of the landscape. Laterborns may have a shallower basin of attraction than firstborns. This shallower basin of attraction may correspond to a lower level of environmental input required to oust the person from that attractor state to another.

Laterborns, having had greater needs to seek out investment in ways different from firstborns, may have been favored to be "chameleon"-like in their personality. Interactions of seeking investments through other sources may foster the development of personality characteristics that aid in pursuit of these alternative investments (e.g., higher scores on openness to experience). Such personality traits may then calibrate internal dynamics, resulting in less environmental input necessary to move them toward the attractor states of other individuals in their social environment. Synchronization is therefore predicted to vary as a function of birth order, with laterborns synchronizing more quickly than firstborns (perhaps revealed by the greater willingness of laterborns to accept revolutionary scientific ideas) (see Sulloway 1996). The tools developed within dynamical social psychology, we believe, will inform future research on family relationships, including the impact of birth order on personality.

CONCLUSIONS

In this chapter, we highlighted a few areas of sibling relationships. There are additional areas of inquiry that were not discussed here but that are equally demanding of research (e.g., incest avoidance) (see Lieberman, this volume). We argue that many important components and studies of sibling relationships have been missed by a failure to incorporate the theoretical power of evolutionary theories and that an evolutionary perspective offers us a means to generate new, untested hypotheses. We believe that much research has yet to be done on topics such as relationships with siblings-in-law, siblicide, sibling conflict, relationships between siblings of varying degrees of relatedness, jealousy, favoritism, examinations of personality differences between siblings as a function of dynamical systems-theory tools, and an exploration of possible mechanisms that function in the minds of siblings to identify putative full siblings from half-siblings. Although many of the predictions reported in this chapter have not been tested, we expect answers to such research questions to emerge in the decades to come. We also expect that a clearer and more comprehensive picture of sibling relationships will emerge with the increased use of evolutionary theories to understand the nature of sibling relationships.

REFERENCES

Anderson, K. G., Kaplan, H., & Lancaster, J. (1999). Paternal care by genetic fathers and stepfathers I: Reports from Albuquerque men. *Evolution & Human Behavior, 20,* 405–431.

Beer, J. M., & Horn, J. M. (2000). The influence of reading order on personality development within two adoption cohorts. *Journal of Personality, 68,* 789–819.

Bray, J. H. (1999). From marriage to remarriage and beyond: Findings from the Developmental Issues in Stepfamilies Research Project. In E. M. Hetherington (Ed.), *Coping with divorce, single parenting, and remarriage* (pp. 295–319). Mayway, NJ: Erlbaum.

Buss, D. M. (2003). *The evolution of desire: Strategies of human mating.* New York: Basic Books.

Cicirelli, V. G. (1995). *Sibling relationships across the life span*. New York: Plenum Press.

Daly, M., & Wilson, M. (1982). Whom are newborn babies said to resemble? *Ethology and Sociobiology, 3*, 69–78.

Daly, M., & Wilson, M. (1987). The Darwinian psychology of discriminative parental solicitude. *Nebraska Symposium on Motivation, 35*, 91–144.

Daly, M., & Wilson, M. (1988). *Homicide*. New York: Aldine de Gruyter.

Daly, M., Salmon, C. A., & Wilson, M. (1997). Kinship: The conceptual hole in psychological studies of social cognition and close relationships (pp. 265–296). In J. A. Simpson and D. T. Kenrick (Eds.), *Evolutionary Social Psychology*. New Jersey: Lawrence Erlbaum Associates.

Daly, M., Wilson, M., Salmon, C. A., Hiraiwa-Hasegawa, M., & Hasegawa, T. (2001). Siblicide and seniority. *Homicide Studies, 5*, 30–45.

Darwin, C. R. (1859). *On the origin of species by means of natural selection*. London: John Murray.

Darwin, C. R. (1871). *The descent of man and selection in relation to sex*. London: John Murray.

Dunn, J., & Kenrick, C. (1982). *Siblings*. Cambridge, MA: Harvard University Press.

Euler, H. A., & Weitzel, B. (1996). Discriminative grandparental solicitude as reproductive strategy. *Human Nature, 7*, 39–59.

Fenigstein, A., & Peltz, R. (2002). Distress over the infidelity of a child's spouse: A crucial test of evolutionary and socialization hypotheses. *Personal Relationships, 9*, 301–312.

Freese, J., Powell, B., & Steelman, L. C. (1999). Rebel without a cause or effect: Birth order and social attitudes. *American Sociological Review, 64*, 207–231.

Hamilton, W. D. (1964). The genetical evolution of social behavior. I and II. *Journal of Theoretical Biology, 7*, 1–52.

Harris, J. R. (1998). *The nurture assumption*. New York: Free Press.

Hartung, J. (1985). Matrilineal inheritance: New theory and analysis. *Behavioral and Brain Sciences, 8*, 661–688.

Hertwig, R., Davis, J., & Sulloway, F. J. (2002). Parental investment: How an equity motive can produce inequality. *Psychological Bulletin, 128*, 728–745.

Horsley, G. C. (1996). *In-laws: A guide to extended-family therapy*. New York: John Wiley & Sons.

Hrdy, S. B. (1999). *Mother nature. Natural selection and the female of the species*. New York: Pantheon Books.

Jankowiak, W., & Diderich, M. (2000). Sibling solidarity in a polygamous community in the USA: Unpacking inclusive fitness. *Evolution and Human Behavior, 21*, 125–139.

Jefferson, T. J., Herbst, J. H., & McCrae, R. R. (1998). Associations between birth order and personality traits: Evidence from self-reports and observer ratings. *Journal of Research in Personality, 32*, 498–509.

Michalski, R. L. (2007). *Upset in response to a sibling's infidelities.* Unpublished manuscript.

Michalski, R. L., Russell, D. P., Shackelford, T. K., & Weekes-Shackelford, V. A. (2007). *Siblicide and genetic relatedness in Chicago, 1870–1930.* Homicide Studies.

Michalski, R. L., & Shackelford, T. K. (2002a). An attempted replication of the relationships between birth order and personality. *Journal of Research in Personality, 36,* 182–188.

Michalski, R. L., & Shackelford, T. K. (2002b). Birth order and sexual strategy. *Personality and Individual Differences, 33,* 661–667.

Michalski, R. L., & Shackelford, T. K. (2005). Grandparental investment as a function of relational uncertainty and emotional closeness with parents. *Human Nature, 16,* 293–305.

Michalski, R. L., & Shackelford, T. K. (2007). *Methods of sibling aggression.* Unpublished manuscript.

Michalski, R. L., Shackelford, T. K., & Salmon, C. A. (2007). *Birth order, sex of child, and perceptions of parental favoritism.* Manuscript submitted for publication.

Michalski, R. L., Shackelford, T. K., & Salmon, C. A. (2007). Upset in response to a sibling's partner's infidelities. *Human Nature, 18,* 74–84.

Mischel, W., & Shoda, Y. (1995). A cognitive-affective system theory of personality: Reconceptualizing situations, dispositions, dynamics, and invariance in personality structure. *Psychological Review, 102,* 246–268.

Norman, W. T. (1963). Toward an adequate taxonomy of personality attributes: Replicated factor structure in peer nomination personality ratings. *Journal of Abnormal and Social Psychology, 66,* 574–583.

Nowak, A., & Vallacher, R. (1998). *Dynamical social psychology.* New York: Guilford.

Nowak, A., Vallacher, R.R., & Zochowski, M. (2002). The emergence of personality: Personal stability through interpersonal synchronization. In D. Cervone & W. Mischel (Eds.), *Advances in personality science* (pp. 292–331). New York: Guilford.

Rohde, P. A., Atzwanger, K., Butovskaya, M., Lampert, A., Mysterud, I., Sanchez-Andres, A., et al. (2003). Perceived parental favoritism, closeness to kin, and the rebel of the family: The effects of birth order and sex. *Evolution and Human Behavior, 24,* 261–276.

Russell, D. E. H. (1984). The prevalence and seriousness of incestuous abuse: Stepfathers vs. biological fathers. *Child Abuse and Neglect, 8,* 15–22.

Russell, D. P., Michalski, R. L., Shackelford, T. K., & Weekes-Shackelford, V. A. (2007). A preliminary investigation of siblicide as a function of genetic relatedness. *Journal of Forensic Sciences, 52,* 738–739.

Salmon, C. A. (1999). On the impact of sex and birth order on contact with kin. *Evolution and Human Behavior, 10,* 183–197.

Salmon, C. A. (2003). Birth order and relationships: Family, friends, and sexual partners. *Human Nature, 14,* 73–88.

Salmon, C. A. (2005). Parental investment and parent–offspring conflict. In D. M. Buss (Ed.), *Handbook of Evolutionary Psychology* (pp. 506–527). Hoboken, NJ: John Wiley & Sons.

Salmon, C. A., & Daly, M. (1998). Birth order and familial sentiment: Middleborns are different. *Evolution and Human Behavior, 19,* 299–312.

Sears, W., Sears, M., & Kelly, C. W. (2001). *What baby needs.* New York: Little, Brown. Shackelford, T. K., Michalski, R. L., & Schmitt, D. P. (2004). Upset in response to a child's partner's infidelities. *European Journal of Social Psychology, 34, 489–497.*

Sulloway, F. J. (1996). *Born to rebel.* New York: Pantheon.

Sulloway, F. J. (2001). Birth order, sibling competition, and human behavior. In J. H. Fetzer & H. R. Holcomb III (Eds.), *Studies in cognitive systems: Vol. 27. Conceptual challenges in evolutionary psychology* (pp. 39–83). Dordrecht, Netherlands: Kluwer Academic.

Trivers, R. L. (1972). Parental investment and sexual selection. In B. Campbell (Ed.), *Sexual selection and the descent of man* (pp. 136–179). Chicago: Aldine.

Trivers, R. L. (1974). Parent–offspring conflict. *American Zoologist, 14,* 249–264.

Trivers, R. L., & Willard, D. E. (1973). Natural selection of parental ability to vary the sex ratio of offspring. *Science, 179,* 90–92.

Underwood, R. C., & Patch, P. C. (1999). Siblicide: A descriptive analysis of sibling homicide. *Homicide Studies, 3,* 333–348.

Weekes-Shackelford, V. A., & Shackelford, T. K. (2004). Methods of filicide: Stepparents and genetic parents kill differently. *Violence and Victims, 19,* 75–81.

Wiehe, V. R. (1997). *Sibling abuse.* Thousand Oaks, CA: Sage.

Wilson, M., & Daly, M. (1987). The risk of maltreatment of children living with stepparents. In R. J. Gelles & J. B. Lancaster (Eds.). *Child abuse and neglect* (pp. 215–232). New York: Aldine de Gruyter.

Zervas, L. J., & Sherman, M. F. (1994). The relationship between perceived parental favoritism and self-esteem. *Journal of Genetic Psychology, 155,* 25–34.

10 Kin Detection and the Development of Sexual Aversions: Toward an Integration of Theories on Family Sexual Abuse

Ilanit Tal and Debra Lieberman

Sexual abuse is a pressing social problem. In the 1990s alone, there were approximately 336,000–429,000 annual reports of child sexual abuse in the United States (Peddle & Wang 2001) with 90,000–150,000 annual cases substantiated by child-protective agencies (Jones & Finkelhor 2001; Jones, Finkelhor, & Kopiec 2001). In a survey of undergraduate students, Finkelhor (1984) found that almost 50% of students reported an unwanted non-penetrative sexual experience, and 16% reported an unwanted penetrative sexual experience before the age of 16. With respect to sexual abuse within the family, specific rates are difficult to assess given the bias against reporting family abuse to authorities. Nevertheless, in a study surveying adult women from the San Francisco area, Russell (1983) found that 16% reported at least one such experience before the age of 18. Given these statistics, it is not surprising that researchers and social workers alike are concerned with understanding *why* sexual abuse occurs and identifying the factors that put children at risk for both intrafamilial and extrafamilial sexual abuse.

Despite decades of research, however, the field of child sexual abuse still lacks an integrative theoretical framework (Cole & Putnam 1992). Consequently, much of the work to date has been descriptive, focusing on, for example, incidence rates (e.g., Finkelhor 1979, 1980; Russell 1983, 1986), how rates have changed over time (e.g., Dunne, Purdie, Cook, Boyle, & Najman

2003; Jones, Finkelhor, & Kopiec 2001), the negative effects on victims (e.g., the development of clinical and psychiatric disorders, Kendall-Tackett, Williams, & Finkelhor 1993; Molnar, Buka, & Kessler 2001; Weiss, Longhurst, & Mazure 1999), and the characteristics of families, victims, and perpetrators of abuse (e.g., Adler & Schutz 1995; Burkett 1991; Hartley 2001; Laviola 1992; Lung & Huang 2004; Smith & Israel 1987; Trepper, Niedner, Mika, & Barrett 1996; Worling 1995).

Although much is known about the sequelae of sexual abuse and the characteristics of the individuals and families involved, these pieces of information have yet to be arranged to form a clear picture of *why* sexual abuse occurs. In this chapter, we provide an account of how an evolutionary computational framework can help organize what is currently known about sexual abuse and provide a set of answers to the question of why. Specifically, we focus on one component of our evolved psychology hypothesized to play a significant role in explaining why familial sexual abuse occurs: mechanisms governing the development of sexual aversions toward close genetic relatives. We suggest that identifying the cues our evolved psychology uses to detect kin and generate sexual aversions toward them can help illuminate why sexual aversions fail to develop, leading, in some circumstances, to an increased risk of sexual abuse. Other concepts also hypothesized to predict patterns of abuse, but not fully explored in this chapter, include mate value (e.g., men with low mate value might target younger females to sidestep the competition for high mate-value females) and inbreeding conflict (e.g., the costs associated with inbreeding are lower for men compared to for women, leading to asymmetric motivations to commit and avoid these sexual encounters). Together, these concepts provide useful guide-rails for organizing our knowledge regarding sexual abuse and generating new avenues of research.

To start, we very briefly discuss two current models of sexual abuse: the family-systems model and the model developed by David Finkelhor, a leading researcher in the field of child sexual abuse. Next, we discuss an evolutionary-computational model of inbreeding avoidance. This entails a discussion of why inbreeding avoidance mechanisms exist and how evolution might have engineered such a system. We focus on the potential cues evolution might have used to detect different types of family members (e.g., offspring, parents, and siblings). We argue that identifying the cues used to guide kin detection can shed light on those circumstances that compromise kin detection and result in a failure to trigger strong sexual aversions. The last section of our paper integrates the features of sexual abuse identified by previous models into an evolutionary-computational framework of kin detection and inbreeding avoidance. Our goal is to demonstrate how an evolutionary framework can help generate new lines of inquiry and inform public policy and programs relating to child sexual abuse.

A SELECTION OF CURRENT MODELS OF SEXUAL ABUSE

Family-Systems Model

As the name suggests, this approach views the family as "a system" and describes the factors that compromise the system and prevent its functioning properly (Friedman 1988, Minuchin 1974). With respect to sexual abuse within the family, the family-systems model was first applied to explain father–daughter and stepfather–stepdaughter incest, and focuses primarily on the health of the marital relationship (Furniss 1983, 1985). Father–daughter sexual abuse is said to occur when the marital relationship breaks down and the mother does not fulfill her duties as mother and wife, causing the father to substitute a daughter for his wife both emotionally and sexually, a process called triangulation (e.g., Greenspun 1994).

More recently, a family systems approach has been applied to explain sibling sexual abuse. As with father–daughter sexual abuse, explanations for sibling sexual behavior focus on the marital relationship. Sibling incest has been found to occur in families with marital conflict or where the parents are neglectful or emotionally distant (e.g., Hardy 2001, Laviola 1992, Pierce & Pierce 1990, Smith & Israel 1987). Specifically, families in which sibling incest has occurred have been characterized as having a neglectful mother (e.g., Laviola 1992).

In general, then, the deterioration of familial relationships is seen as the cause of intrafamilial sexual abuse in the family-systems model. Fathers abuse daughters because the relationship with the mother has deteriorated and the daughter is capable of filling the void; brothers abuse sisters, or siblings engage in consensual incest for comfort when parental relations disintegrate. There have been many criticisms of the family-systems model, including its limitations in explaining extrafamilial sexual abuse (e.g., Finkelhor 1984) and its focus on the mother (e.g., by feminist theories of sexual abuse, which emphasize the power of men over women [Herman 1981]).

The family-systems model also raises important questions: Why is it that the mother plays a key role in mitigating the risk of sexual abuse? Why is the quality of the marital relationship important? And are all seeds of marital conflict factors that contribute to sexual abuse, or only some? As we discuss below, integrating what is known from the family-systems approach with an evolutionary-computational framework can help answer these important questions.

Finkelhor's Preconditions of Sexual Abuse

According to David Finkelhor, a leading researcher and theorist within the field of child sexual abuse, there is a need for a more comprehensive theory of sexual abuse (Finkelhor 1984). Specifically, Finkelhor argues the field has mainly relied on two useful yet disjointed models of sexual abuse: the family-systems model (see above) and models that focus primarily on the attributes of the offender (e.g., the existence of psychopathy and the developmental history of abuse). What is missing, Finkelhor claims, is a general model of sexual abuse that incorporates psychological and also sociological factors related to victims, families, and offenders. In an attempt to unify the disparate theoretical frameworks, Finkelhor proposes a model describing several preconditions that contribute to the occurrence of sexual abuse. These include the presence of motivations to sexually abuse and the ability of the abuser to overcome internal and external inhibitors. We briefly discuss each in turn.

Motivations to Sexually Abuse

According to Finkelhor, an individual's motivation to sexually abuse a child can be influenced by a number of factors. These include: (i) the desire to fulfill an emotional need due to, for example, a lack of emotional development or the need to exert power; (ii) the experience of sexual arousal that can result from a biological abnormality or the recollection of a traumatic (or pleasant) childhood sexual experience; and (iii) the unavailability of alternate sexual partners (termed "blockage"), which might be a function of social skills, marital problems, and traumatic adult sexual experiences.

Overcoming Inhibitors

In addition to the presence of motivations to abuse, abusers must overcome internal and external inhibitors before an instance of sexual abuse occurs; even when motivations to abuse exist, if an individual is dissuaded by any inhibitor, no abuse will occur. Identification of these inhibitors is thus an important component for understanding the occurrence and also the prevention of sexual abuse. Internal disinhibitions can occur when judgments and decision-making processes relating to sexual behavior are impaired. This might be a result of drug or alcohol abuse (e.g., see Famularo, Stone, Barnum, & Wharton 1986; Walsh, MacMillan, & Jamieson 2003), impairments due to clinical abnormalities (e.g., psychosis), or age-related cognitive dysfunctions. Finkelhor also includes the failure of incest-avoidance mechanisms as an internal factor influencing the inhibition of sexual behavior, a topic we turn to in the next section.

External inhibitors of sexual abuse focus on the social environment and family dynamics. Using a method similar to that of the family-systems model discussed above, Finkelhor stresses the importance of the mother when he evaluates a child's risk of being sexually abused. Specifically, Finkelhor found that individuals whose mother was absent, often ill, emotionally distant, or in a sexually or physically abusive relationship (either currently or during her childhood) were more likely to have experienced childhood sexual abuse. In addition, children whose mothers introduced boyfriends or new husbands into the family reported more incidents of sexual abuse. Thus, a consistent finding in the literature is that a healthy, emotionally available mother who maintains a stable relationship with the child's biological father serves as an inhibiting force, protecting the child from the risk of being sexually abused. In addition to mothers, other members of the social environment can be a source of external inhibition. The greater the interaction with siblings, friends, and neighbors, the less likely individuals are to have experienced childhood sexual abuse. Indeed, those with few friends and those who lived in social isolation (e.g., on farms or in the woods) reported greater incidents of sexual abuse compared to those with many friends or those who lived close to neighbors (Finkelhor 1984).

In summary, Finkelhor proposes a general framework that can be applied to any form of sexual abuse, intrafamilial or extrafamilial. Accordingly, each instance of sexual abuse requires an understanding of the motivations to target another sexually and the inhibitors that might have been absent or impaired that otherwise would have prevented the sexual behavior from occurring. By and large, this model catalogues a number of important factors contributing to sexual abuse. But is there a theoretical framework that can organize this information and generate predictions regarding, for example, why certain factors play an inhibitory role or what distinguishes those individuals who sexually target children versus those who do not? Finkelhor's model, though it is much more comprehensive than previous formulations, still leaves unanswered the question of why the mother plays such a critical role in child sexual abuse. Furthermore, what is the structure of inbreeding-avoidance mechanisms and why might they fail to deploy in certain situations? In the next section, we outline an evolutionary-computational model of inbreeding avoidance that identifies the ways in which sexual aversions might fail to develop, introducing the possibility of sexual abuse.

AN EVOLUTIONARY-COMPUTATIONAL MODEL: KIN DETECTION AND SEXUAL AVERSIONS

One approach to understanding why sexual abuse sometimes occurs is to first identify the computational mechanisms that govern sexual avoidance.

One category of individuals for whom there are likely to be mechanisms mediating sexual avoidance is close kin. Indeed, there are sound biological reasons why evolution is expected to have selected for mechanisms that function to prevent sexual relations with close genetic relatives. The selection pressures posed by deleterious recessive mutations (Bittles & Neel 1994) and short-generation pathogens (Tooby 1982) would have meant that, on average, individuals who selected less genetically related individuals as mates would have left a greater number of healthy offspring compared to individuals who mated randomly or with individuals who had a high probability of sharing similar genes. Furthermore, the closer the genetic relatedness between two individuals, the more deleterious the reproductive consequences, with the most severe consequences occurring for mateships between parents and offspring and between siblings (i.e., individuals for whom degree of relatedness equals 0.5). The negative reproductive consequences of inbreeding have been well established in humans and nonhumans. Offspring of close genetic relatives suffer increased rates of mortality, physical defects, and cognitive impairments (e.g., see Adams & Neel 1967; Carter 1967; Charlesworth & Charlesworth 1999; Crnokrak & Roff 1999; Keller, Arcese, James, & Hochachka 1994; Seemanova 1971).

But *how* do humans avoid inbreeding? What cognitive processes are required to avoid genetic relatives as mates? One method for answering this question is to consider what a well-designed inbreeding-avoidance system might look like. From this perspective, at least two psychological procedures are required: (1) the ability to detect kin (i.e., assess for a given individual the probability they share genes identical through common descent), and (2) the ability to regulate sexual motivations based on the probability that an individual is close kin (see Lieberman, Tooby, & Cosmides 2007). This system can function as an inbreeding-avoidance mechanism by monitoring the environment for information indicating an individual is likely to be a close genetic relative and, if such information is present, down-regulating sexual motivations targeting that individual. In the absence of such information, no sexual aversion will develop, and instead, whether that individual is an attractive mate or not will be left to other procedures that guide mate choice. Thus, a key question is: What information does our mind use to detect probable kin and to develop sexual aversions toward them?

How Do We Detect Close Genetic Relatives?

How did evolution engineer systems for learning who counts as a close genetic relative? Since we cannot "see" another person's genes, the best that evolution could have done is to build a system that uses information, or cues, that, over our species' evolutionary history, were correlated with relatedness. A likely source of information regarding relatedness comes from the ecologically valid cues that signaled relatedness in ancestral environments. Indeed, nonhuman animals are capable of detecting kin using a variety of mechanisms (e.g., see Fletcher & Michener 1987, Hepper 1991). But what cues do humans use to carve the social world into kin versus non-kin? And are the same cues used for detecting each category of close kin (e.g., mother, father, offspring, and sibling)? To the extent that different environmental, social, or biological cues correlated with an individual's being a particular type of close genetic relative, different detection systems are expected to exist. What follows is a brief discussion of the stable and recurring cues natural selection could have targeted to detect two specific categories of kin: offspring and siblings.

Female Detection of Offspring

One of the recurring features of our ancestral environment was that women gave birth to their own offspring. Since it was an absolute certainty that the baby coming out of a woman's body was indeed her own, selection could have used this regularity to shape an offspring-detection mechanism in women. To be useful, however, a detection mechanism had to solve the problem of initial detection and also the continued identification throughout childhood and sexual maturity. There are many ways such a detection mechanism could have solved these problems. For example, a woman could imprint on visual, auditory, or olfactory cues derived from her newborn. From a theoretical standpoint, however, visual cues such as facial features might not be the most reliable and consistent source of information because the face of a newborn baby changes rapidly throughout development (Pagel 1997; Porter, Cernoch, & Balogh 1984). Similarly, auditory signatures change throughout the life span and would need to be continually updated to maintain positive identification as kin. Nevertheless, researchers have found that mothers are capable of recognizing their own infants' vocalizations from as early as 48 hours after birth when presented with a number of different infants' cries (Formby 1967; Murray, Hollien, & Muller 1975).

Perhaps the most stable cue available to females for identifying their young is olfactory information that does not change throughout the life cycle. One candidate for this kind of cue is the major histocompatibility complex (MHC). The MHC is a group of cell-surface proteins and are responsible for the self- versus non-self discrimination of the immune system (Janeway 1993, Klein 1986, Snell 1981). Because of the number of different alleles coding for the MHC (some loci have as many as 50–60 alleles), and the increased mutation rate in this part of the genome (Beauchamp, Yamazaki, & Boyse 1985), an individual's MHC composition is unique. As has been shown in mice, MHC can be detected via smell in sweat and urine when it is broken down, making it a potential cue for identifying kin of different types, not just offspring (e.g., see Manning, Wakeland, & Potts 1992; Potts, Manning, & Wakeland 1991; Singer, Beauchamp, & Yamazaki 1997; Singh, Brown, & Roser 1987; Yamazaki, Beauchamp, Curran, Bard, & Boyse 2000). Indeed, a handful of studies have demonstrated that humans are capable of distinguishing between kin and non-kin solely on the basis of smell (Porter, Cernoch, & McLaughlin 1983; Porter & Moore 1981) and might use this information to guide mating preferences (Jacob, McClintock, Zelano, & Ober 2002; Wedekind & Furi 1997; Wedekind, Seebeck, Bettens, & Paepke 1995).

Can women identify their offspring on the basis of smell alone? The answer appears to be yes. Russell, Mendelson, and Peeke (1983) tested whether or not blindfolded mothers could discriminate between their own newborn and two unrelated newborns. They had mothers smell the head of their baby along with those of two unrelated babies and found that mothers could discriminate between their own baby and the others only 6 hours postpartum, having been exposed to the newborn only once for half an hour. Interestingly, the researchers found that fathers could not make the same discrimination, even though they had also been exposed to the newborn for the same amount of time (see Males Detecting Offspring below). Other studies have provided converging lines of evidence that mothers are capable of identifying their own child's odor, in some cases after only a short period of time postpartum (Kaitz, Good, Rokem, & Eidelman 1987; Porter, Cernoch, & McLaughlin 1983; Porter & Moore 1981; Russell et al., 1983; Weisfeld, Czilli, & Phillips 2003).

Given the certainty of relatedness between a mother and her newborn, a kin-detection system that immediately registered cues derived from the newborn (e.g., auditory, visual, and/or olfactory cues) would have functioned as an offspring-detection mechanism. As we discuss below, this would not have been the best design for an offspring-detection mechanism in men.

Male Detection of Offspring

Compared to other primates, men invest heavily in their offspring (Boyd & Silk 1997). However, the benefits men would have accrued from their parental efforts depended critically on the ability to assess their probable relatedness to the child a woman gives birth to. Any design feature that caused a man to regulate his investment in a particular child according to the probability that that child was in fact his offspring would have been selected over alternative design features causing, for example, a man to invest indiscriminately in any offspring he encountered, whether his or not. Unlike a woman, who can be certain that the newborn she bears is her own biological offspring, men cannot be 100% certain as to who their biological offspring are—they lack paternity certainty. Thus, the problem of detecting offspring for men translates into the problem of evaluating paternity certainty.

There are a number of cues that could be used to assess paternity. Children from women a man never had sex with cannot be his. Thus, men should assume the probability of paternity is zero for offspring of women with whom they have not had sex. For women with whom a man has had sex, the frequency of intercourse would have correlated with paternity. That is, the more often a man had sex with a woman during a given period of his life, the greater the likelihood that the children she produced during this period (and during no other) are his.

But frequency of intercourse is insufficient. A woman who is often away from her mate is more likely to have engaged in a sexual liaison with another man than is a woman who is always in the presence of her mate (Baker & Bellis 1993, Buss 2003). Therefore, information as to how much time a man's mate was absent or was known to be with other men might function to estimate the likelihood of paternity. One possible way such a mechanism could be designed is to keep a running total of time a man's mate was absent during the period they maintained a sexual relationship; the greater the total time away, the less certain a man could be of paternity. Or perhaps the mechanism is more targeted and, once cues to pregnancy have been detected, it backtracks to the probable time period of conception and determines the frequency with which the woman was absent back then. Could men have a dedicated memory trace that is activated upon exposure to cues signaling pregnancy? Depending on the evolutionary costs of engineering such a system, this might be one way men solve the problem of assessing paternity.

Another factor that would have provided reliable information about probable paternity is the behavior of a man's mate. Gregarious women with many male friends or a promiscuous sexual history (or reputation) would have posed a greater threat to a man's paternity than would women with few male friends and a reputation for being chaste. Thus, men should be sensitive to the personalities, reputations, and social behaviors of their mates. Indeed, across cultures, chastity is a trait men strongly favor in a mate (Buss 2003). Further, studies by Apicella and Marlowe (2004, 2007) found that male parental investment was a function of a man's perception of mate trustworthiness, fidelity, and clothing style.

Two additional pieces of information that a system designed to assess paternity might take as input are (1) a man's assessment of his own mate value relative to the mate value of other men in his local social environment and, (2) a man's assessment of the mate value of his partner. All else equal, a man with higher status is more attractive to women and may be more certain of paternity than a man of lower status (Symons 1979). In other words, there is a lower probability that a woman will engage in sexual infidelities when she is in a relationship with a higher status man than when she is in a relationship with a lower status man. Similarly, if a man's partner has a high mate value, especially relative to his own, she has a higher probability of being pursued as a mate by other men, opening the door to an increased risk of sexual infidelities. Furthermore, the quality of a mateship (e.g., close and loving versus distant and hostile) may have been a reliable predictor of infidelity. When a relationship is unstable, the man is away a lot, or the woman seems to act promiscuously, paternity certainty might be low and the resulting offspring categorized as non-kin.

Another possible cue that men might use to assess paternity is phenotypic similarity, such as facial resemblance (Daly & Wilson 1982). It has been shown that mothers and maternal relatives remark at the resemblance between a newborn and the mother's mate, presumably in an attempt to assure paternity and evoke greater levels of paternal investment (Daly & Wilson 1982, Regalski & Gaulin 1993). Despite the possibility that visual cues might not have been the most reliable for detecting offspring, men do appear to use facial resemblance as a cue to relatedness. For example, Platek et al. (2003, 2004) have shown that men preferentially favor children whose faces have been morphed with their own. Apicella and Marlowe (2004) showed that men's reports of levels of offspring investment (e.g., attention paid to offspring and help offered with schoolwork) correlated with their perception of offspring resemblance. Whether an offspring-detection mechanism in men relies on phenotypic resemblance or an assessment of cues signaling mate sexual fidelity is still an open question because no study of which we are aware has teased these two classes of cues apart.

What about olfactory cues? The few studies investigating if parents are capable of discriminating between their offspring and other unrelated children via smell indicate that women can identify their offspring with high reliability, but fathers, despite similar times of exposure, are unable to do so (Russell et al., 1983; Weisfeld, Czilli, & Phillips 2003). This suggests that whatever the cues driving offspring detection in men, they may not be the same ones women use to detect offspring. This makes sense since men and women faced different adaptive problems when it came to identifying offspring. In stark contrast to female detection of offspring, male detection of offspring appears to rely on the behavior of the mate. If men assess who their offspring are via female cues of sexual fidelity, then any female behavior that causes a negative assessment might reduce the certainty of relatedness and prevent sexual aversions from developing, thus opening the door to the possibility of sexual abuse.

Sibling Detection

What cues would have signaled that another individual was a sibling? One plausible cue to siblingship would have been duration of shared parental investment. Throughout our evolutionary history, the nutritional demands of breastfeeding, along with the need for protection, would have meant that children of the same mother were typically reared in close proximity during early childhood. Therefore, childhood coresidence would have served as a stable cue that identified probable siblings. This cue was first suggested by Edward Westermarck, a Finnish social scientist. Westermarck, having noted the injurious effects of inbreeding, proposed a mechanism by which humans naturally came to avoid close genetic relatives as sexual partners. He hypothesized that close physical proximity during early childhood leads to the development of a sexual aversion later, during adulthood (Westermarck 1891). This has come to be known as the Westermarck hypothesis.

Perhaps the most famous studies investigating the Westermarck hypothesis are the natural experiments created by the Israeli kibbutzim (Shepher 1971, 1983; Talmon 1964) and Taiwanese minor marriages (Wolf 1995). In both, cultural institutions created situations in which genetically unrelated individuals were co-reared from early childhood. In Israeli kibbutzim, for example, children were reared collectively in mixed-sex peer groups from right after birth. Shepher (1983) found that individuals who married within their own kibbutz rarely chose an individual from the same peer group. And, of the marriages that occurred between individuals of the same peer group, the partners had not lived together for more than 4 of the first 6 years of life. This led Shepher to reason that uninterrupted coresidence during the first 6 years of life is critical for the development of a sexual aversion later, during adulthood.

In Taiwanese minor marriages, a young bride is adopted into her future husband's family and reared alongside him into adulthood until the day they are married. The anthropologist Arthur Wolf has shown that, as the Westermarck hypothesis predicts, the earlier a girl is adopted, the longer her duration of coresidence with her future husband, and, consequently, the lower the rates of marital fertility and the higher the rates of divorce and extramarital affairs (Wolf 1995, 2005). Specifically, Wolf points to the first 3 years of life as the critical age of coresidence. In his data, he finds much lower fertility rates and higher rates of divorce in couples in which the girl was adopted before her third birthday (Wolf 2005).

Though coresidence would have been a good cue for detecting siblings, a better, more stable cue exists: seeing your biological mother caring for a neonate (e.g., breastfeeding). However, this information is available only to older siblings in the environment. (The arrow of time forbids younger siblings from seeing their older siblings breastfed and cared for during infancy.)

For younger siblings, then, coresidence duration might have been the best cue available. Indeed, when younger and older siblings are considered separately, coresidence duration predicts disgust associated with sibling sexual behaviors for younger siblings, not for older siblings (Lieberman et al., 2007). That is, the longer a younger sibling lived with an older opposite-sex sibling, the more disgusting they found the prospect of engaging in sexual behavior with that sibling. For the older sibling in the pair, disgust was not strongly correlated with the length of coresidence with the younger sibling. So long as the older sibling was exposed to his or her mother caring for their younger sibling as an infant, the older sibling reported intense disgust, a level attained after approximately 14–15 years of coresidence for the younger siblings (Lieberman et al., 2007).

In summary, two cues might play prominent roles in sibling detection: for older siblings, seeing one's mother caring for a newborn, and for younger siblings, coresidence during periods of shared parental investment (see also Fessler & Navarrete 2004; Lieberman, Tooby, & Cosmides 2003; McCabe 1983). Of course, additional cues might be used, including MHC-derived olfactory cues (e.g., Porter & Moore 1981, Wedekind & Furi 1997, Wedekind et al. 1995) and phenotypic resemblance (e.g., DeBruine 2005). To tease apart the contribution of each hypothesized cue, we are currently conducting a study that considers all the known possible cues to siblingship: coresidence duration, seeing a newborn being cared for by one's mother, phenotypic resemblance, MHC detection, and genetic similarity. In this way, we will be able to uncover how the mind integrates the various sources of information used to regulate sibling-directed behavior.

Summary

The identification of the cues our mind uses to assess relatedness has important implications for understanding why sexual abuse sometimes occurs. In situations where cues to kinship are absent, sexual aversions might not develop, leaving open the possibility of sexual abuse. In the next section, we discuss how an integration of an evolutionary-computational model of inbreeding avoidance with extant models of sexual abuse can inform future programs of research seeking to understand the factors that contribute to sexual abuse.

CONCEPTUAL INTEGRATION OF MODELS OF SEXUAL ABUSE

Based on the model of inbreeding avoidance discussed above, two procedures are required for the development of sexual aversions toward kin: procedures governing kin detection and procedures that take as input kinship information and regulate sexual motivations accordingly. How might this process shed light on sexual abuse? This model suggests there are (at least) two ways sexual aversions might fail to develop between kin and lead to a greater probability of sexual abuse: (i) cues signaling kinship might be absent or compromised; and (ii) programs regulating sexual motivations (e.g., the emotion of disgust) might be impaired. In this section, we discuss each possibility in turn and, along the way, integrate the factors that contribute to the incidence of sexual abuse as discussed by the family-systems model and David Finkelhor. We then briefly touch on how mate value, a variable distinct from kinship that is also hypothesized to be taken as input by systems regulating sexual motivations, can inform research on sexual abuse.

Cues Mediating Kin Detection Might Be Absent or Compromised

Cues Mediating Sibling Detection and Sexual Abuse

From the discussion above, it is apparent that an important cue found to mediate sibling detection and guide the development of a sexual aversion is coresidence duration. If this is indeed the case and the Westermarck hypothesis is correct, then the interruption or lack of coresidence during childhood should lessen the aversion and contribute to the incidence of sexual behavior or abuse (Erickson 2006; Lightcap, Kurland, & Burgess 1982). This seems to be the case. For example, Bevc and Silverman (1993, 2000) compared a population of college undergraduates who had engaged in sexual relations with a sibling to those who had not to determine whether or not there were any differences in childhood separation. They found that separation from their sibling during childhood was associated with increased consummatory sexual behavior (i.e., acts involving actual or attempted oral or genital penetration) than non-consummatory sexual behavior (i.e., acts including touching and kissing in a sexual manner and pretend intercourse).

In a much earlier evaluation, Weinberg (1955) discusses six cases of sibling sexual behavior. In each case, the siblings had not been reared together throughout childhood. Rather, the majority of the sibling pairs were reunited during adulthood and found each other to be attractive sexual partners. In the absence of the cues signaling relatedness, the mind is left to evaluate potential sexual partners according to the criteria of mate-choice systems (e.g., health and fertility for women; resources and investment inclinations for men). Since one's genetic relatives can be attractive individuals, it is not necessarily surprising that in the absence of any sexual aversions they are considered potential sexual partners. For example, Greenberg and Littlewood (1995) report on an apparently common phenomenon of sexual attraction between family members reunited after being separated by adoption. That kin are perceived as *more* attractive mates under these circumstances does not undermine evolutionary models of inbreeding avoidance. Rather, these examples provide evidence of preferences for individuals who share similar positive affordances such as hobbies, intellectual interests, and lifestyle (e.g., see Tooby & Cosmides 1996 for a discussion on "association value" as a route to the formation of deep engagements).

According to the family-systems model of sexual abuse, families in which sibling incest occurs are typified by a poor marital relationship and a neglectful mother. How might this link to kin detection? If an important cue that older siblings use to assess relatedness is whether or not their own mother cares for a newborn, then when mothers neglect their newborns, this could compromise older siblings' certainty of genetic relatedness. Furthermore, if breastfeeding a newborn is the particular cue older siblings evolved to take as input to assess relatedness, then it is possible that newborns who are wet-nursed or often bottle-fed by women other than their mother would not be as certain of relatedness (it is likely that bottle-feeding mimics breast-feeding cues, given that the positioning of the infant and close contact are quite similar in both cases). Of course, families with a history of sexual abuse are often plagued by many conditions, including drug and alcohol abuse and physical abuse or neglect (Black 1981, Finkelhor 1984, Kellogg & Menard 2003, Liles & Child 1986, Walsh, MacMillan, & Jamieson 2003). Nevertheless, understanding how the parental relationship and the behavior of the mother interfere with the natural categorization of other children as siblings can help us not only understand why sibling incest sometimes occurs but also identify those families at risk.

Cues Mediating Offspring Detection and Sexual Abuse

Within the family, abuse is most common between a mother's mate and her offspring (e.g., see Daly & Wilson 1988, Erickson 2005, Finklehor 1984, Russell 1983). As discussed above, the development of a sexual aversion between a man and the child of a particular woman relies on his assessment of paternity. For those men who lack paternity certainty, young women, for all intents and purposes, represent potential (future) mates. Both the family-systems model and David Finkelhor point to biologically unrelated men introduced into the family (e.g., stepfathers or mother's boyfriends) as posing the greatest threat of sexual abuse (e.g., Finkelhor 1984). These men are certain that any children in the family cannot be their own, and thus motivations to avoid them sexually will not have developed through the kin-detection system.

In contrast to men introduced into the family after the birth of a woman's children (or when she is pregnant), a man who has been sexually active with a woman for a long period of time *could* have fathered her child and can assess his probability of paternity based on cues relating to his mate's sexual fidelity and her patterns of parental investment. For example, if men use the cue "newborn being cared for by the woman I have been having sex with for a prolonged period of time" to assess paternity, then any interruption in maternal parental investment, especially when it occurs early in a child's life, might reduce a man's certainty of relatedness. When a mother has died (perhaps from complications during childbirth) or is often ill, rendering her incapable of caring for her child, this will reduce the frequency with which a man will see a child in an extended care-giving relationship with the mother and might, subsequently, detract from his certainty of relatedness. Indeed, many of the characteristics Finkelhor has found to be linked to sexual abuse fall into this category (Finkelhor 1984; see also Herman & Hirschman 1981).

Both Finkelhor and the family-systems model of sexual abuse indicate that a common feature of families in which sexual abuse occurs is a poor marital relationship. However, a poor marital relationship might not be the cause of sexual abuse per se. Rather, a poor marital relationship is likely the consequence of conflict, and it is the nature of the conflict that is of importance in predicting sexual abuse. An evolutionary framework predicts that poor marital relationships resulting from conflicts relating to female infidelity and male sexual jealousy are more likely to be associated with sexual abuse than poor marital relationships caused by issues unrelated to female mating behavior (e.g., childrearing). This is because the former types of conflict are more likely to compromise paternity certainty. Importantly, what matters is the man's *perception* of sexual infidelity rather than his mate's actual behavior, though of course these two are usually tightly linked. Thus, if a man, for whatever reason, suffers from morbid sexual jealousy, warranted or not, his assessment of paternity might be compromised, leading to a greater probability of sexual abuse.

In addition to considering the nature of the marital discord, an evolutionary perspective suggests that the timing of the conflict might affect paternity assessment. All else equal, marital problems initiating before the time of conception might have a greater likelihood of compromising a man's certainty of paternity than would problems that arise after the child has been born. We are currently exploring these hypotheses, which could have important implications for identifying families at risk of sexual abuse.

What is clear is that the mother, as suggested by Finkelhor and the family-systems model, plays a key role in mitigating the risk of sexual abuse within the family. If a man bases his certainty of paternity on the actions of his mate (e.g., her sexual fidelity, how many male friends she has, how often she is absent, her investment in offspring) and her qualities (e.g., whether her mate value is actually or merely perceived to be higher than his [see below]), then whether or not a sexual aversion develops toward a particular child depends mostly on her. This does not blame women for father–daughter sexual abuse but rather recognizes that a woman's behavior may be critical in shaping how men will interact with her child. Knowledge of how maternal behaviors can affect male paternity certainty can be used to educate teens and new mothers and might help lessen the risk of sexual abuse.

In this section, we stress that the absence of evolutionarily reliable cues signaling paternity are important for identifying children at risk for sexual abuse. These cues might be different from those signaling siblingship. However, previous applications of an evolutionary framework to investigating father–daughter sexual abuse have relied mainly on the Westermarck hypothesis, that is, early childhood exposure, a cue found to mediate sibling detection (e.g., Parker & Parker 1986, Williams & Finkelhor 1995). For example, Williams and Finkelhor (1995) tested the hypothesis that a father's close physical association with his daughter during her childhood leads to the development of a sexual aversion and, consequently, lower rates of incest. The researchers surveyed incestuous and non-incestuous Navy and civilian fathers to determine if any differences existed between incestuous and non-incestuous populations in the level of physical care fathers directed toward their daughters. Collecting data from civilian and Navy incestuous fathers allowed the researchers to determine if time away from home increased the risk of sexual abuse. Though Williams and Finkelhor did not find any difference between incestuous and non-incestuous fathers with respect to the amount of time spent away from the children as infants, they did find that incestuous fathers had lower caretaking scores than did non-incestuous fathers; compared to incestuous fathers, non-incestuous fathers engaged in more non-physical caretaking behaviors (e.g., reading stories and supervising) and also physical care-taking behaviors (e.g., feeding and changing diapers). They interpret these data to mean that care-taking protects the child from later abuse by enhancing positive parenting, protective feelings, and alternative gratifications, not by suppressing sexual arousal.

Based on the evolutionary-computational model discussed above, we posit a different explanation for Williams's and Finkelhor's data. Prolonged close physical association is not necessarily the best cue signaling paternity in the same way it signals siblingship. That is, the Westermarck hypothesis might be specific to siblings. Fathers are hypothesized to use a different set of information to assess relatedness to a child: information relating to paternity certainty (e.g., partner sexual fidelity). In a sense, then, it shouldn't be close physical association with the child but rather prolonged contact with the child's mother around the time of conception that predicts sexual abuse across populations. Though their study did not necessarily consider the cues signaling paternity, Williams and Finkelhor found that men who reported being dissatisfied in their marriage were five times more likely to have sexually abused their daughter. We suspect that marital discord is an important red flag since some of the main causes of conflict within a marriage relate directly to sexual jealousy. We predict that upon further inspection of the causes of marital dissatisfaction, men who suspect sexual infidelity, who are often sexually jealous, or who were absent from their mate around the time of conception will be more likely to sexually abuse a daughter.

Importantly, the cues signaling paternity are hypothesized to shape not only sexual motivations but altruistic motivations as well (e.g., see Daly & Wilson 1988; Lieberman et al., 2007). That non-incestuous fathers display greater patterns of investment is a signal that they have assessed the cues to paternity and estimated the probability of relatedness to be high. Thus care-taking per se does not protect the child from later abuse. Rather, we suggest that it is the cues that indicate to the man that he is the likely father that influence motivations to care as well as motivations to avoid sexual contact.

With respect to the negative results regarding time away, we predict that time away does indeed matter. Whereas Williams and Finkelhor asked if the father had been absent for more than 30 days during the first 12 months of the child's life, we predict the critical time period is before the child is even born. For example, whether or not sexual abuse occurs in Navy families is likely to depend on the time period in which the husband is away from his mate. All else equal, men who depart after their child has been born can be more certain of relatedness than men who depart then return to a pregnant wife! Also, a man's kinship network might help protect his paternity. That is, women who are left close to her mate's kin while he is away might be less apt to seek alternate sexual partners than might a woman left alone or away from the man's kin.

As this discussion reveals, more-focused hypothesis testing that takes into account the cues a man is likely to use to assess paternity holds great promise for shedding light on the factors that contribute to father–daughter sexual abuse. It is our hope that our discussion spurs researchers to shift a portion of their focus from the downstream behaviors that result from paternity certainty to the cues that directly regulate the assessment of paternity.

Programs Regulating Sexual Motivations Might Be Impaired

An evolutionary-computational model of inbreeding avoidance suggests that, even with perfect kin detection, if systems regulating sexual motivations are impaired, intrafamilial sexual abuse might still occur. The emotion of disgust is hypothesized to regulate sexual motivations, specifically sexual avoidance (Angyal 1941; Lieberman et al., 2007). Therefore, impairments to disgust might be linked to greater incidents of sexual abuse. Certainly, alcohol and drug use can affect decision-making processes and likely change disgust sensitivities. In addition, acquired or developmental impairments in neural regions associated with disgust, such as the anterior insula (Phillips et al. 1997) might also be associated with greater incidents of sexual abuse. To date, few if any studies have looked at the relationship between impairments in disgust and sexual abuse. Future investigation of disgust sensitivities, in particular sexual disgust sensitivities, can help illuminate why particular individuals might be targeted as sexual partners.

Beyond Kin Detection: Mate Value, Social Isolation, and Inbreeding Conflict

In the absence of cues signaling kinship, an individual will not categorize another as kin and, consequently, no sexual aversion will develop via this route (e.g., Erickson 2006). Instead, mate-choice systems will use information other than degree of relatedness to guide sexual motivations. Information that should be relevant to mate-choice systems include the mate value of a potential sexual partner (e.g., for women, health and reproductive value; for men, financial status and willingness to invest), one's own mate value, and the availability of potential mates. For example, men with low mate value (e.g., low SES, low symmetry, low testosterone-versus-estrogen levels) most likely experience a smaller mating pool, causing them to shift their focus to more-vulnerable sexual targets. That is, if men are motivated to attain the highest mate-value female they can, then for those dealt a less attractive phenotype, women typically not considered as potential mates by other men might be considered the top choice.

In the presence of cues signaling kinship, sexual aversions are likely to develop, but whether or not sexual motivations still target kin depend on a number of other factors, including the availability of alternate mates (e.g., social isolation) and inbreeding conflict. Perceived social isolation might recalibrate sexual motivations causing men to find their sisters, nieces, and other animals (not necessarily in that order) more attractive sexual partners.

However, because of the asymmetric costs of sexual reproduction in general and incest in particular (e.g., see Haig 1999, Tooby 1977, Walter & Buyske 2003), women are likely to strongly object to incestuous matings, even when there are few men to choose from.

SUMMARY AND CONCLUSIONS

An evolutionary-computational model integrates the themes of current models of sexual abuse into a cogent theoretical framework. It incorporates several of Finkelhor's motivations to abuse and internal and external inhibitors, as well Family Systems' emphasis on the mother and the marital relationship. This model is based on the principles of kin recognition and allows for the generation of specific hypotheses based on the kin recognition cues of each family dyad. For example, mother-offspring recognition is most likely regulated by immediately registered cues because genetic relatedness is assured at birth. Father-offspring recognition, on the other hand, is likely mediated by cues of paternity confidence such as physical resemblance and cues of female fidelity. Finally, sibling recognition is likely regulated by cues of coresidence and witnessing maternal care.

Kin detection plays an important role in how sexual aversions develop. Therefore, understanding how kin detection operates, that is, the cues our mind evolved to use to categorize another as kin, is critical to identifying those situations in which kin detection is likely to fail, leading to a greater probability of sexual abuse. Since procedures for detecting kin influence not only sexual motivations but altruistic motivations as well, understanding how kin detection operates will also shed light on the reasons behind physical abuse and neglect (Daly & Wilson 1988).

In addition to kin detection, the assessment of one's own mate value, one's prospects among potential sexual partners, and the costs associated with different sexual partners are hypothesized to affect sexual motivations. Men with low mate value might be more prone to target more-vulnerable individuals as sexual partners, and once they secure a mate might be less certain of their child's paternity. Social isolation can influence perceptions of potential mating partners, increasing the probability that men but not women (because of the elevated costs women incur from inbreeding) might seek a family member as a sexual partner.

An evolutionary model of all the factors guiding sexual motivations (e.g., kinship and mate value) can help generate predictions of the conditions under which sexual abuse is likely to occur. It is of critical importance that we be able to identify the conditions under which the available kin recognition cues may not inhibit sexual motivation toward morally inappropriate sexual partners, as might be the case in situations of paternity uncertainty. This is especially important given the fact that a large proportion of familial sexual abuse is perpetrated by men, and could have important implications for policy regarding military deployment, for example, and for programs aimed at educating and counseling new families.

References

Adams, M. S., & Neel, J. V. (1967). Children of incest. *Pediactrics, 40*, 55–62.

Adler, N. A., & Schutz, J. (1995). Sibling incest offenders. *Child Abuse & Neglect, 19*, 811–819.

Apicella, C. L., & Marlowe, F. W. (2004). Perceived mate fidelity and paternal resemblance predict men's investment in children. *Evolution & Human Behavior, 25*, 371–378.

Apicella, C. L., & Marlowe, F. W. (2007). Men's reproductive decisions: Mating, parenting and self-perceived mate value. *Human Nature, 18*, 22–34.

Angyal, A. (1941). Disgust and related aversions. *Journal of Abnormal and Social Psychology, 36*, 393–412.

Baker, R. R., & Bellis, M. A. (1993). Human sperm competition: Ejaculate adjustment by males and the function of masturbation. *Animal Behaviour, 46*, 861–885.

Beauchamp, G. K., Yamazaki, K., & Boyse, E. A. (1985). The chemosensory recognition of genetic individuality. *Scientific American, 253*, 86–92.

Bevc, I., & Silverman, I. (1993). Early proximity and intimacy between siblings and incestuous behavior: A test of the Westermarck theory. *Ethology & Sociobiology, 14*, 171–181.

Bevc, I., & Silverman, I. (2000). Early separation and sibling incest: A test of the revised Westermarck theory. *Evolution and Human Behavior, 21*, 151–161.

Bittles, A. H., & Neel, J. V. (1994). The costs of human inbreeding and their implications for variation at the DNA level. *Nature Genetics, 8*, 117–121.

Black, C. (1981). *It will never happen to me.* Denver: M.A.C.

Boyd, R., & Silk, J. B. (1997). *How humans evolved.* New York: W. W. Norton.

Burkett, L. P. (1991). Parenting behaviors of women who were sexually abused as children in their families of origin. *Family Processes, 30*, 421–434.

Buss, D. M. (2003). *The evolution of desire: Strategies of human mating.* New York: Basic Books.

Carter, C. O. (1967). Risk of offspring of incest. *Lancet, 1*, 436.

Charlesworth, D., & Charlesworth, B. (1999). The genetic basis of inbreeding depression. *Genetical Research, 74*, 329–340.

Cole, P. M., & Putnam, F. W. (1992). Effect of incest on self and social functioning: A developmental psychopathology perspective. *Journal of Consulting and Clinical Psychology, 60*, 174–184.

Crnokrak, P., & Roff, D. A. (1999). Inbreeding depression in the wild. *Heredity, 83*, 260–270.

Daly, M., & Wilson, M. I. (1982). Whom are newborn babies said to resemble? *Ethology and Sociobiology, 3,* 69–78.

Daly, M., & Wilson, M. I. (1988). *Homicide.* New York: Aldine de Gruyter.

DeBruine, L. (2005). Trustworthy but not lust-worthy: Context-specific effects of facial resemblance. *Proceedings of the Royal Society B, Biological Sciences, 272,* 919–922.

Dunne, M. P., Purdie, D. M., Cook, M. D., Boyle, F. M., & Najman, J. M. (2003). Is child sexual abuse declining? Evidence from a population-based survey of men and women in Australia. *Child Abuse & Neglect, 27,* 141–152.

Erickson, M. (2005). Evolutionary thought and the current clinical understanding of incest. In A. P. Wolf & W. H. Durham (Eds.), *Inbreeding, incest, and the incest taboo* (pp. 161–189). Stanford, CA: Stanford University Press.

Erickson, M. (2006). Nature disrupted: Evolution, kinship and child sexual abuse. *Clinical Neuropsychiatry, 3,* 100–120.

Famularo, R., Stone, K., Barnum, R., & Wharton, R. (1986). Alcoholism and severe child maltreatment. *American Journal of Orthopsychiatry, 56,* 481–485.

Fessler, D. M. T., & Navarrete, C. D. (2004). Third-party attitudes toward sibling incest: Evidence for Westermarck's hypotheses. *Evolution and Human Behavior, 25,* 277–294.

Finkelhor, D. (1979). *Sexual victimized children.* New York: Free Press.

Finkelhor, D. (1980). Sex among siblings: A survey report on its prevalence its variety and its effects. *Archives of Sexual Behavior, 9,* 171–194.

Finkelhor, D. (1984). *Child sexual abuse: New theory and research.* New York: Free Press.

Fletcher, D. J. C., & Michener, C. D. (1987). *Kin recognition in animals.* New York: Wiley.

Friedman, S. (1988). A family systems approach to treatment. In L. E. A. Walker (Ed.), *Handbook on sexual abuse of children: assessment and treatment issues* (pp. 326–349). New York: Springer.

Formby, D. (1967). Maternal recognition of infant's cry. *Developmental Medicine and Child Neurology, 9,* 293–298.

Furniss, T. (1983). Mutual influence and interlocking professional–family process in the treatment of child sexual abuse and incest. *Child Abuse & Neglect, 7,* 207–223.

Furniss, T. (1985). Conflict-avoiding and conflict-regulating patterns in incest and child sexual abuse. *Acta paedopsychiatrica, 50,* 299–313.

Greenberg, M., & Littlewood, R. (1995). Post-adoption incest and phenotype matching: Experience, personal meanings, and biosocial implications. *British Journal of Medical Psychology, 68,* 29–44.

Greenspun, W. S. (1994). Internal and interpersonal: The family transmission of father–daughter incest. *Journal of Child Sexual Abuse, 3,* 1–14.

Haig, D. (1999). Asymmetric relations: Internal conflicts and the horror of incest. *Evolution and Human Behavior, 20,* 83–98.

Hardy, M. (2001). Physical aggression and sexual behavior among siblings: A retrospective study. *Journal of Family Violence, 16,* 255–268.

Hartley, C. C. (2001). Incest offenders' perceptions of their motives to sexually offend within their past and current life context. *Journal of Interpersonal Violence, 16,* 459–475.

Hepper, P. G. (1991). *Kin recognition.* Cambridge: Cambridge University Press.

Herman, J., & Hirschman, L. (1981). Families at risk for father–daughter incest. *American Journal of Psychiatry, 138,* 967–970.

Herman, J. L. (1981). *Father–daughter incest.* Cambridge: Harvard University Press.

Jacob, S., McClintock, M. K., Zelano, B., Ober, C. (2002). Paternally inherited HLA alleles are associated with women's choice of male odor. *Nature Genetics, 30,* 175–179.

Janeway, C. A. (1993). How the immune system recognizes invaders. *Scientific American, 269,* 72–79.

Jones, L. M., & Finkelhor, D. (2001). *The decline in child sexual abuse cases: Exploring the causes. Bulletin.* Washington, DC: U.S. Department of Justice, Office of Justice Programs, Office of Juvenile Justice and Delinquency Prevention.

Jones, L. M., Finkelhor, D., & Kopiec, K. (2001). Why is sexual abuse declining? A survey of state child protection administrators. *Child Abuse & Neglect, 25,* 1139–1158.

Kaitz, M., Good, A., Rokem, A. M., & Eidelman, A. I. (1987). Mothers' recognition of their newborns by olfactory cues. *Developmental Psychobiology, 20,* 587–591.

Keller, L. F., Arcese, P. S., James, N. M., Hochachka, W. M. (1994). Selection against inbred song sparrows during a natural population bottleneck. *Nature, 372,* 356–357.

Kellogg, N. D., & Menard, S. W. (2003). Violence among family members of children and adolescents evaluated for sexual abuse. *Child Abuse and Neglect, 27,* 1367–1376.

Kendall-Tackett, K. A., Williams, L. M., & Finkelhor, D. (1993). Impact of sexual abuse on children: A review and synthesis of recent empirical studies. *Psychological Bulletin, 113,* 164–180.

Klein, J. (1986). Antigen-major histocompatibility complex-T cell receptors: inquiries into the immunological menage a trois. *Immunological Research, 5,* 173–190.

Laviola, M. (1992). Effects of older brother–younger sister incest: A study of the dynamics of 17 cases. *Child Abuse & Neglect, 16,* 409–421.

Lieberman, D., Tooby, J., & Cosmides, L. (2003). Does morality have a biological basis? An empirical test of the factors governing moral sentiments relating to incest. *Proceedings, Biological Sciences, 270,* 819–826.

Lieberman, D., Tooby, J., and Cosmides, L. (2007). The architecture of human nature. *Nature, 445,* 727–731.

Lightcap, J. L., Kurland, J. A., & Burgess, R. L. (1982). Child abuse: A test of some predictions from evolutionary theory. *Ethology and Sociobiology, 3,* 61–67.

Liles, R. E. & Childs, D. (1986). Similarities in family dynamics of incest and alcohol abuse. *Alcohol-Health & Research World, 11,* 27–38.

Lung, F. W., & Huang, S. F. (2004). Psychosocial characteristics of criminals committing incest and other sex offenses: A survey in a Taiwanese prison. *Journal of Offender Therapy and Comparative Criminology, 48,* 554–560.

Manning, C. J., Wakeland, E. K., & Potts, W. K. (1992). Communal nesting patterns in mice implicate MHC genes in kin recognition. *Nature, 360,* 581–583.

McCabe, J. (1983). FBD marriage: Further support for the Westermarck hypothesis. *American Anthropologist, 85,* 50–69.

Minuchin, S. (1974). *Families and family therapy.* Cambridge: Harvard University Press.

Molnar, B. E., Buka, S. L., & Kessler, R. C. (2001). Child sexual abuse and subsequent psychopathology: Results from the National Comorbidity Survey. *American Journal of Public Health, 91,* 753–760.

Murray, T. Hollien, H., & Muller, E. (1975). Perceptual responses to infant crying: Maternal recognition and sex judgments. *Journal of Child Language, 2,* 199–204.

Pagel, M. (1997). Desperately concealing father: A theory of parent–infant resemblance. *Animal Behaviour, 53,* 973–981.

Parker, H., & Parker, S. (1986). Father–daughter sexual abuse: An emerging perspective. *American Journal of Orthopsychiatry, 56,* 531–549.

Peddle, N., & Wang, C. (2001). *Current trends in child abuse prevention, reporting, and fatalities: The 1999 fifty-state survey.* Chicago: Prevent Child Abuse America.

Phillips, M. L., Young, A. W., Senior, C., Brammer, M., Andrews, C., Calder, A. J., et al. (1997). A specific neural substrate for perceiving facial expressions of disgust. *Nature, 389,* 495–498.

Pierce, L. H., & Pierce, R. L. (1990). Adolescent/sibling incest perpetrators. In A. L. Horton, B. L. Johnson, L. M. Roundy, & D. Williams (Eds.), *The incest perpetrator: A family member no one wants to treat.* Newbury Park, CA: Sage.

Platek, S. M., Critton, S. R., Burch, R. L., Frederick, D. A., Myers, T. E., & Gallup, G. G. (2003). How much paternal resemblance is enough? Sex differences in hypothetical investment decisions but not in the detection of resemblance. *Evolution and Human Behavior, 24,* 81–87.

Platek, S. M., Raines, D. M., Gallup, G. G., Mohamed, F. B., Thomson, J. W., Myers, T. E., et al. (2004). Reactions to children's faces: Males are more affected by resemblance than females are, and so are their brains. *Evolution and Human Behavior, 25,* 394–405.

Porter, R. H., Cernoch, J. M., & Balogh, R. D. (1984). Recognition of neonates by facial–visual characteristics. *Pediatrics, 74,* 501–504.

Porter, R. H., Cernoch, J. M., & McLaughlin, F. J. (1983). Maternal recognition of neonates through olfactory cues, *Physiology and Behavior, 30,* 151–154.

Porter, R. H., & Moore, J. D. (1981). Human kin recognition by olfactory cues. *Physiology and Behavior, 27,* 493–495.

Potts, W. K., Manning, C. J., & Wakeland, E. K. (1991). Mating patterns in seminatural populations of mice influenced by MHC genotype. *Nature, 352,* 619–621.

Regalski, J. M., & Gaulin, S. J. C. (1993). Whom are Mexican infants said to resemble—monitoring and paternal confidence in the Yucatan. *Ethology and Sociobiology, 14,* 97–113.

Russell, D. (1983). Incidence and prevalence of intrafamilial and extrafamilial sexual abuse of female children. *Child Abuse and Neglect, 7,* 133–146.

Russell, D. E. H. (1986). *The secret trauma: Incest in the lives of girls and women.* New York: Basic Books.

Russell, M. J., Mendelson, T., & Peeke, H. V. S. (1983). Mothers' identification of their infant's odors. *Ethology and Sociobiology, 4,* 29–31.

Seemanova, E. (1971). A study of children of incestuous matings. *Human Heredity, 21,* 108–128.

Shepher, J. (1971). Mate selection among second-generation kibbutz adolescents and adults: Incest avoidance and negative imprinting. *Archives of Sexual Behavior, 1,* 293–307.

Shepher, J. (1983). *Incest: A biosocial view.* New York: Academic Press.

Singer, A. G., Beauchamp, G. K., Yamazaki, K. (1997). Volatile signals of the major histocompatibility complex in male mouse urine. *Proceedings of the National Academy of Sciences of the United States of America, 94,* 2210–2214.

Singh, P. B., Brown, R. E., & Roser, B. (1987). MHC antigens in urine as olfactory recognition cues. *Nature, 327,* 161–164.

Smith, H., & Israel, E. (1987). Sibling incest: A study of the dynamics of 25 cases. *Child Abuse & Neglect, 11,* 101–108.

Snell, G. D. (1981). Studies in histocompatibility. *Science, 213,* 172–178.

Symons, D. (1979). *The evolution of human sexuality.* New York: Oxford University Press.

Talmon, G. Y. (1964). Mate selection in collective settlements. *American Sociological Review, 29,* 408–491.

Tooby, J. (1977). Factors governing optimal inbreeding. *Proceedings of the Institute for Evolutionary Studies, 77,* 1–54.

Tooby, J. (1982). Pathogens, polymorphism, and the evolution of sex. *Journal of Theoretical Biology, 97,* 557–576.

Tooby, J., & Cosmides, L. (1996). Friendship and the banker's paradox: Other pathways to the evolution of adaptations for altruism. In W. G. Runciman, J. Maynard Smith, & R. I. M. Dunbar (Eds.), *Evolution of Social Behaviour Patterns in Primates and Man. Proceedings of the British Academy, 88,* 119–143.

Trepper, T., Niedner, D., Mika, L., & Barrett, M. J. (1996). Family characteristics of intact sexually abusing families: An exploratory study. *Journal of Child Sexual Abuse, 5,* 1–18.

Walter, A., & Buyske, S. (2003). The Westermarck effect and early childhood co-socialization: Sex differences in inbreeding avoidance. *British Journal of Developmental Psychology, 21,* 353–365.

Walsh, C., MacMillan, H. L., & Jamieson, E. (2003). The relationship between parental substance abuse and child maltreatment: Findings from the Ontario Health Supplement. *Child Abuse and Neglect, 27,* 1409–1425.

Wedekind, C., & Furi, S. (1997). Body odour preferences in men and women: Do they aim for specific MHC combinations or simply heterozygosity? *Proceedings of the Royal Society of London Series B-Biological Sciences, 264,* 1471–1479.

Wedekind, C., Seebeck, T., Bettens, F., & Paepke, A. J. (1995). MHC-dependent mate preferences in humans. *Proceedings of the Royal Society of London Series B, Biological Sciences, 260,* 245–249.

Weinberg, S. K. (1955). *Incest behavior.* New York: Citadel.

Weisfeld, G. E., Czilli, T., & Phillips, K. A. (2003). Possible olfaction-based mechanisms in human kin recognition and inbreeding avoidance. *Journal of Experimental Child Psychology, 85,* 279–295.

Weiss, E. L., Longhurst, J. G., & Mazure, C. M. (1999). Childhood sexual abuse as a risk factor for major depression in women: Psychosocial and neurobiological correlates. *American Journal of Psychiatry, 156,* 816–828.

Westermarck, E. A. (1891). *The history of human marriage* (5th ed.). London: Macmillan.

Williams, L., & Finkelhor, D. (1995). Paternal caregiving and incest: Test of a biosocial model. *American Journal of Orthopsychiatry, 65,* 101–113.

Wolf, A. P. (1995). *Sexual attraction and childhood association: A Chinese brief for Edward Westermarck.* Stanford, CA: Stanford University Press.

Wolf, A. P. (2005). Explaining the Westermarck effect. In A. P. Wolf & W. H. Durham (Eds.), *Inbreeding, incest, and the incest taboo: The state of knowledge at the turn of the century* (pp. 76–92). Stanford, CA: Stanford University Press.

Worling, J. R. (1995). Adolescent sibling–incest offenders: Differences in family and individual functioning when compared to adolescent nonsibling sex offenders. *Child Abuse & Neglect, 19,* 633–643.

Yamazaki, K., Beauchamp, G. K., Curran, M., Bard, J., & Boyse, E. A. (2000). Parent–progeny recognition as a function of MHC odortype identity. *Proceedings of the National Academy of Sciences of the United States of America, 97,* 10,500–10,502.

11   Grandparental and Extended Kin Relationships

Harald A. Euler and Richard L. Michalski

Modern societies have undergone changes that affect grandparental and other extended-kin relationships. Birth rates and conjugal stability have decreased while life expectancy and residential mobility have increased. State welfare provisions have largely replaced dependence on kin support in many modern states. Extended families have become smaller, with children having fewer siblings, fewer aunts and uncles, and fewer cousins. The breakdown of traditional family structures has been proclaimed repeatedly. But do these demographic changes touch deeper family structures? Scientists with an evolutionary perspective are reluctant to confirm and hesitant to consider the present time unique. Most people have or will have grandchildren, and all have or had grandparents. With rising life expectancy, more people will have living grandparents and will be grandparents for a longer portion of their lives. The plays may change, but the plots remain the same. The mother–daughter relationship will remain the center of the family. With rising divorce rates and child custody typically given to mothers, matrilineal ties are strengthened and men marginalized from the family. The role of the maternal grandmother might therefore become even more important in the future than it has been in the past.

Much family research has been done by sociologists, who traditionally do not address sex differences in human nature. They tend to break families at generations (e.g., parents vs. grandparents) and group grandparents as a homogenous quartet (e.g., Szinovacz 1998). When distinctions are made, grandmothers and grandfathers may be differentiated, but typically without consideration of lineage. Only in rare cases (e.g., Dench & Ogg 2003, Fingerman 2004, Rossi & Rossi 1990) are grandparents categorically distinguished into the four types of grandparents, but even when they are, evolutionary theory provides no guidance about basic sex differences. Evolutionary psychologists heed the advice of Socrates to cut hunted game (meaning nature) at its joints. From this perspective, the differentiation along sex *and* lineage is crucial. There are grandparents and grandparents, and what is good for the goose may not be good for the gander.

In this chapter, we argue that grandparenthood may trigger psychological adaptations with relationship-specific features. Grandparental investment cannot be understood adequately without consideration of its Darwinian fitness consequences. We similarly cannot understand relationships with aunts and uncles and nieces and nephews without such consideration. Because parents are mediators of grandparent and grandchild relationships, the evolutionary analysis of grandparenthood sheds light on the seemingly universal plight of in-law relationships, most conspicuous in the conflict between mothers-in-law and daughters-in-law. Investment in progeny and the emotional closeness of intergenerational dyads is highly and robustly structured. This structure is parsimoniously and to a considerable extent accounted for by a few basic reproductively relevant variables including sex-specific reproductive strategy and relationship uncertainty (Euler, Hoier, & Rohde, in press).

REPRODUCTIVE STRATEGY AND RELATIONSHIP UNCERTAINTY AS BASIC DETERMINANTS OF GRANDPARENTAL INVESTMENT

The reproductive strategy of the female mammal demands high maternal investment. Maximizing genetic replication generally requires maximizing maternal investment, whereas for men, with their high reproductive potential, the opportunity costs of paternal investments are higher. Maternal investment is thus obligatory and paternal investment more facultative, that is, depending on circumstances. This asymmetry between the sexes has far-ranging consequences in the area of intergenerational solidarity as well. The particular consequences are not always straightforward but are mediated by socioecological circumstances, like subsistence conditions, mating and kinship system, division of labor, residence pattern, lineality, resource control, and inheritance rules (Holden, Sear, & Mace 2003; Leonetti, Nath, Hemam & Neill 2005; Voland & Beise 2005).

Juvenile humans, relative to other primates, show the highest demand for parental investment. To be able to fulfill these demands, mothers need help raising offspring and appear to display features that offset children's investment demands (e.g., preferences for mates of high social standing, resources, and ambition) (Buss 2003). The traditional view is that fathers provide help in various forms, including time, food provision, protection, and child socialization. However, even though humans belong to a rare few primate species where paternal investment occurs at all, the absolute investments made by fathers are small relative to those made by mothers. Even among Aka Pygmies, where fathers have been considered most helpful, their investment pales compared to the investment made by mothers (Hewlett 1991). As to food, the caloric contribution of fathers in hunter–gatherer societies is not as impressive as once thought. Hunting successes come unpredictably and are generally shared among the tribe in order to contribute to the status of the hunter, and even the total calories from hunting are less than those from gathering. Above all, Pleistocene men were probably just not around much of the time but were instead roaming and ranging, fighting and philandering. Babies, however, required constant attention.

Help for mothers may therefore have come dependably from closely related females, most notably from the mother's mother, less from her sisters, and some from her preadolescent daughters. Grandmaternal support can help explain the relatively short human inter-birth interval in natural fertility populations (Mace & Sear 2005). In ancestral populations, without modern conveniences such as grocery stores, baby carriages, and baby formula, the inter-birth interval was probably around 3 years if circumstances were good. This appears long, but only when compared to the birthrates of historic times before the modern demographic transition. Compared to other primates, such a birth interval is rather short (Galdikas & Wood 1990). Help from maternal grandmothers is assumed to have enabled human mothers to attain such a short inter-birth interval. In addition to increasing the fertility of her daughter, grandmother's help may also decrease the mortality of her grandchildren (Sear & Mace in press).

Grandmothers can help only if they have a surplus of resources, which they might have if they do not themselves have infants that demand care. Menopause is a unique feature of human female life history that may have enabled this balance between female investment in offspring and in grandchildren. The idea of menopause as a reproductive adaptation was first put forth by Williams (1957) and was later referred to as the "grandmother hypothesis," not quite correctly so, because Williams was apparently considering only the older female as a mother, not as a grandmother: "It may have become advantageous for a woman of forty-five or fifty to stop dividing her declining faculties between the care of extant offspring and the production of new ones" (pp. 407–408). Hamilton (1966) expanded on this notion of "a special value of the old woman as mother or grandmother" (p. 37) but was reluctant to consider it an adaptation. We could, therefore, distinguish between a weak and a strong version of the grandmother hypothesis, the weak one referring merely to the menopausal cessation of reproduction, the strong one adding care of grandchildren.

The grandmother hypothesis is intuitively appealing, but debate continues about if menopause is indeed an adaptation, or only a byproduct or modern artifact (for a summary see Voland, Chasiotis, & Schiefenhövel 2005). There are strong data suggesting that grandmaternal help can contribute to the fitness of the mother and to the survival of the grandchildren (Hawkes, O'Connell, & Blurton-Jones 1989; Hawkes, O'Connell, Blurton-Jones, Alvarez, & Charnov 2000, Lahdenperä, Lummaa, Helle, Tremblay, & Russell 2004), and thus to the inclusive fitness of the grandmother herself. Most convincing are recent data by Sear and Mace (in press) on the effect of the presence of kin on child survival rates among natural fertility populations. The presence of the maternal grandmother contributed to grandchildren's survival in the majority (10 out of 12) of studies. The presence of the other three grandparents was overall less beneficial to grandchildren. Surprisingly, Voland and Beise (2002) even showed that in a historical northern German population it was better for child survival if the paternal grandmother, that is, the mother-in-law, was *not* alive.

To help the adult daughter in her maternal effort is in the inclusive-fitness interest of a postmenopausal woman, and the best she can offer her daughter is her time, food acquisition (in subsistence societies), and child care (in all societies). Her husband, the maternal grandfather, may be of additional help, but his opportunity costs are higher, which means that he can be assumed to be generally less inclined than his spouse to help his daughter. Grandparental resources are limited, and their allocation must be maximized. How much should be invested in the adult son and his children? The son is not as burdened with child care as is the daughter, but he can be aided in his reproductive effort, not by time for child care, but by the transfer of status and wealth, if socioecological conditions permit transformation of status and wealth into sexual access. These conditions lead to the comparably high reproductive variance of men, as seen in traditional pastoral societies with a mating system of optional polygyny. Ancestral Pleistocene environments, however, were presumably to be not characterized by extreme sex differences in reproductive variance. Under conditions of relative pervasive monogamy, be it ecologically imposed, as in the Stone Ages, or culturally imposed, as in modern societies, time investment in the adult daughter and her children rather than in the adult son and his children should be the more desirable option for postmenopausal women. Whether daughter-biased investment is subsumed under matrilateral bias, allomothering, or cooperative breeding, the ultimate cause derives from the sex-specific reproductive strategy of humans.

The role of paternity uncertainty, or more precisely, grandmaternity and grandpaternity uncertainty, was first mentioned by Dawkins (1976). Grandparents throughout human evolutionary history had varying degrees of certainty in their relatedness to grandchildren. Maternal grandmothers could have been more certain about their relatedness to grandchildren than could other grandparents. The maternal grandfather and the paternal grandmother each have one link of paternity uncertainty; the paternal grandfather has two links. The discrepancy between assumed and actual paternity in current Western societies is less than 3%, rather than the ominous 10%, which appears to be more a modern myth than a fact (Euler 2004), but it may have well been around 10% or more in earlier times. Relationship certainty is, therefore, a feature to be considered when evaluating preferential grandpaternal investment, although it has, in our judgment, weaker effects than do sex-specific reproductive strategies. For many researchers in evolutionary accounts of grandparenthood (e.g., Smith 1991), however, paternity uncertainty is the only factor considered. The problem with such a monocausal explanation is the observation that, generally, the maternal grandfather invests more in grandchildren than does the paternal grandmother. This problem has been specifically addressed by Laham, Gonsalkorale, and von Hippel (2005) in "Preferential Investment in More Certain Kin" (see also Beise 2005, pp. 232–233), whose charm is parsimoniousness. Laham et al.'s "outlet theory" will be discussed in more detail below. We take the position that sex-specific reproductive strategy and paternity uncertainty are ultimate causes, which contribute to both the obvious matrilateral bias in human family structures in general and the discriminative grandparental investment in particular (Euler, Hoier, & Rohde 2001).

THE SOLICITUDE RANK ORDER OF GRANDPARENTS

Grandparent–grandchild relationships may be approached from different perspectives. The informant may be the grandchild, the linking parent, or the grandparent. The three information sources appear to be mostly consistent, although grandparents themselves tend to ascribe the greatest importance to and express the highest satisfaction with the grandparental role, feel most closeness to kin, and claim the highest rate of contact (Dench & Ogg 2003). The informant may be questioned about a plethora of proxies for investment, including ratings of grandparental solicitude, favorite grandparents and grandchildren, and contact frequencies. The determinants of grandparental investments, finally, are not restricted to sex-specific reproductive strategy and paternity uncertainty. These two variables are important but nevertheless account for only a fraction of the total variance. We shall present empirical results that cover some aspect of each of the three avenues.

To our knowledge, Smith (1988, 1991) conducted the first study to investigate preferential grandparental investment from an evolutionary perspective. Differential investment among grandparents was predicted on the basis of relationship uncertainty, which yielded equal investment for the paternal grandmother and the maternal grandfather. In a sizeable sample ($N = 587$), however, Smith (1991) found not only maternal grandparents to spend more time with grandchildren than paternal grandparents, and grandmothers more than grandfathers, but also maternal grandfathers more than paternal grandmothers. This pattern was seen in both so-called unilineal grandparents (those who have grandchildren only through daughters or through sons) and in bilineal grandparents (those who have grandchildren through both daughters and sons). Moreover, the difference between the investment of grandmothers and grandfathers should have been the same as the difference between maternal and paternal grandparents, but the latter was larger. The two deviations from the predictions were explained post hoc by resorting to other factors.

Euler and Weitzel (1996) deduced an ordered prediction about grandparental solicitude from the combined effects of both sex-specific reproductive strategy and paternity uncertainty. The former, as the stronger determinant, predicts a higher solicitude for children of daughters than for children of sons. The latter, as the weaker factor, predicts a higher solicitude by grandmothers than by grandfathers. The amount of solicitude was assessed by asking adult participants about the amount of grandparental care received in childhood, under the assumption that ratings by recipients of care are a good, maybe even better, indicator of grandparental solicitude than ratings given by grandparents themselves, because norms of impartiality prevent grandparents from making self-descriptive statements about favored grandchildren. A convenience sample of both student and community participants (720 men, 1,125 women, 12 unspecified; ages 16 –80) were asked how much each grandparent had cared for them (*"gekümmert"*) up to the age of 7. The German verb *kümmern* has both a behavioral and a cognitive–emotional meaning, namely (1) to care for or look after, and (2) to be emotionally and/or cognitively concerned about. From the total sample of 1,857 respondents, a subset of 603 cases were selected for analysis whose four grandparents were all still alive when the participant was 7 years old.

The results confirmed predictions about the discriminative nature of grandparental solicitude. The maternal grandmother was rated as having been the most caring, followed by the maternal grandfather, the paternal grandmother, and the paternal grandfather. Maternal grandparents were significantly more caring than paternal grandparents, and grandmothers significantly more caring than grandfathers. The effect sizes, given as the partial η^2, which denotes the variance attributable to the effect of interest divided by this variance plus error variance, were .11 for the lineage effect (maternal vs. paternal) and .17 for the effect of sex of grandparent. Both effects together account for a sizable proportion of the variance.

Of special interest, apart from the insufficiency of paternity uncertainty as the only basic determinant, is the finding that the maternal grandfather cared more than the paternal grandmother. If grandparental caregiving were solely determined by a social role that ascribes child care predominantly to women, then both types of grandmothers should provide more care than both grandfathers. Accordingly, this argument should apply particularly to the older grandchildren in the sample, whose grandparents presumably subscribe more to traditional gender roles than do grandparents of younger participants. However, the difference was statistically significant in the opposite direction and even more pronounced for the older (40 years or older) than for the younger participants.

This same pattern of discriminative grandparental solicitude has been found in comparable studies in various countries, including the United States (DeKay 1995), France (Steinbach & Henke 1998), Belgium (van Ranst, Verschueren, & Marcoen 1995), and Greece (Pashos 2000). Pashos (2000), who studied within-culture variation in grandparental investment, found that among urban Greeks the pattern of grandparental solicitude was similar to that of other studies, but among rural Greeks it differed, especially for male respondents, who rated the care given by paternal grandparents higher than by maternal grandparents. A similar deviation from the standard pattern of modern Western societies has been reported by King and Elder (1995), who found that paternal grandparents appeared more salient in American farm families. Grandchildren in farm families, as compared to rural non-farm families, lived closer to their paternal grandparents, visited them more frequently, and rated the quality of their relationship as better than that with their maternal grandparents. In pastoral societies with patrilocality, patrilinearity, and corresponding inheritance rules, the investment in sons' children pays the grandparents reproductively more than investment in daughters' children. These findings point to the need to appreciate socioecological conditions that moderate, or even reverse, patterns of grandparental solicitude that might otherwise be missed by predicting effects based only on lineage and sex-specific reproductive strategies.

Various studies of aspects of grandparental investment other than grandchild-rated solicitude were investigated and have confirmed the general pattern of discriminative grandparental investment, including perception of closeness between grandparents and grandchildren (Fischer 1983), time spent with grandchildren (Smith 1988, 1991), interaction frequencies (Eisenberg 1988, Hartshorne & Manaster 1982, Hoffman 1978/1979, Pollet, Nettle, & Nelissen 2006, Salmon 1999), emotional closeness to grandparents (Eisenberg 1988,

Hoffman 1978/1979, Kennedy 1989, Matthews & Sprey 1985, McBurney, Pashos, & Gaulin 2006, Robins & Tomanec 1962, Rossi & Rossi 1990, Russell & Wells 1987), naming favorite (Kahana & Kahana 1970, Steinbach & Henke 1998) or emotionally closest grandparents (Hodgson 1992), gifts received from grandparents (DeKay 1995), grandparental mourning after a grandchild's death (Littlefield & Rushton 1986), and adoption of grandchildren (Daly & Wilson 1980, Schiefenhövel & Grabolle 2005). Missing from this listing are grandparental bequests, about which no data are known to the authors.

Even the informal terms of address used for grandparents are telling. The maternal grandmother is most often of all grandparents addressed with an endearing or diminutive name. For example, in Germany the maternal grandmother might be called "my dear granny" (German: *die liebe Oma*, or *Omilein*), whereas the paternal grandmother is just called "the other grandmother" (Euler, Hoier, & Pölitz 1998).

MODERATING VARIABLES

Sex-specific strategy and paternity uncertainty are not the only determinants of grandparental investment. There are three interacting generations involved, which—together with the socioecological context—open gateways for a variety of variables relevant for an evolutionary analysis, about which data are available. A treatment of constructivistic variables may be found elsewhere (e.g., Szinovacz 1998).

Residential Proximity

The rule "out of sight, out of mind" applies to the grandparent–grandchild relationship. The greater the distance between grandparent and grandchild, the less time spent together (Smith 1991), the less contact (Hodgson 1992), the lower grandchildren's solicitude rating (Euler & Weitzel 1996), and the less closeness (Robins & Tomanec 1962). Salmon (1999), however, found no negative correlation between distance and frequency of visits and phone calls. In many reports, the average residential distance does not differ between the types of grandparent in modern neolocal societies (e.g., Euler & Weitzel 1996, Pashos 2000, Smith 1991, J. L. Thomas 1989), but there are also exceptions of closer proximity to paternal (e.g., King & Elder 1995, Salmon 1999) or to maternal grandparents (Michalski & Shackelford 2005). Considering the role of the maternal grandmother as a source of support and investment in grandchildren, greater residential distance from maternal than from paternal grandparents is somewhat surprising and is at odds with the strong version of the grandmother hypothesis (Hawkes at al. 2000) and the maternal grandmother's role of investing directly in her daughter's off-spring. The problem may be explained by other dispersal determinants in non-natural fertility populations (Koenig 1989), as a mismatch phenomenon, as might be the finding that grandmothers are emotionally closest to daughters even if they are childless (Nosaka & Chasiotis 2005). In any case, the possible confounding influence of residential distance is a necessary control in research on grandparent–grandchild relationships.

The negative correlations between residential distance and the ratings of grandparental investments seem to vary systematically across the four types of grandparents, that is, they have an inverse relationship with the general grand-parent ranking. For maternal grandmothers, the correlation tends to be smallest, for the paternal grandfather, largest (Euler & Weitzel 1996). This may be an indication that the maternal grandmother's investments are the least facultative, and the investments of the paternal grandfather are most facultative.

Marital Status of Grandparent

Grandparents typically come in pairs and show, because of their shared obligations toward kin, a high degree of similarity in care (Euler & Weitzel 1996). This acts as a confound when assessing the independent solicitude of each grandparent type. Therefore, grandparents living alone show a different pattern of solicitude, depending on the reason for their singlehood. Widowed grandparents did not differ from those who were married, but separated or divorced grandparents did differ. The investment of maternal grandmothers was not affected by the presence (or absence) of her mate. The presence of a mate putatively related to the grandchild was a factor for the other grand-parent types—for the paternal grandmother it matters a bit, for the maternal grandfather a lot, and the paternal grandfather the most (see also Dench & Ogg 2003). The family ties of grandfathers, particularly paternal grandfathers, are seriously weakened upon separation from the wife. What is true for fathers is equally and still true for grandfathers: putative (grand)paternal effort is to a large portion mating effort (Anderson, Kaplan, & Lancaster 1999).

Number of Living Grandparents, Number of Grandchildren

Although one might expect that a grandparent's solicitude decreases with the number of other grandparents, such a dilution effect was not found by Euler and Weitzel (1996). Participants did not rate a grandparent's investment differently if the participant had two, three, or four grandparents alive during childhood.

We would assume diminishing returns for investment in a particular grandchild as the number of grandchildren a grandparent has increases. This can be predicted based on the increased attractiveness of alternative investments. A share of investment in all grandchildren pays more than investment in only a subset of grandchildren. We would, therefore, predict that the total investment of grandparents is correlated positively, but the share for each single grandchild negatively, with the number of grandchildren. Smith (1991) found this indeed to be the case. The dilution effect has also been deduced repeatedly from grandchildren's ratings: grandparental investment is rated lower the more cousins (Laham et al. 2005) or the more aunts or uncles (Euler et al. in press) the grandchild reports.

Age of Grandparent, Parent, and Grandchild

As expected, grandparental investment correlates negatively with age of grandchild (e.g., Dench & Ogg 2003), and it also correlates negatively with age of parent (Smith 1991). The findings are unclear as to the effect of grandparent age. Smith (1991, p. 163) reports a small but significantly negative correlation with all grandparents, but this measure appears to be confounded with type of grandparent, because the maternal grandmother is, on average, the youngest, and the paternal grandfather is, on average, the oldest. Euler and Weitzel (1996; see also Pashos 2000) found only small insignificant negative correlations, separate for each grandparent type, between grandparent age and rated grandparental solicitude. However, the age ranges were not large in these between-subject comparisons, and possible cohort confounds were not controlled. We expect changes in overall investment and specific types of investment as a function of the increasing ages of grandparents and grandchildren.

Sibling Constellation of Parent

A puzzling deviation from the dilution effect was found by Euler et al. (in press) and is shown in Figure 1. Contrary to intuition and dilution effect, paternal grandparents care less for the child (that is, the participant giving the rating) of an only son than if the son has a sibling. The data in Figure 1 are from a total sample of 1,696 participants, mostly college students, collected over several years, with the same effect shown in every yearly subsample. The sample sizes for the data points in Figure 1 vary between $N = 136$ (maternal grandfather, daughter with no sibling) and $N = 770$, maternal grandmother,

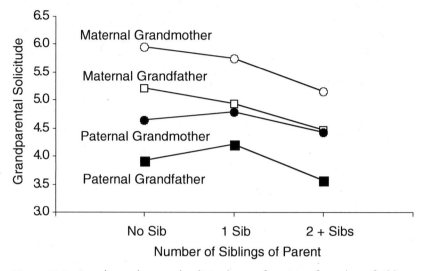

Figure 11.1. Rated grandparental solicitude as a function of number of siblings of parent.

daughter with more than two siblings). All cases were included where either the father or the mother, but not both, have the number of siblings along the horizontal axis.

We tested various hypotheses to account for this only-son deviation from the dilution effect. For paternal grandparents with two adult children, the caregiving for the grandchild did not depend on the sex of the son's sibling. This finding excluded an explanation of the basis of some sort of sibling fairness, such as if the son has a sister, her kids get so much attention and so, for fairness, his kids should get an equal amount. Several possible hypotheses remain to account for these data, for example: (1) the mother-in-law/daughter-in-law conflict hypothesis, (2) the son-as-heir hypothesis, and (3) the sibling-competition hypothesis.

The relationship between the mother-in-law (MiL) and the daughter-in-law (DiL) is burdened with conflict (see the next section for more detail). If parents have a son as the only child, there is only one woman in the next generation, the son's spouse, and she is an in-law. The conflict cannot be attenuated or made less salient by additional children or other in-laws. Whatever the dynamic details of this conflict problem, the hypothesis would predict that the MiL–DiL relationship, but not the father-in-law (FiL)–daughter-in-law (DiL) relationship, should be poorer if the son is an only child than if the son has one or more siblings. This prediction was indeed supported. The rating of the MiL–DiL relationship in cases where the son is an only child was numerically lower than was rating of the MiL–DiL relationship in cases where the son has a brother, a sister, only brothers, or only sisters. It was significantly poorer than if the son had at least one brother and at least one sister. No comparable differences were found for the FiL–DiL relationships.

The son-as-heir hypothesis relies on data selection artifact and originates from the following observation. According to the 1989 census in Germany, the sex ratio at birth (boys to 100 girls) was 105.2 for one-child families within the lower half of income (less than 4,000 German marks), 104.6 for families with two children, and 104.1 for families with three or more children. For the upper half of income (more than 4,000 marks) it was, respectively, 118.8, 110.1, and 112.9 (Müller 1992). The difference between the poorer and the richer families demonstrates the Trivers–Willard effect. Notable is the extremely high male-biased sex ratio in families with only one male child. This high ratio (118.8) may be due to the desire for a male heir. Many couples want a male child. If the first child is a boy, the desire is satisfied. If the first child is a girl, they try again. This means that among families with a boy as the only child, there is a larger proportion of couples with an interest less in children per se than there is among families with other offspring combinations, including families with a daughter as an only child. Couples who have only one male child may on average be less inclined toward parental investment. Extending this argument, they may be less inclined for later grandparental investment. This latter extension, however, may be debatable if one argues that there are relationship-specific adaptations and that parental investment cannot be generalized sweepingly into grandparental investment. The son-as-heir hypothesis of the lowered grandparental investment in offspring of a male singleton has not been tested empirically so far.

An alternative explanation of lowered grandparental investment in the grandchildren of only sons may be based on the sex-specific sibling competition of parents over their parents' investments in their children. If (a) siblings compete with each other over grandparental investments, and (b) sons compete more intensely for parental resources than daughters do, then the pattern may be interpretable based on this conjecture. Grandchildren through sons without siblings may receive less investment than grandchildren through sons with siblings because psychological mechanisms are not activated in the mind of the only child, here the adult son, to trigger his motivation to secure resources from his parents for his children. This effect might be predicted not to hold for women because sisters may not compete as intensely with siblings for access to parental resources. Although speculative, the impact of parental competitiveness for grandparental resources deserves a closer look. Parents may not be explicitly competitive with siblings about grandparental resources, but they may emphasize to their children the importance of spending time with grandparents as a means of extracting more grandparental resources for their children than for their sibling's children.

The sex constellation of the extended family is the central aspect of the outlet theory of Laham et al. (2005). To explain why maternal grandfathers are emotionally closer to grandchildren than are paternal grandmothers, the authors point to differences in paternity-certain outlets between these grandparents. The maternal grandfather has the more certain outlet in the children of his daughter than he does in the children of his son, for whom he would be the paternal grandfather. The paternal grandmother, however, who might also be a maternal grandmother, may prefer to invest as the maternal grandmother in the children of her daughter rather than as the paternal grandmother in the children of her son. This outlet bias adds to the investment of the maternal grandfather and detracts from the investment of the paternal grandmother. Laham et al. (2005) present empirical support for this hypothesis. If the maternal grandfather has other grandchildren through daughters, but the paternal grandmother does not, the investment bias of the maternal grandfather over the paternal grandmother should be most evident. If, in contrast, the paternal grandmother has other grandchildren through daughters, but the maternal grandfather does not, the outlet theory would predict an investment bias of the paternal grandmother over the maternal grandfather. Laham et al. did indeed find an investment bias of the maternal grandfather only in the first case but not in the second one. However, an investment bias reversal in the second case was not observed.

Laham et al. (2005) concede that their outlet considerations amount to small effect sizes. They certainly need to be considered as moderating variables, but they cannot account by themselves for the generally found higher solicitude of the maternal grandfather over the paternal grandmother, and thus discount the effect of sex-specific reproductive strategy. Our database does not contain information about the existence of other grandchildren but rather about parents' siblings. If the father has only a sister and the mother only a brother, the solicitude of the paternal grandmother is not rated higher than that of the maternal grandfather, nor is it if the father has as siblings only sisters and the mother only brothers.

The higher solicitude of the maternal grandfather over the paternal grandmother is only to a minor extent determined by the availability of paternity-certain outlets. A larger determinant is laterality (matrilateral vs. patrilateral) and thus a sex-specific reproductive strategy. The largest determinant, however, is simply the sex-specificity of the particular care behavior. To identify features of grandparental investment, the authors have developed an inventory including various acts that grandparents may do for their grandchildren. In an initial examination of these acts, 230 German students (59 male, 171 female) were asked to use a 10-point scale to rate how much of 55 specific activities each of their four grandparents had done with or for them. To quantify the grandparental sex-specificity of each activity, we calculated the difference between the mean for both grandmothers and the mean for both grandfathers. For the item-specific laterality difference, we calculated the difference between maternal and paternal grandparents. Across items, the maternal grandfather/paternal grandmother difference correlated $r = .31$ ($p = .02$) with the laterality difference, and $r = .89$ with the sex-specificity of the behavior. Only for extremely female-gendered behaviors, like cooking for the grandchild or making clothes for him or her, does the paternal grandmother overtake the paternal grandfather.

Birth Rank

Salmon (1999) reported a marked effect based on the birth order of the linking parent. According to reports of adult grandchildren, grandparents had significantly less contact with the grandchildren of their middleborn daughters or sons than with the grandchildren of their firstborn and lastborn offspring, a finding explained by the fact that middleborns show less attachment to their parents and less kinship ties than do firstborns or lastborns (see Sulloway, this volume). With respect to the global grandparental solicitude rating by adult grandchildren, we could not replicate the clear V-shaped pattern (firstborn high, middleborn low, lastborn high) in a sample of 1,696 student participants (507 males, 1,182 females, 7 undeclared), collected over three consecutive years. The sample sizes for the 12 cells (four grandparent types, three birth-rank types) ranged from $N = 114$ (paternal grandparent, lastborn father) to $N = 302$ (paternal grandmother, middleborn father). No effect of parental rank on grandparental caregiving could be observed, except that parents of lastborn children were rated as numerically more solicitous than parents of middleborn children, statistically significant for maternal grandparents (maternal grandmother $t = 2.86$, $df = 430$, $p < .01$, $d = .29$; maternal grandfather $t = 2.39$, $df = 391$, $p < .05$, $d = .25$).

With respect to grandchild birth rank, we are aware of no published data except that Leonetti et al. (2005) found, among the Bengali in India, that the presence of the paternal grandmother was positively related to grandchild weight, but with no child birth-rank differences.

Sex of Grandchild

If grandparents are asked about their overall investment or their emotional closeness to a grandchild, the sex of the grandchild generally does not matter (e.g., Robins & Tomanec 1962, J. L. Thomas 1989), owing perhaps to a reluctance to express favoritism. Evolutionary theories would not predict a general preference by the grandchild's sex (Daly & Wilson 1990), except in interaction with other factors, like parental resource capacity (Trivers & Willard 1973). Euler and Weitzel (1996) reported support for a Trivers–Willard effect only for the maternal grandparents; Leek and Smith (1991) found no clear support. However, overall investment does not tell us if specific acts are done preferentially for female or for male grandchildren.

If adult grandchildren are reporting grandparental investment, women give somewhat higher ratings in some studies (e.g., Euler & Weitzel 1996, Salmon 1999), but not in others (e.g., Laham et al. 2005, Pashos 2000, Robins & Tomanec 1962, Spitze & Ward 1998). A sex difference could be due to a grandparental preference for females, or to the higher family sentiment of females compared to males (Salmon & Daly, 1996), which would result in a positive-rating bias in female grandchildren. A general rating bias would be expected to affect all grandparents equally. This, however, is not the case, as the analysis of the first authors' cumulative data file ($N = 3,545$) showed. Women rate only the care of the maternal grandparents and of the paternal grandmother higher than male participants do—all significant but with very small effect sizes ranging from $d = .08$ (maternal grandfather) to $d = .19$ (maternal grandmother). Paternal grandfathers, in contrast, were not rated differently by male and female grandchildren.

The preferential treatment of a certain gender of grandchild is activity-specific. From the above data sample concerning 55 specific grandparental activities, we calculated the mean ratings for all four grandparents for each item. On 14 out of the 55 items, women gave a significantly higher rating than did men. The collection of the 14 items revealed that there seems not to be a primary positive bias for the female grandchild, but rather a secondary one. Girls are socially and emotionally more responsive than are boys (item example: grandparent "smooched or cuddled with me"), are considered more in need of surveillance ("picked me up from school"), and more often ask for help than do boys ("taught me skills, e.g., bicycling, swimming"). What is true for parents seems also true for grandparents: girls get more (grand)parental attention because they accept care more readily and reward the caregiver more than boys do. This explains the finding that paternal grandfathers are the only grandparent not to get higher ratings from female than from male grandchildren: Paternal grandfathers do not invest enough to produce a difference.

A theoretical possibility for a particular statistical interaction between grandparent and grandchild sex was suggested by Chrastil, Getz, Euler, and Starks (2006). Ignoring paternity uncertainty, grandparents are equally related to male and female grandchildren only with respect to autosomal genes, not genes on the sex chromosomes. Because males are heterozygous for sex chromosomes, paternal grandparents are not symmetrically related to male and female grandchildren. The Y chromosome is directly passed from the paternal grandfather to his grandson, and passed only along this route. This allows for the prediction that paternal grandfathers favor grandsons over granddaughters. The prediction was tested with two different data sets and found no clear support. Sex-chromosome selection, if it produces differential effects at all, is not strong enough to override paternity-uncertainty effects.

Across generations, same-sex dyads tend to show higher investments than cross-sex dyads (Godoy et al. 2006, D. Thomas 1994). The principle "like father, like son; like mother, like daughter" applies to grandparent–parent dyads (Euler et al. 2001) and grandparent–grandchildren dyads (Salmon 1999). We calculated the ratings given on the 55 activity items for both grandmothers combined and both grandfathers combined, and found a numerical same-sex preference on 51 items, 17 of which were significant.

Phenotypical Similarity

Unlike some of the moderating variables discussed so far, the phenotypical similarity between investment provider and investment receiver is a variable of unique importance to adaptationist thinking because resemblance is a cue of genetic relatedness. Grandparents should use such cues and be influenced by their resemblance to their grandchild. It has been shown that men are more affected by resemblance to children than women are (e.g., Platek, Burch, Panyavin, Wasserman, & Gallup 2002). Likewise, we should expect that the more links of paternity uncertainty, the higher should be the correlation between grandparental investment and perceived resemblance, whether in looks, behavior, or both. Thus, maternal grandmothers should be least affected, paternal grandfathers most, with the other two grandparents in between. Also, the resemblance to adult children could be a factor guiding investment decisions. Grandparents should make their investment in grandchildren more dependent on similarity to sons than to daughters.

There is meager empirical support for these predictions and more evidence would be desirable. Leek and Smith (1991) found positive correlations between help given and personality similarity to adult children and to grandchildren. However, without differentiation as to sex this finding is too vague to counter the influence of paternity uncertainty. Euler (1994) reported that the correlation between resemblance in behavior and/or appearance and grandchildren-rated solicitude were—across the four grandparent types—inversely related to solicitude. The correlations were $r = .37$ for the maternal grandmother, $r = .39$ for the maternal grandfather, $r = .42$ for the paternal grandmother, and $r = .47$ for the paternal grandfather.

The differences between the coefficients, however, were not statistically significant.

Type of Investment Activity

The type of grandparental investment activity, like parental effort, is strongly determined by the gender of the investor. Grandmothers tend to do the time-consuming, empathic, caring, and consoling activities, whereas grandfathers tend to do the repairs, teach skills (except for cooking), and spend money. Whether the difference in caregiving ratings between maternal grandfathers and paternal grandmothers is large, small, or even reversed is determined solely by the general grandparental gender difference in behavior.

To assess the activities that serve as best predictors of grandparental solicitude, we correlated the overall solicitude rating with the 55 activity ratings and obtained the highest correlations (mostly $r > .60$) for activities that consume time (e.g., "spent time with me," "played games with me") and for activities indicating empathy and emotional closeness (e.g., "was proud of me," "complimented me," "encouraged me"). Devoted time and emotional closeness are the best behavioral and subjective proxies of kin investment.

Quality of Grandparent–Parent Relationship

Parents, particularly the mother, act as gatekeepers who regulate grandparental access to grandchildren. Grandparental solicitude should therefore depend on the quality of the grandparent–parent relationship. We correlated the relationship-quality ratings that our adult participants retrospectively gave to each of the eight grandparent–parent dyads with the solicitude ratings for each grandparent. The coefficients were between $r = .35$ (maternal grandmother–father) and $r = .54$ (maternal grandfather–mother; sample sizes between $N = 1,107$ and $N = 1,557$). For each grandparent type, the correlation with the relationship to the mother was significantly larger than with the relationship to the father. The size of the difference (z values) was ordered along the rank of grandparents (highest for the maternal grandmother and lowest for the paternal grandfather). This might mean that the relationship of the grandparent with the mother of the grandchild is most important for the maternal grandmother because her grandmaternal investment is the strongest, in decreasing order for the other three grandparent types. Comparable findings have been reported by Michalski and Shackelford (2005) and McBurney et al. (2006).

similarity to the niece and/or nephew and closeness ratings were slightly higher for twins with male co-twins than for twins with female co-twins.

The relationship with cousins, finally, differs due to paternity certainty. Comparatively, the relationship is genetically most certain with children of one's mother's sister and least certain with children of one's father's brother. Closeness of relationship, as measured by willingness to help, empathic concern, and contact frequency covary accordingly (Jeon & Buss 2007).

CONCLUDING REMARKS

The reproductive asymmetry between the sexes is evident in various asymmetries of intergenerational family relationships. The matrilineal bias bestows on the maternal grandmother a unique and prominent role in grandparental relationships, as evident in many different forms of investment in grandchildren and particularly in feelings of emotional closeness, which can be considered the proximate process mediating the various forms of investment.

The data are consistent with the hypothesis of grandparent-specific adaptations (Daly, Salmon, & Wilson 1997). Mothers in ancestral environments often lived long enough to become grandmothers and make relationship-specific contributions to their inclusive fitness. For example, whereas parental investment is largely insensitive to the sex of offspring (Daly & Wilson 1990), grandparental investment is clearly sensitive to the parental sex and at the same time insensitive to grandchild's sex. Likewise, we would not be surprised if future studies reveal that grandparents' fondness for their grandchildren is not congruent with the grandparents' fondness for their own children. Grandparents frequently seem to take a particular grandparental pride in the sheer number of their grandchildren, which appears not to be equalled by parental pride in the number of children. If lineage is one of the joints at which nature is to be cut, grandparental pride in number of grandchildren might be more pronounced for paternal than for maternal grandparents.

Because organisms are equipped with reward mechanisms to motivate execution of problem-specific adaptations in the appropriate situations, most grandparents appear happy to be able to invest in grandchildren. Indeed, almost all grandparents find grandchildren and investment in them rewarding (Dench & Ogg 2003), even at an age when acedia typically takes its toll.

The approach to intergenerational relations guided by evolutionary theory and adaptationist hypotheses has already furthered our understanding of kin structures, and promises to yield more. Such an approach can help researchers clear blurs, to integrate contributions from separate disciplines, to ask meaningful questions, to guide research, to inform public policies, and to provide personal insights into our own family lives. Nearly a century ago, William McDougall (1908/1960) admonished the "philosophers" for their lack of interest in kin matters like parental instincts. The topic of grandparental investment still does not have a place in standard textbooks of motivational or social psychology, but having a close grandparent and having grandchildren adds to life quality. Grandchildren are, after all, tangible tokens of genetic posterity.

REFERENCES

Anderson, K. G., Kaplan, H., & Lancaster, J. B. (1999). Paternal care by genetic fathers and stepfathers I: Reports from Albuquerque men. *Evolution and Human Behavior, 20,* 405–431.

Beise, J. (2005). The "helping" and the "helpful" grandmother: The role of maternal and paternal grandmothers in child mortality in the seventeenth- and eighteenth-century population of French settlers in Québec, Canada. In E. Voland, A. Chasiotis, & W. Schiefenhövel (Eds.), *Grandmotherhood: The evolutionary significance of the second half of female life* (pp. 215–238). New Brunswick, NJ: Rutgers University Press.

Burt, A., & Trivers, R. (2006). *Genes in conflict: The biology of selfish genetic elements.* Cambridge, MA: Belknap Press of Harvard University Press.

Buss, D. M. (2003). *The evolution of desire: Strategies of human mating.* New York: Basic Books.

Chrastil, E. R., Getz, W. M., Euler, H. A., & Starks, P. T. (2006). Paternity uncertainty overrides sex chromosome selection for preferential grandparenting. *Evolution and Human Behavior, 27,* 206–223.

Daly, M., Salmon, C., & Wilson, M. (1997). Kinship: The conceptual hole in psychological studies of social cognition and close relationships. In J. A. Simpson & D. T. Kenrick (Eds.), *Evolutionary social psychology* (pp. 265–296). Mahwah, NJ: Lawrence Erlbaum.

Daly, M., & Wilson, M. (1980). Discriminative parental solicitude: A biological perspective. *Journal of Marriage and the Family, 42,* 277–288.

Daly, M., & Wilson, M. (1990). Is parent–offspring conflict sex-linked? Freudian and Darwinian models. *Journal of Personality, 58,* 163–189.

Dawkins, R. (1976). *The selfish gene.* Oxford: Oxford University Press, 1976.

DeKay, W. T. (1995, July). *Grandparent investment and the uncertainty of kinship.* Paper presented at the seventh annual meeting of the Human Behavior and Evolution Society, Santa Barbara, CA.

Dench, G., & Ogg, J. (2003). *Grandparenting in Britain: A baseline study* (2nd ed.). Eastbourne, England: Antony Rowe.

Eisenberg, A. R. (1988). Grandchildren's perspectives on relationships with grandparents: The influence of gender across generations. *Sex Roles, 19,* 205–217.

Euler, H. A. (1994, October). *Diskriminative großelterliche Fürsorge* [Discriminative grandparental solicitude]. Paper presented at the Congress "Anthropologie Heute" of the Gesellschaft für Anthropologie, Humboldt-University of Berlin and University Potsdam, Potsdam, Germany.

Euler, H. A. (2004). Genspur aus der Steinzeit. Psychologie der Vaterschaftsungewissheit [Gene trace from the Stone Age. The psychology of paternity uncertainty]. In H. Haas & C. Waldenmaier (Eds.), *Der Kuckucksfaktor [The cuckoo factor]* (pp. 34–82 & 323–330). Prien, Germany: Gennethos e. K. Verlag.

Euler, H. A., Hoier, S., & Pölitz, E. (1998, May 31–June 3). *Kin investment of aunts and uncles: Why is the matrilateral bias stronger in women?* Paper presented at the 21st annual meeting of the European Sociobiological Society (ESS), Russian State University for the Humanities, Moscow.

Euler, H. A., Hoier, S., & Rohde, P. A. (2001). Relationship-specific closeness of intergenerational family ties: Findings from evolutionary psychology and implications for models of cultural transmission. *Journal of Cross-Cultural Psychology, 32,* 163–174.

Euler, H. A., Hoier, S., & Rohde, P. (in press). Relationship-specific intergenerational family ties: An evolutionary approach to the structure of cultural transmission. In U. Schönpflug (Ed.), *Cultural transmission: Developmental, psychological, social, and methodological perspectives.* Cambridge, UK: Cambridge University Press.

Euler, H. A., & Weitzel, B. (1996). Discriminative grandparental solicitude as reproductive strategy. *Human Nature, 7,* 39–59.

Fingerman, K. L. (2004). The role of offspring and in-laws in grandparents' ties to their grandchildren. *Journal of Family Issues, 25,* 1026–1049.

Fischer, L. R. (1983). Transition to grandmotherhood. *International Journal of Aging and Human Development, 16,* 67–78.

Galdikas, B. M. F., & Wood, J. W. (1990). Birth spacing patterns in humans and apes. *American Journal of Physical Anthropology, 83,* 185–191.

Gaulin, S. J. C., McBurney, D. H., & Brakeman-Wartell, S. L. (1997). Matrilateral biases in the investment of aunts and uncles. *Human Nature, 8,* 139–151.

Godoy, R., Reyes-García, V., McDade, T., Tanner, S., Leonard, W. R., Huanca, T., et al. (2006). Why do mothers favor girls and fathers, boys? A hypothesis and a test of investment disparity. *Human Nature, 17,* 169–189.

Hamilton, W. D. (1966). The moulding of senescence by natural selection. *Journal of Theoretical Biology, 12,* 12–45.

Hartshorne, T. S., & Manaster, G. L. (1982). The relationship with grandparents: Contact, importance, role conceptions. *International Journal of Aging and Human Development, 15,* 233–245.

Hawkes, K., O'Connell, K. J. F., & Blurton-Jones, N. G. (1989). Hardworking Hadza grandmothers. In V. Standen & R. A. Foley (Eds.), *Comparative socioecology: The behavioral ecology of humans and other mammals* (pp. 341–366). Oxford: Blackwell.

Hawkes, K., O'Connell, K. J. F., Blurton-Jones, N. G., Alvarez, H., & Charnov, E. (2000). The grandmother hypothesis and human evolution. In L. Cronk, N. Chagnon, & W. Irons (Eds.), *Adaptation and human behavior: An anthropological perspective* (pp. 237–258). Hawthorne, NY: Aldine de Gruyter.

Hewlett, B. S. (1991). *Intimate fathers: The nature and context of Aka pygmy paternal care.* Ann Arbor, MI: University of Michigan Press.

Hodgson, L. G. (1992). Adult grandchildren and their grandparents: The enduring bond. *International Journal of Aging and Human Development, 34,* 209–225.

Hoffman, E. (1978/1979). Young adults' relations with their grandparents: An exploratory study. *International Journal of Aging and Human Development, 10,* 299–310.

Hoier, S., Euler, H. A., & Hänze, M. (2000). Diskriminative verwandtschaftliche Fürsorge von Onkeln und Tanten. Eine evolutionspsychologische Analyse [Discriminative solicitude of aunts and uncles. An evolutionary analysis]. *Zeitschrift für Differentielle und Diagnostische Psychologie, 22,* 206–215.

Holden, C., J., Sear, R., & Mace, R. (2003). Matriliny as daughter-biased investment. *Evolution and Human Behavior, 24,* 99–112.

Jeon, J., & Buss, D. M. (2007). Altruism towards cousins. *Proceedings of the Royal Society B: Biological Sciences, 274,* 1181–1187.

Kahana, B., & Kahana, E. (1970). Grandparenthood from the perspective of the developing grandchild. *Developmental Psychology, 3,* 98–105.

King, V., & Elder, G. H. (1995). American children view their grandparents: Linked lives across three rural generations. *Journal of Marriage and the Family, 57,* 165–178.

Koenig, W. D. (1989). Sex-biased dispersal in the contemporary United States. *Ethology and Sociobiology, 10,* 263–278.

Laham, S. M., Gonsalkorale, K., & von Hippel, W. (2005). Darwinian grandparenting: Preferential investment in more certain kin. *Personality and Social Psychology Bulletin, 31,* 63–72.

Lahdenperä, M., Lummaa, V., Helle, S., Tremblay, M., & Russell, A. F. (2004). Fitness benefits of prolonged post-reproductive lifespan in women. *Nature, 428,* 178–181.

Leek, M., & Smith, P. K. (1991). Cooperation and conflict in three-generation families. In P. K. Smith (Ed.), *The psychology of grandparenthood: An international perspective* (pp. 177–194). London: Routledge.

Leonetti, D. L., Nath, D. C., Hemam, N. S., & Neill, D. B. (2005). Kinship organization and the impact of grandmothers on reproductive success among the matrilineal Khasi and patrilineal Bengali of Northeast India.

In E. Voland, A. Chasiotis, & W. Schiefenhövel (Eds.), *Grandmotherhood: The evolutionary significance of the second half of female life* (pp. 194–214). New Brunswick, NJ: Rutgers University Press.

Littlefield, C. H., & Rushton, J. P. (1986). When a child dies: The sociobiology of bereavement. *Journal of Personality and Social Psychology, 51*, 797–802.

Mace, R., & Sear, R. (2005). Are humans cooperative breeders? In E. Voland, A. Chasiotis, & W. Schiefenhövel (Eds.), *Grandmotherhood: The evolutionary significance of the second half of female life* (pp. 143–159). New Brunswick, NJ: Rutgers University Press.

Matthews, S. H., & Sprey, J. (1985). Adolescents' relationships with grandparents: An empirical contribution to conceptual clarification. *Journal of Gerontology, 40*, 621–626.

McBurney, D. H., Pashos, A., & Gaulin, S. J. C. (2006, June 7–11). *Family relationships and kin investment biases: A two-generational questionnaire study.* Paper presented at the 18th annual meeting of the Human Behavior Evolution Society, Philadelphia, PA.

McBurney, D., Simon, J., Gaulin, S. J. C., & Geliebter, A. (2001). Matrilateral biases in the investment of aunts and uncles: Replication in a population presumed to have high paternity uncertainty. *Human Nature, 13*, 391–402.

McDougall, W. (1960). *An introduction to social psychology* (31st ed.). London, UK: Methuen.

Michalski, R. L., & Shackelford, T. K. (2005). Grandparental investment as a function of relational uncertainty and emotional closeness with parent. *Human Nature, 16*, 293–305.

Müller, M. (1992). *Determinanten der sekundären Sexualproportion und Verteilung der Geschlechter in Familien* [Determinants of the secondary sex ration and distribution of the sexes in families]. Unpublished master's thesis, Department of Statistics, University of Dortmund, Germany.

Nosaka, A., & Chasiotis, A. (2005). Exploring the variation in intergenerational relationships among Germans and Turkish immigrants: An evolutionary perspective of behavior in a modern social setting. In E. Voland, A. Chasiotis, & W. Schiefenhövel (Eds.), *Grandmotherhood: The evolutionary significance of the second half of female life* (pp. 256–276). New Brunswick, NJ: Rutgers University Press.

Pashos, A. (2000). Does paternal uncertainty explain discriminative grandparental solicitude? A cross-cultural study in Greece and Germany. *Evolution and Human Behavior, 21*, 97–109.

Platek, S. M., Burch, R. L., Panyavin, I. S., Wasserman, B. H., & Gallup, G. G., Jr. (2002). Reactions to children's faces: Resemblance affects males more than females. *Evolution and Human Behavior, 23*, 159–166.

Pollet, T. V., Nettle, D., & Nelissen, M. (2006). Contact frequencies between grandparents and grandchildren in a modern society: estimates of the impact of paternity uncertainty. *Journal of Cultural and Evolutionary Psychology, 4*, 203–214.

Robins, L. N., & Tomanec, M. (1962). Closeness to blood relatives outside the immediate family. *Marriage and Family Living, 24,* 340–346.

Rossi, A. S., & Rossi, P. H. (1990). *Of human bonding: Parent–child relations across the life course.* New York: Aldine de Gruyter.

Russell, R. J. H., & Wells, P. A. (1987). Estimating paternity confidence. *Ethology and Sociobiology, 8,* 215–220.

Salmon, C. A. (1999). On the impact of sex and birth order on contact with kin. *Human Nature, 10,* 183–197.

Salmon, C. A., & Daly, M. (1996). On the importance of kin relations to Canadian women and men. *Ethology and Sociobiology, 17,* 289–297.

Schiefenhövel, W., & Grabolle, A. (2005). The role of maternal grandmothers in Tobriand adoptions. In E. Voland, A. Chasiotis, & W. Schiefenhövel (Eds.), *Grandmotherhood: The evolutionary significance of the second half of female life* (pp. 177–193). New Brunswick, NJ: Rutgers University Press.

Sear, R., & Mace, R. (in press). Who keeps children alive? A review of the effects of kin on child survival. *Evolution and Human Behavior.*

Segal, N., Seghers, J., Marelich, W., Mechanic, M., & Castillo, R. (in press). Social closeness of MZ and DZ twin parents toward nieces and nephews. *European Journal of Personality.*

Smith, M. S. (1988). Research in developmental sociobiology: Parenting and family behavior. In K. B. MacDonald (Ed.), *Sociobiological perspectives on human development* (pp. 271–292). New York: Springer.

Smith, M. S. (1991). An evolutionary perspective on grandparent–grandchild relationships. In P. K. Smith (Ed.), *The psychology of grandparenthood: An international perspective* (pp. 157–176). London: Routledge.

Spitze, G., & Ward, R. A. (1998). Gender variations. In M. E. Szinovacz (Ed.), *Handbook on grandparenthood* (pp. 113–127). Westport, CT: Greenwood Press.

Steinbach, I., & Henke, W. (1998). Grosselterninvestment—eine empirische interkulturelle Vergleichsstudie [Grandparental investment—An empirical cross-cultural comparative study]. *Anthropologie, 36,* 293–301.

Szinovacz, M. E. (Ed.). (1998). *Handbook on grandparenthood.* Westport, CT: Greenwood Press.

Szydlik, M. (1995). Die Enge der Beziehung zwischen erwachsenen Kindern und ihren Eltern—und umgekehrt [The closeness of relationship between adult children and their parents—and vice versa]. *Zeitschrift für Soziologie, 24,* 75–94.

Thomas, D. (1994). Like father, like son; like mother, like daughter: Parental resources and child height. *The Journal of Human Resources, 29,* 950–988.

Thomas, J. L. (1989). Gender and perceptions of grandparenthood. *International Journal of Aging and Human Development, 24,* 269–282.

Trivers, R. L., & Willard, D. E. (1973). Natural selection of parental ability to vary the sex ratio of offspring. *Science, 179,* 90–91.

van Ranst, N., Verschueren, K., & Marcoen, A. (1995). The meaning of grandparents as viewed by adolescent grandchildren: An empirical study in

Belgium. *International Journal of Aging and Human Development, 41*, 311–324.

Voland, E., & Beise, J. (2002). Opposite effects of maternal and paternal grandmothers on infant survival in historical Krummhörn. *Behavioral Ecology and Sociobiology, 52*, 435–443.

Voland, E., & Beise, J. (2005). "The husband's mother is the devil in the house": Data on the impact of the mother-in-law on stillbirth mortality in historical Krummhörn (1750–1874) and some thoughts on the evolution of the postgenerative female life. In E. Voland, A. Chasiotis, & W. Schiefenhövel (Eds.), *Grandmotherhood: The evolutionary significance of the second half of female life* (pp. 239–255). New Brunswick, NJ: Rutgers University Press.

Voland, E., Chasiotis, A., & Schiefenhövel, W. (2005). Grandmotherhood: A short overview of three fields of research on the evolutionary significance of postgenerative female life. In E. Voland, A. Chasiotis, & W. Schiefenhövel (Eds.), *Grandmotherhood: The evolutionary significance of the second half of female life* (pp. 1–17). New Brunswick, NJ: Rutgers University Press.

Williams, G. C. (1957). Pleiotropy, natural selection, and the evolution of senescence. *Evolution, 11*, 398–411.

Young, M., & Willmott, P. (1957). *Family and kinship in East London*. Harmondsworth, England: Penguin.

PART IV

Applications to Specific Issues

12 Violence and Abuse in Families: The Consequences of Paternal Uncertainty

Aaron T. Goetz

To some, it may seem paradoxical that members of a family are often violent and abusive toward one another. Why, for example, would an individual harm another in whom they have a vested interest? One whom they love? One answer that might be offered is that violence and abuse occurs only in families that lack intimacy, love, and care. This answer, however, is wrong. Violence and abuse can occur in even the most loving families and between the most satisfied couples (reviewed in, e.g., Campbell & Ellis 2005; Miller 1997). This chapter discusses why violence and abuse occurs in families, particularly between intimate partners. My goal is not to detail all causes of intimate-partner violence but to discuss the root of most partner violence: paternal uncertainty. Moreover, I focus the discussion on physical and sexual intimate-partner violence.

PATERNAL UNCERTAINTY AND THE FUNCTION OF MALE SEXUAL JEALOUSY

Jealousy is an emotion experienced when a valued relationship is threatened by a real or imagined rival, and generates contextually contingent responses aimed at stifling the threat. It functions to maintain relationships by activating behaviors that deter rivals from mate poaching and deter mates from infidelity or outright departure from the relationship (Buss, Larsen, Westen, & Semmelroth 1992; Daly, Wilson, & Weghorst 1982; Symons 1979). Because ancestral men and women faced the adaptive problems of retaining partners and maintaining relationships, men and women do not differ in the frequency or intensity of their jealousy (Shackelford, LeBlanc, & Drass 2000; White 1981). A sex difference, however, emerges when considering the two types of jealousy—emotional and sexual—and this sex difference coincides with men's and women's differing adaptive problems regarding relationships (Buss 2000, Symons 1979). Ancestral women's challenge of securing the paternal investment needed to raise offspring exerted a significant selection pressure for women to be more sensitive to and more distressed by cues associated with a partner's emotional infidelity. Ancestral men's challenge of paternal uncertainty, however, exerted a significant selection pressure for men to be more sensitive to and more distressed by cues associated with a partner's sexual infidelity. Because emotional and sexual infidelity were highly correlated throughout evolutionary history (i.e., if an individual were engaging in one form, he or she was often engaging in the other), researchers studying sex differences in jealousy have employed forced-choice methods in which participants are asked to select which infidelity type upsets them most; however, some researchers, such as Sagarin, Becker, Guadagno, Nicastle, and Millevoi (2003) and Wiederman and Allgeier (1993) have found a sex difference using a continuous measure. At least two dozen empirical studies have shown the sex difference in jealousy, documenting that men experience more jealousy and distress in response to the sexual aspects of an infidelity, whereas women experience more jealousy and distress in response to the emotional aspects of an infidelity. These data are corroborated by experimental data (e.g., Schützwohl & Koch 2004), physiological data (Buss et al. 1992), patterns of divorce (Betzig 1989), and the behavioral output of jealousy (e.g., Buss & Shackelford 1997).

Men's sensitivity, distress, and reactions to sexual infidelity are not surprising, given the serious reproductive costs associated with cuckoldry—the unwitting investment of resources into genetically unrelated offspring. Some of the costs associated with cuckoldry include loss of the time, effort, and resources the man spent attracting his partner, the potential misdirection of his resources to a rival's offspring, the loss of his mate's investment in offspring he may have had with her in the future, and reputational damage if such information becomes known to others. Perhaps aside from death, cuckoldry is the most profound reproductive cost, and it is clear how selection could have favored the evolution of strategies and tactics aimed at avoiding cuckoldry and decreasing paternal uncertainty.

INTIMATE-PARTNER VIOLENCE
AND SEXUAL JEALOUSY

Male sexual jealousy is one of the most frequently cited causes of intimate-partner violence, both physical and sexual (e.g., Buss 2000, Daly & Wilson 1988, Daly et al. 1982, Dobash & Dobash 1979, Dutton 1998, Dutton & Golant 1995, Frieze 1983, Gage & Hutchinson 2006, Russell 1982, Walker 1979). Intimate-partner violence is a tactic used by men to limit a partner's sexuality (Buss & Malamuth 1996, Daly & Wilson 1988, Wilson & Daly 1996) and is best understood as behavioral output of male sexual jealousy. A man will afford his partner many freedoms, with the exception of those related to her sexual behavior (Buss 1996, 2000). Men are hypothesized to have evolved psychological mechanisms dedicated to generating risk assessments of a partner's sexual infidelity. These information-processing mechanisms include, for example, assessments of time spent apart from the partner, the presence of potential mate poachers, the partner's reproductive value and fertility, and the partner's likelihood of committing infidelity (e.g., Goetz & Shackelford 2006; Peters, Shackelford, & Buss 2002; Shackelford & Buss 1997; Shackelford et al. 2002; Trivers 1972; Wilson & Daly 1993). Moreover, the male mind might be designed to be hypersensitive to cues of sexual infidelity, motivating more false positives than false negatives because the benefits of the former outweigh the costs of the latter (Haselton & Nettle 2006). Together with risk assessment of a partner's sexual infidelity, contextual factors—such as social and reputational costs, proximity of the partner's kin capable of retaliation, and economic dependency (Figueredo & McClosky 1993, Wilson & Daly 1993)—are processed during decisions to inflict violence on a partner.

Occasionally, men's use of violence toward their partner is lethal. As with non-lethal partner violence, male sexual jealousy is the most frequently cited cause of spousal homicide across cultures (Daly & Wilson 1988, Serran & Firestone 2004). Killing an intimate partner is certainly costly, but under specific circumstances could its benefits have outweighed its costs enough for selection to produce psychology associated with mariticide? According to Daly and Wilson (Daly & Wilson 1988; Wilson & Daly 1998; Wilson, Daly, & Daniele 1995), killing an intimate partner is not the product of evolved psychological mechanisms but is a byproduct of mechanisms selected for their non-lethal outcomes. The byproduct, or "slip-up" hypothesis, as it has been termed, argues that men who kill their partners have "slipped up" in that their violence—which was intended to control their partner—inadvertently resulted in their partners' death. Although Daly and Wilson argue against the notion that male psychology might be designed to kill a partner in certain contexts, they hold that lethal intimate-partner violence is ultimately the result of male sexual jealousy stemming from paternal uncertainty.

The byproduct hypothesis is attractive in that it would seem too costly to kill an intimate partner. Why kill a partner and risk facing its enormous costs, when you can simply leave her? But consider this: If killing an intimate partner is a slip-up or accident, as argued by Daly and Wilson, why are so many spousal homicides premeditated? Hiring someone to kill your partner, aiming at and shooting your partner with a firearm, slitting your partner's throat, and poisoning your partner are not accidents. Although some spousal homicides are accidental, far too many are premeditated. This is one observation that led Buss and Duntley (1998, 2003; see also Buss 2005) to suggest that many spousal homicides result from evolved psychological mechanisms specifically designed to motivate killing under certain conditions. Discovering a partner's sexual infidelity, Buss and Duntley argue, may be a special circumstance that might motivate spousal homicide. Homicide-adaptation theory does not argue that discovering a partner's infidelity invariably leads to homicidal behavior but that this situation would activate mechanisms associated with weighing the costs and benefits of homicide, and that under certain circumstances, spousal homicide might be the best solution (for full treatment, see Buss 2005).

Daly and Wilson (1988; Wilson & Daly 1998, Wilson et al. 1995) and Buss and Duntley's (1998, 2003; Buss 2005) competing hypotheses have not yet been examined concurrently to give a single hypothesis that best accounts for the data (but see Shackelford, Buss, & Weekes-Shackelford 2003), and my intention here was not to critically evaluate their hypotheses. I intended to argue that spousal homicide, by design or byproduct, is often the behavioral output of male sexual jealousy stemming from paternal uncertainty.

Men's mate-retention behavior is another example of the behavioral output of jealousy. Buss (1988) identified specific mate-guarding behaviors such as vigilance (e.g., dropping by unexpectedly to check up on a partner), concealment of mate (e.g., taking a partner away from a social gathering where other men are present), and monopolization of time (e.g., insisting that a partner stay home rather than go out). These mate-guarding behaviors vary in ways that suggest they have evolved as paternity guards. For example, a man guards his partner more intensely when she is of greater reproductive value (as indexed by her youth and attractiveness) and when the perceived probability of her extra-pair copulation is greater (Buss & Shackelford 1997). In addition, men who are mated to women who possess characteristics that make them more likely to commit sexual infidelity guard their partners more intensely (Goetz et al. 2005), and men guard their partners more intensely near ovulation—a time when an extra-pair copulation would be most costly for the in-pair man (Gangestad, Thornhill, & Garver 2002).

Recognizing that men's mate-retention behaviors are manifestations of jealousy, Shackelford, Goetz, Buss, Euler, and Hoier (2005) investigated the associations between men's mate-retention behaviors and intimate-partner violence, specifically how some mate-retention behaviors and seemingly innocuous romantic gestures may be harbingers of violence. Securing self-reports from men, partner reports from women, and cross-spouse reports from married couples, Shackelford and his colleagues found that, across three studies, men's use of particular mate-retention behaviors was related to partner violence in predictable ways. For example, men who dropped by unexpectedly to see what their partner was doing or who told their partner that they would "die" if their partners ever left were most likely to use serious violence against their partners, whereas men who attempted to retain their partners by expressing affection and displaying resources were least likely to use violence against their partners. These findings corroborated those by Wilson, Johnson, and Daly (1995), who found that women who affirmed statements such as, "He insists on knowing who you are with and where you are at all times" and "He tries to limit your contact with family or friends" were twice as likely to have experienced serious violence by their partners.

SEXUAL ABUSE IN INTIMATE RELATIONSHIPS AND SEXUAL JEALOUSY

Between 10% and 26% of women experience rape in marriage (Abrahams, Jewkes, Hoffman, & Laubscher 2004; Dunkle et al. 2004; Finkelhor & Yllo 1985; Hadi 2000; Painter & Farrington 1999; Russell 1982; Watts, Keough, Ndlovu, & Kwaramba 1998). Rape also occurs in non-marital intimate relationships. Goetz and Shackelford (2006) secured prevalence estimates of rape in intimate relationships from a sample of young men and from an independent sample of young women who were in a committed relationship, but not necessarily married, for at least one year. Goetz and Shackelford documented that 7.3% of men admitted to raping their current partner at least once, and 9.1% of women reported that they had experienced at least one rape by their current partner. Although these percentages are astonishingly high, they likely don't reflect the true incidence of partner rape. Questions concerning sexual coercion and rape in relationships are emotionally laden and can be subject to social desirability, and thus, these percentages could be underestimates of the prevalence of rape in intimate relationships among young men and women who are not married.

Hypotheses have been generated to explain why, across cultures, reliable percentages of women are sexually coerced by their partners. Some researchers have hypothesized that sexual coercion in intimate relationships is motivated by men's attempts to dominate and control their partners (e.g., Basile 2002; Bergen 1996; Frieze 1983; Gage & Hutchinson 2006; Gelles 1977; Meyer, Vivian, & O'Leary 1998; Watts et al. 1998) and that this expression of power is the product of men's social roles (e.g., Brownmiller 1975; Johnson 1995; Yllo & Straus 1990). Results relevant to this hypothesis are mixed. Several studies have found that physically abusive men are more likely than non-abusive men to sexually coerce their female partners (Apt & Hurlbert 1993; DeMaris 1997; Donnelly 1993; Finkelhor & Yllo 1985; Koziol-McLain, Coates, & Lowenstein 2001; Shackelford & Goetz 2004), supporting the domination-and-control hypothesis. Gage and Hutchinson (2006), however, found that women's risk of sexual coercion by their partners is not related significantly to measures assessing the relative dimensions of power in a relationship, such as who maintains control over decision making and his/her partner's actions. That is, women mated to men who maintained the dominant position in the relationship were not more likely to experience sexual coercion than women mated to men who did not maintain the dominant position in the relationship, thus contradicting the domination-and-control hypothesis. Although many researchers agree that *individual men* may sexually coerce their partners to maintain dominance and control, proponents of the domination-and-control hypothesis often argue that men are motivated *as a group* to exercise "patriarchal power" or "patriarchal terrorism" over women (e.g., Brownmiller 1975; Johnson 1995; Yllo & Straus 1990).

An alternative hypothesis has been advanced by researchers studying sexual coercion from an evolutionary perspective: sexual coercion in intimate relationships may be related to paternal uncertainty, with its occurrence related to a man's suspicions of his partner's sexual infidelity (Camilleri 2004, Goetz & Shackelford 2006, Lalumière et al. 2005, Thornhill & Thornhill 1992, Wilson & Daly 1992). Sexual coercion in response to cues of his partner's sexual infidelity might function to introduce a male's sperm into his partner's reproductive tract at a time when there is a high risk of cuckoldry (i.e., when his partner has recently been inseminated by a rival male). This sperm-competition hypothesis was proposed following recognition that forced in-pair copulation (i.e., partner rape) in nonhuman species followed female extra-pair copulations (e.g., Barash 1977; Cheng, Burns, & McKinney 1983; Lalumière, Harris, Quinsey, & Rice 2005; McKinney, Cheng, & Bruggers 1984) and that sexual coercion and rape in human intimate relationships often followed accusations of female infidelity (e.g., Finkelhor & Yllo 1985, Russell 1982). Before considering the case of partner rape in humans, I review briefly the animal literature on forced in-pair copulation (FIPC).

Examining the adaptive problems and resultant evolved solutions to these problems in nonhuman animals may provide insight into the adaptive problems and evolved solutions in humans (and vice versa). Shackelford and Goetz (2006), for example, argued that because humans share with some avian species a similar mating system (social monogamy) and similar adaptive problems (e.g., paternal uncertainty, mate retention, cuckoldry), humans and some birds may have evolved similar solutions to these adaptive problems. Identifying the contexts and circumstances in which FIPC occurs in nonhuman species may help us understand why FIPC occurs in humans.

Forced In-pair Copulation in Nonhuman Animals

Instances of FIPC are relatively rare in the animal kingdom, primarily because males and females of most species (more than 95%) do not form long-term pair bonds (Andersson 1994). Without the formation of a pair bond, FIPC, by definition, cannot occur. Many avian species form long-term pair bonds, and researchers have documented FIPC in several of these species (Bailey, Seymour, & Stewart 1978; Barash 1977; Birkhead, Hunter, & Pellatt 1989; Cheng, Burns, & McKinney 1983; Goodwin 1955; McKinney et al. 1984; McKinney & Stolen 1982). FIPC is not performed randomly, however. FIPC reliably occurs immediately after extra-pair copulations, intrusions by rival males, and female absence, in many species of waterfowl (e.g., Bailey et al. 1978; Barash 1977; Cheng et al. 1983; McKinney, Derrickson, & Mineau 1983; McKinney & Stolen 1982; Seymour & Titman 1979) and in other avian species (e.g., Birkhead et al. 1989; Goodwin 1955; Valera, Hoi, & Kristin 2003). FIPC following observed or suspected extra-pair copulation in these avian species is often interpreted as a sperm-competition tactic (Barash 1977; Cheng et al. 1983; Lalumière, Harris, Quinsey, & Rice 2005; McKinney et al. 1984).

Sperm competition is a form of male–male postcopulatory competition. Sperm competition occurs when the sperm of two or more males simultaneously occupy the reproductive tract of a female and compete to fertilize her egg (Parker 1970). Males can compete for mates, but if two or more males have copulated with a female within a sufficiently short period of time, males must compete for fertilizations. Thus, the observation that in many avian species FIPC immediately follows extra-pair copulations has been interpreted as a sperm-competition tactic because the in-pair male's FIPC functions to place his sperm in competition with sperm from an extra-pair male (Birkhead et al. 1989, Cheng et al. 1983). Reports of FIPC in nonhuman species are theoretically beneficial in that they make it difficult to claim that males rape their partners to humiliate, punish, or control them—as is often argued by some social scientists who study rape in humans (e.g., Pagelow 1988).

But was sperm competition a significant selective force in our species' evolutionary history? Mounting evidence suggests that sperm competition has been a recurrent and important feature of human evolutionary history. Psychological, behavioral, physiological, anatomical, and genetic evidence reveals that ancestral women sometimes mated with multiple men within sufficiently short time periods so that sperm from two or more men simultaneously occupied the reproductive tract of one woman (Baker & Bellis 1993; Gallup et al. 2003; Goetz et al. 2005; Kilgallon & Simmons 2005; Pound 2002; Shackelford & Goetz 2006, 2007; Shackelford & Pound 2006; Shackelford, Pound & Goetz, 2005; Shackelford et al. 2002; Smith 1984; Wyckoff, Wang, & Wu 2000). This adaptive problem led to the evolution of adaptive solutions to sperm competition. For example, men display copulatory urgency, perform semen-displacing behaviors, and adjust their ejaculates to include more sperm when the likelihood of female infidelity is high (Baker & Bellis 1993, Goetz et al. 2005, Shackelford et al. 2002).

The selective importance of sperm competition in humans, however, is an issue of scholarly debate. Those questioning the application of sperm competition to humans (e.g., Birkhead 2000; Dixson 1998; Gomendio, Harcourt, & Roldán 1998) do not contend that sperm competition in humans is not possible or unlikely but that it may not be as intense as in other species with adaptations to sperm competition. Recent work on the psychological, physiological, behavioral, anatomical, and genetic evidence of human sperm competition (cited above), however, was not considered in these previous critiques of human sperm competition. When considering all the evidence of adaptations to sperm competition in men and current nonpaternity rates (see Anderson 2006; Bellis, Hughes, Hughes, & Ashton 2005), it is reasonable to conclude that sperm competition may have been a recurrent and selectively important feature of human evolutionary history. Below, I discuss theory and research related to forced in-pair copulation in humans. In keeping with the established animal literature and a comparative evolutionary psychological perspective, from here out I will refer to partner rape in humans as forced in-pair copulation—the forceful act of sexual intercourse by a man against his partner's will.

Forced In-pair Copulation in Humans

Noting that instances of FIPC follow extra-pair copulations in waterfowl and that documentation that FIPC in humans often follows accusations of female infidelity (e.g., Finkelhor & Yllo 1985, Russell 1982), Wilson and

Daly (1992) suggested in a footnote that "sexual insistence" in the context of a relationship might act as a sperm-competition tactic in humans as well. Sexual coercion in response to cues of his partner's sexual infidelity might function to introduce a man's sperm into his partner's reproductive tract at a time when there is a high risk of cuckoldry.

Thornhill and Thornhill (1992) also hypothesized that FIPC may be an anti-cuckoldry tactic designed over human evolutionary history by selective pressures associated with sperm competition. They argued that a woman who resists or avoids copulating with her partner might thereby be signaling to him that she has been sexually unfaithful and they suggest that the FIPC functions to decrease his paternal uncertainty. Thornhill and Thornhill argued that the fact that the rape is more likely to occur during or after a breakup—times in which men express great concern about female sexual infidelity—provides preliminary support for the hypothesis. For example, they cited research by Frieze (1983) indicating that women who were physically abused and raped by their husbands rated them to be more sexually jealous than did women who were abused but not raped. Similar arguments were presented by Thornhill and Palmer (2000), and Lalumière et al. (2005) suggested that antisocial men who suspect that their female partner has been sexually unfaithful may be motivated to engage in FIPC.

Both indirect and direct empirical evidence supporting this hypothesis has been documented. Frieze (1983) and Gage and Hutchinson (2006), for example, found that husbands who raped their wives were more sexually jealous than husbands who did not rape their wives. Shields and Hanneke (1983) documented that victims of FIPC were more likely to have reported engaging in extramarital sex than were women who were not raped by their in-pair partner. Studying men's partner-directed insults, Starratt, Goetz, Shackelford, McKibbin, and Stewart-Williams (2006) found in two studies that a man's accusations of his partner's sexual infidelity were a reliable predictor of sexual coercion. Specifically, men who accused their partners of being unfaithful (nominating items such as "I accused my partner of having sex with many other men" and "I called my partner a 'whore' or a 'slut'") were more likely to sexually coerce them.

Direct empirical evidence supporting this hypothesis is accumulating. Camilleri (2004), for example, found that risk of a partner's infidelity predicted sexual coercion among male participants but not among female participants. It is biologically impossible for women to be cuckolded, so one would not expect women to possess sperm-competition psychology that would generate sexually coercive behavior in response to a male partner's sexual infidelity. Goetz and Shackelford (2006) documented in two studies that a man's sexual coercion in the context of an intimate relationship is related positively to his partner's infidelities. According to men's self-reports and women's partner reports, men who used more sexual coercion in their relationship were mated to women who had been or were likely to be unfaithful, and these men also were likely to use more mate-retention behaviors.

Because cuckoldry poses a substantial reproductive cost for males of paternally investing species, men are expected to have evolved a host of adaptations to confront the adaptive problem of paternal uncertainty. One such adaptation may be a sperm-competition tactic whereby sexual coercion and FIPC function to increase the likelihood that the in-pair male, and not a rival male, sires the offspring that his partner might produce. It may be that a proportion of sexually coercive behaviors (in the context of an intimate relationship) are performed by antisocial men who aim to punish, humiliate, or control their partners *independent of their perception of cuckoldry risk*. I am not arguing that all sexual coercion and FIPCs are the output of evolved psychological mechanisms designed to reduce the risk of being cuckolded. Instead, I am suggesting that sexual coercion might sometimes be the result of evolved psychology in men that is associated with male sexual jealousy.

CONCLUDING REMARKS

It is unsettling that a simple asymmetry in reproductive biology can cause such conflict between the sexes. But one must bear in mind that natural selection is neither a moral nor an immoral process; it is amoral. The products of selection are not subject to any code of ethics or rules of conduct; neither is selection concerned with the rightness and wrongness of actions or the goodness and badness of motives. Selection simply favors alleles that provide higher reproductive success in their current environment. Because selection is indifferent to moral standards and principles, it may produce adaptations for survival and reproduction that are judged by cultures and societies to be abhorrent. Physical and sexual intimate-partner violence are detestable products of an amoral selection process. Other morally reprehensible tactics associate with paternal uncertainty that were not discussed here include stalking, genital mutilation such as clitoridectomy and infibulation, pregnancy abuse, infanticide, and child abuse. That selection produces and maintains these anti-cuckoldry tactics, by increasing the frequency of genes that are associated with such behaviors, may be unsettling but is also undeniable. It is the consequences of paternal uncertainty that prompted Duntley (2005) to suggest that "perhaps the most dangerous human a woman will encounter in her lifetime is her own romantic partner" (p. 243).

References

Abrahams, N., Jewkes, R., Hoffman, M., & Laubscher, R. (2004). Sexual violence against intimate partners in Cape Town: Prevalence and risk factors reported by men. *Bulletin of the World Health Organisation, 82*, 330–337.

Anderson, K. G. (2006). How well does paternity confidence match actual paternity? Results from worldwide nonpaternity rates. *Current Anthropology, 48*, 511–518.

Andersson, M. (1994). *Sexual selection.* Princeton, NJ: Princeton University Press.

Apt, C., & Hurlbert, D. F. (1993). The sexuality of women in physically abusive marriages: Comparative study. *Journal of Family Violence, 8*, 57–69.

Bailey, R. O., Seymour, N. R., & Stewart, G. R. (1978). Rape behavior in blue-winged teal. *Auk, 95*, 188–190.

Baker, R. R., & Bellis, M. A. (1993). Human sperm competition: Ejaculate adjustment by males and the function of masturbation. *Animal Behaviour, 46*, 861–885.

Barash, D. P. (1977). Sociobiology of rape in mallards (*Anas platyrhynchos*): Response of the mated male. *Science, 197*, 788–789.

Basile, K. C. (2002). Prevalence of wife rape and other intimate partner sexual coercion in a nationally representative sample of women. *Violence and Victims, 17*, 511–524.

Bellis, M. A., Hughes, K., Hughes, S., & Ashton, J. R. (2005). Measuring paternal discrepancy and its public health consequences. *Journal of Epidemiology and Community Health, 59*, 749–754.

Bergen, R. K. (1996). *Wife rape: Understanding the response of survivors and service providers.* Thousand Oaks, CA: Sage.

Betzig, L. (1989). Causes of conjugal dissolution: A cross-cultural study. *Current Anthropology, 30*, 654–676.

Birkhead, T. (2000). *Promiscuity.* London: Faber & Faber.

Birkhead, T. R., Hunter, F. M., & Pellatt, J. E. (1989). Sperm competition in the zebra finch, *Taeniopygia guttata*. *Animal Behaviour, 38*, 935–950.

Brownmiller, S. (1975). *Against our will: Men, women, and rape.* New York: Simon & Schuster.

Buss, D. M. (1988). From vigilance to violence: Tactics of mate retention in American undergraduates. *Ethology and Sociobiology, 9*, 291–317.

Buss, D. M. (1996). Sexual conflict: Evolutionary insights into feminism and the "battle of the sexes." In D. M. Buss & N. M. Malamuth (Eds.), *Sex, power, conflict* (pp. 296–318). New York: Oxford University Press.

Buss, D. M. (2000). *The dangerous passion.* New York: The Free Press.

Buss, D. M. (2005). *The murderer next door.* New York: Penguin.

Buss, D. M., & Duntley, J. D. (1998, July 10). *Evolved homicide modules.* Paper presented at the annual meeting of the Human Behavior and Evolution Society, Davis, CA.

Buss, D. M., & Duntley, J. D. (2003). Homicide: An evolutionary perspective and implications for public policy. In N. Dress (Ed.), *Violence and public policy* (pp. 115–128). Westport, CT: Greenwood.

Buss, D. M., Larsen, R. J., Westen, D., & Semmelroth, J. (1992). Sex differences in jealousy: Evolution, physiology and psychology. *Psychological Science, 3,* 251–255.

Buss, D. M., & Malamuth, N. M. (1996). *Sex, power, conflict.* New York: Oxford University Press.

Buss, D. M., & Shackelford, T. K. (1997). From vigilance to violence: Mate retention tactics in married couples. *Journal of Personality and Social Psychology, 72,* 346–361.

Camilleri, J. A. (2004). Investigating sexual coercion in romantic relationships: A test of the cuckoldry risk hypothesis. Unpublished master's thesis, University of Saskatchewan, Saskatoon, Saskatchewan, Canada.

Campbell, L., & Ellis, B. J. (2005). Commitment, love, and mate retention. In D. M. Buss (Ed.), *The handbook of evolutionary psychology* (pp. 419–442). Hoboken, NJ: John Wiley & Sons.

Cheng, K. M., Burns, J. T., & McKinney, F. (1983). Forced copulation in captive mallards III. Sperm competition. *Auk, 100,* 302–310.

Daly, M., & Wilson, M. (1988). *Homicide.* Hawthorne, NY: Aldine de Gruyter.

Daly, M., Wilson, M., & Weghorst, J. (1982). Male sexual jealousy. *Ethology and Sociobiology, 3,* 11–27.

DeMaris, A. (1997). Elevated sexual activity in violent marriages: Hypersexuality or sexual extortion? *Journal of Sex Research, 34,* 361–373.

Dixson, A. F. (1998). *Primate sexuality.* Oxford: Oxford University Press.

Dobash, R. E., & Dobash, R. P. (1979). *Violence against wives.* New York: The Free Press.

Donnelly, D. A. (1993). Sexually inactive marriages. *Journal of Sex Research, 30,* 171–179.

Dunkle, K. L., Jewkes, R. K., Brown, H. C., Gray, G. E., McIntyre, J. A., & Harlow, S. D. (2004). Gender-based violence, relationship power and risk of prevalent HIV infection among women attending antenatal clinics in Soweto, South Africa. *Lancet, 363,* 1415–1421.

Duntley, J. D. (2005). Adaptations to dangers from humans. In D. M. Buss (Ed.), *The handbook of evolutionary psychology* (pp. 224–249). Hoboken, NJ: John Wiley & Sons.

Dutton, D. G. (1998). *The abusive personality.* New York: Guilford Press.

Dutton, D. G., & Golant, S. K. (1995). *The batterer.* New York: Basic Books.

Figueredo, A. J., & McClosky, L. A. (1993). Sex, money, and paternity: The evolution of domestic violence. *Ethology and Sociobiology, 14,* 353–379.

Finkelhor, D., & Yllo, K. (1985). *License to rape: Sexual abuse of wives.* New York: Holt, Rinehart, & Winston.

Frieze, I. H. (1983). Investigating the causes and consequences of marital rape. *Signs: Journal of Women in Culture and Society, 8,* 532–553.

Gage, A. J., & Hutchinson, P. L. (2006). Power, control, and intimate partner sexual violence in Haiti. *Archives of Sexual Behavior, 35*, 11–24.

Gallup G. G., Burch, R. L., Zappieri, M. L., Parvez, R. A., Stockwell, M. L., & Davis, J. A. (2003). The human penis as a semen displacement device. *Evolution and Human Behavior, 24*, 277–289.

Gangestad, S. W., Thornhill, R., & Garver, C. E. (2002). Changes in women's sexual interests and their partner's mate-retention tactics across the menstrual cycle: Evidence for shifting conflicts of interest. *Proceedings of the Royal Society of London, 269*, 975–982.

Gelles, R. (1977). Power, sex and violence: The case of marital rape. *Family Coordinator, 26*, 339–347.

Goetz, A. T., & Shackelford, T. K. (2006). Sexual coercion and forced in-pair copulation as sperm competition tactics in humans. *Human Nature, 17*, 265–282.

Goetz, A. T., Shackelford, T. K., Weekes-Shackelford, V. A., Euler, H. A., Hoier, S., Schmitt, D. P., et al. (2005). Mate retention, semen displacement, and human sperm competition: A preliminary investigation of tactics to prevent and correct female infidelity. *Personality and Individual Differences, 38*, 749–763.

Gomendio, M., Harcourt, A. H., & Roldán, E. R. S. (1998). Sperm competition in mammals. In T. R. Birkhead and A. P. Møller (Eds.), *Sperm competition and sexual selection* (pp. 667–756). New York: Academic Press.

Goodwin, D. (1955). Some observations on the reproductive behavior of rooks. *British Birds, 48*, 97–107.

Hadi, A. (2000). Prevalence and correlates of the risk of martial sexual violence in Bangladesh. *Journal of Interpersonal Violence, 15*, 787–805.

Haselton, M. G., & Nettle, D. (2006). The paranoid optimist: An integrative evolutionary model of cognitive biases. *Personality and Social Psychology Review, 10*, 47–66.

Johnson, M. P. (1995). Patriarchal terrorism and common couple violence: Two forms of violence against women. *Journal of Marriage and the Family, 57*, 283–294.

Kilgallon, S. J., & Simmons, L. W. (2005). Image content influences men's semen quality. *Biology Letters, 1*, 253–255.

Koziol-McLain, J. Coates, C. J., & Lowenstein, S. R. (2001). Predictive validity of a screen for partner violence against women. *American Journal of Preventative Medicine, 21*, 93–100.

Lalumière, M. L., Harris, G. T., Quinsey, V. L., & Rice, M. E. (2005). *The causes of rape: Understanding individual differences in male propensity for sexual aggression.* Washington, DC: APA Press.

McKinney, F., Cheng, K. M., & Bruggers, D. J. (1984). Sperm competition in apparently monogamous birds. In R. L. Smith (Ed.), *Sperm competition and evolution of animal mating systems* (pp. 523–545). New York: Academic Press.

McKinney, F., Derrickson, S. R., & Mineau, P. (1983). Forced copulation in waterfowl. *Behavior, 86,* 250–294.

McKinney, F., & Stolen, P. (1982). Extra-pair-bond courtship and forced copulation among captive green-winged teal (*Anas crecca carolinensis*). *Animal Behaviour, 30,* 461–474.

Meyer, S., Vivian, D., & O'Leary, K. D. (1998). Men's sexual aggression in marriage: Couple's reports. *Violence against Women, 4,* 415–435.

Miller, R. S. (1997). We always hurt the ones we love: Aversive interactions in close relationships. In R. Kowalski (Ed.), *Aversive interpersonal interactions* (pp. 11–29). New York: Plenum.

Pagelow, M. (1988). Marital rape. In V. B. V. Hasselt, R. Morrison, A. Bellack, & M. Hersen (Eds.), *Handbook of family violence* (pp. 207–232). New York: Plenum.

Painter, K., & Farrington, D. P. (1999). Wife rape in Great Britain. In R. Muraskin (Ed.), *Women and justice: Development of international policy* (pp.135–164). New York: Gordon and Breach.

Parker, G. A. (1970). Sperm competition and its evolutionary consequences in the insects. *Biological Reviews, 45,* 525–567.

Peters, J., Shackelford, T. K., & Buss, D. M. (2002). Understanding domestic violence against women: Using evolutionary psychology to extend the feminist functional analysis. *Violence and Victims, 17,* 255–264.

Pound, N. (2002). Male interest in visual cues of sperm competition risk. *Evolution and Human Behavior, 23,* 443–466.

Russell, D. E. H. (1982). *Rape in marriage.* New York: Macmillan.

Sagarin, B. J., Becker, D. V., Guadagno, R. E., Nicastle, L. D., & Millevoi, A. (2003). Sex differences (and similarities) in jealousy: The moderating influence of infidelity experience and sexual orientation of the infidelity. *Evolution and Human Behavior, 24,* 17–23.

Schützwohl, A., & Koch, S. (2004). Sex differences in jealousy: The recall of cues to sexual and emotional infidelity in personally more and less threatening context conditions. *Evolution and Human Behavior, 25,* 249–257.

Serran, G., & Firestone, P. (2004). Intimate partner homicide: A review of the male proprietariness and the self-defense theories. *Aggression and Violent Behavior, 9,* 1–15.

Seymour, N. R., & Titman, R. D. (1979). Behaviour of unpaired male black ducks (*Anas rupribes*) during the breeding season in a Nova Scotia tidal marsh. *Canadian Journal of Zoology, 57,* 2412–2428.

Shackelford, T. K., & Buss, D. M. (1997). Cues to infidelity. *Personality and Social Psychology Bulletin, 23,* 1034–1045.

Shackelford, T. K., Buss, D. M., & Weekes-Shackelford, V. A. (2003). Wife killings committed in the context of a "lovers triangle." *Basic and Applied Social Psychology, 25,* 137–143.

Shackelford, T. K., & Goetz, A. T. (2004). Men's sexual coercion in intimate relationships: Development and initial validation of the Sexual Coercion in Intimate Relationships Scale. *Violence and Victims, 19,* 21–36.

Shackelford, T. K., & Goetz, A. T. (2006). Comparative psychology of sperm competition. *Journal of Comparative Psychology, 120,* 139–146.

Shackelford, T. K., & Goetz, A. T. (2007). Adaptation to sperm competition in humans. *Current Directions in Psychological Science, 16,* 47–50.

Shackelford, T. K., Goetz, A. T., Buss, D. M., Euler, H. A., & Hoier, S. (2005). When we hurt the ones we love: Predicting violence against women from men's mate retention tactics. *Personal Relationships, 12,* 447–463.

Shackelford, T. K., LeBlanc, G. J., & Drass, E. (2000). Emotional reactions to infidelity. *Cognition and Emotion, 14,* 643–659.

Shackelford, T. K., LeBlanc, G. J., Weekes-Shackelford, V. A., Bleske-Rechek, A. L., Euler, H. A., & Hoier, S. (2002). Psychological adaptation to human sperm competition. *Evolution and Human Behavior, 23,* 123–138.

Shackelford, T. K., & Pound, N. (Eds.). (2006). *Sperm competition in humans.* New York: Springer.

Shackelford, T. K., Pound, N., & Goetz, A. T. (2005). Psychological and physiological adaptations to sperm competition in humans. *Review of General Psychology, 9,* 228–248.

Shields, N. M., & Hanneke, C. R. (1983). Battered wives' reactions to marital rape. In R. Gelles, G. Hotaling, M. Straus, and D. Finkelhor (Eds.), *The dark side of families* (pp. 131–148). Thousand Oaks, CA: Sage.

Smith, R. L. (1984). Human sperm competition. In R. L. Smith (Ed.), *Sperm competition and the evolution of animal mating systems* (pp. 601–660). New York: Academic Press.

Starratt, V. G., Goetz, A. T., Shackelford, T. K., McKibbin, W. F., & Stewart-Williams, S. (2006). Men's partner-directed insults and sexual coercion in intimate relationships. Manuscript under editorial review.

Symons, D. (1979). *The evolution of human sexuality.* New York: Oxford University Press.

Thornhill, R., & Palmer, C. T. (2000). *A natural history of rape.* Cambridge, MA: MIT Press.

Thornhill, R., & Thornhill, N. W. (1992). The evolutionary psychology of men's coercive sexuality. *Behavioral and Brain Sciences, 15,* 363–421.

Trivers, R. L. (1972). Parental investment and sexual selection. In B. Campbell (Ed.), *Sexual selection and the descent of man 1871–1971* (pp. 136–179). Chicago: Aldine.

Valera, F., Hoi, H., & Kristin, A. (2003). Male shrikes punish unfaithful females. *Behavioral Ecology, 14,* 403–408.

Walker, L. E. (1979). *The battered woman.* New York: Harper & Row.

Watts, C., Keogh, E., Ndlovu, M., & Kwaramba, R. (1998). Withholding of sex and forced sex: Dimensions of violence against Zimbabwean women. *Reproductive Health Matters, 6,* 57–65.

White, G. L. (1981). Some correlates of romantic jealousy. *Journal of Personality, 49,* 129–147.

Wiederman, M. W., & Allgeier, E. R. (1993). Gender differences in sexual jealousy: Adaptionist or social learning explanation? *Ethology and Socio-biology, 14*, 115–140.

Wilson, M., & Daly, M. (1992). The man who mistook his wife for a chattel. In J. H. Barkow, L. Cosmides, & J. Tooby (Eds.), *The adapted mind* (pp. 289–322). New York: Oxford University Press.

Wilson, M., & Daly, M. (1993). An evolutionary psychological perspective on male sexual proprietariness and violence against wives. *Violence and victims, 8*, 271–294.

Wilson, M., & Daly, M. (1996). Male sexual proprietariness and violence against women. *Current Directions in Psychological Science, 5*, 2–7.

Wilson, M., & Daly, M. (1998). Lethal and nonlethal violence against wives and the evolutionary psychology of male sexual proprietariness. In R. E. Dobash & R. P. Dobash (Eds.), *Rethinking violence against women* (pp. 199–230). Thousand Oaks, CA: Sage.

Wilson, M., Daly, M., & Daniele, A. (1995). Familicide: The killing of spouse and children. *Aggressive Behavior, 21*, 275–291.

Wilson, M., Johnson, H., & Daly M. (1995). Lethal and nonlethal violence against wives. *Canadian Journal of Criminology, 37*, 331–361.

Wyckoff, G. J., Wang, W., & Wu, C. (2000). Rapid evolution of male reproductive genes in the descent of man. *Nature, 403*, 304–308.

Yllo, K., & Straus, M. A. (1990). Patriarchy and violence against wives: The impact of structural and normative factors. In M. A. Straus & R. J. Gelles (Eds.), *Physical violence in American families: Risk factors and adaptations to violence in 8145 families* (pp. 383–399). New Brunswick, NJ: Transaction.

13 Temperament as a Biological Mechanism for Mate Choice: A Hypothesis and Preliminary Data

Helen E. Fisher, Heide D. Island, Daniel Marchalik, and Jonathan Rich

There is a growing interest in behavioral syndromes. Bell writes, "A behavioral syndrome occurs when individuals behave in a consistent way through time or across contexts and is analogous to 'personality' or 'temperament.' Interest is accumulating in behavioural syndromes owing to their important ecological and evolutionary consequences" (Bell 2007). This chapter reports on two pilot studies of questionnaire data, on 3,000 men and women and 2,766 men and women, respectively, collected from a current dating/relationship Web site, Chemistry.com, with the supposition that four broad behavioral syndromes are prevalent in *Homo sapiens*.

These investigations are based on Fisher's hypothesis that men and women tend to be attracted to potential mates who have a somewhat different genetic profile associated with different cognitive and behavioral traits, an unconscious attraction mechanism that enables mating partners to create more genetic variety in their offspring and co-parent their young with a wider array of parenting skills. The paper concludes that the results of these pilot projects provide enough preliminary data to warrant further pursuit of this line of investigation. But the ideas are speculative; they are offered in the hope of stimulating further empirical work on the biological mechanisms associated with mate choice.

A NEURAL MECHANISM FOR "COURTSHIP ATTRACTION"

The phenomenon of "mate choice" is so common in nature that the etho-logical literature regularly uses several terms to describe it, including "individual preference," "favoritism," "female choice," "sexual choice," "selective proceptivity," and "courtship attraction." Despite variations in the duration of courtship attraction, many species display similar characteristics of attraction as they court. Most important, attracted individuals *focus* their courtship attention on a *preferred* mating partner. They also express heightened energy; obsessive following; sleeplessness; loss of appetite; impulsivity; possessive "mate guarding;" affiliative courtship gestures such as patting, stroking, licking, and nuzzling; goal-oriented courtship behaviors, and intense motivation to win this *particular* individual (Fisher 2004). Moreover, many creatures express this attraction instantly, what may be the forerunner of human "love at first sight."

Scientists have described many physical and behavioral traits in birds and mammals that evolved to "attract" a mate (Andersson 1994, Miller 2000). The peacock's tail is the standard example. But the corresponding brain mechanism by which the "display chooser" responds to these traits, comes to *prefer* a *specific* individual, and displays the above-mentioned suite of traits associated with courtship attraction has not been examined until recently (Fisher, Aron, & Brown 2005). However, current data on prairie voles (Gingrich, Liu, Cascio, Wang, & Insel 2000), sheep (Fabre-Nys 1997), and rats (Robinson, Heien, & Wightman 2002) indicate that the dopaminergic reward system is involved in mammalian courtship attraction.

Human romantic love shares several of the behavioral and physiological traits characteristic of mammalian courtship attraction, including intense focus on a preferred individual, elevated energy, hyperactivity, sleeplessness, loss of appetite, impulsivity, goal-oriented behaviors and strong motivation to pursue and win the beloved (Harris 1995, Hatfield & Sprecher 1986, Liebowitz 1983, Tennov 1979). All these traits can be seen in other mammalian (and avian) species during courtship (Fisher 2004). Men and women also report feelings of euphoria and mood swings into despair during a romantic setback. Adversity heightens romantic passion, known as "frustration attraction" (Fisher 2004). Lovers also become emotionally dependent; they feel empathy for their amour, and they think obsessively about the beloved. Lovers crave emotional union with their sweetheart, and express intense sexual desire and sexual possessiveness. As a result, rejected lovers often go to inappropriate, even dangerous, efforts to win back a departing sweetheart. Many spurned lovers suffer "abandonment rage" and depression as well (Fisher, Aron, & Brown 2006). Romantic love is also involuntary, difficult to control, and often impermanent.

These behavioral data suggest that human romantic love shares several primary traits with mammalian courtship attraction (Fisher et al. 2005).

The physiological underpinnings of human romantic love and mammalian courtship attraction also have similarities. Using functional magnetic resonance imaging (fMRI), Fisher et al. collected data on the neural mechanisms associated with early-stage intense romantic love (Aron et al. 2005, Fisher et al 2003, Fisher et al 2006), as did Bartels and Zeki (2000, 2004). Both groups found evidence that human romantic love is associated with the subcortical dopaminergic reward system. Moreover, recent fMRI data indicate that romantic love engages a different, but overlapping, constellation of neural correlates than does the sex drive (see Fisher 2005), indicating that this neural network is associated with a specific function: mate preference. But this brain system is triggered by some conspecifics and not by others. So the neural mechanism for romantic love must act in tandem with many other neural systems, including those for sensory perception, discrimination, and memory, to enable courting individuals to feel attraction for some individuals and indifferent to or repelled by others. This article explores what may be one of the unconscious biological mechanisms that stimulates the brain system for romantic love: temperament.

PSYCHOLOGICAL MECHANISMS OF MATE CHOICE

In humans, many social, economic, and psychological forces contribute to mate choice. Timing and proximity affect mate choice (Fiore & Donath 2004, Hatfield 1988, Pines 1999). Mystery plays a role; people tend to be less attracted to those they know well, particularly those with whom they had regular contact as a child (Shepher 1971). Men and women are also attracted to individuals from the same socioeconomic and ethnic background (Buston & Emlen 2003; Byrne, Clore, & Smeaton 1986; Cappella & Palmer 1990; Galton 1884; Pines 1999; Sussman & Reardon 1987), those with a similar level of education and intelligence (Buston & Emlen 2003; Byrne, Clore, & Smeaton 1986; Cappella and Palmer 1990; Galton 1884; Pines 1999), those who share their religious views and have other similar attitudes and values (Krueger & Caspi 1993, Laumann, Gagnon, Michael, & Michaels 1994, Shaikh & Suresh 1994), and those with a similar sense of humor and degree of financial stability (Buston & Emlen 2003). Data indicate that men and women also gravitate to individuals with similar social and communication skills (Buston & Emlen 2003; Byrne, Clore, & Smeaton 1986; Cappella & Palmer 1990; Pines 1999).

Reik (1964) proposed that men and women choose mates who satisfy an important need, including the qualities they lack. Others have proposed that this "need complementarity" drives mating and marriage (Aron & Aron 1989, Hinde 1997, Winch 1958). Proponents of "social exchange theory," a variant of this hypothesis, hold that men and women are attracted to those who can provide the resources they seek in exchange for the assets they can provide (Blau 1964; Dryer & Horowitz 1997; Foa & Foa 1980; Huston & Burgess 1979; Murstein 1976; Roloff 1981; Sprecher 2001; Sprecher & Regan 2002; Walster, Walster, & Berscheid 1978). Psychologists also propose that men and women tend to fall in love with people who are in love with them (Aronson 1998, Aron & Aron 1989, Hoyt & Hudson 1981, Pines 2005). Murstein (1976) hypothesizes that attraction has several stages, and during the "role stage" one becomes more attracted (or repelled) as they consider whether or not they can fit into the role they are likely to play in the relationship.

People are also attracted to those who show signs of bodily and facial symmetry (Gangestad & Thornhill 1997; Gangestad, Thornhill & Yeo 1994; Jones & Hill 1993), and those with specific bodily proportions (Singh 1993, Lavrakas 1975). Women are drawn to men with rank, money, and other resources (Buss 1994, Ellis 1992) and to those who are self-confident, assertive, and smart (Kenrick, Sadalla, Groth, & Trost 1990), whereas men are drawn to women exhibiting signs of youth, health, and beauty (Buss 1994). Yet, both sexes tend to choose mates of their level of attractiveness (Buston & Emlen 2003).

Freud (and many others) proposed that one's parents affect one's romantic choices. Hazan and Shaver (1987) build on the theories of Bowlby (1969) and Ainsworth, Blehar, Waters, and Wall (1978), proposing that humans seek attachments that mirror the type of infant attachment they made with mother, be it secure, anxious–ambivalent, or avoidant. And Harris (1999) hypothesizes that individuals are attracted to a partner who reflects the values, interests, and goals of childhood friends.

Zentner (2005) proposes that people gradually develop a psychological model of their ideal mate, what he refers to as one's ideal mate personality concept (IMPC). He defines this template as a "unique ordering and configuration of personality characteristics" that an individual regards as ideal for him or her (Zentner 2005, 245). This idiosyncratic psychological chart is subtle and unique and varies considerably from one individual to the next (Zentner 2005). Moreover, one's IMPC is not fixed or rigid; individuals change their image of their ideal mate over time, being most likely to alter this template when they become dissatisfied with a current partnership (Zentner 2005, 253). Zentner reports that women have a more incisive ideal mate personality concept than men do, and that women are better than men at picking a romantic partner who fits within their ideal type (Zentner 2005).

The process of attraction appears to operate like a funnel (Murstein 1976, Pines 2005, Winch 1958, Zentner 2005). Looks, values, background, needs, roles, and one's unique psychological chart all contribute to partner attraction, and at specific points in this trajectory, the process can fail, at what some regard as hidden "breaking points" (Sunnafrank 1986, Walther & Parks 2002). But the role of personality in this process is complex and controversial.

Several investigations of American couples, married and unmarried, homosexual and heterosexual, have shown that men and women are attracted to those with a similar personality (Byrne 1997; Caspi & Harbener 1990; Gottman, Murray, Tyson, & Swanson 2002; Holman 2001; Karney & Bradbury 1995; Keller & Young 1996; Kurdek and Schmitt 1987; Marioles, Strickert, & Hammer 1996; Phillips, Fulker, Carey, & Nagoshi 1988; Pines 2005; Richards, Wakefield, & Lewak 1990). However, attraction to specific similar personality traits is often contingent on attraction to other personality traits. For example, extroverts are regularly attracted to other extroverts, but only extroverts with high self-esteem are attracted to one another; extroverts with low self-esteem are less drawn to people like themselves (Zentner 2005). Thus, similarity in one personality dimension can influence, or even override, similarities in other dimensions. As Zentner writes, "Preference for similarity in personality characteristics varies substantially across traits and individuals" (2005, p. 252).

Moreover, other psychologists who have given extensive personality tests to long-married couples report that few patterns of similarity in personality emerge (Klohnen & Mendelsohn 1998, Zentner 2005). When Zentner reexamined 470 personality studies done since the 1930s, he concluded that under most circumstances men and women do not marry partners with a similar personality (Zentner 2005). Other investigators agree (e.g., Luo & Klohnen 2005); in fact, many have concluded that humans are regularly attracted to individuals who are very different from themselves (Hinde 1997, Winch 1958, Zentner 2005), specifically those who complement them in their personality traits (Beach, Whitaker, Jones, & Tesser, 2001; Houran, Lange, Rentfrow, & Bruckner 2004; Houts, Huston, & Robins 1996; Pilkington, Tesser, & Stephens 1991).

It appears that individuals are attracted to potential mates with similarity in some traits and complementarity in others. As Pines writes, "The evidence for an attraction between people with similar personalities is far weaker than the evidence for an attraction between people with similar attitudes" (Pines 2005, p. 137). She concludes, "It seems that we are attracted to partners to whom we are similar in general—in background, values, interests, and intelligence—but who complement us in a particular, significant personality dimension" (Pines 2005, p. 145). Luo and Klohnen come to a similar conclusion, reporting that an interest in a partner's financial stability, good looks, education, or sense of humor are ultimately more important to most people than are the personality traits they share (Luo & Klohnen 2005). And after reviewing several decades of this literature, Zentner concluded, "How two personalities may be best combined in a relationship remains at present an unresolved issue" (2005, p. 242)." Klohnen concurs, writing, "The temptation to throw in the towel, to conclude that personality does not systematically and importantly influence partner selection is understandable" (Klohnen & Mendelsohn 1998, p. 269).

How can one explain the dearth of clear patterns in psychological studies of human mate choice, an essential aspect of human reproduction? Perhaps biological forces play influential roles. Current data suggest that several of these neural mechanisms exist. For example, humans tend to be attracted to those who are biologically symmetrical (Gangestad & Thornhill 1997). Women tend to be attracted to men with a chiseled jaw and rugged cheekbones, signs of an active testosterone system (Grammer & Thornhill 1994). Men tend to be attracted to women with clear smooth skin, full lips, and neotenous facial features, signs of estrogen activity (Johnston 1999). Most important to this paper, women are attracted to men with a *different* cluster of genes in the major histocompatibility complex (MHC), an aspect of the immune system (Wedekind, Seebeck, Bettens, & Paepke 1995, Ziegler, Kentenich, & Uchanska-Ziegler 2005). Moreover, in a recent study of 48 couples, those women who shared the same cluster of genes in the MHC system as their long-term partner were more likely to be adulterous; the more genes in the MHC system that a woman shared with her mate, the more extra partners she engaged (Garver-Apgar, Gangestad, Thornhill, Miller, & Olp 2006).

This article hypothesizes that both sexes also gravitate to individuals with differences in other biological systems, specifically the systems for dopamine, serotonin, testosterone, and estrogen, variations associated respectively with different suites of cognitive and behavioral traits. This biological attraction to mates with a different genetic profile, Fisher hypothesizes, operates in tandem with the myriad cultural forces that affect mate choice, and most likely evolved to motivate ancestral hominids to produce greater genetic diversity in their young and co-parent these young with a wider array of parenting skills. First we explore data from behavior genetics and related fields that are relevant to this hypothesis, then we report on two pilot studies that offer very preliminary support of this hypothesis.

FOUR PRIMARY TEMPERAMENT SYNDROMES: A HYPOTHESIS

Cloninger defines personality as distinct clusters of thoughts and feelings that color all of a person's actions. He proposes that personality is a mix of biologically based traits, dimensions of "temperament," and traits that an individual acquires, dimensions of "character" (Cloninger 1987). It is now believed that 50% (or more) of the observed variance in personality traits is due to genetic influence (Bouchard 1994, Robins 2005). Cross-cultural surveys, brain imaging studies, twin studies, and population and molecular genetics suggest that traits of temperament are heritable, relatively stable across the life course and linked to specific genes, hormones, neurotransmitters, and/or patterns of brain activity (Bouchard 1994, Roberts & DelVecchio 2000, Terracciano et al. 2005). These traits of temperament also appear to be universal among humans. A study of 49 cultures has shown that cross-culturally people share the same array of personality traits, regardless of age, financial status, or social class (Terracciano et al. 2005).

Individuals within a society vary, however. Some are more agreeable, shy, impulsive, or cautious, or express some other traits more regularly and/or more intensely than others. The most commonly discussed traits of temperament are the "big five," openness to new experiences, conscientiousness, extroversion, agreeableness, and neuroticism or anxiety (Gosling, Rentfrow, & Swann 2003, Zentner 2005). Although the expression of these traits can be situation dependent, studies in behavior genetics suggest that their expression is due, in part, to genetic influence (Bouchard 1994); moreover, they are expressed cross-culturally (McCrae et al. 2005), recorded in many species (Gosling & John 1999), and linked with specific lifestyles in humans, including variations in health, life span, success in school and work, ability to sustain a romantic relationship, and likelihood of addiction or criminality (Robins 2005).

Many other traits have been linked with specific alleles, neurotransmitters, and/or hormones. However, the genes associated with specific behavioral and cognitive traits express themselves in complex combinations and interactions (Reif & Lesch 2003). So the activities and levels of these neurotransmitters and neurohormones are most likely not as significant as the functional ratios between them and their interactions with many other neural systems. Nevertheless, data suggest that specific variations in the neural systems for dopamine, serotonin, testosterone, and estrogen are associated with specific suites of behavioral and cognitive traits.

DOPAMINE: THE "EXPLORER"

A cluster of specific behavioral and cognitive traits are associated with activity in dopamine pathways. The DRD4 gene controls much of the dopamine activity in the forebrain, and a polymorphism in the type 4 dopamine receptor gene (DRD4) has been associated with several varieties of novelty seeking, including impulsivity and exploratory excitability (the tendency to approach novel situations). Age and gender do not contribute to the differences in the expression of these traits (Keltikangas-Jarvinen et al. 2003). Zuckerman (1994) has reported four components of sensation seeking: thrill and adventure seeking; experience seeking (often involving unconventional or innovative mental or social activities); boredom susceptibility; and disinhibition, expressed by alcohol and/or drug use, risky sex, or gambling. Cloninger associates novelty seeking with several other traits, including exploratory excitability, impulsiveness, quick-temperedness, extravagance, and disorderliness (Cloninger, Przybeck, & Svrakic 1991). Many of these novelty-seeking people have one version of the D4 dopamine receptor gene, D4DR (Ebstein et al 1996).

Other traits have been linked with activity in the dopamine system, including sex drive (Meston & Frohlic 2000, Pearson 2006), mania and hypersocial behaviors (La Cerra & Bingham 2002), social dominance, enthusiasm, energy, assertiveness, ambitiousness, and achievement striving (Depue & Collins 1999, Wacker, Chavanon, & Stemmler 2006), and verbal and non-linguistic creativity and idea generation (Flaherty 2005, Reuter, Roth, Holve, & Hennig 2006). When a Parkinson's disease patient was treated with drugs that elevate central dopamine, the patient began to express poetic talent (Schrag & Trimble 2001).

The above data suggest that a suite of biologically based traits can be associated with the central dopamine system, including risk taking, novelty seeking, impulsivity, boredom susceptibility, disinhibition, sex drive, energy, enthusiasm, excitability, curiosity, idea generation, and creativity. The degree to which these traits correlate has not yet been established; and the expression of these genes is highly influenced by myriad other biological and environmental forces. But the above genetic data suggest that, theoretically, a human can inherit a specific matrix of genetic traits associated with a predisposition for a particular suite or syndrome of related cognitions and behaviors. For the purposes of discussion, we label individuals with this possible temperament syndrome as "Explorer."

SEROTONIN: THE "BUILDER"

A different cluster of specific behavioral and cognitive traits is associated with activity in serotonin pathways. Polymorphic alleles of the serotonin 2A receptor gene (5–HTR2A), T102C and A1438G, are associated with variations in emotionality, activity, and sociability (Golimbet, Alfimova, & Mityushina 2004). Individuals with one variation in the T102C gene display lower levels of anxiety and have higher scores on the scale of hypomania (mild mania); whereas those with the A1438G heterozygote A/G (rather than the homozygote G/G) are also more extroverted and have lower scores on the scale of "no close friends" (Golimbet et al. 2004). Extroversion and positive mood have also been associated with increased central serotonin (Flory, Manuck, Matthews, & Muldoon, 2004), as has persistence (Davidge et al. 2004).

Allele polymorphisms involved in serotonin metabolism produce individual variations in degree of anxiety, neuroticism, and harm avoidance as well (Golimbet et al. 2004, Parks et al. 1998). Harm avoidance is also associated with blood platelet 5–HT2 receptor sensitivity (Peirson et al. 1999); and degree of fear of uncertainty, shyness, anticipatory worry, and harm avoidance have been associated with a polymorphism in a gene for serotonin receptor type 3 (Melke et al. 2003). Among laboratory rats, elevated central 5–HT inhibits exploration (Wilson, Gonzalez, & Farabollini 1992), supporting the link between elevated serotonin activity, cautiousness, and harm avoidance.

There is an inverse relationship between central serotonin activity and human aggression (Davidge et al. 2004). Selective serotonin reuptake inhibitors (SSRIs) increase affiliative behavior during a cooperative task, including giving more suggestions and fewer commands, and making fewer attempts at unilateral solutions, correlating with increased plasma levels of these serotonin agonists (Knutson et al. 1998). SSRI treatment in male vervet monkeys also enhances a suite of affiliative behaviors, leading to increased social status (Knutson et al. 1998). People with elevated plasma levels of serotonin also exhibit higher socioeconomic status and live in more affluent neighborhoods (Manuck et al. 2005). Individuals who score lower than average on Cloninger's Novelty Seeking scale (Cloninger et al. 1991) tend to be rigid, loyal, stoic, and frugal (Ebstein et al. 1996). Because genes associated with novelty seeking are in the dopamine system, and the dopamine and serotonin systems are negatively correlated in many brain regions (Stahl 2000), it is likely that the tendencies toward mental inflexibility, loyalty, stoicism, and frugality are also associated with elevated activity in serotonin pathways.

A PET study of 15 normal male subjects showed a correlation between self-transcendence (religiosity) and elevated serotonin activity (Borg, Andree, Soderstrom, & Farde 2003, Golimbet et al. 2004). So Borg et al. (2003) argue that variability in 5–HT1A receptor density may explain why people vary in their degree of religious and/or spiritual fervor. Self-transcendence or religiosity is also associated with other polymorphisms in the serotonin system (Bachner-Melman et al. 2005, Ham et al. 2004). When given tests of emotional intensity, patients taking SSRIs also report being less able to cry; feeling less irritable; caring less about others' feelings; and feeling less sadness, less surprise, less anger, and less worry over things or situations; and being less able to express their feelings (Opbroek et al. 2002); these drugs also inhibit sexual desire, sexual function, and sexual pleasure (Rosen, Lane, & Menza 1999), exploratory behavior (Wilson et al. 1992), and general creativity (Opbroek et al. 2002).

The above data suggest that specific genetic variables associated with the central and peripheral serotonin system contribute to a suite of cognition and behavioral traits, including lower levels of anxiety, elevated mood, extroversion, sociability, popularity, elevated social status, conventionality, cautiousness and harm avoidance, religiosity, loyalty, stoicism, frugality, figural and numeric creativity, persistence, and managerial qualities, including being more socially cooperative, giving suggestions, giving fewer commands, and making fewer attempts at unilateral solutions. For the purpose of discussion, individuals who express this broad suite of genetically based cognitive and behavioral traits and its associated temperament syndrome are labeled "Builders."

TESTOSTERONE: THE "DIRECTOR"

Data suggest that a different constellation of characteristics is associated with specific activity in the testosterone system. Both men and women can express the traits associated with the activities of testosterone; however, the data on testosterone-related traits have largely been collected via studies of gender differences.

Among those traits associated with testosterone activity is spatial acuity. In a meta-analysis of 150,000 Americans aged 13 to 22 and tested across 32 years, the overwhelming majority of those whose scores fell in the top 5–10% in science, math, mechanical reasoning, and engineering were male (Hedges & Nowell 1995; Hyde, Fennema, & Lamon 1990). In another meta-analysis of 10,000 seventh- and eighth-grade boys and girls, 260 boys and 20 girls scored above 700 (out of 800) on the standard Scholastic Aptitude Test, and studies in several other countries have yielded similar results (Benbow & Stanley 1983, Mann, Sasanuma, Sakuma, & Masaki 1990).

The brain architecture associated with these spatial skills is created by fetal testosterone (Grimshaw, Bryden, & Finegan 1995). But bodily levels of testosterone continue to contribute to men's (and women's) spatial dexterity across the life course (Nyborg 1994). When healthy male senior citizens receive infusions of testosterone, their spatial acuity increases (Janowsky, Oviatt, & Orwoll 1994), and women become more skilled at finding their car in a parking lot just before and during menstruation, when estrogen levels decline and levels of testosterone become unmasked (Hampson 1990). Animal studies support this association between spatial skills and the activity of testosterone (De Vries & Simerley 2002).

Baron-Cohen, Knickmeyer, and Belmonte (2005) distinguish two specific sex differences in cognition, what they refer to as empathizing (E) and systemizing (S). Systemizing is "the drive to analyze a system in terms of the rules that govern the system, in order to predict the behavior of the system"; whereas "empathizing is the drive to identify another's mental states and to respond to these with an appropriate emotion, in order to predict and respond to the behavior of another person" (Baron-Cohen et al. 2005, 820). These researchers propose that humans have evolved three specific brain types: S (S > E), which is more common in men; E (E > S), which is more common in women; and B (E = S), which is characteristic of men and women who are equally proficient at both empathizing and systemizing (Baron-Cohen et al. 2005).

They also report that the "extreme" androgenic brain is also associated with less emotion recognition, less empathy, less eye contact, and less social sensitivity. These individuals also have fewer friends and other social relationships, poorer quality of social relations, and fewer language skills (Baron-Cohen et al. 2005, Knickmeyer, Baron-Cohen, Raggatt, & Taylor 2005). However, these individuals express a superior understanding of machines and an obsession for rule-based systems (Baron-Cohen et al. 2005). Baron-Cohen et al. propose that this hyper-masculinity is the result of more short-range connectivity and less long-distance connectivity in the brain, due to prenatal androgens (Baron-Cohen et al. 2005, Knickmeyer, Baron-Cohen, Raggatt, Taylor, & Hackett 2006).

Another aspect of hyper-masculinity is heightened attention to detail and intensified focus on narrow interests (Baron-Cohen et al. 2005), a suite of related traits that Baron-Cohen et al. associate with systemizing (Knickmeyer et al. 2005). Psychological data corroborate this association between testosterone and a narrow focus on the details of a system. Faced with a business problem, men tend to focus on the immediate dilemma rather than putting the issue into a larger context; then they progress in a straightforward, linear, causal path toward a specific goal, the solution (Duff 1993, Hampden-Turner 1994, Helgesen 1990, Rosener 1995).

Baron-Cohen proposes that men compartmentalize their attention, focus narrowly, and have restricted interests because the male brain is more lateralized and less integrated, due to fetal testosterone (Baron-Cohen et al. 2005, Knickmeyer et al. 2005). Testosterone injections in adults can also produce these traits, however. After three months of testosterone infusions, a female-to-male sex-change patient reported that "he" had begun to have problems expressing himself verbally; his thinking was more concrete; he now acted more quickly; he imagined less; he saw visual images more intensely; he lost fine motor control; he no longer saw the "overall picture"; and he changed "in mental focus from broad to narrow" (Dabbs 2000, 43). Related to this mental compartmentalization and narrow focus may be other traits: men tend to think and plan according to abstract principles more regularly than do women; they also tend to become wedded to these principles

(Gilligan 1982, Kohlberg 1969, Lever 1976, Tannen 1990). Men are, on average, more rule-bound, indicating mental inflexibility (Kohlberg 1981).

Another trait associated with the activity of testosterone is sensitivity to social dominance. Men tend to place themselves within real or perceived hierarchies; then they strive to achieve rank (Gilligan 1982, Hoyenga & Hoyenga 1980, Tannen 1990). Boys' games have clear winners and losers, and boys sort themselves into hierarchical packs and compete to be "top dog" (Lever 1976, Tannen 1990, Thorne 1993). Businessmen assign greater value to titles, office space, and high salary (Browne 1995, Duff 1993, Helgesen 1990), and men are more willing to endure exhausting workloads and sacrifice their health, safety, and spare time to win status, money, and prestige (Duff 1993, Helgesen 1990, Rosener 1995). Men and women exhibit no difference in "internal competitiveness," the desire to meet personal goals and display excellence. But men score higher in "external competitiveness," the willingness to elbow others aside to gain rank (Sassen 1980).

In almost all primate communities where more than one male resides, males also form a male–male dominance hierarchy (Smuts, Cheney, Seyfarth, Wrangham, & Struhsaker 1986), and testosterone has been associated with this drive for rank in many species (Mazur, Susman, & Edelbrock 1997). High levels of testosterone are commonly associated with rank in men and women as well (Booth, Shelley, Mazur, Tharp, & Kittok 1989; Mazur, Booth, & Dabbs 1992; Mazur et al. 1997). There is no simple correlation between androgens and status (Dabbs 1992); nevertheless, cross-culturally men are more likely than women to compete aggressively for rank (Halpern 1992). Testosterone has also been regularly associated with aggressiveness. For centuries, farmers have castrated roosters, bulls, and stallions to curtail physical aggressiveness (Knickmeyer et al. 2005), and approximately half of America's violent crimes are committed by men under age 24, a period of life when the activity of testosterone is greatest (Dabbs 1990).

The above data suggest that a suite of traits is associated with the androgens, specifically testosterone. Included are spatial skills; competency with machines and other rule-based systems; the ability to systemize; the ability to focus one's attention, often narrowly; the tendency to construct and adhere to abstract rules; mental inflexibility; sensitivity to rank and dominance; aggressiveness; outward competitiveness; and poorer linguistic and interpersonal social skills. Although this suite of behavioral and cognitive traits is recorded more regularly in men than in women, both sexes can potentially express these qualities (Baron-Cohen et al. 2005), most likely for a biological reason: the androgens and estrogens are produced in several diverse bodily regions, so an individual can potentially express elevated activity of both the estrogens and the androgens, or low activity of both these steroids, or any other ratio of these hormones. Those exhibiting this constellation of traits and their associated temperament syndrome are referred to as "Directors."

ESTROGEN: THE "NEGOTIATOR"

Available data suggest that a suite of specific traits is also associated with elevated activity in the estrogen system. Once again, both men and women can express the traits associated with the activities of estrogen; however, the data on estrogen-related traits have largely been collected via studies of gender differences.

For example, psychologists report that girls and women (more regularly than boys and men) think contextually and holistically (Baron-Cohen et al. 2005, Hall 1984); they generalize, synthesize, and integrate more details and connect these details faster, details ranging from the nuances of body posture (Hall 1984) to the position of objects in a room (Silverman & Eals 1992). This tendency to take a holistic perspective most likely derives from brain architecture (Baron-Cohen et al. 2005, Dabbs 2002, Fisher 1999). The splenium, the posterior section of the corpus callosum, is more extensive in women than in men (Holloway, Anderson, Defendini, & Harper 1993); also, the anterior commissure is 12% thicker in women (Allen, Richey, Chai, & Gorski 1991), data that indicate greater interhemispheric connectivity (Baron-Cohen et al. 2005). In most women, the two hemispheres are also more symmetrical and similar in function, while in men the brain is more asymmetrical, lateralized, and specialized (Geschwind & Galaburda 1985). These features of brain architecture are configured during fetal life by sex hormones (Nyborg 1994) and contribute to women's holistic, contextual view (Baron-Cohen et al. 2005, Dabbs 2000, Fisher 1999). However, women also have greater intrahemispheric long-range connectivity (Braeutigam, Rose, Swithenby, & Ambler 2004), which may also contribute to the ability to integrate a broad range of information.

Specific genes may contribute to this contextual perspective, and also to a related trait of many women, mental flexibility. Skuse et al. (1997) reported that a gene or gene cluster on the X chromosome influences the formation of the prefrontal cortex. This segment of DNA is silenced in all men but active in 50% of women, and it contributes to several cognitive traits, including the ability to pick up the nuances of social interactions (a contextual skill) and mental flexibility (Skuse et al. 1997). Psychological studies support this gender difference in mental flexibility; women are less rule-bound (Kohlberg 1969), perhaps because they envision a wider range of alternatives (Fisher 1999).

Language skills are also linked with estrogen and brain architecture. Infant girls listen more intently to music, pay greater attention to people's voices (McGuinness & Pribram 1979), and speak sooner (Halpern 1992). By age 12, most girls excel at grammar, punctuation, spelling, and understanding and remembering what they read (McGuinness 1985). Girls and women also excel at verbal memory and verbal fluency, finding the right word rapidly (Baron-Cohen 2002). A meta-analysis of studies done between 1960 and 1992 reports that women excelled at several language skills in all three decades; the average differences between the sexes were small, but significantly more women scored in the top 5–10% range in reading comprehension, writing, perceptual speed, and associative memory (Hedges & Nowell 1995). Girls and women also excel at several verbal skills in other countries (Mann et al. 1990).

The activity of estrogen is associated with these linguistic skills. Verbal memory, the ability to find the right word rapidly, and the capacity to pronounce words increase during mid-cycle ovulation when estrogen levels peak (Halpern 1992), and girls with Turner's Syndrome, the genetic disorder wherein females are missing one of the two Xs in the chromosomal pair, have difficulty remembering verbal information and speaking quickly and appropriately (Skuse et al. 1997). Two fMRI studies suggest that the gender difference in the corpus callosum contributes to women's efficiency with words (Hines, Allen, & Gorski 1992, Shaywitz et al. 1995). But genes also enable some women to speak more effectively than men. As mentioned above, Skuse et al. (1997) have located a gene or gene cluster on the X chromosome that influences several language skills, including reading ability and speech disorders; this gene is active in 50% of women and silenced in all men. This explains, Skuse writes, why "males are substantially more vulnerable to a variety of developmental disorders of speech, language impairment and reading disability" (Skuse et al. 1997, 707).

The literature describes another suite of attributes that are likely to be associated with estrogen, specifically the interest in social contacts, the drive to achieve interpersonal harmony, and the tendency to work and play in egalitarian teams (Hoyenga & Hoyenga 1980, Tannen 1990). During informal play, girls form "flat packs," small, non-hierarchical, leaderless groups (Tannen 1990). Girls seek social stability and non-combative interactions (Gilligan 1982, Lever 1976, Thorne 1993). In business, women's style of management is also based on inclusion, consultation, consensus, and collaboration (Duff 1993, Helgesen 1990, Rosener 1995). These traits have been widely linked with the activity of estrogen. At puberty, as estrogen activity increases, the feminine urge to connect, cooperate, and sustain a system of support intensifies (Brown & Gilligan 1992).

Women in 10 countries also excel at recognizing emotions in a face (Babchuk, Hames, & Thompson 1983; Hall 1984), another ability associated with estrogen (McCauley, Kay, Ito, & Treder 1987). Women, on average, perform better on tests of facial recognition (Herlitz & Yonker 2002), and women in 19 countries excel at reading a person's emotions from their tone of voice, posture, gestures, and other nonverbal cues (Hall 1984, McGuinness & Pribram 1979). Women also display more patience than men (McGuinness 1985), a trait also common to female chimpanzees (McGrew 1981). This feminine patience is also linked to estrogen, via its positive correlation with serotonin: low serotonin activity is associated with impulsivity, and estrogen stimulates the increase of 5–HT2A binding sites (Fink, Sumner, McQueen, Wilson, & Rosie,1998), thereby increasing serotonin activity to produce less impulsivity and more patience.

"Executive social skills" include awareness of others' feelings, the ability to pick up emotional expressions in faces, an aptitude for noticing and integrating body language cues, mental flexibility, and the abilities to make friends, maintain social ties, and override the impulses that distract one from completing one's social goals (Skuse et al. 1997). These social aptitudes have also been associated with this specific gene or gene cluster on the X chromosome, which is active in about 50% of women but silenced in all men, leading Skuse et al. (1997) to conclude that women, on average, excel at these executive social skills.

Girls and women excel at making inferences about what another person is thinking or feeling, "theory of mind"; they develop this ability earlier and excel at adjusting their behavior accordingly (Baron-Cohen, Jolliffe, Mortimore & Robertson, 1997). And on cross-cultural tests of empathy, emotional responsiveness, nurturance, and affection, girls and women achieve higher scores than do boys and men (Baron-Cohen 2002, McGuinness & Pribram 1979). Because empathy activates brain regions that integrate data from multiple neural sources (Ochsner et al. 2004), this feminine compassion may result from the greater long-range connectivity of the female brain (Baron-Cohen et al. 2005). But empathizing, nurturing, and other prosocial skills and behaviors have also been associated directly with estrogen in humans and other mammals (Baron-Cohen 2002, Knickmeyer et al. 2005).

The above data suggest that a suite of traits is associated with activity in the estrogen system, including the ability to synthesize, integrate, and contextualize information to "see the big picture"; verbal fluency, memory, and articulation; executive social skills, including the ability to read faces, postures, gestures, and tone of voice; the ability to pick up on the nuances of social interactions; prosocial behaviors, including mental flexibility, social cooperation, consensus building, egalitarian team playing, and the drive to seek social harmony and non-combative interactions; emotional expressivity;

the ability to discern the emotions and thoughts of others (important components of compassion); patience; and nurturing behaviors. Although this proposed constellation of behavioral and cognitive traits is recorded more regularly in women than in men, both sexes express a range of these traits (Baron-Cohen et al. 2005). Those with this suite of traits and associated temperament syndrome are referred to as "Negotiators."

TEMPERAMENT: A PILOT PROJECT

Using many of the aforementioned traits as domains, Fisher designed a 56-question instrument with 14 questions to explore the degree to which men and women expressed activity in each of these genetic systems: dopamine, serotonin, testosterone, and estrogen. This test was administered to members of Chemistry.com, an Internet dating/relationship service that is part of the parent companies Match.com and InterActiveCorp (IAC). Chemistry.com was launched in the United States in February, 2006; it has served 1.6 million members who are seeking romantic love leading to a long-term attachment to a single partner; 94% of members are between the ages of 20 and 59; 35% are in their 20s, and 30% are in their 30s.

An example of a question designed to measure the expression of activity in the dopamine system was "Do you have more energy than most people?" A question designed to measure a trait associated with the serotonin system was "In general, do you think it's important to follow the rules?" A question designed to measure a trait associated with the estrogen system was "In conversation, can you find the right words rapidly?" A question designed to measure the degree to which an individual expressed elevated activity in the testosterone system was "Does it take a lot of evidence to make you change your mind on an important issue?" Using a 4-point Likert-like scale, participants were requested to respond to all 56 questions with one of four answers: 1 (*almost never*), 2 (*sometimes*), 3 (*most of the time*), or 4 (*all the time*). Responses to these 56 questions were tabulated using a 0–3 scale, with 0 points for the response "almost never," and 3 points for the response "all the time."

After a participant's scores on all 56 questions were tabulated, respondents received their questionnaire results on all four scales; For example: Negotiator 38%, Director 30%, Builder 19%, Explorer 13%. This individual was then registered primarily as a Negotiator and secondarily as a Director (Negotiator–Director). Thus, participants ($N = 523,622$) were placed in 1 of 12 categories: Explorer–Builder. Explorer–Director, Explorer–Negotiator, Builder–Explorer, Builder–Director, Builder–Negotiator, Director–Explorer, Director–Builder, Director–Negotiator, Negotiator–Explorer, Negotiator–

Builder, and Negotiator–Director. The distribution of these 12 types is seen in Table 13.1.

Preliminary analysis of the questionnaire responses in an initial sample of 1,500 men and 1,500 women suggests patterns of trait association. Cronbach's alpha coefficients were calculated for each 14-item scale, and these calculations yielded the following results: Explorer .692, Builder .723, Director .702, and Negotiator .604. A factor analysis was performed on all 56 items (4 scales with 14 items each), using a varimax rotation. A scree test suggested that 6 factors adequately explained the item variance. However, the establishment and refinement of this measure will take multiple iterations (Fisher, Island, Rich, & Zava, in preparation). This preliminary investigation suggests only that we have enough data to proceed with this line of investigation. When we have established higher reliability scores, we plan to administer the questionnaire to 200 participants (not members of the site) and collect from each participant samples of blood, urine, and saliva to investigate the biological validity of these four proposed styles of temperament (Fisher et al., in preparation).

However, preliminary data indicate the validity of this instrument. One question unrelated to the 56-item questionnaire asks members to describe the individuals typical of their circle of friends: adventurers, social intellectuals, activists. Explorers chose Adventurers; Builders chose Social;

Table 13.1. Personality Type Distributions for Men, Women, and the Full Population

Major Profile	Minor Profile	Male%	Female%	Population%
Explorer	Builder	2.3	2.74	2.52
	Director	2.57	2.63	2.60
	Negotiator	2.98	3.42	3.21
Explorer Total		7.86	8.79	8.33
Builder	Explorer	3.43	4.18	3.81
	Director	19.6	19.82	19.71
	Negotiator	17.45	19.62	18.55
Builder Total		40.48	43.62	42.07
Director	Explorer	3.67	3.71	3.69
	Builder	15.51	13.00	14.24
	Negotiator	11.01	8.82	9.90
Director Total		30.19	25.52	27.82
Negotiator	Explorer	4.08	4.61	4.35
	Builder	10.12	11.51	10.82
	Director	7.28	5.98	6.61
Negotiator Total		21.47	22.07	21.78
Total		100.00	100.00	100.00

Note: Total 523,622 individuals: 45.01% male, 54.99% female.

Directors chose Intellectuals; Negotiators chose Activists (F [3, 2996] = 16.39, 3.57, 11.79, 4.72 respectively Explorers, Builders, Directors, and Negotiators; p < .05 for Builders, p < .01 for the other three scales). These results would be expected if these four behavioral profiles reflect biological mechanisms; and they suggest that the four scales show both convergent and divergent validity.

TEMPERAMENT AS A MECHANISM FOR MATE CHOICE: ANOTHER PRELIMINARY INVESTIGATION

The Chemistry.com Web site endeavors to introduce appropriate individuals to one another for the purpose of triggering the brain system associated with romantic love and initiating a long-term pair-bond. During a process known as "1-2-3 Meet," a member on this site first reads the specific written responses of five potential "matches" presented to them by the company; next the member interacts via the Internet with one (or more) of these individuals whom he or she finds interesting; then, if two members express an interest in one another, they meet in person, generally in a coffee house for twenty minutes of conversation. After this first meeting, each member is then requested to return to the Internet site and report on the degree of romantic attraction they feel for the individual just met. Specifically, they respond to the question: "Was there any chemistry between you and _____?" They register the degree of their romantic interest by choosing one of four options: "Not at all," "A little," "Quite a lot," or "A lot." Fisher collected preliminary data on 2,766 of these initial responses, specifically the responses of 1,331 men and 1,435 women.

The first meeting (often the first 3 minutes of the first meeting) makes a significant difference in relationship development and outcome (Pines 2005, Sunnafrank & Ramirez 2004). With no contradictory or temporizing information about a novel individual, men and women tend to weight heavily those few traits they first encounter (Walther & Parks 2002). In one study, love at first sight was reported by 11% of 93 individuals queried (Pines 2005); however, many relationships fail at the first meeting. Hence, the first meeting is an important escalation point in the process of mate choice, perhaps a pivotal node in the trajectory of courtship.

Table 13.2 reflects the degree to which reported attraction to other members after a first meeting varied across different pairs of the proposed personality types (N = 2,766). These numbers are shown relative to the overall population of those having a first meeting. A score of zero means that the proportion of people with the indicated personality types who reported attraction was no different from the percent of attractions in the population of those having first meetings; positive scores reflect a higher percent of

Table 13.2. Relative Attraction by Personality Type After "First Meeting"; Population Normalized

Match: Women Who Found Men Attractive: (N = 1,435 female responses)

| | Male | | | |
Female	Explorer	Builder	Director	Negotiator
Explorer	–0.636	–0.005	–0.041	0.307
Builder	0.031	–0.012	–0.065	0.100
Director	–0.223	–0.214	0.059	0.401
Negotiator	–0.173	–0.291	0.139	0.414

Match: Men Who Found Women Attractive: (N = 1,331 male responses)

| | Female | | | |
Male	Explorer	Builder	Director	Negotiator
Explorer	–0.505	0.116	–0.067	0.049
Builder	0.319	0.043	–0.079	–0.122
Director	0.088	–0.156	0.062	0.205
Negotiator	0.185	–0.206	0.123	0.196

reported attraction than in the overall sample; lower scores indicate a lower percent of attraction than in the overall sample (Charts 1–8).

These tables suggest several patterns. For example, all proposed temperament types appear to gravitate to the Negotiator, with the exception of male Builders. Most important, these preliminary data suggest that when seeking a long-term (in many cases, potentially reproductive) partnership, both men and women of several proposed personality types are more attracted to individuals with a *different* behavioral and cognitive profile and less attracted to individuals with a *similar* biological constitution.

Once again, the data in this pilot study are preliminary. They suggest only that continued investigation using a similar research design may eventually yield some significant data on a biological mechanism associated with mate choice.

POSSIBLE EVOLUTION OF FOUR TEMPERAMENT CONSTELLATIONS

The four suites of temperament traits suggested in the literature on behavior genetics (cited above) correspond roughly to four basic temperaments noted

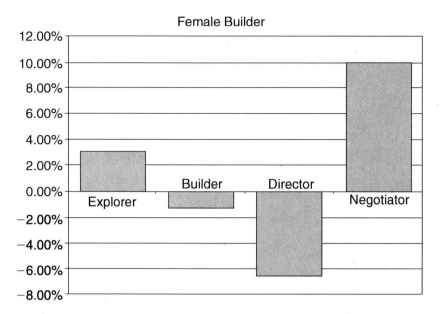

Chart 1. Relative attraction by personality type after "first meeting"; population normalized. Chart of Table 13.2: Female Builder attraction to male Explorers, Builders, Directors, and Negotiators. 0.00%=degree of attraction by chance.

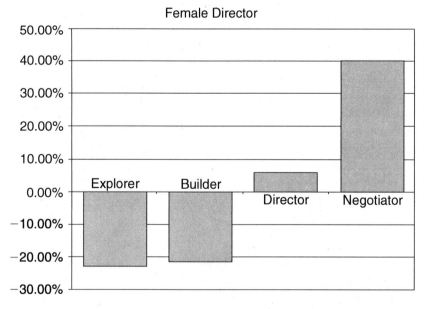

Chart 2. Relative attraction by personality type after "first meeting"; population normalized. Chart of Table 13.2: Female Director attraction to male Explorers, Builders, Directors, and Negotiators. 0.00%=degree of attraction by chance.

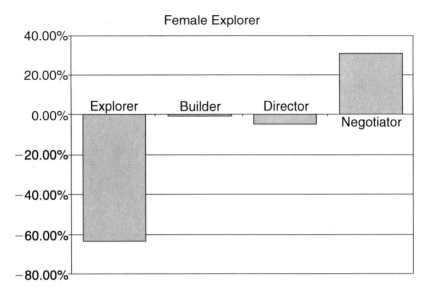

Chart 3. Relative attraction by personality type after "first meeting"; population normalized. Chart of Table 13.2: Female Explorer attraction to male Explorers, Builders, Directors, and Negotiators. 0.00% = degree of attraction by chance.

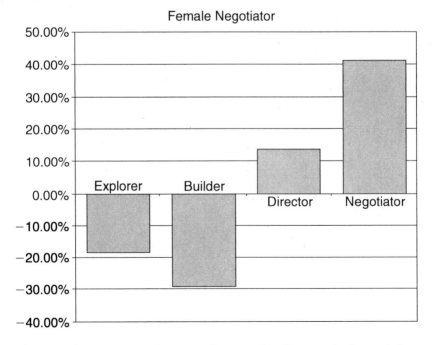

Chart 4. Relative attraction by personality type after "first meeting"; population normalized. Chart of Table 13.2: Female Negotiator attraction to male Explorers, Builders, Directors, and Negotiators. 0.00% = degree of attraction by chance.

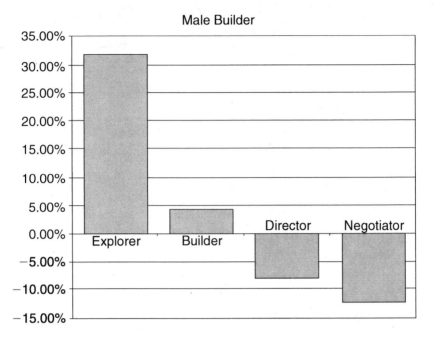

Chart 5. Relative attraction by personality type after "first meeting"; population normalized. Chart of Table 13.2: Male Builder attraction to female Explorers, Builders, Directors, and Negotiators. 0.00%=degree of attraction by chance.

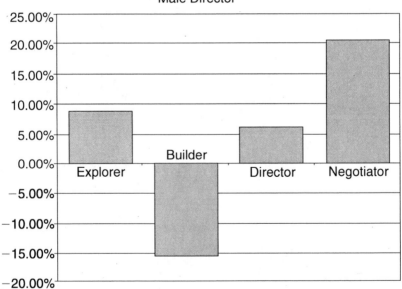

Chart 6. Relative attraction by personality type after "first meeting"; population normalized. Chart of Table 13.2: Male Director attraction to female Explorers, Builders, Directors, and Negotiators. 0.00%=degree of attraction by chance.

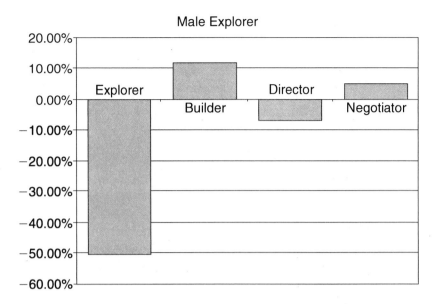

Chart 7. Relative attraction by personality type after "first meeting"; population
normalized. Chart of Table 13.2: Male Explorer attraction to female Explorers,
Builders, Directors, and Negotiators. 0.00% = degree of attraction by chance.

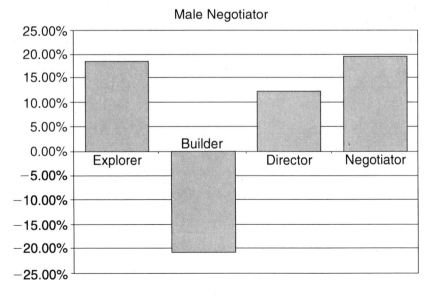

Chart 8. Relative attraction by personality type after "first meeting"; population
normalized. Chart of Table 13.2: Male Negotiator attraction to female Explorers,
Builders, Directors, and Negotiators. 0.00% = degree of attraction by chance.

since antiquity (Keirsey 1998). In *The Republic,* Plato used the terms "Artisan," "Guardian," "Idealist," and "Rational" to distinguish what Fisher refers to as the Explorer, Builder, Negotiator, and Director. Aristotle, Galen (the 2nd-century Roman doctor), and Paracelsus (the 16th-century Swiss doctor) also categorized people roughly into these four biological types (Keirsey 1998). By the early 20th century, many other scientists and laymen began to divide humankind into broad types, most notably Carl Jung in his text *Psychological Types.* In the 1940s, Myers and Briggs developed a measure of personality based largely on Jung's theories of type, the Myers–Briggs Type Indicator (MBTI) (Myers & Myers 1980). Keirsey (1998) has reinterpreted the MBTI, reducing it to a measure of the four essential types first proposed by Plato. All these investigators roughly described at least three (and often all four) of the possible trait clusters that appear to be associated with the neural systems for dopamine, serotonin, estrogen, and testosterone.

Because these four basic suites of temperament traits are described in the biological literature, because they have been described by physicians, philosophers and laymen for centuries, because preliminary analysis of an initial sample of 523,622 men and women on the Chemistry.com Internet dating/relationship site appear to fall within these four proposed broad dispositional categories, and because preliminary data suggest that several of these dispositional types show disproportional attraction to individuals of a different temperament syndrome than their own, we believe it is acceptable to regard these pilot projects as a first initiative in a continued, more precise investigation.

It is premature to explore how, when, or why the genetic underpinnings of these four proposed syndromes of temperament might have evolved in hominid prehistory. Perhaps these four proposed syndromes will show hallmarks of adaptation; perhaps they are more parsimoniously explained as by-products of the natural variation that occurs in these neurochemical systems. Nevertheless, Ding et al. have proposed that the specific allele for novelty seeking (DRD4*7R) "originated as a rare mutational event that nevertheless increased to high frequency in human populations by positive selection" (Ding et al. 2002, 309). Moreover, Higley et al. (1996) have reported on two versions of a gene in the serotonin system that may shed light on the evolution of genetic temperament syndromes within ancestral hominid populations. Rhesus monkeys who inherit the short version of this gene express less serotonin activity and are more likely to be aggressive and impulsive. Some 5–10% of rhesus monkeys inherit this short version, and many die young because they take too many risks in aggressive encounters with conspecifics (Higley et al. 1996). But Higley et al. propose that this gene has been maintained in the population because aggressive, impulsive male Rhesus monkeys are also more exploratory, an important quality for a species that (like humans) lives in harsh environments. Nettle (2006) describes genetic variations among members of other species that also enhance individual fitness, and the costs and benefits of variations in the big five personality traits.

Buss (1991) has proposed that humans may have evolved several equally adaptive alternative behavioral strategies, underlain by genetic polymorphisms, which are maintained in the population because no one strategy is optimal at all times; thus, genetic variation is maintained. MacDonald (1995) hypothesizes that individuals expressing different degrees of specific personality traits may differ in the ways they achieve survival and reproduction. It is not difficult to envision the social and reproductive advantages of each of the above proposed temperament syndromes in the shifting ecological and social environment of hominid prehistory. In fact, Bouchard writes of human variation in personality traits: "The purpose of this variation is undoubtedly rooted in the fact that humans have adapted to life in face-to-face groups (sociality)" (Bouchard 1994). The four proposed temperament syndromes discussed above could have evolved by means of sexual selection, as have many other complex constellations of human traits (Miller 2000).

How ancestral individuals would have recognized those with different genetic profiles and associated temperament syndromes is unknown. As noted above, Wedekind has reported that women are attracted to men with a different immune system (Wedekind et al. 1995); they select these men unconsciously, using smell. Women also tend to be attracted to men with specific facial features associated with testosterone (Grammer & Thornhill 1994), whereas men tend to be attracted to women with facial features associated with estrogen (Johnston 1999). Perhaps the dopamine and serotonin systems also have facial and/or odor signals that enable individuals to identify these attributes. A recent study on the iris suggests a marker for the dopamine system. The furrows (lines curving around the outer edge) and crypts (pits) in the iris have been correlated with aspects of personality. Individuals with more furrows are more regularly impulsive and willing to indulge their cravings (traits associated with dopamine activity), while those with more crypts are more likely to be trusting, warm, and tender (traits associated with estrogen activity) (Larsson, Pedersen, Stattin, in press).

Future research on the facial features of the individuals on the Chemistry.com site may illuminate some of the facial signals specific to these proposed four personality syndromes. But it is parsimonious to hypothesize that in prehistory all four temperament types also displayed aspects of their biological predispositions as they verbalized their values and beliefs, moved their faces and bodies in specific ways, and/or pursued specific personal, social, and economic goals.

CONCLUSION

Fisher (1998) has proposed that romantic love is one of three discrete, inter-related emotion/motivation systems that mammalian (and avian) species have evolved to direct courtship, mating, reproduction, and parenting. The other two are the sex drive and attachment. The sex drive evolved to motivate our ancestors to seek coitus with a *range* of appropriate partners. Courtship attraction (and its developed human form, romantic love) evolved to motivate individuals to focus their courtship attention on a preferred mating partner, thereby conserving courtship time and metabolic energy. Partner attachment evolved primarily to motivate individuals to sustain this affiliative connection at least long enough to complete species-specific parental duties.

It is hypothesized here that human romantic love (and mammalian courtship attraction) evolved in tandem with many other biological mechanisms (and cultural mechanisms) that serve to guide an individual to prefer one conspecific rather than another and stimulate the brain system for attraction. This chapter discusses two exploratory pilot projects designed to investigate one of these unconscious mechanisms: a biological appetite to become attracted to individuals with different genetic profiles. It is hypothesized that humans, a socially monogamous species, evolved four very broad genetically based temperament syndromes for a variety of social and ecological reasons and that humans tend to select romantic partners with a different suite of cognitive and behavioral traits in order to create more genetic variety in their offspring and engage in the job of co-parenting with a wider array of parenting skills. This hypothesized unconscious appetite is most likely one of many biological mechanisms that contribute to this central aspect of human reproduction, mate choice.

REFERENCES

Ainsworth, M. D. S., Blehar, M. C., Waters, E., & Wall, S. (1978). *Patterns of attachment: A psychological study of the strange situation.* Hillsdale, NJ: Erlbaum.

Allen, L. S., Richey, M. F., Chai, Y. M., & Gorski, R. A. (1991). Sex differences in the corpus callosum of the living human being. *Journal of Neuroscience, 11,* 933–942.

Andersson, M. (1994). *Sexual selection.* Princeton, NJ: Princeton University Press.

Aron, A. & Aron, E. N. (1989). The Heart of Social Psychology. Lexington, MA: Lexington Books.

Aron, A., Fisher, H., Mashek, D. J., Strong, G., Li, H. F., & Brown, L. L. (2005). Reward, motivation and emotion systems associated with early-stage intense romantic love: An fMRI study. *Journal of Neurophysiology, 94,* 327–337.

Aronson, E. (1998). *The social animal* (7th ed.). San Francisco: Freeman.

Babchuk, W. A., Hames, R. B., & Thompson, R. A. (1983). Sex differences in the recognition of infant facial expressions of emotion: The primary caretaker hypothesis. *Ethology and Sociobiology, 6,* 89–102.

Bachner-Melman, R., Dina, C., Zohar, A. H., Constantini, N., Lerer, E., Hoch, S., et al. (2005). Polymorphisms are associated with creative dance performance. *PLoS Genetics, 1,* 42.

Baron-Cohen, S. (2002). The extreme male brain theory of autism. *Trends in Cognitive Sciences, 6,* 248–254.

Baron-Cohen, S., Jolliffe, T., Mortimore, C., & Robertson, M. (1997). Another advanced test of theory of mind: Evidence from very high functioning adults with autism or Asperger Syndrome. *Journal of Child Psychology and Psychiatry, 38,* 813–822.

Baron-Cohen, S., Knickmeyer, R. C., & Belmonte, M. K. (2005). Sex differences in the brain: Implications for explaining autism. *Science, 310,* 819–823.

Bartels, A., & Zeki, S. (2000). The neural basis of romantic love. *Neuroreport, 11,* 3829–3834.

Bartels, A., & Zeki, S. (2004). The neural correlates of maternal and romantic love. *NeuroImage, 21,* 1155–1166.

Beach, S. R. H., Whitaker, D., Jones, D. J., & Tesser, A. (2001). When does performance feedback prompt complementarity in romantic relationships? *Personal Relationships, 8,* 232–248.

Bell, A. M. (2007). Future directions in behavioural syndromes research. Proceedings of the Royal Society B: Biological Sciences, 274(1611), 755–761.

Benbow, C. P., & Stanley, J. C. (1983). Sex difference in mathematical reasoning ability: More facts. *Science, 222,* 1029–1031.

Blau, P. (1964). *Exchange and power in social life.* New York: John Wiley.

Booth, A., Shelley, G., Mazur, A., Tharp, G., & Kittok, R. (1989). Testosterone and winning and losing in human competition. *Hormones and Behavior, 23,* 556–571.

Borg, J., Andree, B., Soderstrom, H., & Farde, L. (2003). The serotonin system and spiritual experiences. *American Journal of Psychiatry, 160,* 1965–1969.

Bouchard, T. J. (1994). Genes, environment, and personality. *Science, 264,* 1700–1701.

Bowlby, J. (1969). *Attachment and loss: Attachment* (Vol. 1). New York: Basic Books.

Braeutigam S., Rose, S. P., Swithenby, S. J., & Ambler, T. (2004). The distributed neuronal systems supporting choice-making in real-life situations: Differences between men and women when choosing groceries detected using magnetoencephalography. *European Journal of Neuroscience, 20,* 293–302.

Brown, L. M., & Gilligan, C. (1992). *Meeting at the Crossroads: Women's psychology and girls' development*. Cambridge, MA: Harvard University Press.

Browne, K. R. (1995). Sex and temperament in modern society: A Darwinian view of the glass ceiling and the gender gap. *Arizona Law Review, 37,* 973–1106.

Buss, D. M. (1991). Evolutionary personality psychology. *Annual Review of Psychology, 42,* 459–491.

Buss, D.M. (1994). *The evolution of desire: Strategies of human mating*. New York: Basic Books.

Buston, P. M., & Emlen, S. T. (2003). Cognitive processes underlying human mate choice: The relationship between self-perception and mate preference in Western society. *Proceedings of the National Academy of Sciences, 100,* 8805–8810.

Byrne, D. (1997). An overview (and underview) of research and theory within the attraction paradigm. *Journal of Social and Personal Relationships, 14,* 417–431.

Byrne, D., Clore, G. L., & Smeaton, G. (1986). The attraction hypothesis: Do similar attitudes affect anything? *Journal of Personality and Social Psychology, 51,* 1167–1170.

Cappella, J. N., & Palmer, M. T. (1990). Attitude similarity, relational history, and attraction: The mediating effects of kinesic and vocal behaviors. *Communication Monographs, 57,* 161–183.

Caspi, A., and Harbener, E. S. (1990). Continuity and change: Assortive marriage and the consistency of personality in adulthood. *Journal of Personality and Social Psychology 58,* 250–258.

Cloninger, C. R. (1987). A systematic method for clinical description and classification of personality variants: A proposal. *Archives of General Psychiatry, 44,* 573.

Cloninger C. R., Przybeck, T. R., & Svrakic, D. M. (1991). The Tridimensional personality questionnaire: U.S. normative data. *Psychological Reports, 69,* 1047–1057.

Dabbs, J. (1990). Age and seasonal variation in serum testosterone concentration among men. *Chronobiology International, 7,* 245–49.

Dabbs, J. (1992). Testosterone and occupational achievement. *Social Forces, 70,* 813–824.

Dabbs, J. M., & Dabbs, M. G. (2000). *Heroes, rogues, and lovers: Testosterone and behavior*. New York: McGraw-Hill.

Davidge K. M., Atkinson, L., Douglas, L., Lee, V., Shapiro, S., Kennedy, J. L., et al. (2004). Association of the serotonin transporter and 5HT1Kß receptor genes with extreme persistent and pervasive aggressive behaviour in children. *Psychiatric Genetics, 14,* 143–146.

De Vries, G., & Simerley, R. B. (2002). Anatomy, development, and function of sexually dimorphic neural circuits in the mammalian brain. In D. W. Pfaff, A. P. Arnold, A. M. Etgen, S. E. Fahrbach, R. L. Moss, & R. T. Rubin, (Eds.), *Hormones, Brain and Behavior* (Vol 4, pp. 137–191). San Diego: Academic Press.

Depue, R. A., & Collins, P. F. (1999). Neurobiology of the structure of personality: Dopamine, facilitation of incentive motivation, and extraversion. *Behavioral and Brain Sciences, 22,* 491–569.

Ding, Y. C., Chi, H. C., Grady, D. L., Morishima, A., Kidd, J. R., Kidd, K. K., et al. (2002). Evidence of positive selection acting at the human dopamine receptor D4 gene locus. *Proceedings of the National Academy of Sciences, 99*(1), 309–314.

Dryer, D. C., & Horowitz, L. M. (1997). When do opposites attract? Interpersonal complementarity versus similarity. *Journal of Personality and Social Psychology, 72,* 592–603.

Duff, C. S. (1993). When women work together: Using our strengths to overcome our challenges. Berkeley, CA: Conari Press.

Ebstein, R. P., Novick, O., Umansky, R., Priel, B., Osher, Y., Blaine, D., et al. (1996). Dopamine D4 receptor (D4DR) exon III polymorphism associated with the human personality trait of novelty seeking. *Nature Genetics, 12,* 78–80.

Ellis, B. J. (1992). The evolution of sexual attraction: Evaluative mechanisms in women. In J. H. Barkow, L. Cosmedes, & J. Tooby (Eds.), *The adapted mind: Evolutionary psychology and the generation of culture* (pp. 267–288). New York: Oxford University Press.

Fabre-Nys, C. (1997). Steroid control of monoamines in relation to sexual behaviour. *Reviews of Reproduction, 3,* 31–41.

Fink, G., Sumner, B. E., McQueen, J. K., Wilson, H., and Rosie, R. (1998) Sex steroid control of mood, mental state and memory. *Clinical and Experimental Pharmacology and Physiology* 25(10), 764–775.

Fiore, A. T., & Donath, J. S. (2004). Online personals: An overview. *CHI,* 1395–1398.

Fisher, H. (1998). Lust, attraction, and attachment in mammalian reproduction. *Human Nature, 9*(1), 23–52.

Fisher, H. (1999). *The first sex: The natural talents of women and how they are changing the world.* New York: Random House.

Fisher, H. (2004). Why we love: The nature and chemistry of romantic love. New York: Henry Holt.

Fisher, H. (2005). The drive to love: The neural mechanism for mate selection. In R. J. Sternberg & K. Weis (Eds.), *The new psychology of love..* New Haven, CT: Yale University Press.

Fisher, H., Aron, A., & Brown, L. L. (2005). Romantic love: An fMRI study of a neural mechanism for mate choice. *Journal of Comparative Neurology, 493,* 58–62.

Fisher, H., Aron, A., & Brown, L. L. (2006). Romantic love: A mammalian brain system for mate choice. *Philosophical Transactions of the Royal Society: Biological Sciences, 361,* 2173–2186.

Fisher, H., Aron, A., Mashek, D., Strong, G., Li, H., & Brown, L. L. (2003, November 11). Early-stage intense romantic love activates cortical-basal-ganglia reward/motivation, emotion and attention systems: An fMRI study of a dynamic network that varies with relationship length, passion intensity and gender. Poster presented at the annual meeting of the Society for Neuroscience, New Orleans.

Fisher, H. F., Island, H. D., Rich, J., & Zava, D. (in preparation). Manuscript in preparation. Rutgers University, Department of Anthropology, New Brunswick, NJ.

Flaherty, A. W. (2005). Frontotemporal and dopaminergic control of idea generation and creative drive. *Journal of Comparative Neurology, 493,* 147–153.

Flory, J. D., Manuck, S.B., Matthews, K. A., & Muldoon, M. F. (2004). Serotonergic function in the central nervous system is associated with daily ratings of positive mood. *Psychiatry Research, 129,* 11–19.

Foa, E. B., & Foa, U. G. (1980). Resource theory: interpersonal behavior as exchange. In K. J. Gergen, M. S. Greenberg, & R. H. Willis (Eds.), *Social exchange: Advances in theory and research* (pp. 77–94). New York: Plenum.

Galton, F. (1884). The measurement of character. *Fortnightly Review, 36,* 179–185.

Gangestad, S. W., & Thornhill, R. (1997). The evolutionary psychology of extra pair sex: The role of fluctuating asymmetry. *Evolution and Human Behavior, 18,* 69–88.

Gangestad, S.W., Thornhill, R., & Yeo, R. A. (1994). Facial attractiveness, developmental stability, and fluctuating asymmetry. *Ethology and Sociobiology, 15,* 73–85.

Garver-Apgar, C. E., Gangestad, S. W., Thornhill, R., Miller, R. D., Olp, J. J. (2006). Major histocompatibility complex alleles, sexual responsivity, and unfaithfulness in romantic couples. *Psychological Science, 17,* 830–835.

Geschwind, N., & Galaburda, A. M. (1985). Cerebral lateralization, biological mechanisms, associations, and pathology. Cambridge, MA: MIT Press.

Gilligan, C. (1982). *In a different voice.* Cambridge, MA: Harvard University Press.

Gingrich, B, Liu, Y., Cascio, C., Wang, Z., & Insel, T. R. (2000). D2 receptors in the nucleus accumbens are important for social attachment in female prairie voles (Microtus ochrogaster). *Behavioral Neuroscience, 114,* 173–183.

Golimbet, V. E., Alfimova, M. V., & Mityushina, N. G. (2004). Polymorphism of the serotonin 2A receptor gene (5HTR2A) and personality traits. *Molecular Biology, 38*(3), 337–344.

Gosling, S. D., & John, O. P. (1999). Personality dimensions in non-human animals: A cross-species review. *Current Directions in Psychological Science, 8,* 69–75.

Gosling, S. D., Rentfrow, P. J., & Swann, W. B., Jr. (2003). A very brief measure of the big-five personality domains. *Journal of Research in Personality, 37,* 504–528.

Gottman, J. M., Murray, J. D., Tyson, R., & Swanson, K. R. (2002). The mathematics of marriage: Dynamic nonlinear models. Cambridge MA: MIT Press.

Grammer, K., & Thornhill, R. (1994). Human (Homo sapiens) facial attractiveness and sexual selection: The role of symmetry and averageness. *Journal of Comparative Psychology, 108*, 233–242.

Grimshaw, G. M., Bryden, M. P., & Finegan, J. K. (1995). Relations between prenatal testosterone and cerebral lateralization in children. *Neuropsychology, 9*, 68–79.

Hall, J. A. (1984). Nonverbal sex differences: Communication accuracy and expressive style. Baltimore: Johns Hopkins University Press.

Halpern, D. F. (1992). *Sex differences in cognitive abilities.* Hillsdale, NJ: Lawrence Erlbaum Associates.

Ham, B. J., Kim, Y. H., Choi, M. J., Cha, J. H., Choi, K. Y., & Lee, M. S. (2004). Serotonergic genes and personality traits in the Korean population. *Neuroscience Letters, 354*, 2–5.

Hampden-Turner, C. (1994). The structure of entrapment: Dilemmas standing in the way of women managers and strategies to resolve these. *The Deeper News, 5*, 142.

Hampson, E. (1990). Variations in sex-related cognitive abilities across the menstrual cycle. *Brain and Cognition, 14*, 26–43.

Harris, H. (1995). Rethinking heterosexual relationships in Polynesia: A case study of Mangaia, Cook Island. In W. Jankowiak (Ed.), *Romantic passion: A universal experience?* (pp. 95–127). New York: Columbia University Press.

Harris, J. R. (1999). *The nurture assumption: Why children turn out the way they do.* New York: Touchstone.

Hatfield, E. (1988). Passionate and companionate love. In R. J. Sternberg & M. L. Barnes (Eds.). *The psychology of love* (pp. 191–217). New Haven, CT: Yale University Press.

Hatfield, E., & Sprecher, S. (1986). Measuring passionate love in intimate relationships. *Journal of Adolescence, 9*, 383–410.

Hazan, C., & Shaver, P. (1987). Romantic love conceptualized as an attachment process. *Journal of Personality and Social Psychology, 52*, 511–524.

Hedges, L. V., & Nowell, A. (1995). Sex differences in mental test scores, variability, and numbers of high-scoring individuals. *Science, 269*, 41–45.

Helgesen, S. (1990). *The female advantage: Women's ways of leadership.* New York: Doubleday/Currency.

Herlitz, A., & Yonker, J. E. (2002). Sex differences in episodic memory: The influence of intelligence. *Journal of Clinical and Experimental Neuropsychology, 24*, 107–114.

Higley, J. D., Mehlman, P. T., Higley, S. B., Fernald, B., Vickers, J., Lindell, S. G., et al. (1996). Excessive mortality in young free-ranging male nonhuman primates with low cerebrospinal fluid 5–hydroxyindoleacetic acid concentrations. *Archives of General Psychiatry, 53*, 537–543.

Hinde, R. (1997). *Relationships: A dialectical perspective.* Hove, England: Psychology Press.

Hines, M., Allen, L. S., & Gorski, R. A. (1992). Sex differences in subregions of the medial nucleus of the amygdala and the bed nucleus of the stria terminalis of the rat. *Brain Research, 579*, 321–326.

Holloway, R. L., Anderson, P. J., Defendini, R., & Harper, C. (1993). Sexual dimorphism of the human corpus callosum from three independent samples: Relative size of the corpus callosum. *American Journal of Physical Anthropology, 92*, 481–498.

Holman, T. B. (2001). *Premarital prediction of marital quality or break up: Research, theory, and practice.* New York: Kluwer.

Houran, J., Lange, R., Rentfrow, P. J., & Bruckner, K. H. (2004). Do online matchmaking tests work? An assessment of preliminary evidence for a publicized "predictive model of marital success." *North American Journal of Psychology, 6*, 507–526.

Houts, R., Huston, T. L., & Robins, E. (1996). Compatibility and the development of premarital relationships. *Journal of Marriage and the Family, 58*, 7–20.

Hoyenga, K. B., & Hoyenga, K. T. (1980). *The question of sex differences.* Boston: Little, Brown.

Hoyt, L. L., & Hudson, J. W. (1981). Personal characteristics important in mate preference among college students. *Social Behavior and Personality, 9*, 93–96.

Huston, T. L., & Burgess, R. L. (1979). Social exchange in developing relationships: An overview. In T. Huston and R. Burgess (Eds.), *Social exchange in developing relationships* (pp. 3–28). New York: Academic Press.

Hyde, J. S., Fennema, E., & Lamon, S. J. (1990). Gender differences in mathematics performance: A meta-analysis. *Psychological Bulletin, 107*, 139–155.

Janowsky, J. S., Oviatt, S. K, Orwoll, E. S. (1994). Testosterone influences spatial cognition in older men. *Behavioral Neuroscience, 108*, 325–332.

Johnston, V. S. (1999). *Why we feel: The science of human emotions.* Cambridge, MA: Perseus Books.

Jones, E., & Hill, K. (1993). Criteria of facial attractiveness in five populations. *Human Nature, 4*, 271–296.

Karney, B. R., & Bradbury, T. N. (1995). The longitudinal course of marital quality and stability: A review of theory, methods and research. *Psychological Bulletin, 118*, 3–34.

Keirsey, D. (1998). *Please understand me II: Temperament, character intelligence.* Del Mar, CA: Prometheus Nemesis.

Keller, M. C., & Young, R. K. (1996). Mate assortment in dating and married couples. *Personality and Individual Differences, 21*, 217–221.

Keltikangas-Jarvinen, L., Elovainio, M., Kivimaki, M., Lichtermann, D., Ekelund, J., & Peltonen, L. (2003). Association between the type 4 dopamine receptor gene polymorphism and novelty seeking. *Psychosomatic Medicine, 65*, 471–476.

Kenrick, D.T., Sadalla, E.K., Groth, G.E., & Trost, M. R. (1990). Evolution, traits and the states of human courtship: Qualifying the parental investment model. *Journal of Personality, 58*, 97–116.

Klohnen, E. C., & Mendelsohn, G. (1998). Partner selection for personality characteristics: A couple-centered approach. *Journal of Personality and Social Psychology, 24*, 268–278.

Knickmeyer, R., Baron-Cohen, S., Raggatt, P., & Taylor, K. (2005). Foetal testosterone, social relationships and restricted interests in children. *Journal of Child Psychology and Psychiatry, 46*, 198–210.

Knickmeyer, R., Baron-Cohen, S., Raggatt, P., Taylor, K., & Hackett, G. (2006). Fetal testosterone and empathy. *Hormones and Behavior, 49*, 282–292.

Knutson B., Wolkowitz, O. M., Cole, S. W., Chan, T., Moore, E. A., Johnson, R. C., et al. (1998). Selective alteration of personality and social behavior by serotonergic intervention. *American Journal of Psychiatry, 155*, 373–378.

Kohlberg, L. (1969). Stage and sequence: The cognitive-developmental approach to socialization. In D. A. Goslin (Ed.), *Handbook of socialization: Theory and research* (pp. 383–432). Chicago: Rand McNally.

Kohlberg, L. (1981). *The philosophy of moral development*. San Francisco: Harper.

Krueger, R. F., & Caspi, A. (1993). Personality, arousal, and pleasure: A test of competing models of interpersonal attraction. *Personality and Individual Differences, 14*, 105–111.

Kurdek, L. A., & Schmitt, J. P. (1987). Partner homogamy in married, heterosexual, cohabiting, gay, and lesbian couples. *Journal of Sex Research, 23*, 212–232.

La Cerra, P., & Bingham, R. (2002). *The origin of minds: Evolution, uniqueness and the new science of the self.* New York: Harmony.

Larsson, M., Pederson, N. L., & Stattin, H. (in press). Associations between iris characteristics and personality in adulthood, *Biological Psychology*.

Laumann, E.O., Gagnon, J. H., Michael, R.T., & Michaels, S. (1994). *The social organization of sexuality: Sexual practices in the United States.* Chicago: University of Chicago Press.

Lavrakas, P. J. (1975). Female preferences for male physique. *Journal of Research in Personality, 9*, 324–334.

Lever, J. (1976). Sex differences in the games children play. *Social Problems, 23*, 478–487.

Liebowitz, M. R. (1983). *The chemistry of love.* Boston: Little Brown.

Luo, S., & Klohnen, E. (2005). Assortative mating and marital quality in newlyweds: A couple-centered approach. *Journal of Personality and Social Psychology, 88*, 304–326.

MacDonald, K. (1995). Evolution, the 5–factor model, and levels of personality. *Journal of Personality, 63*, 525–567.

Mann, V. A., Sasanuma, S., Sakuma, N., & Masaki, S. (1990). Sex differences in cognitive abilities: A cross-cultural perspective. *Neuropsychologia, 28*, 1063–1077.

Manuck, S. B., Bleil, M. E., Petersen, K. L., Flory, J. D., Mann, J. J., Ferrell, R. E., et al. (2005). The socio-economic status of communities predicts variation in brain serotonergic responsivity. *Psychological Medicine, 35*, 519–528.

Marioles, N. S., Strickert, D. P., & Hammer, A. L. (1996). Attraction, satisfaction, and psychological types of couples. *Journal of Psychological Type, 26*, 16–27.

Mazur, A., Booth, A., & Dabbs, J. M., Jr. (1992). Testosterone and chess competition. *Social Psychology Quarterly, 55*, 70–77.

Mazur, A., Susman, E. J., & Edelbrock, S. (1997). Sex differences in testosterone response to a video game contest. *Evolution and Human Behavior, 18*, 317–326.

McCauley, E., Kay, T., Ito, J., & Treder, R. (1987). The Turner syndrome: Cognitive deficits, affective discrimination and behavior problems. *Child Development, 58*, 464–473.

McCrae, R. R., Terracciano, A., and 78 Members of the Personality Profiles of Cultures Project (2005). Universal features of personality traits from the observer's perspective: Data from 50 cultures. *Journal of Personality and Social Psychology, 88*, 547–561.

McGrew, W. C. (1981). The female chimpanzee as a human evolutionary prototype. In F. Dahlberg (Ed.), *Woman the gatherer* (pp. 35–73). New Haven, CT: Yale University Press.

McGuinness, D. (1985). Sensorimotor biases in cognitive development. In R. L. Hall, P. Draper, M. E. Hamilton, D. McGuinness, C. M. Otten, & E. A Roth (Eds.), *Male–female differences: A bio-cultural perspective.* (pp. 57–126). New York: Praeger.

McGuinness, D., & Pribram, K. H. (1979). The origin of sensory bias in the development of gender differences in perception and cognition. In M. Bortner (Ed.), *Cognitive growth and development: Essays in memory of Herbert G. Birch.* New York: Brunner/Mazel.

Melke, J., Westberg, L., Nilsson, S., Landén, M, Soderstrom, H., Baghaei, F. et al. (2003). A polymorphism in the serotonin receptor 3A (HTR3A) gene and its association with harm avoidance in women. *Archives of General Psychiatry, 60*, 79–85.

Meston, C. M., & Frohlic, P. F. (2000). The neurobiology of sexual function. *Archives of General Psychiatry, 57*, 1012–1030.

Miller, G. F. (2000). *The mating mind: How sexual choice shaped the evolution of human nature.* New York: Doubleday.

Murstein, B. (1976). Who will marry whom. New York: Springer.

Myers, I. B., & Myers, P. B. (1980). *Gifts differing.* Palo Alto, CA: Consulting Psychologists Press.

Nettle, D. (2006). The evolution of personality variation in humans and other animals. *American Psychologist, 61*, 622–631.

Nyborg, H. (1994). *Hormones, sex and society.* Westport, CT: Praeger.

Ochsner, K. N., Knierim, K., Ludlow, D. H., Hanelin, J., Ramachandran, T., Glover, G., et al. (2004). Reflecting upon feelings: An fMRI study of neural systems supporting the attribution of emotion of self and other. *Journal of Cognitive Neuroscience, 16*, 1746–1772.

Opbroek, A., Delgado, P. L., Laukes, C., McGahuey, C., Katsanis, J., Moreno, F. A., et al. (2002). Emotional blunting associated with SSRI-induced sexual dysfunction. Do SSRIs inhibit emotional responses? *International Journal of Neuropsychopharmacology, 5*, 415–416.

Parks, C. L., Robinson, P. S., Sibille, E., Shenk, T., & Toth, M. (1998). Increased anxiety of mice lacking the serotonin 1A receptor. *Proceedings of the National Academy of Sciences, 95*(18), 10,734–10,739.

Pearson, H. (2006, May 31). Sexual desire traced to genetics: Differences in sexual appetite might be partly determined by our genes. Retrieved May 31, 2006 at http://www.nature.com/news/index.html

Peirson, A. R., Heuchert, J. W., Thomala, L., Berk, M., Plein, H., & Cloninger, C. R. (1999). Relationship between serotonin and the temperament and character inventory. *Psychiatry Research, 89*, 29–37.

Phillips, K., Fulker, D. W., Carey, G., & Nagoshi, C. T. (1988). Direct marital assortment for cognitive and personality variables. *Behavior Genetics, 18*, 347–356.

Pilkington, C. J., Tesser, A., & Stephens, D. (1991). Complementarity in romantic relationships: A self-evaluation maintenance perspective. *Journal of Social and Personal Relationships, 8*, 481–504.

Pines, A. M. (1999). *Falling in love: Why we choose the lovers we choose.* New York: Routledge.

Pines, A. M. (2005). *Falling in love: Why we choose the lovers we choose* (2nd ed.). New York: Routledge.

Reif, A. and Lesch, K. L. (2003) Toward a molecular architecture of personality. *Behavioral Brain Research, 139*, 74–89.

Reik, T. (1964). *The need to be loved.* New York: Bantam.

Reuter, M., Roth, S., Holve, K., & Hennig, J. (2006). Identification of first candidate genes for creativity: A pilot study. *Brain Research, 1069*, 190–197.

Richards, L. S., Wakefield, J. A., & Lewak, R. (1990). Similarity of personality variables as predictor of marital satisfaction: Minnesota Multiple Personality Inventory (MMPI) item analysis. *Personality and Individual Differences, 11*, 39–43.

Roberts, B. W., & DelVecchio, W. F. (2000). The rank-order consistency of personality traits from childhood to old age: A quantitative review of longitudinal studies. *Psychological Bulletin, 126*, 3–25.

Robins, R. W. (2005). The nature of personality: Genes, culture, and national character. *Science, 310*, 62–63.

Robinson, D. L., Heien, M. L. & Wightman, R. M. (2002). Frequency of dopamine concentration transients increases in dorsal and ventral striatum of male rats during introduction of conspecifics. *Journal of Neuroscience, 22*, 10,477–10,486.

Roloff, M. E. (1981). *Interpersonal communication: The social exchange approach.* Thousand Oaks, CA: Sage.

Rosen, R. C., Lane, R. M., & Menza, M. (1999). Effects of SSRIs on sexual function: A critical review. *Journal of Clinical Psychopharmacology, 19,* 67–85.

Rosener, J. B. (1995). *America's competitive secret: Women managers.* New York: Oxford University Press.

Sassen, G. (1980). Success anxiety in women: A constructivist interpretation of its sources and its significance. *Harvard Educational Review, 50,* 13–25.

Schrag, A. & Trimble, M. (2001). Poetic talent unmasked by treatment of Parkinson's disease. *Movement Disorders, 16,* 1175–1176.

Shaikh, T., & Suresh, K. (1994). Attitudinal similarity and affiliation needs as determinants of interpersonal attraction. *Journal of Social Psychology, 134,* 257–259.

Shaywitz, B. A., Shaywitz, S. E., Pugh, K. R., Constable, R. T., Skudlarski, P., Fulbright, R. K., et al. (1995). Sex differences in the functional organization of the brain for language. *Nature, 373,* 607–609.

Shepher, J. (1971). Mate selection among second generation kibbutz adolescents and adults: Incest avoidance and negative imprinting. *Archives of Sexual Behavior, 1,* 293–307.

Silverman, I., & Eals, M. (1992). Sex differences in spatial abilities: Evolutionary theory and data. In Jerome Barkow, Leda Cosmides, & John Tooby (Eds.), *The adapted mind: Evolutionary psychology and the generation of culture* (pp. 533–549). New York: Oxford University Press.

Singh, D. (1993). Adaptive significance of waist-to-hip ratio and female physical attractiveness. *Journal of Personality and Social Psychology, 65,* 293–307.

Skuse, D. H., James, R. S., Bishop, D. V. M., Coppin, B., Dalton, P., Aamodt-Leeper, G., et al. (1997). Evidence from Turner's syndrome of an imprinted X-linked locus affecting cognitive function. *Nature, 387,* 705–708.

Smuts, B. B., Cheney, D. L., Seyfarth, R. M., Wrangham, R. M. & Struhsaker, T. T. (Eds.). (1986). *Primate societies.* Chicago: University of Chicago Press.

Sprecher, S. (2001). A comparison of emotional consequences of and changes in equity over time using global and domain-specific measures of equity. *Journal of Social and Personal Relationships, 18,* 477–501.

Sprecher, S., & Regan, P. (2002). Liking some things (in some people) more than others: Partner preferences in romantic relationships and friends. *Journal of Social and Personal Relationships, 19,* 463–481.

Stahl, S. M. (2000). *Essential psychopharmacology* (2nd ed.). New York: Cambridge University Press.

Sunnafrank, M. (1986). Predicted outcome value during initial interactions: A reformulation of uncertainty reduction theory. *Human Communication Research, 13,* 3–33.

Sunnafrank, M., & Ramirez, A. (2004). At first sight: Persistent relational effects of get-acquainted conversations. *Journal of Social and Personal Relationships. 21,* 361–379.

Sussman, S., & Reardon, K. K. (1987). Asset equality or similarity as determinants of perceived marital effectiveness: A rules perspective formulation. *Representative Research in Social Psychology, 17*, 37–52.

Tannen, D. (1990). You just don't understand: Women and men in conversation. New York: Ballantine.

Tennov, D. (1979). Love and limerence: The experience of being in love. New York: Stein & Day.

Terracciano, A., Abdel-Khalek, A. M., Ádám, N., Adamovová, L., Ahn, C.-k., Ahn, H.-n., et al. (2005). National character does not reflect mean personality trait levels in 49 cultures. *Science, 310*, 96–100.

Thorne, B. (1993). *Gender play*. New Brunswick, NJ: Rutgers University Press.

Wacker, J., Chavanon, M. L., & Stemmler, G. (2006). Investigating the dopaminergic basis of extraversion in humans: A multilevel approach. *Journal of Personality and Social Psychology 91*, 171–187.

Walster E., Walster, G., & Berscheid, E. (1978). *Equity: Theory and research.* Boston: Allyn and Bacon.

Walther, J. B., & Parks, M. R. (2002). Cues filtered out, cues filtered in: Computer-mediated communication and relationships. In M. L. Knapp and J. A. Daly (Eds.), *Handbook of interpersonal communication* (3rd ed., pp. 529–563). Thousand Oaks, CA: Sage.

Wedekind, C., Seebeck, T., Bettens, F., & Paepke, A. J. (1995). MHC-dependent mate preferences in humans. *Proceedings of the Royal Society of London, 260*, 245–249.

Wilson, C. A., Gonzalez, I., & Farabollini, F. (1992). Behavioural effects in adulthood of neonatal manipulation of brain serotonin levels in normal and androgenized females. *Pharmacology Biochemistry and Behavior, 41*, 91–98.

Winch, R. F. (1958). *Mate selection: A study of complementary needs.* New York: Harper.

Zentner, M. R. (2005). Ideal mate personality concepts and compatibility in close relationships: A longitudinal analysis. *Journal of Personality and Social Psychology, 89*, 242–256.

Ziegler, A., Kentenich, H, & Uchanska-Ziegler, B. (2005). Female choice and the MHC. *Trends in Immunology, 26*, 496–502.

Zuckerman, M. (1994). *Behavioral expressions and biosocial bases of sensation seeking.* New York: Cambridge University Press.

14 Twin Research: Evolutionary Perspective on Social Relations

*Nancy L. Segal, Kevin A. Chavarria,
and Joanne Hoven Stohs*

Evolutionary psychology (EP) aims to identify physical and psychological features contributing to individual survival and reproduction during the course of human history. It focuses on how and why the human mind was shaped as it was, and how the mind transforms environmental inputs (mostly social) into behavior (Buss 2004). It also offers a framework for unifying observations across disciplines (Mealey 2001, McAndrew 2002). EP thus brings a new level of analysis to human behavior, yet does not supplant other more proximally based views (Segal 2003).

The late evolutionary psychologist Linda Mealey asserted that for evolutionary psychologists, "kinship, via the effect of inclusive fitness, constitutes a core construct of relevance to all social interaction" (Mealey 2001, p. 23). This concept, formally developed in a set of seminal papers by Hamilton (1964), offers fresh answers to questions concerning the bases of cooperative social behavior. Hamilton reasoned that alleles predisposing individuals to act in ways favoring the transmission of those alleles would be selected for. Cooperative behavior directed toward individuals likely to carry copies of these alleles would be an indirect way to transmit those alleles into future generations. Thus, biological fitness was redefined as inclusive fitness, that is, one's reproductive success, augmented by one's effects on relatives other than children. Hamilton's theory, in addition to solving an enduring evolutionary dilemma, spawned a series of exciting research programs aimed at understanding the nature and development of social relations.

Assessing evolutionary-based hypotheses relevant to social processes and outcomes within families requires studying pairs of individuals who vary in their genetic and environmental relatedness. Behavioral genetics (BG), a discipline concerned with identifying genetic and environmental influences underlying individual differences in behavior, offers investigators a vast assortment of research designs. Many of these designs are well suited to evaluating evolutionary-based questions and hypotheses. BG, once known for its controversial history, now enjoys a brighter future. In the 1950s and 1960s, critics argued that such work would support theories of genetic determinism and value judgments of racial variation. However, advances in human genetics and dissatisfaction with environmental explanations of behavior resurrected behavioral genetics as an informative psychological discipline. Behavioral genetics was finally accepted into the mainstream of psychology in the early 1980s. Recent progress in identifying the approximately 25,000 genes in the human genome (International Human Genome Sequencing Consortium, 2004), and efforts to associate specific genes with specific behaviors (Plomin, DeFries, McClearn, & McGuffin 2001) have given new direction to behavioral genetic studies.

Behavioral genetics and evolutionary psychology stand to benefit considerably from closer association with one another. Behavioral genetics offers a rich array of research designs to evolutionary psychologists. Evolutionary psychologists, in turn, can provide insights into the differential heritabilities of selected traits. However, given the different foci of these two disciplines (BG is concerned with within-species variation, whereas EP is concerned with cross-species variation and within-species uniformities), the two disciplines have generally engaged in parallel play. This situation is showing some signs of change, given the growing number of empirical studies combining the two approaches (see Mealey, Bridgstock, & Townsend 1999; Miller 2004). A positive outcome has been more interdisciplinary thinking about behavioral development.

Twin studies, in particular, provide novel approaches to old problems regarding human social relations. The following section reviews the biological differences between twin types, then outlines ways of incorporating twins in evolutionary psychological research.

TWINS AND TWIN-RESEARCH DESIGNS: A BRIEF OVERVIEW

Biology of Twinning

Twins occur in two varieties: monozygotic (identical, or MZ) and dizygotic (fraternal, or DZ). MZ twins share all their genes, whereas DZ twins share half their genes, on average, by descent. MZ twins form when a zygote (fertilized egg) divides during the first 14 days after conception. DZ twins result when two simultaneously released eggs are fertilized by separate sperm. DNA analysis is the most accurate scientific method for establishing zygosity or twin type. In the event that DNA testing is precluded, a standard physical resemblance questionnaire (that correlates highly with results from extensive serological testing), may be completed by twins or their parents (see Nichols & Bilbro 1966). Placental examination may not be informative with respect to twin type, given that both DZ twins and one third of MZ twins have separate placentae and fetal membranes (Segal 2000b). Documenting the methods by which zygosity was established is a crucial first step in research using twins (Segal 2006a).

Despite sharing the same genes, MZ twins are neither physically nor behaviorally identical. DZ twins, despite sharing an average of half their genes, may vary in their degree of resemblance for selected traits. Figures 14.1 and 14.2 illustrate these points by depicting the different degrees of physical similarity and dissimilarity possible in both types of twins.

There are several explanations for discordance between MZ co-twins. MZ twins may differ in midline congenital malformations, associated with zygotic splitting (Machin & Keith 1999; also see Segal 2000b). Shared circulation (fetal anastomoses) variously affects approximately two thirds of MZ twins (pairs that share chorions and, in rare cases, amnions). In such cases, outcomes range from co-twin differences in size and health to cardiac failure or the demise of one or both twins. Different patterns of X-inactivation in female MZ twins may underlie differences in X-linked conditions, such as Duchenne muscular dystrophy (Burn et al. 1986), color-blindness (Jørgensen et al. 1992; also see Segal 2000a) and Lesch–Nyhan syndrome (De Gregorio et al. 2005). MZ co-twins can also show discordance for chromosomal anomalies (e.g., Turner's syndrome: 45, XO) associated with chromosomal loss in one twin during embryogenesis (Uchida, DeSa, & Whelan 1983). Differences in gene imprinting can explain MZ co-twin differences in diseases such as Beckwith–Widemann syndrome (Machin & Keith 1999).

There is also considerable biological variety among DZ twin pairs. Fertilization of a mature ovum and a polar body produces polar body twins (Bulmer 1970; also see Segal 2000a). Such twins may show varying degrees of genetic relatedness, depending on the timing of cellular events. Arranged from least alike to most alike genetically, such twins would be: pairs derived from fertilization of the first polar body and mature ovum, DZ twins, pairs derived from fertilization of the second polar body and mature ovum, uniovular dispermatic twins (twins thought to result from division of the mature ovum, prior to or during fertilization), and MZ twins (Machin & Keith 1999). If two eggs are fertilized on different occasions

Figure 14.1. Two pairs of monozygotic twins.
A. Monozygotic twins who are highly similar in appearance. Photo by
Dr. Nancy L. Segal.

B. Monozygotic twins who are highly dissimilar in appearance. The twin
on the right experienced adverse birth effects. Photo by Dr. Nancy L. Segal.

Figure 14.2. Two pairs of dizygotic twins.
A. Dizygotic twins who are highly similar in appearance.
Photo courtesy the twins' family.

B. Dizygotic twins who are highly dissimilar in appearance.
Photo by Dr. Nancy L. Segal.

(but near in time) by different men, DZ co-twins will be genetically equivalent to half-siblings. This event, known as superfecundation, is thought to be rare, but some cases are difficult to detect (Segal 2000b). It has also been shown that twins born to interracial couples can look very different physically, even to the point of appearing unrelated (see, for example, Laing 2006).

Twinning Rates

Twin births are relatively rare in human and in most nonhuman mammalian populations (Segal 2000b). The natural twinning rate is approximately 1 of 80 to 1 of 100 births in Western nations. The MZ twinning rate is fairly constant worldwide (1 of 300), but the DZ twinning rate varies across populations (e.g., Japan: 2.3 of 100; South Africa/Bantu: 17.5 of 100; Great Britain, among Caucasians: 8.9 of 100) (see Machin & Keith 1999). However, the twinning rate in Western countries has risen over the last few decades, from approximately 1 of 53 births in 1980 to 1 of 32 births in 2002 (Martin, Kochanek, Strobino, Guyer, & MacDorman, 2005). It is estimated that one-third of this increase (mostly in DZ twins) is explained by mothers' older age at conception, and the other two thirds is explained by the increased availability of artificial reproductive technologies (Martin & Park 1999).

An evolutionary perspective would explain twins' infrequency with reference to their higher rate of congenital anomalies and lower birth weight, factors that strain parental care and resources. Multiple-birth pregnancies also pose physical risks for expectant mothers (Krotz, Fajardo, Ghandi, Patel, & Keith 2002). Note, however, that the natural occurrence of DZ twins is twice that of MZ twins. Forbes (1997) proposed that increases in DZ twinning with maternal age may represent an adaptive tradeoff. Specifically, the benefits of delivering two children (who may transmit genes to future generations, thereby increasing maternal reproductive fitness) may offset the cost of producing defective children. (Down's syndrome is more common in children born to mothers aged 35 years and older than to younger mothers; see Crane & Morris 2006). Additional discussion of twinning rates is available in Segal (2005a, 2005b) and in Segal and Hill (2005).

The varieties of both MZ and DZ twin pairs offer a rich but largely untapped source for exploring social relatedness vis-à-vis genetic overlap of the social partners. Ways in which twins can be used to test evolutionarily derived hypotheses on family relationships are presented below.

Logic of Twin Research Designs

The simple yet elegant logic of the classic twin design derives from the difference in genetic relatedness between MZ and DZ twins. Greater resemblance within MZ than DZ twin pairs indicates genetic influence on the trait under study. A key assumption in twin research is that environmental effects operate similarly for both types of twins. This concept, while questioned by some individuals, has withstood rigorous testing. The conclusion is that there is scant evidence linking similar or different parental treatment of twins to similarities or differences in their behavioral outcomes (Hettema, Neale, & Kendler 1995; also see Segal 2000b).

There are approximately 10 variants of the classic twin study (Segal 1990). Designs that would especially inform evolutionary analyses of family relations are described below.

Twins as "Couples" contrasts the behavioral processes and outcomes of MZ and DZ twins in joint problem-solving situations or other interactional circumstances. This model shows how the genetic backgrounds of the interactants (genetically homogenous or heterogeneous) affect social behaviors. The expectation is that MZ co-twins will be more cooperative toward one another, relative to DZ co-twins.

Twins Reared Apart includes the rare group of MZ (MZA) and DZ (DZA) twins separated at birth and reared in different families. Such twins have been used mostly to derive direct estimates of genetic influence on intelligence, personality, and health measures (Bouchard, Lykken, McGue, Segal, & Tellegen 1990; Ripatti, Gatz, Pedersen, & Palmgren 2003). However, their potential utility in evolutionary studies of behavioral development has been recognized.

Crawford and Anderson (1989) noted that selective breeding is a way to tease apart associations among life histories, strategies, and tactics. (Life history refers to a genetically organized life course involving allocation of energy, time, or resources to reproduction, growth, or survival. Strategies include decision processes and rules that affect how developmental events affect life-history trajectories. Tactics are variable behavioral patterns caused by applying decisions and rules (see Crawford & Anderson 1989 and references therein). However, selective breeding studies are not possible with human populations. These investigators, therefore, reasoned that MZA twins could be organized according to hypotheses about genetic life-history traits to test predictions about how environmentally contingent tactics develop in certain environments for each life history. This method is illustrated with a hypothetical test of how father absence affects MZ female twins' age at menarche.

Subsequent to the publication of Crawford and Anderson's paper and papers by other investigators promoting BG–EP links (e.g., Buss 1990, Segal 1993), several evolutionary psychological studies using reared-apart twins have appeared. One such study addressed the heritability of repro-duction-related variables and reproductive success (Mealey & Segal 1993). Interestingly, an evolutionary-based twin study of father absence and age at menarche was recently reported, although it did not use MZA twins; this study by Mendle et al. (2006) is reviewed in a later section of this chapter). Only a single study, also described below, has used twins raised apart to study social closeness and familiarity (Segal, Hershberger, & Arad 2003).

Virtual Twins (VTs) are same-age unrelated siblings raised together since early infancy (Segal 2005a, 2005b). These unique pairs replicate twinship, but without the genetic link. VTs are composed of two adopted children, or one biological child and one adoptee. These pairs directly complement MZA twins because they yield direct estimates of environmental influence on measured traits. IQ studies from the Fullerton Virtual Twin Study have found modest shared environmental effects on general intelligence in early childhood (Segal & Hershberger 2005). Height and weight analyses showed both genetic and shared environmental effects on body size in a combined twin–virtual twin analysis (Segal & Allison 2002). VTs also provide an informative comparison group for assessing the effects of genetic relatedness, rearing, and familiarity on social relations. A pair of virtual twins is shown in Figure 14.3.

The *Twin-Family Design* (also called the MZ half-sib method) consists of two intact families, created when MZ twins marry and have children (Segal 1997, 2000b). Twin aunts and uncles in MZ twin families are "genetic parents" to their nieces and nephews, and nieces and nephews are their "genetic children."

Figure 14.3. Virtual twins—same-age unrelated siblings raised together since birth, born 4 months apart. Photo courtesy of the twins' family.

In contrast, the usual aunt–uncle and niece–nephew relationships are maintained when DZ twins marry and have children. Many informative kin comparisons are generated by such families. For example, comparing height similarity of MZ twin aunts and nieces with that of MZ twin mothers and daughters separates genetic and shared environmental effects on stature.

Behavioral geneticists have used MZ and DZ twin families to study factors affecting birth weight (Magnus 1984), nonverbal skills (Rose, Harris, Christian, & Nance 1979), predisposition to schizophrenia (Gottesman & Bertelsen 1989), child behavioral outcomes (D'Onofrio et al. 2003, D'Onofrio et al. 2005, 2006), and conduct disorder (Haber, Jacob, & Heath 2005). The first evolutionary-based studies of social relatedness to use this design are reviewed below.

Families generated by the rare marriages of two MZ twin pairs enable further tests contrasting biological and cultural relationships (Segal 2000b, 2005a). This is because both twin aunts and twin uncles are genetic "mothers" and "fathers" to their co-twin's children, who are genetically equivalent to their own children. Furthermore, pairs of first cousins become genetic "full siblings." It would, for example, be possible to compare parental involvement of mothers and aunts, and fathers and uncles to each set of children, within MZ families and between MZ and DZ families. Aside from summaries of such cases in the popular press, only one report of 50 families (mostly descriptive and mostly MZ) is available in the scientific literature (Taylor 1971).

In *DZ Twin Designs*, DZ twin pairs are typically used as a comparison group for MZ twins. Low resemblance between DZ twins and high resemblance between MZ twins has been interpreted as evidence of emergenesis— emergenic traits are those influenced by complex configurations of genes at multiple loci (Lykken 1982). MZ twins would be expected to show concordance for such traits since they share all their genes, but it would be rare for DZ twins to inherit the same complex gene combination.

An alternative explanation for low DZ twin resemblance might be an overrepresentation of superfecundated twins and/or certain polar-body pairs in the sample. Clearly, the variety of DZ twin types makes them attractive to evolutionary researchers interested in associations between genetic relatedness and social affiliation.

Twin Studies of Social Relatedness

The common theme emerging from twin studies of social relatedness is that MZ twins are, on average, socially closer than DZ twins. It is also the case that the social context affects interactional processes and outcomes. As such, specific relationship features may not necessarily differ between twin types.

Researchers using the classic twin design have relied largely on social relationship surveys to compare MZ and DZ twin relations. Loehlin and Nichols (1976) found that MZ twins were in greater agreement than were DZ twins with respect to relationship satisfaction, although some ratings (e.g., regarding frequency of fighting) did not differ. Foy, Vernon, and Jang (2001) found that MZ twins were more likely than DZ twins to name their co-twin as their best friend, but the two twin types did not differ in expressed levels of intimacy. Neyer (2002a) found higher MZ than DZ twin agreement in dyadic attachment (to the co-twin), suggesting genetic influence. In a more recent twin study, Tancredy and Fraley (2006) found that both genetic and relational processes affect the development of attachment.

Some studies have compared average levels of closeness between twins and other sibling pairs. Findings support closer MZ than DZ twins across all measured age groups.

Danby and Thorpe (2006) found greater compatibility between young MZ than young DZ co-twins. DZ same-sex twins in that study viewed their co-twin less favorably than did MZ or opposite-sex twins. Mowrer (1954) found that MZ twin adolescents chose their co-twin as a preferred social partner more often than did DZ twins. Furthermore, a higher proportion of MZ than DZ twins indicated that their co-twin was the family member who best understood them. Reiss, Neiderhauser, Hetherington, and Plomin (2000) reported greater "positivity" and less "negativity" between adolescent MZ twins, relative to DZ twins, full siblings, half-siblings and unrelated siblings. An interesting exception concerned unrelated siblings in step-families, who showed less negativity (and less positivity) than MZ twins. It was suggested that adoptive siblings are especially disengaged from one another.

Studies examining adult twin relationships have found that after adolescence, MZ twins live closer to one another than do DZ twins and experience more frequent contact, emotional closeness, and social support (Neyer 2002b). In contrast with DZ twins, MZ twins indicated that relationship satisfaction and attachment security were independent of contact frequency. Tomassini, Juel, Holm, Skytthe, and Christensen (2003) reported a lower suicide rate in Danish twins than in non-twins, suggesting that strong family ties might be responsible; the risk for suicide did not differ between MZ and DZ twins.

The "twins as couples" design extends and elaborates questionnaire data by observing twins interacting in semi-naturalistic and naturalistic settings. Von Bracken's (1934) study of school-age twins is exemplary in this regard. MZ and DZ twins were observed while working independently on arithmetic and coding tasks, in the same room and by themselves. MZ co-twins expended more-similar efforts when working close to one another. In contrast,

DZ co-twins who perceived that they were equally skilled competed with each other, whereas DZ twins who perceived that they were not equally skilled were not motivated to work very hard. It was proposed that "the understanding between the two members of an identical pair is much greater than that between either member and other persons. With fraternals, on the other hand, centrifugal tendencies have greater play since the intimate understanding due to similar hereditary disposition is not present to the same degree" (Von Bracken 1934, p. 305).

Segal (1984, 1997) observed higher frequencies of cooperative behaviors and a higher success rate within young MZ than young DZ twin pairs during joint puzzle completion. Several judges' global impressions of these filmed sequences indicated greater mutuality, cooperation, accommodation, involvement, and contribution among MZ than among DZ twin pairs. The only measure on which DZ twins outscored MZ twins was role division (Segal 2002).

Studies conducted in Singapore by Loh and Elliott (1998) found that MZ twin children were more cooperative during joint activity than were DZ twins, but only when reward equality was uncertain. In contrast, MZ twins competed to a greater degree than DZ twins when conditions guaranteed equal outcomes for both co-twins. The authors suggested that reward equality for MZ twins offered an opportunity for "dominance testing" (p. 408), given minimal challenge to their relationship.

Comparison of young MZ and DZ twins' play preferences in unstructured settings are consistent with laboratory findings (Segal 1997). The nearest-neighbor technique, developed for studying spatial and social affinities of sex–age classes within hamadryas baboon troops (Kummer 1968), was used to record "nearest neighbors" of MZ and DZ target twins in playgrounds. MZ co-twins were more closely situated spatially and showed evidence of more meaningful interaction, relative to DZ co-twins.

Non-zero-sum games (games in which players may both benefit or lose, and in which gains and losses do not sum to zero) offer informative glimpses into social relationships. Few experiments have involved relatives, but two have involved twins. Segal (1984) administered a differential productivity task (DPT) to pairs of young MZ and DZ twins. Separated from their co-twin, children traced rows of small figures with a red pen such that the more work they completed, the higher their score. They also completed the task under the condition that the points they earned would be awarded to their twin sibling. Both MZ and DZ twins worked harder for themselves than for their co-twin; however, the self–twin difference was significantly smaller for MZ than for DZ twins. This outcome suggests that, in some circumstances, MZ twins' greater within-pair cooperation may be achieved via their greater restraint of selfishness, a concept proposed by Axelrod and Hamilton (1981).

The prisoner's dilemma game (PDG) shares features with the DPT in that individual gains may be increased or decreased relative to group gains. Segal and Hershberger (1999) administered a PDG to MZ and DZ twins between the ages of 10 and 82 years. MZ twins showed higher levels of cooperation and continuity of cooperation, as expected. Neither co-twin differences in IQ nor in social-closeness ratings were associated with co-twin differences in cooperative choices.

The studies reviewed above have focused on twins raised together. Twins raised apart and reunited as adults bring a different perspective to social interactions within families because these twins lack a shared childhood history. More importantly, many of the twins were raised with unrelated siblings in their adoptive home. This situation allows comparison of social relations in pairs connected by genes alone versus environment alone.

The classic studies of separated MZA twins included detailed biographical sketches of each pair together with quantitative (individual and group) analyses of behavioral data (Juel-Nielsen 1966; Newman, Freeman, & Holzinger 1937; Shields 1962; Popenoe 1922). The quality of the twins' relationship with one another was never systematically assessed, although information is variously provided in some cases. Forty of the 76 pairs developed close social relations; 14 pairs did not; and 22 pairs were difficult to judge. The striking finding is that 40 of 54 pairs (nearly 75%) developed close relations following reunion (Segal et al. 2003). Unfortunately, these studies did not include DZA twins, nor did they explore the nature of the twins' social relations with the unrelated siblings with whom they were raised. A twin-relationship survey, administered to participants in the Minnesota Study of Twins Reared Apart, offered an opportunity to do both (Segal et al. 2003).

Main findings from the Minnesota study were that MZA twins' ratings indicated significantly higher social closeness and familiarity than did those of DZA twins. These measures showed negligible associations with contact time before assessment. Additionally, both types of twins felt closer to and more familiar with their newly found co-twin than their unrelated sibling. Few associations emerged between closeness and similarity in personality, interests, values, and education. It is, however, possible that twins' perceptions of their similarities, rather than their similarities in self-ratings, may provide the underlying explanatory mechanisms.

Virtual twins provide a better comparison group for MZA twins than do ordinary unrelated siblings because VTs are matched in age. As part of the Fullerton study, parents provide ratings of social relatedness for young children, and adults provide such ratings for themselves. Relevant data are also gathered from participants in TAPS (Twins, Adoptees, Peers, and Siblings), a collaborative project between California State University, Fullerton (CSUF) and the University of San Francisco (McGuire & Segal 2005; Segal, McGuire,

Havlena, Gill, & Hershberger 2007). This study explores genetic and environmental influences on general intelligence, social relations, and behavioral adjustment in pairs of 8- to 13-year-old MZ twins, DZ twins, full siblings, virtual twins, and best friends.

Social relatedness data for VTs have not yet been analyzed, but ratings from two young adult VT pairs (DZ male co-twins raised with an unrelated same-age brother) exemplify the kinds of relations predicted by evolutionary psychological theorizing. Both DZ co-twins indicated that they were "as close as best friends" to each other, but "as close as a casual friend" to their unrelated sibling. Their unrelated brother indicated that he was "between best friends and casual friends" to one twin, and "as close as a best friend" to the other twin. Despite their common rearing, the non-biological relationships are characterized by reduced closeness and discordant ratings, whereas the biological relationships are characterized by relatively increased closeness and concordant ratings.

Like VT methods, the MZ Twin-Family Study is well suited to studying social relationships within families. This design has recently captured the attention of evolutionary investigators.

Only two recent studies have used MZ and DZ twin families to study social relatedness. In the first study, the main hypothesis, generated by Hamilton's inclusive-fitness theory, was that MZ twin aunts and uncles would express greater social closeness toward nieces and nephews (their co-twins' children), relative to DZ twin aunts and uncles (Segal, Seghers, Chavarria, Marelich, & Mechanic in press). A second hypothesis was based on the paternity-uncertainty concept, namely that men can never be certain that their spouse's children are truly their own biological children because of possible female infidelity. Thus, it was anticipated that twins with female co-twins would express greater closeness toward nieces and nephews, relative to twins with male co-twins. Both hypotheses were supported, based on more than 300 individual twins' responses to an Internet survey.

A recent, creative use of the twin-family design tested the finding by Belsky, Steinberg, and Draper (1991) that stressful family environments (including biological father absence, psychological conflict, and limited resources) predispose daughters to early menarche. Mendle et al. (2006) found that cousins (children of twins) discordant for having stepfathers did not differ in age at menarche. In fact, girls in both types of families achieved relatively early menarche, and mothers' age at menarche was a strong predictor of daughters' age at menarche. It was suggested that being genetically related to someone with a stepfather, rather than experiencing a stepfather situation directly, was sufficient to affect pubertal events. It was also suggested that a genetic or environmental confound may explain the family conflict–early menarche relationship reported by Belsky et al. (1991).

The only study of twins married to twins (mostly MZ) suggested that genetic factors may affect marital stability and genetic similarities between spouses may be associated with understanding and congeniality (Taylor 1971). This design and other twin-family designs have considerable potential to test hypotheses generated by the wide range of genetically informative relationships; some examples of possible studies are presented below. A final area of research that deserves attention concerns findings from DZ twin designs.

Few studies have attempted to link behavioral and physical resemblance in DZ twins, and none have considered links to social relations. Bock, Vandenberg, Bramble, and Pearson (1970) found that DZ twins sharing selected blood groups showed greater resemblance on some Wechsler IQ subtests, relative to twins who matched on fewer groups. Pakstis, Scarr-Salapatek, Elston, and Siervogel (1972) found that DZ twins who were more physically similar had fewer blood-group differences than did less physically similar DZ twins. Plomin, Willerman, and Loehlin (1976) observed that judgments of DZ twins' physical resemblance was positively associated with their personality resemblance. Dumont-Driscoll and Rose (1983) found that genotyped DZ twins with higher estimates of shared genes were mistaken or less certain of their twin type than were DZ pairs with lower estimates. However, recent advances in molecular genetic techniques have moved such efforts forward, with exciting results.

Visscher et al. (2006) obtained genome scans and height measurements on 4,401 full sibling pairs (who, like DZ twins, share half their genes, on average). They then used genome-wide identity-by-descent sharing to estimate the heritability of height as .80, consistent with values reported from traditional twin and family studies. In contrast with previous research, Montgomery et al. (2006) did not detect excess allele sharing in DZ twin pairs at the human leukocyte antigen (HLA) locus. This result has implications for linkage studies concerned with diseases that use DZ twin data. Such approaches can potentially be used to assess relationships between shared genes and other behavioral phenotypes, including cognition, social relatedness, and marital satisfaction. An advantage is elimination of confounding non-genetic effects.

Potential applications of DZ twin designs will be revisited in the final section. First, it is important to consider possible mechanisms underlying the observed MZ–DZ twin differences in social relatedness.

Mechanisms Underlying Differences in MZ–DZ Twin Relations

The MZ–DZ twin comparisons described thus far allow numerous tests of inclusive fitness. However, mechanisms for recognizing and reacting to relatives as a function of proportion of shared genes, and discriminating between kin and non-kin, are necessary. Twinning is relatively rare in human populations, such that a mechanism specific to MZ co-twin relations would be unlikely. Instead, it is proposed that the mechanisms underlying social relations among non-twin relatives would be operative for twins as well (Segal 2005a).

Phenotypic matching (comparing phenotypes of the self with those of others) has been proposed as a mechanism facilitating kin recognition. This would entail learning information about one's own characteristics and/or those of close relatives. Such processes would yield "images," "templates" (Sherman & Holmes 1985), or "learned standards of appearance" against which the phenotypes of unfamiliar individuals could be assessed (Trivers 1985). For example, physical proximity may provide clues about relatedness, given that relatives tend to be situated relatively close together. Olfactory-based mechanisms may also mediate favoritism of blood relatives (Weisfeld, Czilli, Phillips, Gall, & Lichtman 2003).

Individuals' perceived similarities may exert more powerful effects on interaction than might more objective behavioral measures or self-ratings, as indicated above. Social bonding may thus be fostered by neurological mechanisms affecting attraction between individuals who perceive similarities between themselves (Freedman 1979). Associations between various forms of recognition and emotions have been observed, triggering a series of psychological and physiological events (McGuire, Fawzy, Spar, Weigel, & Troisi 1994). Tancredy and Fraley (2006) suggested that MZ twins' identical genes "may affect relational dynamics, such as a heightened sense of empathy, that promote the development of attachment." Consistent with this view are findings from a non-twin study that identified emotional closeness as partially mediating the influence of genetic relatedness on willingness to perform altruistic acts (Korchmaros & Kenny 2001).

CLOSING COMMENTS AND FUTURE DIRECTIONS

Behavioral–genetic methods, especially twin studies, offer informative approaches for evaluating evolutionary hypotheses and predictions concerning family relationships. Recent advances in molecular genetics should increase the efficacy and fruitfulness of such efforts. In fact, associations between self-report measures of human altruism and dopaminergic polymorphisms have been reported (Bachner-Melman et al. 2005). Several studies underway will yield new results in coming years and, one hopes, suggest new directions for future research.

Investigators associated with TAPS and with the CSU Fullerton projects are comparing tacit coordination in pairs of young MZ and DZ twins, siblings, and adoptees, and in adult twins. Tacit coordination refers to the case in which two or more parties have identical interests and face the problem not of reconciling interests but of coordinating their actions for their mutual benefit when communication is impossible (Schelling 1960). It is anticipated that MZ twin pairs will show greater success in these tasks than will DZ twin pairs, suggesting a mechanism facilitating the expression of some cooperative acts.

Behaviors in other domains invite exploration via twin research. A potentially informative study would compare MZ and DZ twins' willingness to serve as organ donors for their co-twin versus non-twin relatives. Especially sensitive comparisons could come from MZ twins married to MZ twins, asked to rate feelings in reference to a child versus a niece or nephew ("genetic child"), spouse versus genetically identical in-law, and twin versus non-twin sibling. Data gathered from actual twin donors might be even more revealing with respect to altruistic acts that pose serious costs to one's physical health. Burnstein, Crandall, and Kitayama (1994) showed that people prefer to help close relatives over distant relatives in hypothetical life-and-death situations.

Frequency of gift-giving and cost of gifts given by MZ and DZ twin aunts and uncles to their nieces and nephews are being compared as part of the Fullerton study of social relationships in twin families. Parallel family designs involving MZA and DZA twins have never been studied but could produce exciting results. Children of MZA twins, while cousins, are really half-siblings reared apart. Children of DZA twins are ordinary cousins who have never met. Comparing social affinities (e.g., degree of attraction, frequency of contact) between these two types of cousins would isolate the genetic contribution to relationships between members of a culturally, but not biologically, equivalent kinship category.

A new study of behavioral similarities and social relatedness in young Chinese twin girls, adopted separately under China's one-child policy, is currently underway (see Segal 2006b). These particular MZA and DZA twins provide the best comparison group for virtual twins (siblings with shared genes and different environments vs. siblings with shared environments and different genes), because the twins and VTs are young children; separated twins in existing studies are mostly adults. There are also other ways to involve VTs in family relationship studies. One such study could focus on the subset of adoptive-biological pairs whose families had other biological children. This would allow comparison of cooperation and affiliation between unrelated same-age children and related different-age children living together. Evolutionary theory would anticipate greater closeness within related than unrelated pairs. Comparing parent–child relationships in these families and in ordinary biological families would be insightful with respect to closeness and caring (Segal & Hill 2005).

Many exciting studies could involve DZ twins, organized according to genetic overlap. Social closeness could be compared in superfecundated pairs and in ordinary DZ twin pairs. The varying degrees of genetic relatedness associated with the different types of polar body twins is also conducive to exploring more direct associations between common genes and social behavior. The future availability of a centralized human genetic database should assist such efforts (Kean 2006).

Evolutionary psychology brings new levels of analysis and interpretation to current psychological findings. It can also benefit from creative use of twin study methods and from discoveries in the molecular genetics field. All three disciplines, both individually and collectively, have reconceptualized families and family relationships. Examined through these multiple lenses, parents and children, aunts and nieces, uncles and nephews, and twins and siblings can offer fresh insights into human relationships, just by acting naturally.

ACKNOWLEDGMENTS

This work was supported, in part, by a National Science Foundation award (SBR–9712875), a stipend for Research, Scholarship and Creative Activity from California State University, Fullerton, and an NIMH grant (R01 MH63351).

REFERENCES

Axelrod, R., & Hamilton, W. D. (1981). The evolution of cooperation. *Science, 211*, 1390–1396.

Bachner-Melman, R., Gritsenko, I., Nemanov, L., Zohar, A. H., Dina, C., & Ebstein, R. P. (2005). Dopaminergic polymorphisms associated with self-report measures of human altruism: A fresh phenotype for the dopamine D4 receptor. *Molecular Biology, 10*, 333–335.

Belsky, J., Steinberg, L., & Draper, P. (1991). Childhood experience, interpersonal development, and reproductive strategy: An evolutionary theory of socialization. *Child Development, 62*, 647–670.

Bock, R. D., Vandenberg, S. G., Bramble, W., & Pearson, W. (1970). A behavioral correlate of blood-group discordance in dizygotic twins. *Behavior Genetics, 1*, 89–98.

Bouchard, T. J., Jr., Lykken, D. T., McGue, M., Segal, N. L., & Tellegen, A. (1990). Sources of human psychological differences: The Minnesota Study of Twins Reared Apart. *Science, 250*, 223–228.

Bulmer, M. G. (1970). *The biology of twinning in man.* Oxford: Oxford University Press.

Burn, J., Povey, S., Boyd, Y., Munro, E. A., West, L., Harper, K., et al. (1986). Duchenne muscular dystrophy in one of monozygotic twin girls. *Journal of Medical Genetics, 23,* 494–500.

Burnstein, E., Crandall, C., & Kitayama, S. 1994. Some neo-Darwinian rules for altruism: Weighing cues for inclusive fitness as a function of the biological importance of the decision. *Journal of Personality and Social Psychology, 67,* 773–789.

Buss, D. M. (1990). Toward a biologically informed psychology of personality. *Journal of Personality, 58,* 1–16.

Buss, D. M. (2004). *Evolutionary psychology: The new science of the mind* (2nd ed.). Boston: Allyn and Bacon.

Crane, E., & Morris, J. K. (2006). Changes in maternal age in England and Wales: Implications for Down's syndrome. *Down's Syndrome Research and Practice, 10,* 41–43.

Crawford, C. B., & Anderson, J. L. (1989). Sociobiology: An environmentalist discipline? *American Psychologist, 44,* 1449–1459.

Danby, S., & Thorpe, K. (2006). Compatibility and conflict: Negotiation of relationships by dizygotic same-sex twin girls. *Twin Research and Human Genetics, 9,* 103–112.

De Gregorio, L., Jinnah, H. A., Harris, J. C., Nyhan, W. L., Schretlen, D. J., Trobley, L. M., et al. (2005). Lesch–Nyhan disease in a female with a clinically normal monozygotic twin. *Molecular Genetics and Metabolism, 85,* 70–77.

D'Onofrio, B. M., Turkheimer, E., Eaves, L. J., Corey, L. A., Berg, K., Solaas, M. H., et al. (2003). The role of the children of twins design in elucidating causal relations between parent characteristics and child outcomes. *Journal of Child Psychology and Psychiatry, 44,* 1130–1144.

D'Onofrio, B. M., Turkheimer, E., Emery, R. E., Slutske, W. S., Heath, A. C., Madden, P. A., et al. (2005). A genetically informed study of marital instability and its association with offspring psychopathology. *Journal of Abnormal Psychology, 14,* 570–586.

D'Onofrio, B. M., Turkheimer, E., Emery, R. E., Slutske, W. S., Heath, A. C., Madden, P. A., et al. (2006). A genetically informed study of the processes underlying the association between parental marital instability and offspring adjustment. *Developmental Psychology, 42,* 486–499.

Dumont-Driscoll, M., & Rose, R. J. (1983). Testing the twin model: Is perceived similarity due to genetic identity? *Behavior Genetics, 13,* 531–532.

Forbes, L. S. (1997). The evolutionary biology of spontaneous abortion in humans. *Trends in Ecology and Evolution, 12,* 446–450.

Foy, A. K., Vernon, P. A., & Jang, K. (2001). Examining the dimensions of intimacy in twin and peer relationships. *Twin Research, 4,* 443–452.

Freedman, D. G. (1979). *Human sociobiology.* New York: Free Press.

Gottesman, I. I., & Bertelsen, A. (1989). Confirming unexpressed genotypes for schizophrenia. *Archives of General Psychiatry, 46,* 867–872.

Haber, J. R., Jacob, T., & Heath, A. C. (2005). Paternal alcoholism and offspring conduct disorder: Evidence for the "common genes" hypothesis. *Twin Research and Human Genetics, 8,* 120–131.

Hamilton, W. D. (1964). The genetical evolution of social behavior. I and II. *Journal of Theoretical Biology, 7,* 1–52.

Hettema, J. M., Neale, M. C., & Kendler, K. S. (1995). Physical similarity and the equal-environment assumption in twin studies of psychiatric disorders. *Behavioral Genetics, 25,* 327–335.

International Human Genome Sequencing Consortium (2004). Finishing the euchromatic sequence of the human genome. *Nature, 385,* 931–945.

Jørgensen, A. L., Philip, J., Raskind, W. H., Matsushita, M., Christensen, B., Drever, V., et al. (1992). Different patterns of X inactivation in MZ twins discordant for red–green color-vision deficiency. *American Journal of Human Genetics, 51,* 291–298.

Juel-Nielsen, N. (1966). *Individual and environment: Monozygotic twins reared apart.* New York: International Universities Press.

Kean, S. (2006, August 31). NIH proposes centralized database of human genetic data to advance health research. *Chronicle of Higher Education,,* http://chronicle.com/daily/2006/08/2006083101n.htm. Retrieved August 31, 2006.

Korchmaros, J. D., & Kenny, D. A. (2001). Emotional closeness as a mediator of the effect of genetic relatedness on altruism. *Psychological Science, 12,* 262–265.

Krotz, S., Fajardo, J., Ghandi, S., Patel, A., & Keith, L. G. (2002). Hypertensive diseases in twin pregnancies: A review. *Twin Research, 5,* 8–14.

Kummer, H. (1968). Social organization of hamadryas baboons: A field study. Chicago: University of Chicago Press.

Laing, L. (2006, March 2). Black and white Twins. *Daily Mail.* http://www.daily mail.co.uk/pages/live/articles/news/news.html?in_article_id=377839&in_ page_id=1770&in_a_source=&ct=5. Retrieved March 2, 2006.

Loehlin, J., & Nichols, R. (1976). *Heredity, environment and personality: A study of 850 sets of twins.* Austin: University of Texas Press.

Loh, C. Y., & Elliott, J. M. (1998). Cooperation and competition as a function of zygosity in 7- to 9-year-old twins. *Evolution and Human Behavior, 19,* 397–411.

Lykken, D. T. (1982). Research with twins: The concept of emergenesis. *Psychophysiology, 19,* 361–373.

Machin, G. A., & Keith, L. G. (1999). *An atlas of multiple pregnancy.* New York: Parthenon.

Magnus, P. (1984). Causes of variation in birth weight: A study of offspring of twins. *Clinical Genetics, 25,* 15–24.

Martin, J. A., Kochanek, K. D., Strobino, D. M., Guyer, B., & MacDorman, M. F. (2005). Annual summary of vital statistics—2003. *Pediatrics, 115,* 619–634.

Martin, J. A., & Park, M. M. (1999). Trends in twin and triplet births: 1980–97. *National Vital Statistics Reports, 47,* 1–17.

McAndrew, F. T. (2002). New evolutionary perspectives on altruism: Multi-level- selection and costly-signaling theories. *Current Directions in Psychological Science, 11,* 79–82.

McGuire, M. T., Fawzy, F. I., Spar, J. E., Weigel, R. M., & Troisi, A. (1994). Altruism and mental disorders. *Ethology and Sociobiology, 15*, 299–321.

McGuire, S., & Segal, N. L. (2005, April 7–10). *Parental differential treatment of siblings in three twin contexts: MZs, DZs and VTs.* Symposium: "The Ecologies of Parental Differential Treatment of Siblings." Society for Research in Child Development, Atlanta.

Mealey, L. (2001). Kinship: The ties that bind (disciplines). In Holcomb III, H. R. (Ed.), *Conceptual challenges in evolutionary psychology: Innovative research strategies.* (pp. 19–38). Dordrecht, Netherlands: Kluwer.

Mealey, L., Bridgstock, R., & Townsend, G. C. (1999). Symmetry and perceived facial attractiveness: A monozygotic co-twin comparison. *Journal of Personality and Social Psychology, 76*, 157–165.

Mealey, L., & Segal, N. L. (1993). Heritable and environmental variables affect reproduction-related behaviors, but not ultimate reproductive success. *Personality & Individual Differences, 14*, 783–794.

Mendle, J., Turkheimer, E., D'Onofrio, B. M., Lynch, S. K., Emery, R. E., Slutske, W. S., et al. (2006). Family structure and age at menarche: A children-of-twins approach. *Developmental Psychology, 42*, 533–542.

Miller, G. (2004, July 22–25). Fitness indicator theory predicts genetic correlation patterns among intelligence and personality traits in 2,144 pairs of British 7-year-old twins. Paper presented to Human Behavior and Evolution Society, Berlin, Germany.

Montgomery, G. W., Zhu, G., Hottenga, J. J., Duffy, D. L., Heath, A. C., Boomsma, D. I., et al. (2006). *HLA and genome-wide allele sharing in DZ twins.* Unpublished manuscript.

Mowrer, E. (1954). Some factors in the affectional adjustment of twins. *American Sociological Review, 19*, 468–471.

Newman, H. H., Freeman, F. N., & Holzinger, K. J. (1937). *Twins: A study of heredity and environment.* Chicago: University of Chicago Press.

Neyer, F. J. (2002a). Twin relationships in old age: A development perspective. *Journal of Personality and Social Relationships, 19*, 155–177.

Neyer, F. J. (2002b). The dyadic interdependence of attachment security and dependency: A conceptual replication across older twin pairs and younger couples. *Journal of Personality and Social Relationships, 19*, 483–503.

Nichols, R. C., & Bilbro, W. C. (1966). The diagnosis of twin zygosity. *Acta Genetica et Statistica Medica, 16*, 265–275.

Pakstis, A., Scarr-Salapatek, S., Elston, R. C., & Siervogel, R. (1972). Genetic contributions to morphological and behavioral similarities among sibs and dizygotic twins: Linkages and allelic differences. *Social Biology, 19*, 185–192.

Plomin, R., DeFries, J. C., McClearn, G. E., & McGuffin, P. (2001). *Behavioral Genetics* (4th ed.). New York: Worth.

Plomin, R., Willerman, L., & Loehlin, J. (1976). Resemblance in appearance and the equal environment's assumption in twin studies of personality traits. *Behavior Genetics, 6*, 43–52.

Popenoe, P. (1922). Twins reared apart. *Journal of Heredity, 5*, 142–144.

Reiss, D., Neiderhauser, J. M., Hetherington, E. M., & Plomin, R. (2000). *The relationship code.* Cambridge, MA: Harvard University Press.

Ripatti, S., Gatz, M., Pedersen, N. L., & Palmgren, J. (2003). Three-state frailty model for age at onset of dementia and death in Swedish twins. *Genetic Epidemiology, 24,* 139–149.

Rose, R. J., Harris, E. L., Christian, J. C., & Nance, W. E. (1979). Genetic variance in nonverbal intelligence: Data from the kinships of identical twins. *Science, 205,* 1153–1155.

Schelling, T. C. (1960). *The strategy of conflict.* Cambridge, MA: Harvard University Press.

Segal, N. L. (1984). Cooperation, competition and altruism within twin sets: A reappraisal. *Ethology & Sociobiology, 5,* 163–177.

Segal, N. L. (1990). The importance of twin studies for individual differences research. *Journal of Counseling and Development, 68,* 612–622.

Segal, N. L. (1993). Twin, sibling and adoption methods: Tests of evolutionary hypotheses. *American Psychologist, 48,* 943–956.

Segal, N. L. (1997). Twin research perspective on human development. In N. L. Segal, G. E. Weisfeld, & C. C. Weisfeld (Eds.), *Uniting psychology and biology: Integrative perspectives on human development* (pp. 145–173). Washington, DC: APA Press.

Segal, N. L. (2000a). *Entwined lives: Twins and what they tell us about human behavior.* New York: Plume.

Segal, N. L. (2000b). Forgotten twins. *Twin Research, 3,* 58–63.

Segal, N. L. (2002). Co-conspirators and double-dealers: A twin film analysis. *Personality and Individual Differences, 33,* 621–631.

Segal, N. L. (2005a). Evolutionary studies of cooperation, competition and altruism: A twin-based approach. In R. L. Burgess & K. B. MacDonald (Eds.), *Evolutionary perspectives on human development.* (2nd ed., pp. 275–304). Thousand Oaks, CA: Sage.

Segal, N. L. (2005b). *Indivisible by two: Lives of extraordinary twins.* Cambridge, MA: Harvard University Press.

Segal, N. L. (2006a). Letter to the editor: Twin zygosity must be established. *Journal of Developmental and Behavioral Pediatrics, 27,* 426.

Segal, N. L. (2006b). Fullerton Virtual Twin Study. *Twin Research and Human Genetics, 9,* 963–964.

Segal, N. L., & Allison, D. B. (2002). Twins and virtual twins: bases of relative body weight revisited. *International Journal of Obesity, 26,* 437–441.

Segal, N. L., & Hershberger, S. L. (1999). Cooperation and competition in adolescent twins: Findings from a prisoner's dilemma game. *Evolution and Human Behavior, 20,* 29–51.

Segal, N. L., & Hershberger, S. L. (2005). Virtual twins and intelligence: updated and new analyses of within-family environmental influences. *Personality and Individual Differences, 39,* 1061–1073.

Segal, N. L., Hershberger, S. L., & Arad, S. (2003). Meeting one's twin: Perceived social closeness and familiarity. *Evolutionary Psychology, 1,* 70–95.

Segal, N. L., & Hill, E. M. (2005). Developmental behavioral genetics and evolutionary psychology: Tying the theoretical and empirical threads. In B. J. Ellis & D. F. Bjorkland (Eds.), *Origins of the social mind: Evolutionary psychology and child development* (pp. 108–136). New York: Guilford.

Segal, N. L., McGuire, S. A., Havlena, J., Gill, P., & Hershberger, S. L. (2007). Intellectual similarity of virtual twin pairs: Developmental trends. *Personality and Individual Differences, 42,* 1209–1219.

Segal, N. L., Seghers, J. P., Chavarria, K., Marelich, W., Mechanic, M., & Castillo, R. (in press). Social closeness between twin parents and their nieces and nephews. American Psychological Society, New York City, NY, May 25–28.

Sherman, P. W., & Holmes, W. G. (1985). Kin recognition: Issues and evidence. In B. Hölldobler & M. Lindauer (Eds.), *Experimental behavioral ecology and sociobiology. In Memoriam Karl von Frisch 1886–1982* (pp. 437–460). Sutherland, MA: Sinauer.

Shields, J. (1962). *Monozygotic twins: Brought up apart and brought up together.* London: Oxford University Press.

Tancredy, C. M., & Fraley, R. C. (2006). The nature of adult twin relationships: An attachment-theoretical perspective. *Journal of Personality and Social Psychology, 90,* 78–93.

Taylor, C. C. (1971). Marriages of twins to twins. *Acta Geneticae Medicae et Gemelologiae, 20,* 96–113.

Tomassini, C., Juel, K., Holm, N. V., Skytthe, A., & Christensen, J. (2003). Risk of suicide in twins: 51-year follow-up study. *British Medical Journal, 327,* 373–374.

Trivers, R. L. (1985). *Social evolution.* Menlo Park, CA: Benjamin/Cummings.

Uchida, I. A., DeSa, D. J., & Whelan, D. T. (1983). 45,X/46XX mosaicism in discordant monozygotic twins. *Pediatrics, 71,* 413–417.

Visscher, P. M., Medland, S. E., Ferreira, M. A. R., Morley, K. I., Zhu, G., Cornes, B. K., et al. (2006). Assumption-free estimation of heritability from genome-wide identity-by-descent sharing between full siblings. *PLOS Genetics, 2,* 316–325.

Von Bracken, H. (1934). Mutual intimacy in twins. *Character and Personality, 2,* 293–309.

Weisfeld, G. E., Czilli, T., Phillips, K. A., Gall, J. A., & Lichtman, C. M. (2003). Possible olfactory-based mechanisms in human kin recognition and inbreeding avoidance. *Journal of Experimental Child Psychology, 85,* 279–295.

PART V

Conclusions and Future Directions

15 All in the Family: An Evolutionary Developmental Perspective

Amy Gardiner and David F. Bjorklund

Human children evolved to grow up in human families. Families are the near-inevitable consequence of children's prolonged immaturity and dependency, and families, in turn, fostered the extension of such immaturity. The human juvenile period extends far beyond that of most other species to permit the development of a very large brain, which was of great importance in providing a survival advantage to our ancestors. During this period, children undergo essential psychological development to prepare them for life in a socially complex environment (see Bjorklund & Bering 2003; Flinn, Quinlan, Coe, & Ward, this volume). The necessity and value of childhood development cannot be overemphasized (see Bjorklund & Pellegrini 2002); but with great benefits come great costs, and an extended maturational period leaves children with a significant chance of dying from predation, starvation, or disease before they reach reproductive age.

The solution to this problem was the human family. Humans are among about 3% of bird and mammal species that live in families, and one of only a handful of primates in which the father provides any substantial childcare. Moreover, they do it while living in complex, multi-male social groups, something that no other species is known to do (Flinn et al., this volume; Geary, this volume).

Because of the lengthy period of dependence, it is very costly to raise a human child, requiring many more resources than can be provided by a single individual. While mothers are the primary caregivers across cultures, they receive assistance from mates and kin while raising their children (see Hrdy, this volume). Together, a mother, her relatives, and her mate comprise the family, a distinct group of individuals with a common goal of ensuring the survival of her children. As mentioned above, this social structure likely evolved in response to the substantial care needed to rear a child, an overwhelming task for one individual but manageable for a family. Families provide children with people upon whom they can rely for protection and also physical and psychological nourishment.

Being a good parent (or at least "good enough," Scarr 1992) is essential for the survival of one's children and, ultimately, one's genes. The unique demands of big-brained, slow-developing offspring required the evolution of a suite of adaptations, both in parents and children, in order to ensure survival. As noted, directly or indirectly, by the contributors to this volume, most of these adaptations can be "explained" by reference to inclusive-fitness theory (Hamilton 1964), in which the amount of resources one invests in a child is a function of the percentage of shared genes, and parental-investment theory (R. Trivers 1972), which postulates differences in the amount of effort men and women devote to mating versus parenting (see further discussion below). However, these adaptations should not be conceived as being hardwired in the brains of parents or children, but rather thought of as developed strategies that will vary as a function of early experiences and general ecological conditions. Given the diversity of human physical and social environments, children and parents must have the behavioral flexibility to respond to often-uncertain circumstances (Geary 2005a), making untenable the evolution of a single, or "best" species-typical parenting style. Instead, natural selection favored children and parents who were sensitive to ecological conditions and could modify their behaviors accordingly, producing children who were apt to grow up to be well adapted to similar environments.

In this chapter, we first look briefly at evolutionary theory applied to human families, in particular inclusive-fitness and parental-investment theories, and also some assumptions derived from evolutionary developmental psychology, including the concepts of ontogenetic, deferred, and conditional adaptations. We then examine factors that influence the investment decisions that mothers, fathers, grandparents, and stepparents make with regard to children. We conclude by looking at issues related to living with siblings, including factors that influence both sibling conflict and cooperation and mechanisms responsible for incest avoidance.

SOME THEORETICAL CONSIDERATIONS

Inclusive-Fitness and Parental-Investment Theories

Much of modern evolutionary theory is based on Hamilton's (1964) inclusive-fitness theory, developed initially to explain the paradoxical phenomenon of altruism. Basically, Hamilton's rule holds that the cost of helping others should correspond to the degree to which individuals are related. Parents and their children share 50% of their genes, as do siblings; grandparents and grandchildren share, on average, 25% of their genes, as do half-siblings; and stepchildren and stepparents share no genes in common. (They are, of course, both members of the same species, but they are not "blood relatives.") Inclusive fitness is defined not solely in terms of the number of children one has (Darwin's definition of classical fitness), but as the number of copies of one's genes that are represented in future generations, including one's own progeny and also the progeny of genetic relatives. According to inclusive-fitness theory, the care, or investment, one provides children should be influenced by genetic relatedness (see Hrdy; Michalski & Euler; Segal, Chavarria, & Stohs, all from this volume).

Many factors other than genetic commonality influence how much people invest in children. For example, a child's mother and father each contribute 50% of nuclear DNA to their children, but mothers typically invest far more in a child than do fathers. This phenomenon is addressed by Robert Trivers's (1972) parental-investment theory. Throughout life, individuals make mating and parenting decisions in the interest of maximizing their inclusive fitness. Individuals must decide when it is in the best interest of their inclusive fitness to pursue mating opportunities in lieu of investing in children and vice versa. The decisions surrounding mating strategies and parenting effort are generally different for men and women, and these sex differences are largely due to differential amounts of parental investment. Investment begins with conception for both the male, investing sperm, and the female, investing an egg. Obligatory investment for the male can also end here, but for the female it requires at least nine months of gestation (for humans) followed by several more years of lactation (see Keller & Chasiotis, this volume).

The differing amounts of parental investment required of men and women predict certain sex differences in behavior. For example, because sexual intercourse carries the possibility of substantial parental investment for women, they tend to be cautious in agreeing to sex (Oliver & Hyde 1993), waiting to see if their partner is able and willing to take care of a family. Men, on the other hand, need not worry about high obligatory investment and can instead focus primarily on their partner's genetic fitness, which is signified by attractiveness. Women are also concerned about a mate's genetic fitness but are more willing to compromise on attractiveness for the sake of investment.

Another sex difference concerns parental certainty, a non-issue for women because maternity is always certain. Men, however, can never be absolutely positive about paternity, and when they invest their time and resources in a child they risk being cuckolded by supporting children who are not genetically related to them (see Geary, this volume). Therefore, men tend to become jealous over women's sexual infidelity and exhibit mate-retention tactics when they believe they are in danger of investing in another man's children. As detailed by Goetz (this volume), these tactics sometimes have tragic consequences. Women, on the other hand, are more likely to become jealous over a partner's emotional infidelity because they suspect a mate may withdraw investment (e.g., Buss, Larsen, Westen, & Semmelroth 1992).

In most mammals, fathers contribute little if anything to their mate and offspring following birth. Humans are one of a handful of species in which fathers make considerable contributions, although in all societies they provide less childcare than do mothers (Eibl-Eibesfeldt 1989). As we commented, life-history characteristics of children increase the need for paternal support, although how much fathers (and mothers) invest in their children differs as a function of a variety of factors related to characteristics of the children, the parents, and the local ecology (see discussion below). Moreover, although both inclusive-fitness and parental-investment theories purport to explain the actions of men and women toward one another and their children, these behaviors do not arise fully formed in the phenotypes of adults; rather, they must develop. As developmentalists, we ask how these behaviors come to be expressed through the interaction of an individual and his or her environment. We next examine some assumptions and concepts of evolutionary developmental psychology and how they may relate to family life.

CONCEPTS OF EVOLUTIONARY DEVELOPMENTAL PSYCHOLOGY

An evolutionary developmental psychological perspective holds that "development matters," that important, evolutionarily influenced aspects of adult psychological functioning do not arise de novo but emerge via complex, dynamic interactions between children and their environments at all levels of organization, from the genetic through the cultural. Proponents of this perspective argue that both children and adults have been prepared by evolution for life in a human group and that natural selection has operated as forcefully on the behaviors and cognitions of children as it has on those of adults (see Bjorklund & Hernández Blasi 2005, Bjorklund & Pellegrini 2002). In this section we focus on three types of hypothesized adaptations of infancy and childhood and how they might affect children's adjustment to living in families.

Adaptations refer to reliably developing, inherited characteristics that solved some problems of survival or reproduction for our ancestors. Adaptations, of course, can be functional at any point during the lifespan, but we are particularly interested in those characterizing infancy and childhood. Three types of developmental adaptations can be identified: deferred, ontogenetic, and conditional. *Deferred adaptations* refer to aspects of children's learning or social behavior that have been shaped by natural selection to facilitate later adult functioning (Hernández Blasi & Bjorklund 2003). *Ontogenetic adaptations* refer to behaviors that play a functional role at a particular time in development, fostering children's adaptation to the niche of childhood, rather than preparing them for life in the future (Bjorklund 1997, Oppenheim 1981). *Conditional adaptations* refer to a young organism's sensitivity to environmental conditions and modifications of its morphology or behavior in anticipation of adult life (Boyce & Ellis 2005).

Some sex differences in social and cognitive functioning are good candidates for deferred adaptations. For example, as described by parental-investment theory, men and women invest differentially in children and have different traditional roles in caring for children as adults. One robust sex difference is children's interest in infants and caregiving. Across cultures (Hrdy 1999, Maestripieri & Pelka 2002), girls show greater interest in childcare than do boys, a pattern that is also found in many juvenile nonhuman mammals (Maestripieri & Roney 2006). Similar to nearly all female mammals, women have greater responsibility for childcare than men do, and the experience of caring for younger brothers and sisters may serve them well (and served ancestral women well) as preparation for becoming mothers themselves.

In contrast to deferred adaptations, ontogenetic adaptations serve an adaptive function at a particular time in development and are lost after they are no longer necessary. Some aspects of prenatal functioning, such as the yoke sack in birds and the umbilical cord and placenta in mammals, are clear examples of ontogenetic adaptations, as are some early postnatal reflexes (e.g., sucking, rooting, grasping). One candidate for a behavioral–cognitive ontogenetic adaptation is neonatal imitation. Infants copy some facial gestures (e.g., tongue protrusion, mouth opening) shortly after birth (e.g., Meltzoff & Moore 1977, Nagy & Molnar 2004), although such matching behaviors decline to chance values by about 2 months of age (e.g., Jacobson 1979). Although some have proposed that neonatal imitation reflects symbolic functioning (e.g., Meltzoff & Moore 1992), others have argued that it serves a specific function early in life and disappears when it is no longer needed. Proposed functions include facilitating nursing (Jacobson 1979) and fostering the interactions between the mother and her newborn infant when the baby lacks intentional control over its gaze and head movements (Bjorklund 1987, Legerstee 1991). Consistent with this latter argument, infants who show higher rates of neonatal imitation have higher levels of social interactions with their mothers 3 months later (Heimann 1989). Also, newborns are just as likely to provoke imitation from adults as to imitate adults

(Nagy & Molnar 2004), suggesting that the purpose of such mutual imitation is to synchronize and consolidate the social interaction (see Byrne 2005).

Central to evolutionary developmental psychology is the idea that children show a high degree of plasticity, or flexibility, and the ability to adapt to different contexts (see Geary 2005a). Plasticity is not unrestricted, however, but limited to a range of likely outcomes, depending on ecological conditions. More specifically, children's early experiences influence their particular developmental pathway, anticipating, in a sense, what adult life will be like. If early environments are predictive of later ones, children may develop relatively permanent dispositions well suited to the contexts in which they will (likely) find themselves as adults. Boyce and Ellis (2005) developed the concept of conditional adaptations to capture this phenomenon, which they defined as "evolved mechanisms that detect and respond to specific features of childhood environments—features that have proven reliable over evolutionary time in predicting the nature of the social and physical world into which children will mature—and entrain developmental pathways that reliably matched those features during a species' natural selective history" (p. 290).

One application of this concept is the quality of the family environment and subsequent development of mating and parenting strategies (see Johns & Belsky, this volume). For example, Belsky, Steinberg, and Draper (1991, p. 650) proposed that "a principal evolutionary function of early experience—the first 5 to 7 years—is to induce in the child an understanding of the availability and predictability of resources (broadly defined) in the environment, of the trustworthiness of others, and of the enduringness of close interpersonal relationships, all of which will affect how the developing person apportions reproductive effort." Children who experience harsh early conditions, including father absence, inadequate resources, high stress, and insecure attachment, were predicted to attain puberty earlier, begin sexual activity sooner, and follow a mating strategy that emphasized short-term bonds and limited parental investment, relative to children living in more favorable homes. Aspects of this model have been confirmed, at least for girls. For example, significant relationships have been found between age of menarche and: (1) socioeconomic stress (e.g., Ellis, McFadyen-Ketchum, Dodge, Pettit, & Bates 1999), (2) maternal depression (Ellis & Graber 2000), and (3) father absence (e.g., Wierson, Long, & Forehand 1993). Father absence is also associated with increased sexual activity and adolescent pregnancy (Ellis et al. 2003), and the earlier a father leaves the family, the earlier his daughters reach puberty (Surbey 1990) (see Ellis 2004 for a review). Maestripieri et al. reported that not only was father absence associated with earlier menarche, but also with greater interest in infants, suggesting that such girls are becoming "prepared" for early reproduction and parenting (Maestripieri,

Roney, DeBias, Durante, & Spaepen 2004). Although early sexual activity and a "low-investment" parenting strategy may be viewed as maladaptive in contemporary culture, it is a strategy that is likely to result in greater inclusive fitness in some environments, and surely would have for our ancestors.

Family life is complicated and highly variable across cultures, and an evolutionary perspective is not sufficient for understanding the dynamics and consequences for children of living in a family. But an evolutionary perspective is likely necessary if one is to appreciate the significance of the family to children and their development. Moreover, the concepts we have provided here are not the only useful ones for gaining an understanding of family life from an evolutionary perspective; but they form the core, we believe, for such an understanding, making much of family life comprehensible and (relatively) predictable.

INVESTING IN CHILDREN

Although modern sensibilities may tell us that all parents (or at least mothers) should love and invest heavily in all their children, this may be a luxury afforded those living in affluent societies where access to essential resources is not an issue. In actuality, allocating resources to a child limits one's own development, restricts mating efforts (at least for women), and also affects opportunities to invest in other children, both born and unborn (see Keller & Chasiotis, this volume). And biological parents are not the only people who invest in children. In this section, we look through the lens of evolutionary theory at some of the factors that influence the amount of care that mothers, fathers, grandparents, and stepparents provide to children.

Maternal Investment

A mother is the most important individual in an infant's life. A newborn depends on his or her mother for food, protection, and comfort. As children are her genetic passport into future generations, a mother also places considerable value on her children. However, the amount of value she places on each child is not invariable. Some children are more genetically valuable than others, and mothers will perform unconscious cost–benefit analyses to decide how much to invest. Keller and Chasiotis (this volume) detail several factors that mothers take into account in making this calculation. Although it may sound immoral that she would not invest equally in all of her children, the amount of investment she can be expected to give varies according to factors related to the child, herself, and her social situation.

A child's health is the most obvious indicator of his or her reproductive fitness. It is in a mother's best interest to invest in healthy children who are likely to live until reproductive age, rather than to invest heavily in sickly children who may have slim chances of making it through childhood. Such reduced investment in high-risk children is accepted practice in many societies. Even in those societies in which such attitudes are abhorred, mothers may be unable to escape adaptive biases. For example, children born mentally retarded or with physical congenital defects are abused at rates 2 to 10 times higher than are normal children (see Daly & Wilson 1981 for review). While not typical, an action that goes far beyond neglect and reflects parental divestment to the extreme is infanticide. Using data from the Human Relations Area Files (HRAF), Daly and Wilson (1988) reported that, of the 60 major cultures analyzed, 35 described instances of infanticide. In societies that sanction this practice, it is often seen as a right or obligation of the parents. Other child factors, such as the age of the child (older children are typically valued more) or the sex of the child (boys are typically valued more), can influence the amount of investment mothers provide their children, particularly in environments where resources are scare (e.g., Daly & Wilson 1988; Sulloway, this volume).

Characteristics of mothers themselves also influence investment decisions. For example, younger women have more childbearing years ahead of them than do older women and thus more opportunities to produce healthy children whom they can raise to maturation. A decision to withhold investment in an infant may not be very risky in terms of inclusive fitness for a young mother (and fact, it may be in the woman's best inclusive-fitness interest); in contrast, older mothers are more limited in their reproductive prospects and are likely to invest in whatever children they have. A considerable amount of data support this evolutionary interpretation. In the United States, younger mothers are more likely to abuse their children than are older mothers (Lee & George 1999). Mother's age also predicts infanticide both in developed (e.g., Daly & Wilson 1988) and traditional (e.g., Bugos & McCarthy 1984) cultures. Women who lack adequate resources are also likely to reduce their investment in children. For instance, Daly and Wilson (1988) reported that, of women who commit infanticide, single women are represented in proportions greater than expected by chance, even after controlling for maternal age.

Even when mothers make the decision to invest, the parent–child relationship is far from harmonious. This may seem counterintuitive because both parties have much to gain from each other, but the logic is explained by R. L. Trivers's (1974) theory of parent–offspring conflict. Based on Hamilton's (1964) concept of inclusive fitness, Trivers proposed that because a child is related to his mother and siblings only half as much as he is related to himself, he will attempt to garner more parental resources than his mother, who must also invest in herself and other children, is willing to give. A parent's curtailment of investment leads the child to attempt to withdraw resources using evolved psychological and physiological mechanisms. As discussed by Salmon (this volume), conflict begins prenatally and extends through childhood and adolescence.

Given the burden that mammal mothers (including humans) bear in raising their offspring, it is understandable that they should be the primary focus of research and discussion (see, e.g., Maestripieri & Mateo, in press). However, as we mentioned earlier, the demands of a slow-developing and dependent child required greater resources than a single *Homo sapiens* mother could provide, necessitating that others provide some support. Any individual other than the mother who provides care to a child is called an *alloparent*. In humans, fathers and also mostly female kin serve as alloparents in all cultures of the world, and likely always have. Hrdy (this volume) proposed the cooperative-breeding model, arguing that humans evolved a system of parenting in which mothers shared the responsibility for childcare with others in the family and the larger social group. According to Hrdy, this increased social support permitted women to space their slow-developing children more closely, allowing them to care for and nourish more children than they possibly could if they alone were responsible for childcare.

Hrdy further argued that this need for alloparents had a profound effect on the evolution of children's social cognition. Because they needed to attract alloparents, children became skilled at soliciting care through intersubjective engagement and reading the intentions of potential caregivers. These social abilities develop in the first years of a child's life, when it is of greatest importance in procuring care from others. Along similar lines, others have argued that differences in maternal behavior may have been especially important for ancient humans' acquisition of symbolic functioning, particularly within the realm of social cognition, leading to new selective pressures furthering the evolution of symbolic abilities (e.g., Bjorklund 2006). Given the social–cognitive abilities seen in great apes, modifications in mothers' behaviors toward their young children could have fostered the development of joint attention, the treatment of others as intentional agents, imitation, and perspective taking, which are the foundations for theory of mind. Hrdy's proposal that such developments were further promoted by infants' and young children's need to interact with and "read the minds" of a variety of conspecifics bolsters this argument, we believe.

Paternal Investment

One of the most important alloparents is a child's father. During their reproductive lifespan, men must make decisions about when to mate and when to invest in children, taking into account the goal of maximizing their inclusive fitness. Geary (this volume) asserts that in species in which men provide support for their children, their investment varies with the risk of cuckoldry and mating opportunity. In species characterized by high paternity certainty and low chances of additional mating, such as humans, men are expected to invest because doing so will increase their inclusive fitness.

Human fathers invest in their children to a degree far greater than fathers of most other mammals. This high degree of paternal investment likely co-evolved with the extended human juvenile period because investment by fathers increased the survival chances of their long-dependent, slow-developing children. High paternal investment is made possible by the relatively low level of cuckoldry, and thus relatively high level of paternity certainty, found in humans. Across varied cultures, it is estimated that 2–30% of domestic fathers are not the genetic fathers of their children (see Shackelford & Goetz, 2007). Men should be sensitive to cues that signify paternity, particularly the child's physical resemblance, and be more likely to invest in children to whom they believe they are genetically related than in those they suspect were fathered by another man. When paternity is ambiguous, women are expected to attempt to convince men of relatedness by using social cues, such as suggesting greater paternal than maternal resemblance (e.g., Christenfeld & Hill 1995).

Geary (2005b) examined a wide range of cross-cultural evidence from traditional, industrialized, and historical societies and found a consistent pattern with regard to paternal investment and the well-being of offspring: children's mortality rates are higher and their social status is lower when fathers are absent. Additionally, data from contemporary U.S. households shows that high-quality support and involvement from fathers is positively associated with academic achievement, emotional regulation, and social competence (see Cabrera, Tamis-LeMonda, Bradley, Hofferth, & Lamb 2000). Paternal investment is most important in conditions of limited resources, high stress, and intense competition. Socially competent children will be better able to navigate the social landscape later in life than will incompetent individuals and will therefore have increased chances of surviving future risks and taking advantage of future mating and resource opportunities (Geary 2005b). Therefore, the reproductive strategies of men should reflect an evolved tendency to enhance their inclusive fitness by investing during times of high stress rather than pursuing mating opportunities (Lancaster & Lancaster 1983).

Grandparental Investment

Grandparents, particularly grandmothers, are an important source of support in rearing children, in some cultures playing a role that is as, or more, important than that of the father. Of the four possible grandparents children can have, maternal grandmothers provide the most support, followed by maternal grandfathers, paternal grandmothers, and paternal grandfathers (see Euler & Michalski, this volume; Euler & Weitzel 1996). This pattern is expected based on the grandparent's degree of parental certainty in relation to his or her grandchildren. Maternal grandmothers can be certain that both their daughters and their grandchildren are genetically related to them. However, because there is some degree of paternity uncertainty for maternal grandfathers (they can't be 100% certain that their daughter is genetically related to them), they have a similar degree of grandpaternal uncertainty. Paternal grandparents must also factor paternity certainty into their investment decisions because they can be only as certain of their grandchildren's paternity as their son is. Paternal grandfathers have an even greater degree of uncertainty than do paternal grandmothers because of the combined effect of paternity uncertainty in relation to their sons and their son's uncertainty in relation to his own children. These parental-certainty effects are found in the self-reports of grandchildren, who rate maternal grandmothers as giving the most care, followed by maternal grandfathers, paternal grandmothers, and then paternal grandfathers (Euler & Weitzel 1996). This result held even when considering that, on average, the grandchildren lived within equal distances from their maternal and paternal grandparents. Similar findings have been reported for maternal and paternal aunts and uncles, with college students viewing their maternal aunts and uncles as expressing more concern for them than did their paternal equivalents (e.g., Gaulin, McBurney, & Brakeman-Wartell 1997).

As alloparents, grandmothers in particular provide a level of care that significantly increases their grandchildren's chances of survival. Known as the grandmother hypothesis (Alexander 1974, Hamilton 1966), this perspective holds that as fertility declines and women reach an age at which reproduction becomes risky for both themselves and any new children, it is in their best inclusive-fitness interests to discontinue investing in children of their own and to begin investing in their grandchildren. Thus, women who are no longer fertile can still act to further their genetic legacy by assisting in the development and survival of their grandchildren.

That maternal grandmothers in particular are important in the nurturance and survival of children is illustrated by evidence from a broad range of cultures and over the course of history. For example, in contemporary Ethiopia, help provided by maternal grandmothers is associated with lower child mortality (Gibson & Mace 2005). Similarly, the presence of a maternal grandmother was associated with higher fertility and survival rates for Canadian and Finnish farm families (Lahdenpera, Lumma, Helle, Tremblay, & Russell 2004). Among the Hadza, a small group of foragers from the African Rift Valley, the health of weaned children whose mothers were nursing was positively related to the foraging efforts of their grandmothers (Hawkes, O'Connell, & Blurton Jones 1997); and an examination 150 years of German births (1720–1874) showed that children without a living maternal grandmother were more likely to die than were those without a living paternal grandmother. In some age intervals, the difference in death rate was as much as 60% (Beise & Voland 2002).

Stepparent Investment

In contemporary societies, divorce and remarriage are common occurrences, and remarriage was also likely common, in one form or another, for our ancestors. This means that some adults invested in children who were not genetically related to them. This seems at odds with inclusive-fitness theory that predicts investment only in biological children. Indeed, investing in another individual's child appears wasteful because it provides no immediate benefit to one's inclusive fitness. However, stepparents consistently show significant levels of care toward their stepchildren.

Most research has investigated the relationships between stepfathers and stepchildren because children tend to remain with their mothers if their parents separate. In terms of men, stepparental investment is seen not as parenting effort but as a mating strategy (e.g., Anderson, Kaplan, Lam, & Lancaster 1999). Women are likely to mate with men who will assist them in raising their children, and therefore men should demonstrate a willingness to invest in stepchildren in order to take advantage of such mating opportunities. This investment also serves as an indicator that he will be willing and able to invest in any children he and his mate may have in the future.

Researchers have consistently reported that stepparents (usually stepfathers) provide less support and/or care than do biological parents. These patterns have been found in a variety of cultures and include money for college (e.g., Anderson et al. 1999), time spent interacting with children (e.g., Anderson et al. 1999, Marlowe 1999), and even money for food (Case, Lin, & McLanahan 2000).

Keep in mind that many stepparents do form strong emotional bonds with their stepchildren. Many others, however, find it difficult to form a relationship that parallels the level of attachment felt toward their biological children. For instance, in a study of middle-class U.S. stepfamilies, Duberman (1975) found that only 53% of stepfathers and 25% of stepmothers held any "parental feelings" toward their stepchildren. While many stepparents do genuinely love and care for their stepchildren, cross-cultural evidence supports a clear pattern: stepchildren are invested in less than are biological children.

Sadly, because stepparents feel less desire to invest in stepchildren, these children are at a greater risk for abuse, neglect, and even filicide. In an extensive study of child abuse, Daly and Wilson (1985) found that children were 40 times more likely to be abused if they lived with a stepparent versus with two birth parents, even after controlling for factors related to stepfamilies, including poverty, mother's age, and family size. This and similar findings led Daly and Wilson (1996) to conclude that having a stepparent is the most powerful single risk factor for child abuse. A similar pattern is found for the most extreme form of child abuse, filicide. Daly and Wilson (1988) reported that the risk of being killed by a stepparent was far greater than that of filicide by a genetic parent, even higher than the risk of abuse. Children under the age of 2 were at particularly high risk, with the chance of being killed by a stepparent 70 times greater than of dying at the hands of a biological parent. Other research reports that even the risk of unintentional death (e.g., drowning) is greater in stepfamilies than in biologically intact families. In an Australian study examining fatal injuries of children 5 years of age and younger, stepchildren were found to be at a greater risk for unintentional death of any type relative to children in intact families or children in single-parent families (Tooley, Karakis, Stokes, & Ozanne-Smith 2006).

This wealth of data reveals the reality of stepparenthood. Although stepparents make considerable efforts to form loving and caring bonds with their stepchildren, they often find this task more difficult than that of forming an attachment to a natural child. This often leads to less investment in stepchildren than in biological children, which in some extreme cases escalates to abuse or even homicide. It should be noted that cases of abuse are not typical but do reflect the overall trend of decreased care for stepchildren. However, while it is important to identify stepparenthood as a significant risk factor for children, it is also important to realize that most stepparents are an asset rather than a drawback to their children. We perhaps should be impressed with how flexible human behavior can be and with the vast majority of stepparents who provide loving care to their stepchildren.

LIFE WITH SIBLINGS

Most children grow up with siblings, and these relationships can have many positive effects on development but may also serve as a source of conflict. A mother is equally related to all of her children, sharing 50% of her genes with each child, and it is to her benefit to encourage cooperation and altruism among her children. Siblings share, on average, 50% of their genes and should therefore be inclined to cooperate with and assist their siblings in many situations. However, each child is related to him- or herself twice as closely as to his or her siblings and is expected to act selfishly at times, attempting to garner more attention and resources from parents than are received by his or her brothers and sisters.

The exception to typical sibling relationships is relationships between monozygotic twins, who share 100% of their genes. While this relationship is certainly not without conflict, as Segal et al. note (this volume), identical twins enjoy a closer, more cooperative lifelong relationship than do single-born siblings, adoptive siblings, or dizygotic twins, consistent with the tenets of inclusive-fitness theory.

Conflict and Cooperation Among Siblings

Conflict between siblings is inevitable, beginning with the birth of the second child. The firstborn is now no longer the sole benefactor of his or her parents' investment and must share resources with a brother or sister. In an attempt to regain former levels of parental attention, many children exhibit signs of regression, displaying behavior characteristic of younger children that requires parental involvement, such as having toileting accidents or wanting to be fed or clothed by a parent.

One effect of having a new baby in the house is to decrease the security of attachment between the firstborn and his or her mother. In one study of preschoolers, security of attachment declined for the children between late in the mother's pregnancy and 4–8 weeks after the baby was born (Teti, Sakin, Kucera, Corns, & Eiden 1996). This decline was greatest for children 2 years of age and older, possibly because these children are cognitively advanced enough to feel threatened by the new addition, whereas their younger counterparts have not yet developed this cognitive ability. Along the same lines, Dunn and Kendrick (1981) found that firstborn preschool girls who had strong positive relationships with their mothers before the birth of a new sibling had particularly strong negative reactions toward their new brother or sister, and these feelings persisted for at least 14 months after the birth.

Although conflict may be inevitable, it does not mean that sibling relations have to be negative. In fact, siblings are frequently the best of friends and a major source of support for one another. Both younger and older siblings also have much to learn from each other. By interacting with and watching one another, they learn to cooperate, share, help, and empathize. Older siblings, in particular, act as teachers and models for their younger brothers and sisters, who learn by mimicking older siblings' actions (e.g., Dunn & Kendrick 1982), asking them for suggestions (e.g., Azmita & Hesser 1993), and complying with their instructions (e.g., Abramovitch, Corter, Pepler, & Stanhope 1986). Additionally, older siblings may serve to advance younger siblings' development and competency by modeling appropriate social and problem-solving behavior, using language differently than adults, and showing care and nurturing behaviors (e.g., Dunn & Kendrick 1982). These interactions benefit older siblings as well because they can enhance their own intellect playing the role of teacher (Zajonc & Marcus 1975).

In addition to encouragement from their parents, siblings often receive signals from society that advocate cooperative and caring relationships (see Michalski & Euler, this volume). This can make it extremely difficult to determine if positive sibling relationships are due to evolved psychological mechanisms or cultural influences. Jankowiak and Diderich (2000) attempted to disentangle these factors by examining the relationships among adults in a polygamous Mormon society of the American Southwest. Throughout such communities, it is emphasized that the father is the official head of the family, and all his children are equal, regardless of whom their mother is. Distinctions between full-siblings and half-siblings are not made, and cooperation between all children within the family is expected. These egalitarian values were not expressed, however, in the siblings' responses to questions related to sibling solidarity, such as whom one would invite to attend a wedding reception or birthday party, give money to, or ask to babysit. In all such cases, individuals chose full-siblings more often than they chose half-siblings, despite their all growing up in the same house and despite the continually emphasized cultural values.

As in the twin studies described by Segal et al. (this volume), these results are consistent with inclusive-fitness theory and show that genetic relatedness plays a significant part in the development of sibling relationships. This particular connection, however, appears to be mediated by environmental, and not strictly genetic, causes. Jankowiak and Diderich reported that mothers show preferential treatment to their own children, such as inviting them into their bedrooms to watch television or to read. Children themselves were more likely to congregate with their own mothers and full-siblings. Thus, it appears that the behavior of mothers in this polygamous community promoted solidarity among full-siblings. This is also consistent with inclusive-fitness theory because mothers are related to their own children and are therefore expected to have a greater interest in their care than in the care of children of other mothers to whom they are not related.

Because children cannot anticipate how many siblings they will have, or what the nature of these relationships will be, it is unlikely that children evolved mechanisms to deal with specific instances, such as being firstborn or laterborn (see Michalski & Euler, this volume; and Sulloway, this volume). A more tenable possibility is that children acquired mechanisms that promote kin recognition and the ability to compete with siblings of varying status (older or younger) for parental resources early in life.

Incest Avoidance Among Siblings

In any species, inbreeding has serious disadvantages. Two primary deleterious effects are recessive-gene expression and loss of genetic variability. Humans and other mammals seem to have evolved mechanisms to identify and prefer members of the opposite sex that differ in terms of aspects of the immune system, specifically the major histocompatibility complex (MHC). The source of such identification and preference is olfactory. Nonhuman animals prefer mates with immune systems that are different from their own, and they make these judgments based on odor (Apanius, Penn, Slev, Ruff, & Potts 1997). There is some evidence that a similar mechanism is functioning in humans. For example, women prefer the smell of men who differ from them in terms of the MHC region of their genome (Wedekind & Füri 1997). These differences can sometimes lead to marriage. For example, one study reported that of 411 Hutterite couples, people tended to marry those whose MHC types were different from their own (Ober et al. 1997). Fisher, Island, and Zava (this volume) similarly propose that romantic attraction is based on a preference for a partner with a different genetic profile as reflected by differences in personality.

The greatest danger of recessive-gene expression and loss of genetic variability would come from mating between siblings. Because members of the same family have similar genotypes, it is likely that each possesses some of the same recessive alleles. If two family members choose to mate, they run the substantial risk of these alleles being paired in the single genotype of their children and expressing an undesirable, possibly lethal, trait. Inbreeding also reduces genetic variability between generations, which is important for parasite resistance (Ridley 1993) and essential in providing natural selection with a variety of traits from which to choose.

With dangers as significant as these, it is important and indeed expected that incest-avoidance mechanisms would have evolved to protect individuals from squandering their reproductive potential by mating with family members. In 1891, the Finnish anthropologist Edward Westermarck noticed that people who had extensive contact with one another during childhood rarely married, even if they were available as mates. Known as the Westermarck effect, he proposed that because it is likely that individuals who grow up together are related, close proximity during early childhood leads to sexual aversion once individuals reach maturity.

Support for the Westermarck effect was reviewed by Tal and Lieberman (this volume), and we will only highlight it here. Looking at minor marriages in Taiwan, in which a future bride was raised by her future husband's family, Wolf (1995) noted that many such couples were reluctant to marry as adults, and, relative to major marriages, these marriages produced fewer children, and wives admitted more extramarital affairs. Similarly, Shepher

(1983) documented the lack of sexual intercourse and marriages between men and women who grew up together in Israeli kibbutzim. Bevc and Silverman (1993, 2000) showed that siblings who cohabited early in life rarely engaged in mature sexual behaviors (e.g., genital or oral intercourse), whereas siblings who were separated early in life were more apt to do so. That once-separated siblings may find one another attractive is supported by evidence from adopted biological siblings who meet only as adults. One survey of post-adoption counselors in London indicated that about 50% of clients who had been reunited with kin as adults experienced "strong, sexual feelings" toward their newly discovered siblings (Greenberg & Littlewood 1995). These findings support Westermarck's original contention that early cohabitation (before the age of 3) produces later sexual aversion.

A number of possible mechanisms for the effects of early cohabitation and later incest aversion have been suggested (see Tal & Lieberman, this volume), one particularly promising one being olfactory cues. Weisfeld, Czilli, Phillips, Gal, and Lichtman (2003) asked family members to wear T-shirts on 2 consecutive nights and to avoid using perfumes or scented soaps. Family members were later given the T-shirts to smell and asked to identify who had worn each one and whether the odor was aversive. People were generally able to identify the T-shirts worn by their genetic relatives. Important for the issue of incest avoidance were the patterns of aversion. Mothers did not show any aversions, whereas fathers displayed aversions to their daughters' (but not to their sons') odors. Brothers and sisters showed aversions to each other's odors, although no aversions were noted among same-sex siblings. Finally, daughters displayed aversions to their fathers' odors. The only cases in which aversions were mutual were the father–daughter and brother–sister pairs, which represent the greatest danger of incest. These patterns of aversion were found whether or not the source of the odor was recognized. The findings by Weisfeld et al. make a strong argument that the Westermarck effect is mediated, at least in part, by olfactory cues. Moreover, given the previous findings of the effects of early cohabitation on incest avoidance, it appears that it is exposure to these cues early in life that sets the stage for later sexual aversion.

CONCLUSION

Children evolved to grow up in families because they need families to survive. Without adults to care for them, children would neither survive physically nor develop psychologically. Families prepare children for mature lives in socially complex surroundings by providing them with an environment in which to develop competencies to navigate the landscape of human society.

Just as caring adults are indispensable to children, children are essential for adults, who wish to see their genes survive within the species. Parents and alloparents place great value on the children for which they care because these children are the key to genetic representation in future generations.

This mutual need shaped the adaptations that allow children to develop within families and that prepare adults to provide the kind of family that children need to survive. Although these mechanisms have emerged from hundreds of thousands of years of evolution, they are not without environmental sensitivity. Behaviors evolved for family life are sensitive to ecological conditions and develop within the family itself; variations among families produce variations in children's adaptive behaviors.

The relationships between the individuals who comprise a family are not always pleasant, at times being marked by conflict and competition. Such incidents are often important in preserving the genetic fitness of individuals; but of even greater importance is the cooperation that family members must exhibit. Children, fathers, mothers, sisters, brothers, aunts, uncles, grandmothers, and grandfathers are all in the family together, and they must cooperate to ensure their genetic progeny, the potential for which lies within the developing child.

REFERENCES

Abramovitch, R., Corter, C., Pepler, D. J., & Stanhope, L. (1986). Sibling and peer interaction: A final follow-up and a comparison. *Child Development, 57,* 217–229.

Alexander, R. D. (1974). The evolution of social behavior. *Annual Review of Ecology and Systematics, 5,* 325–384.

Apanius, V., Penn, D., Slev, P. R., Ruff, L. R., & Potts, W. (1997). The nature of selection on the major histocompatibility complex. *Critical Reviews in Immunology, 17,*179–224.

Azmita, M., & Hesser, J. (1993). Why siblings are important agents of cognitive development: A comparison of siblings and peers. *Child Development, 64,* 430–444.

Beise, J., & Voland, E. (2002). A multilevel event history analysis of the effects of grandmothers on child mortality in a historical German population (Krummhorn, Ostfriesland, 1720–1987). *Demographic Research, 7,* 469–498.

Bevc, I., & Silverman, I. (1993). Early proximity and intimacy between siblings and incestuous behavior: A test of the Westermarck theory. *Ethology and Sociobiology, 14,* 171–181.

Bevc, I., & Silverman, I. (2000). Early separation and sibling incest: A test of the revised Westermarck theory. *Evolution and Human Behavior, 21,* 151–161.

Bjorklund, D. F. (1987). A note on neonatal imitation. *Developmental Review, 7,* 86–92.

Bjorklund, D. F. (1997). The role of immaturity in human development. *Psychological Bulletin, 122,* 153–169.

Bjorklund, D. F. (2006). Mother knows best: Epigenetic inheritance, maternal effects, and the evolution of human intelligence. *Developmental Review, 26,* 213–242.

Bjorklund, D. F., & Bering, J. M. (2003). Big brains, slow development, and social complexity: The developmental and evolutionary origins of social cognition. In M. Brüne, H. Ribbert, & W. Schiefenhövel (Eds.). *The social brain: Evolutionary aspects of development and pathology* (pp. 133–151). New York: Wiley.

Bjorklund, D. F., & Hernández Blasi, C. (2005). Evolutionary developmental psychology. In D. Buss (Ed.), *The handbook of evolutionary psychology* (pp. 828–850). New York: Wiley.

Bjorklund, D. F., & Pellegrini, A. D. (2002). *The origins of human nature: Evolutionary developmental psychology.* Washington, DC: American Psychological Association.

Boyce, W. T., & Ellis, B. J. (2005). Biological sensitivity to context: I. An evolutionary-developmental theory of the origins and functions of stress reactivity. *Development & Psychopathology, 17,* 271–301.

Bugos, P. E., & McCarthy, L. M. (1984). Ayoreo infanticide: A case study. In G. Hausfater & S. B. Hrdy (Eds.), *Infanticide: Comparative and evolutionary perspectives* (pp. 503–520). New York: Aldine de Gruyter.

Buss, D. M., Larsen, R. J., Westen, D., & Semmelroth, J. (1992). Sex differences in jealousy: Evolution, physiology, and psychology. *Psychological Science, 3,* 251–255.

Byrne, R. W. (2005). Social cognition: Imitation, imitation, imitation. *Current Biology, 15,* 498–499.

Cabrera, N. J., Tamis-LeMonda, C. S., Bradley, R. H., Hofferth, S., & Lamb, M. E. (2000). Fatherhood in the twenty-first century. *Child Development, 71,* 127–136.

Case, A., Lin, I-F., & McLanahan, S. (2000). How hungry is the selfish gene? *Economic Journal, 110,* 781–804.

Christenfeld, N., & Hill, E. (1995). Whose baby are you? *Nature, 378,* 669.

Daly, M., & Wilson, M. (1981). Abuse and neglect of children in evolutionary perspective. In R. D. Alexander & D. W. Tinkle (Eds.), *Natural selection and social behavior* (pp. 405–416). New York: Chiron.

Daly, M., & Wilson, M. (1985). Child abuse and other risks of not living with both parents. *Ethology and Sociobiology, 6,* 197–210.

Daly, M., & Wilson, M. (1988). *Homicide.* New York: Aldine.

Daly, M., & Wilson, M. (1996). Violence against children. *Current Directions in Psychological Science, 5,* 77–81.

Duberman, L. (1975). *The reconstituted family: A study of remarried couples and their children.* Chicago: Nelson-Hall.

Dunn, J., & Kendrick, C. (1981). Interaction between young siblings: Association with the interaction between mother and firstborn child. *Developmental Psychology, 17,* 336–343.

Dunn, J., & Kendrick, C. (1982). *Siblings: Love, envy, and understanding.* Cambridge, MA: Harvard University Press.

Eibl-Eibesfeldt, I. (1989). *Human ethology.* Hawthorne: NY: Aldine de Gruyter.

Ellis, B. J. (2004). Timing of pubertal maturation in girls: An integrated life history approach. *Psychological Bulletin, 130,* 920–958.

Ellis, B. J., Bates, J. E., Dodge, K. A., Fergusson, D. M., Horwood, L. J., Pettit, G. S., et al. (2003). Does father absence place daughters at special risk for early sexual activity and teenage pregnancy? *Child Development, 74,* 801–821.

Ellis, B. J., & Graber, J. (2000). Psychosocial antecedents of variation in girls' pubertal timing: Maternal depression, stepfather presence, and marital and family stress. *Child Development, 71,* 485–501.

Ellis, B. J., McFadyen-Ketchum, S., Dodge, K. A., Pettit, G. S., & Bates, J. E. (1999). Quality of early family relationships and individual differences in the timing of pubertal maturation in girls: A longitudinal test of an evolutionary model. *Journal of Personality and Social Psychology, 77,* 387–401.

Euler, H. A., & Weitzel, B. (1996). Discriminative grandparental solicitude as reproductive strategy. *Human Nature, 7,* 39–59.

Gaulin, S. J. C., McBurney, D. H., & Brakeman-Wartell, S. L. (1997). Matrilateral biases in the investment of aunts and uncles: A consequence and measure of paternity certainty. *Human Nature, 8,* 139–151.

Geary, D. C. (2005a). *The origin of mind: Evolution of brain, cognition, and general intelligence.* Washington, DC: American Psychological Association.

Geary, D. C. (2005b). Evolution of paternal investment. In D. M. Buss (Ed.), *The handbook of evolutionary psychology* (pp. 483–505). New York: Wiley.

Gibson, M. A., & Mace, R. (2005). Helpful grandmothers in rural Ethiopia: A study of the effect of kin on child survival and growth. *Evolution and Human Behavior, 26,* 469–482. Greenberg & Littlewood, 1995.

Greenberg, M., & Littlewood, R. (1995). Post-adoption incest and phenotypic matching: Experience, personal meanings and biosocial implications. *British Journal of Medical Psychology, 68,* 29–44.

Hamilton, W. D. (1964). The genetical theory of social behavior. *Journal of Theoretical Biology, 7,* 1–52.

Hamilton, W. D. (1966). The moulding of senescence by natural selection. *Journal of Theoretical Biology, 12,* 12–45.

Hawkes, K., O'Connell, J. F., & Blurton Jones, N. G. (1997). Hadza women's time allocation, offspring provisioning, and the evolution of postmenopausal lifespans. *Current Anthropology, 38,* 551–578.

Heimann, M. (1989). Neonatal imitation gaze aversion and mother-infant interaction. *Infant Behavior & Development, 12,* 495–505.

Hernández Blasi, C., & Bjorklund, D. F. (2003). Evolutionary developmental psychology: A new tool for better understanding human ontogeny. *Human Development, 46,* 259–281.

Hrdy, S. B. (1999). Mother nature: A history of mothers, infants, and natural selection. New York: Pantheon.

Jacobson, S. W. (1979). Matching behavior in the young infant. *Child Development, 50,* 425–430.

Jankowiak, W., & Diderich, M. (2000). Sibling solidarity in a polygamous community in the USA: Unpacking inclusive fitness. *Evolution and Human Behavior, 21,* 125–139.

Lahdenpera, M., Lumma,V., Helle,S., Tremblay, M., & Russell, A. F. (2004). Fitness benefits of prolonged post-reproductive lifespan in women. *Nature, 428,* 178–181.

Lee, B. J., & George, R. M. (1999). Poverty, early childbearing and child maltreatment: A multinomial analysis. *Children & Youth Services Review, 21,* 755–780.

Legerstee, M. (1991). The role of person and object in eliciting early imitation. *Journal of Experimental Child Psychology, 51,* 423–433.

Maestripieri, D. & Mateo, J. (Eds.) (in press). *Maternal effects in mammals.* Chicago: Chicago University Press.

Maestripieri, D., & Pelka, S. (2002). Sex differences in interest in infants across the lifespan: A biological adaptation for parenting? *Human Nature, 13,* 327–344.

Maestripieri, D., & Roney, J. R. (2006). Evolutionary developmental psychology: Contributions from comparative research with nonhuman primates. *Developmental Review, 26,* 120–137.

Maestripieri, D., Roney, J. R., DeBias, N., Durante, K. M., & Spaepen, G. M. (2004). Father absence, menarche and interest in infants among adolescent girls. *Developmental Science, 7,* 560–566.

Marlowe, F. (1999). Showoffs or providers? The parenting effort of Hazda men. *Evolution and Human Behavior, 20,* 391–404.

Meltzoff, A. N., & Moore, M. K. (1977). Imitation of facial and manual gestures by human neonates. *Science, 198,* 75–78.

Meltzoff, A. N., & Moore, M. K. (1992). Early imitation within a functional framework: The importance of person identity, movement, and development. *Infant Behavior and Development, 15,* 479–505.

Nagy, E. & Molnar, P. (2004). Homo imitans or homo provocans? Human imprinting model of neonatal imitation. *Infant Behavior and Development, 27,* 54–63.

Ober, C., Weitkamp, L. R., Cox, N., Dytch, H., Kostyu, D., & Elias, S. (1997). HLA and mate choice in humans. *American Journal of Human Genetics, 61,* 497–504.

Oliver, M. B., & Hyde, J. S. (1993). Gender differences in sexuality: A meta-analysis. *Psychological Bulletin, 114,* 29–36.

Oppenheim, R. W. (1981). Ontogenetic adaptations and retrogressive processes in the development of the nervous system and behavior. In K. J. Connolly

& H. F. R. Prechtl (Eds.), *Maturation and development: Biological and psychological perspectives* (pp. 73–108). Philadelphia: International Medical Publications.

Ridley, M. (1993). *The red queen.* London: Viking.

Scarr, S. (1992). Developmental theories for the 1990s: Development and individual differences. *Child Development, 63,* 1–19.

Shackelford, T. K., & Goetz, A. T. (2007). Adaptation to sperm competition in humans. *Current Directions in Psychological Science, 16,* 47–50.

Shepher, J. (1983). *Incest: A biosocial view.* New York: Academic Press.

Surbey, M. K. (1990). Family composition, stress, and the timing of human menarche. In T. E. Ziegler & F. B. Bercovitvch (Eds.), *Socioendocrinology of primate reproduction* (pp. 11–32). New York: Wiley-Liss.

Teti, D. M., Sakin, J. W., Kucera, E., Corns, K. M., & Eiden, R. D. (1996). And baby makes four: Predictors of attachment security among preschool-age firstborns during the transition to siblinghood. *Child Development, 67,* 579–596.

Tooley, G. A., Karakis, M., Stokes, M., & Ozanne-Smith, J. (2006). Generalizing the Cinderella effect to unintentional childhood fatalities. *Evolution and Human Behavior, 27,* 224–230.

Trivers, R. (1972). Parental investment and sexual selection. In B. Campbell (Ed.), *Sexual selection and the descent of man* (pp. 136–179). New York: Aldine de Gruyter.

Trivers, R. L. (1974). Parent–offspring conflict. *American Zoologist, 14,* 249–264.

Wedekind, C., & Füri, S. (1997). Body odour preferences in men and women: do they aim for specific MHC combinations of simply heterozygosity? *Proceedings of the Royal Society of London, Series B, 265,* 1471–1479.

Weisfeld, G. E., Czilli, T., Phillips, K. A., Gal, J. A., & Lichtman, C. M. (2003). Possible olfaction-based mechanisms in human kin recognition and inbreeding avoidance. *Journal of Experimental Child Psychology, 85,* 279–295.

Wierson, M., Long, P. J., & Forehand, R. L. (1993). Toward a new understanding of early menarche: The role of environmental stress in pubertal timing. *Adolescence, 23,* 913–924.

Wolf, A. (1995). *Sexual attraction and childhood association: A Chinese brief for Edward Westermarck.* Stanford, CA: Stanford University Press.

Zajonc, R. B., & Marcus, G. B. (1975). Birth order and intellectual development. *Psychological Review, 82,* 74–88.

INDEX